"There are many books on short-term psychotherapy, but *Co-Creating Change* stands out. The clarity of Frederickson's thought and writing is striking, and the multiple clinical transcripts are inspiring, helpful, and often tremendously moving. No one does a better job explaining how and when to focus on emotions, anxiety, and defenses or in integrating psychotherapeutic technique with the latest research on neurobiology, attachment, and emotion. *Co-Creating Change* deserves to be read by both novice and experienced psychotherapists alike."

> —Stephen E. Finn, PhD, founder, Center for Therapeutic Assessment, Austin, Texas

"This is the clearest and most clinically useful exposition of Davanloo's Short-Term Dynamic Psychotherapy on the market. It is chock-full of compelling clinical vignettes that bring the reader directly into the session in a wonderfully engaging and evocative way. Practitioners of all forms of psychodynamic therapy will profit greatly by delving into the pages of this outstanding volume."

> —Stanley B. Messer, PhD, Dean and Distinguished Professor, Graduate School of Applied and Professional Psychology, Rutgers University

"*Co-Creating Change* is an insightful and well-written guide that enables the therapist to build an effective collaboration to lead the client into an awareness of the biobehavioral shifts that constitute feelings. The book is a road map with excellent examples of how the therapist can 'co-create' a therapeutic alliance to stop the suffering by enabling the client to become aware of feelings."

> —Stephen W. Porges, PhD, author of *The Polyvagal Theory*

"Frederickson integrates the emerging brain sciences of affective feelings and the dynamics of the inner life with a detailed analysis of how to manage clinical relationships. With a rich blend of the emerging understanding of our brains' emotional processes, brought to life in skilled therapeutic engagements, we are led to experience how the strengths and weaknesses of clients can be steered toward harmonious ways of living. Anyone interested in the breadth and depth of mental life will find this to be an exceptional guide to therapeutic progress."

> —Jaak Panksepp, Baily Endowed Professor of Animal Well-Being Science, Washington State University, and author of *Affective Neuroscience* and *The Archaeology of Mind*

"This book synthesizes research and theory in a clear and straightforward way, compatible with modern ideas from the fields of neuroscience, attachment theory, interpersonal communication, and developmental theories. Change requires a well-equipped store of knowledge about ways to confront anxiety and defenses. This is exactly what *Co-Creating Change* offers. It is a practical guide for change through the dyadic relationship—an integrated model to help people break the chains of their suffering."

> —Marion Solomon, PhD, coauthor of *Love and War in Intimate Relationships*

"*Co-Creating Change* is an invaluable source book for all therapists wanting to do work that is highly collaborative and deeply affecting. From a solid base in theory and research, Jon Frederickson deals with the nitty-gritty of therapy, outlining treatment strategies and interventions that can help therapists increase their effectiveness across a wide spectrum of patients."

> —Patricia Coughlin, PhD, faculty, University of New Mexico, and author of *Intensive Short-Term Dynamic Psychotherapy*

"Jon Frederickson's *Co-Creating Change: Effective Dynamic Therapy Techniques* is a must-read for every practitioner of psychotherapy. This may very well be the most cogent and compelling distillation of the technical processes of dynamic psychotherapy. Clearly written, with abundant case material and patient-therapist vignettes, Frederickson illuminates the process of dynamic psychotherapy with concise descriptions and clinical decision trees, which serve as excellent clinical guides for any psychotherapist, regardless of theoretical orientation."

> —Jeffrey J. Magnavita, PhD, ABPP, Past President, Division of Psychotherapy, American Psychological Association, and Lecturer in Psychiatry, Yale University

"*Co-Creating Change* can serve both as a scholarly text and as a remarkable clinical guide. I found Frederickson's integration with neuroscience, numerous clinical interchanges, moment-to-moment attunement, and work with fragile and highly resistant patients to be especially valuable."

> —Michael Stadter, PhD, faculty, International Psychotherapy Institute and Washington School of Psychiatry, and author of *Presence and the Present*

"A fascinating contribution to working with emotion in psychotherapy. Frederickson opens up contemporary psychodynamic theory, putting it in concrete terms for therapists of all orientations. Written in a personable and highly accessible style, this book is chock-full of concise and practical illustrations for moment-by-moment intervention! This volume invites the curious reader into fresh dialogues on psychotherapy integration."

> —Antonio Pascual-Leone, PhD, Clin Psych, Director, Emotion Change Lab, University of Windsor, and coauthor of *Emotion-Focused Therapy for Complex Trauma*

"A tour de force. . . . This book covers a dazzling sweep of topics indispensable to a clinician hoping to do profoundly transformational work. I only wish I'd had this available as I was struggling to manage difficult, rapidly occurring defenses and significant anxiety reactions. Jon's style is warm, personal, and exceedingly clear, and he equips the therapist with detailed interventions to handle every confounding defense, manifestation of anxiety, or problem that can present itself in a therapist's office. This is the most detailed, clear, and all-inclusive treatment manual I have had the pleasure to read. And unlike many scholarly texts, this one is enjoyable to read!"

> —Susan Warshow, MSW, founder, DEFT Institute

"From the brilliant and beautiful opening paragraphs on accomplishment and suffering, Jon Frederickson carries us right into the process of effective psychotherapy. He tells us just what we want to know about the theory of technique, but he never loses touch with our need to know what to do to convert our patients' sticky places into centers of growth. He shows us how to keep going in the face of obstacles put up by the keen and hurt minds we encounter. With *Co-Creating Change*, Frederickson has created a classic resource on the most modern of psychotherapies, Intensive Short-Term Dynamic Psychotherapy."

> —Thomas Brod, MD, Associate Clinical Professor of Psychiatry, University of California, Los Angeles

"This valuable resource presents a masterful blend of theoretical knowledge and applied material in a clear, accessible style and format. It captures the essence of the therapy process, deftly illustrated by therapist-patient scenarios and practical tools. A 'must-have' for both aspiring therapists-in-training and seasoned practitioners who wish to hone their skills to effect lasting change."

—Theresa DiNuzzo, PhD, Former President, International Association of Counseling Services

Co-Creating Change

Effective Dynamic Therapy Techniques

Jon Frederickson

Seven Leaves Press
Kansas City, MO

Seven Leaves Press, LLC
4550 Belleview
Kansas City, MO 64111
www.sevenleavespress.com

Ordering Information

Quantity sales. Special discounts are available on quantity purchases
by corporations, associations, and others. For details, contact the
"Special Sales Department" at the address above.

Orders by US trade bookstores and wholesalers. Please contact BCH:
(800) 431-1579 or visit www.bookch.com for details.

Printed in the United States of America

Frederickson, Jon.
 Co-creating change : effective dynamic therapy
 techniques / Jon Frederickson.
  p. cm.
 Includes bibliographical references and index.
 LCCN 2013901623
 ISBN 978-0-9883788-4-1

 1. Psychodynamic psychotherapy--Technique.
 I. Title.

RC489.P72F74 2013   616.89'14

                                    QBI13-60026

First Edition

In memory of my father,
Laurence Frederickson, a blacksmith
who taught me the meaning of art and craft
at the anvil and forge.

Acknowledgments

A book of this scope is truly the work of a community since so many helped me along the way. I'd like to thank Bruce Ammons, Joal Bennet-Stenzel, Jean Braun, Thomas Brod, Linda Campbell, F. Barton Evans, Joe Gorin, Jeanne Isaaksen, Nat Kuhn, Allan Larsen, Maureen Lyon, Tom Marup, Olga and Michael Meerson, Tobias Nyqvist, Monroe Pray, Ollie Russell, Maggie Silberstein, Monica Urru, Susan Warshow, and Tor Wennerberg for reading and critiquing chapters of the book. Rowan Blackmon deserves thanks for her transcriptions of videotapes and library research. Maurice Joseph deserves thanks for his research assistance. I would also like to thank Suzanne Kunkel for her transcriptions of videotapes. And thanks are due Penelope Burt, who did research for this book and critiqued the entire book. Special thanks go to Linda Gilbert, Carolyn Ammons, and Diane Byster, who also read and critiqued the entire book. And of course, I want to thank my trainees whose questions have made me think more deeply and precisely. Their questions have always helped me grow. If I have forgotten anyone who helped me, please accept my gratitude.

I have been very fortunate to have an intellectual home within the Washington School of Psychiatry, and I thank all my teachers and supervisors there. As Martin Buber once said, "It is a place that keeps the questions open." In particular, I would like to thank Gordon Kirschner, mentor, friend, and colleague, who exemplifies the ideal of intellectual curiosity and integrity, and Rochelle Kainer, whose support as a mentor has been a model for me. And thanks must go to Anne Stephansky, who introduced me to this model of treatment.

Of course, this book would not have been written were it not for the supervision and training I received from the man who developed intensive short-term dynamic psychotherapy, Habib Davanloo. I have also benefitted immensely from the training and presentations of my colleagues and friends Allan Abbass, Allen Kalpin, Robert Neborsky, and Josette Ten Have de Labije. And my work on moment-to-moment processing would never have become what it is today were it not for my relationships with Terry Sheldon and Beatriz Winstanley. My biggest thanks must go to my dear friend, mentor, supervisor, and colleague, Patricia Coughlin, whose work with me over years of supervision transformed my vision of what psychotherapy could be.

And finally, my profound gratitude goes to my wife, Kath, without whom none of this would have been possible.

Contents

Dynamic Psychotherapy

I walked into the well-appointed office, glancing at the paintings on the wall. The analyst shook my hand. I sat down, and he began our interview. He said he and his colleagues were delighted by my application to the institute to become a psychoanalyst, but they had only one concern: "We're not sure you are analyzable, given the amount of trauma in your history."

I was shocked. I was being judged on what had been done to me in the past, not what I had done with it. What had been done to me was impersonal. I had just been the accidental location where bad things had happened. The analysts were paying attention to the impersonal, not to me, the person.

During later interviews, most of the analysts asked about the traumas in my background, but no one asked, "How did you get to where you are today?" "How did you overcome these difficulties and get this far?" In short, no one asked a question about what I did, only about what others had done to me.

When they judged me based on what had been done to me, for the first time I began to feel proud of what I had done in spite of that past. Like everyone else, I had to make choices throughout my life to overcome those past obstacles. Now I had a new appreciation for the acts of will (Rank 1936) by which we create ourselves (Berdyaev 1944) and give meaning to our lives (Frankl 1959).

In the end, this experience was a gift. It highlighted the basic tension in the psychotherapy field between freedom and determinism. Patients come to us because they have lost their freedom to engage in self-creation. They have become determined, in part, by defenses of which they are unaware. They know they want something different in their lives but are unable to see what inhibits their freedom. Our task as therapists is to help them recover their freedom to love, to live, and to create a life that matters. Their past, their diagnoses, and their genetics are easy to mistake as factors that completely determine their lives. But then we relate to dead concepts rather than living persons. Our overarching task is to recognize those determining forces while mobilizing patients' self-creative capacity to act.

The acts by which we create our lives and meaning will be the focus of this book. What we do can create a beautiful life full of meaning or a desperate life full of suffering. At each moment in therapy we have a choice: to face our inner life or run from ourselves, to engage in the therapeutic task or avoid it. When we run from our inner life, we create suffering. Usually, we do not consciously pursue suffering, but we may automatically engage in actions that create it. Our task as therapists is to help patients see how they hurt themselves so they can stop suffering. To do that, we must understand what causes suffering.

From the Buddha thousands of years ago to neuroscientists today, people have tried to answer that question. Cognitive therapists say we suffer because of maladaptive cognitions. Emotion-focused therapists say we suffer because of avoided feelings. Psychoanalysts say we suffer because of unresolved conflicts and transference reactions in relationships. Body workers say we suffer because of adaptive action tendencies, which have become frozen in the body. Behavior therapists say we suffer because of all these maladaptive behaviors. Mindfulness therapists say we suffer because we are unable to pay attention to our experience at each moment. And the Buddha? He said we suffer because we resist reality.

We have all these answers and therapies, each of which has helped patients. Now that its first hundred years have passed, the field of psychotherapy is undergoing a scientific revolution (Kuhn 1970). Clinicians widely recognize the need for an integrative model of treatment. This book will present an integrative theory and a model of intervention based on moment-to-moment assessment of a patient's needs.

THE NATURE OF SUFFERING

To begin, we must first address the fundamental question: why do we suffer? Only by understanding suffering can we develop a coherent model for treating it. And to understand suffering, we must understand the difference between pain and suffering. In life, pain is inevitable. Everyone we love will die, and everything we have we will lose, either before or at the moment of death. We can respond to the inevitable pain of life in two ways. The person whose heart has been broken and gives up loving ends up with an empty heart. The person with a broken heart who continues to love has a full heart, knowing that everyone we love we lose through death or abandonment. That is why there are only two kinds of hearts: empty hearts and loving hearts. It takes courage to face the inevitable losses and yet, in spite of it all, to keep on loving and being open to life.

The reality of loss and disappointment is built into every relationship. Each of us wants something from every person in our life. Yet our loved ones can do only one of three things. They can deliver, delay, or disappoint. They cannot always want what we want. And even if they want to give us what we want, they may not have the ability. The conflict between desire and reality is inherent in human existence. So we avoid the pain of life by using defenses, which bring us suffering. Rather than face reality, we avoid it, no longer able to deal with it effectively. That is why the Buddha said that our relationship to desire is the source of suffering: desiring what we cannot have, what does not exist in reality, makes us suffer. When our desires bump into reality, we realize people do not want what we want, they cannot always give us what we want, and our fantasy is different from reality.

In response, we experience feelings and anxiety. We can face all the feelings and anxiety evoked by reality so we can deal with it adaptively. Or we can avoid facing reality and our feelings. However, avoidance creates our suffering. The pain of loss, illness, and death is inevitable, but suffering from our defenses is optional—if we learn to see and turn against them.

What do we mean by *defenses*? They are the ways we resist reality and our feelings in response to it. We avoid feelings through maladaptive thoughts (cognitive therapy), behaviors (behavior therapy), relational patterns (psychoanalysis, cognitive and behavior therapy), or inattention (mindfulness therapy).

When we use a defense to avoid reality, we cannot deal with reality effectively. If we avoid our feelings through self-critical thoughts, we become depressed. When we use defenses to avoid reality and feelings, we become out of touch with life and ourselves. If we avoid feelings through avoidant behaviors, our relationships fail. The man who projects onto other people suffers from tormenting relationships and a life of loneliness. The housewife who excuses her husband for hitting her traps herself in an abusive marriage. It turns out the Buddha was right. Defenses, our resistance to what is, create our symptoms and presenting problems.

CAUSALITY

We have seen that pain in life is inevitable, but suffering from defenses is optional. So let us examine the causality of suffering. First, a stimulus in reality triggers our feelings (Damasio 1999). Those feelings make us anxious (Damasio 1999; S. Freud 1923a, 1961, 1926; LeDoux 1998). We can face our feelings and anxiety to deal with reality effectively (Hartmann 1964). Or we can avoid our feelings and anxiety through defenses, which create our symptoms and presenting problems (S. Freud 1923a, 1961). For instance, a man verbally abuses his fiancée (stimulus). In response, she feels angry. However, she grew up with people who condemned her expressions of anger. So instead of feeling angry at her fiancé, she becomes anxious. Rather than use her anger to set a limit to his verbal abuse, she wards her anger off with defenses. She rationalizes, "He was angry because he didn't receive a raise from his boss." She minimizes what he did and what she felt by saying, "It was no big deal." She turns the anger onto herself by saying, "I deserved what he said because I did something stupid." These defenses create her symptoms: by turning the anger on herself, she becomes depressed, and by rationalizing away her feelings and minimizing what her fiancé did, she keeps herself stuck with a series of abusive men. After all, she tells herself that her fiancé's verbal abuse is "no big deal."

How do we help her? First, we must find out what she suffers from. We do so by asking her what problem she wants us to help her with. Then we ask about her difficulties, their origin, and their history.

Her answers tell us a great deal. Perhaps she answers our questions readily. Maybe she floods with anxiety as soon as she shares her inner life with us. She could even claim to have no problem at all! Every answer is good. It tells us what she needs help with and her ability to co-create a relationship for change. Once we have surveyed the patient's problem and she declares her will to explore it, we explore a specific example of her problem to get a clear picture of what causes it.

As we explore, a surprising pattern occurs in therapy. The patient comes to your office seeking help. Yet as soon as you ask about her problem, her will to explore it, or a specific example, the patient often becomes anxious (S. Freud 1926/1961 A. Freud 1936) and uses defenses (S. Freud 1923a/1961). Why?

Sadly, most patients who seek therapy have been hurt in previous relationships. They have learned that closeness and sharing lead to pain (Bowlby 1973, 1980). Patients want help, but their anxiety signals that this relationship, like earlier ones, could be painful. So patients use defenses to avoid sharing their feelings, hopes, and desires. We call this pattern of feeling-anxiety-defense the *triangle of conflict* (Malan 1979). (See chapter 5 for an elaboration on the triangle of conflict.)

Every conflict creating the patient's symptoms has this form: (1) the patient has a feeling, (2) he automatically becomes anxious physically in his body, (3) a moment later he uses a defense to ward off that feeling, and (4) that defense creates his symptoms and presenting problems. Every statement you make invites the patient to co-create a relationship for change. By sharing a feeling, the patient dares to co-create a relationship for change based on emotional closeness. By becoming anxious or sharing a defense, the patient unwittingly creates a past relationship. His anxiety and defenses are not a problem for the therapist. They are the history of the patient's suffering, what he implicitly is asking you to heal.

If he expresses a feeling, we encourage him to feel that feeling more deeply to get to the bottom of his difficulties. If he is too anxious, we regulate his anxiety and then explore his feeling. If he uses a defense, we help him see the defense and its cost so he can let go of it and face his feeling. These are the three basic principles of all psychotherapy interventions. Although the principles are simple, their application can be complex, as the rest of the book will illustrate.

When patients respond with anxiety or defense, we do not follow these detours. Instead, we identify each detour and invite the patient to focus on his feeling. Maintaining a consistent focus on feelings is one of the most important skills for therapists to learn. Feelings express our primary motivations and drives (Tomkins 1962). Without them, we lack a compass to show us where we want to go in life (P. Coughlin, personal communication).

Here is an analogy. Suppose I was teaching you to drive and you drive into a ditch. I'll say, "Could you turn the wheel so we can get back on the road toward your destination?" You might tell me, "I want to drive in the ditch!" I'll reply, "That is certainly your right, but as long as you drive in the ditch, you won't reach your destination." If you tell me that driving in the ditch is just the way you are, I'll say, "It's not the way you are, but it is the way you drive your car. You say you want us to drive north toward New York, but you have a habit of driving the car into the ditch, onto the beach, and into the ocean. If you drive that way, we'll get stuck, and you won't end up in New York." If the patient goes on a detour to anxiety, regulate his anxiety and then return to the focus on his feeling. If the patient goes on a detour to defense, help him see the defense, let go of it, and return to focusing on his feeling. If he continues to detour to anxiety and defense, he will not achieve his goals in therapy.

THE RELATIONSHIP BETWEEN SUFFERING AND THE THERAPEUTIC TASK

As mindfulness practices have shown, we do not avoid reality or our feelings once in a while (Safran 2003). *We create our suffering and symptoms moment by moment all day long.* Thus, moment by moment we must help the patient see the defenses that create his suffering. One might think of therapy as a form of guided mindfulness meditation. We help the patient pay attention to reality in this moment, his internal experience. Each time he ignores his inner life by using a defense, we help him see his defense and return to his feeling. As he lets go of his defenses, they no longer cause his suffering, and he becomes in touch with himself. Each time he pays attention to reality in this moment, he becomes more present (Eigen 1998). And he becomes at one with the emotional truth of this moment (Bion 1970).

To do this, the patient must relinquish his defenses and face the feelings he fears and has avoided. Through these two choices, the patient joins the therapist to co-create a relationship for change: the therapeutic alliance.

With this understanding of causality, the therapeutic task becomes clear: help the patient see and relinquish the defenses that cause his suffering. By feeling his feelings as deeply as possible, he will be able to channel them into adaptive action, and he will gain insight into the reasons he used those defenses in the first place.

In every therapy session we see the following sequence: (1) the therapist invites the patient to form a closer relationship, (2) the patient has a feeling, (3) he becomes anxious, (4) he uses a defense, and (5) he experiences a symptom or presenting problem. This sequence happens every time you invite a closer relationship, anywhere up to 150 times an hour! From this perspective, we do not say a patient "has" depression. Instead, defenses create and sustain his depression all day.

This gives us hope. If we can stop every defense that hurts the patient and help him see and relinquish them, his symptoms will diminish and disappear. From this point of view, defense interruption is an act of compassion toward the patient (S. Warshow, personal communication). Collaboration with the patient's defenses hurts the patient. Let me give an example.

One day a patient had not shown up for her session. I wondered if she might be in the hallway. I went out there and sure enough, there she was, sitting on the floor, cutting her wrist with an X-Acto knife while watching the blood drip onto a pile of napkins on the floor. I did not just watch her defense, cutting her wrist. I took the knife away from her and brought her into my office. Every defense is a cut to the soul. If these defenses are not blocked, the patient may die the death of a thousand cuts. In this model of therapy, we take a firm stand with the patient against defenses that cause her suffering.

By helping the patient relinquish her defenses, we help her embrace herself and her inner life. In short, we help her have compassion for herself by demonstrating our compassion for her. In a letter to Carl Jung, Sigmund Freud once wrote, "Psychoanalysis is a cure through love" (S. Freud and Jung, 1994). And that love is itself an act of faith. As one patient said to me, "You saw who I was underneath all the chaos and defenses before I knew there was a me there to be found." Through our constant attention to the patient's inner life and our blockage of the defenses that strangle it, we embrace the patient's inner life and encourage her to do the same.

In this book you will learn many techniques to help patients. *Technique* often refers to the way we manipulate an object, for example, sculpting a piece of wood. In contrast, *psychotherapy techniques are ways of relating to the patient*, of demonstrating our love and compassion. Techniques are not merely ways of "doing" but ways of "being together." Our constant attention to the patient's feelings demonstrates our belief that she has the right to become free from the defenses that have perpetuated her suffering. Then she can take up the path of self-creation that is personality itself (Berdyaev 1944).

To begin this journey of psychotherapy, we must explore the patient's presenting problems to develop a consensus on the problem, its causes, and the therapeutic task, which will resolve the problem. But to do this, the therapist needs to understand how to explore feeling, regulate anxiety, identify defenses, and assess the patient. Only with those tools will the therapist be able to develop a conscious therapeutic alliance effectively. So let us begin by learning how to explore feelings.

RECOMMENDED READINGS

Abbass, A., Town, J., and Driessen, E. (2012). Intensive short-term dynamic psychotherapy: A systematic review and meta-analysis of outcome research. *Harvard Review of Psychiatry, 20*(2), 97–108. http://www.istdpinstitute.com/resources/.

Coughlin Della Selva, P. (1996). The integration of theory and technique in Davanloo's intensive short-term dynamic psychotherapy. In *Intensive short-term dynamic psychotherapy: Theory and Technique* (pp. 1–25). New York: Wiley.

Malan, D., and Coughlin Della Selva, P. (2006). Empirical support for Davanloo's ISTDP. In *Lives transformed: A revolutionary method of dynamic psychotherapy* (pp. 34–74). London: Karnac.

Neborsky, R. (2001). Davanloo's method of intensive short-term dynamic psychotherapy. In M. Solomon, R. Neborsky, L. McCullough, M. Alpert, F. Shapiro, and D. Malan (Eds.), *Short-term therapy for long-term change* (pp. 16–53). New York: W. W. Norton.

RECOMMENDED MATERIALS

For information on forming a therapeutic alliance presented in videos by Jon Frederickson, visit the URLs below.

Intensive short-term dynamic psychotherapy part 1 (October 5, 2011).
http://www.youtube.com/watch?v=cKzmk2-xnzY

Intensive short-term dynamic psychotherapy part 2 (October 5, 2011).
http://www.youtube.com/watch?v=dK2x906ptWA.

Intensive short-term dynamic psychotherapy part 3 (January 18, 2012),
http://www.youtube.com/watch?v=sDmVgoKPVkw.

PART ONE

Establishing an Effective Focus

CHAPTER ONE

Feelings: Where We Focus in Therapy

L izards, lions, and humans are all moved by the bodily activations known as *emotions* (Darwin 1872/1998; Panksepp 1998). These emotions organize animal behavior. Unlike reptiles and mammals, however, we can become conscious of those physical activations in the body and label them as feelings. Subjectively, becoming aware of our feelings gives us a sense of a core self (Damasio 1994, 1999), the basis for our identity. Intersubjectively, feelings allow us to know others and be intimate (Kelly 1996; Nathanson 1996). And culturally, feelings allow us to have shared values, which we express through laws, religions, and art. Feelings allow for the intergenerational transmission of culture by which we connect to the accumulated consciousness of humankind (Trevarthen 2009, 57).

Feelings are the fundamental way we make sense of the world. They tell us what we want and what we do not, what gives us pleasure and what gives us pain. They mobilize us to act adaptively on our own behalf, to pursue our goals in life (Tomkins 1962). Like a GPS unit, feelings tell us where we are, where we want to go, and how to get there.

HOW TO FOCUS ON FEELINGS

When we do not know what we feel, we go through life without an emotional compass (P. Coughlin, personal communication). Evolution provided us with feelings, which organize the body, so we can act adaptively. Patients who use defenses to ignore their feelings lose the information feelings provide. Feelings and desire no longer mobilize their actions; anxiety and defenses do (Schore 2009). Therapy helps patients let go of their defenses so they can face their feelings. By learning to "feel and deal" (Fosha 2000), they can channel their feelings into adaptive actions rather than maladaptive defenses. Thus, we intervene to help patients experience previously avoided feelings.

Seemingly everyone knows what feelings are. Suppose you ask a patient, "What is the feeling toward your boyfriend for slapping you in the face?" She might offer one of the following comments as descriptions of her feeling:

- "I feel he shouldn't have done that."
- "I feel he did that because of his upbringing."
- "I feel betrayed."
- "I feel detached."
- "I feel like leaving him."
- "I feel tense."
- "I feel sad."
- "I feel angry."

Only the last statement is the feeling toward her boyfriend. Let's examine these responses in detail to understand what feelings are.

- "I feel he shouldn't have done that." *This is not a feeling but the way the patient avoids a feeling: the defense of intellectualization.* The patient offers a thought rather than her feeling. She does not distinguish between her thought and her feeling toward her boyfriend. The therapist might respond, "Well, that's your thought, but your thought is not a feeling. If you don't cover your feeling with a thought, what is the feeling toward him for slapping you in the face?"
- "I feel he did that because of his upbringing." *This is not a feeling but the defense of rationalization.* The patient tries to explain the *reason* her boyfriend hit her rather than describe the *feeling* toward him for doing so. She does not differentiate her explanation from her feeling. The therapist might respond, "Well, that's the reason he slapped you, but that doesn't say what the feeling is toward him for slapping you. If we don't go off to reasons, what is the feeling toward him for slapping you?"
- "I feel betrayed." *This is not a feeling but the stimulus.* He betrayed her by slapping her (stimulus). Naturally, she has a feeling in response. She does not recognize the difference between

the stimulus (the slap, the act of betrayal) and her feeling toward her boyfriend. The therapist might differentiate the stimulus from the feeling by responding, "Of course! He betrayed you. That's what he did by slapping you. So what is the feeling toward him for betraying you?"

- "I feel detached." *This is not a feeling but how she avoids her feeling using the defense of detaching*. The patient does not see the difference between her feeling and the way she wards it off. The therapist might differentiate the defense from the feeling by responding, "*Detached* is not your feeling. Detaching is how you avoid your feeling. You detach. If you don't detach, could we look at the feeling toward him for slapping you?"

- "I feel like leaving him." *This is not a feeling but the action mobilized by her feeling*. She does not differentiate her feeling from the impulse, her intended action. The therapist might respond, "It makes sense you want to leave him. What is the feeling toward him that makes you want to leave?"

- "I feel tense." *This is not a feeling but the anxiety triggered by her feeling*. She does not differentiate her feeling from her anxiety. The therapist might differentiate the anxiety from the feeling by responding, "That's your anxiety, but anxiety is not the feeling toward him. If we don't cover the feeling with anxiety and tension, what is the feeling toward him that makes you tense?"

- "I feel sad." *Sadness is a feeling, but it is not the feeling toward the boyfriend*. She does not differentiate her reactive feeling toward him from the sadness that covers it. The therapist might respond, "This sadness is a feeling between you and you. If we don't cover this other feeling with sadness, can we take a look at the feeling toward him for slapping you?" In this case, we would consider the sadness a defensive affect because it functions as a defense to cover up her anger.

- "I feel angry." *This is the patient's feeling* toward *someone who hit her*. She might feel sad that he hit her. She might be afraid to be close to him again in the future, but anger would be the reactive feeling toward someone who hit her. In clinical practice, patients often describe their sadness or anxiety, not their reactive feeling of anger.

In these examples, the patient could not differentiate her feeling from a defense, the stimulus, anxiety, an impulse, or a defensive affect. We must help patients make these differentiations so they can become conscious of their feelings.

CONSCIOUSNESS OF FEELINGS

By becoming conscious of our feelings, we can perceive, reflect upon, express, and channel them into healthy actions (Monsen et al. 1995, 1996). To acquire this self-knowledge, we must pay attention to the emotions in the body rather than use a defense to avoid them. We must tolerate the experience of emotion in the body long enough to label and understand our feelings. Patients who do not know what they feel do not know what they want.

We used two words above: *emotions* and *feelings*. The brain nonconsciously assesses the environment. This message goes to the limbic system in the brain, mobilizing the bodily reactions known as *emotions* (Damasio 1999). Humans can become conscious of bodily emotions and label them as *feelings*.

Emotion researchers have found six basic feelings: anger, fear, disgust, sadness, surprise, and happiness (Ekman 2003; Izard 1994; Tomkins 1962). These feelings are unique because they are identified by specific facial expressions recognized around the world (Ekman 1992, 2003; Keltner et al. 2003), specific autonomic nervous system (ANS) activation (Davidson 2004; Ekman and Davidson 1994; Levenson 2003), and specific adaptive action tendencies (Frijda 1986), motoric routines activated by the feelings. Other feelings, known as *social emotions*, involve more cognition and have no specific biological markers. We will focus only on the six basic feelings plus guilt and shame because they are the primary generators of conflict.

Based on what we have learned so far, we must help the patient: (1) pay attention to her feelings, (2) label her feelings accurately, (3) experience her feelings in the body, and (4) experience the action tendency of her feelings. To do so, she must see and turn against anxiety and defenses, which prevent her from becoming aware of her feelings.

INVITING FEELINGS: MAINTAINING THE FOCUS

We feel feelings all day long. Sometimes these feelings can trigger anxiety based on previous experiences. If sharing feelings was danger-ous in a past relationship, the body reacts as if it is still dangerous. The patient who learned to hide her feelings in the past may do so today. Hiding feelings may have been adaptive then, but now it creates pre-senting problems and symptoms. Thus, the therapeutic task is to help patients see and let go of their defenses so they can face their feelings.

To do this, we ask the patient to tell us the problems for which he seeks help. With his permission, we explore a specific example to find out the feelings he has and the defenses he uses to avoid them. Suppose he mentions a boss who humiliated him. To explore a specific situa-tion, we ask, "What is the feeling toward your boss for doing that?" Thus begins the phase of inviting feeling.

We must constantly focus on feeling while addressing anxiety and defenses as detours. This brings up a common misunderstand-ing about "free association." Freud initially thought that unconscious feelings would rise if he invited a patient to say what comes to mind. But he discovered that, rather than freely associate *to* difficult issues, patients often associate *away from* them by using defenses (S. Freud 1923/1961c). That is why we must systematically point out the patient's defenses and block them.

The therapist must be active. Defenses do not occur only once or twice a session. A highly resistant patient can use 150 defenses in a fifty-minute session. With so many defenses, no access to feelings and no therapeutic alliance will be possible. Defenses create an insecure attachment, symptoms, and presenting problems. We must show com-passion by blocking every single defense that destroys the possibility of treatment. Never interrupt the patient's feelings, the outpouring of his inner life. Always interrupt defenses that block his inner life.

As soon as the patient responds with anxiety or defense, help him see the difference between (1) a feeling and a stimulus, and then invite the feeling, (2) a feeling and anxiety, and then invite the feeling, or (3) a feeling and a defense, and then invite the feeling. Always address the "detour," and then explore the feeling. Patients usually respond ei-ther with anxiety or defense. To help the patient, point out his detour to anxiety or defense, then invite him to face his feeling instead. By doing so, we co-create a better relationship, both of us paying close attention to his inner life. In the following vignette, a moderately resistant patient has just reported that his fiancée in a fit of rage threw her engagement ring into the gutter.

> Therapist (Th): What's the feeling toward her for doing that? [*Invite the feeling.*]

> Patient (Pt): I think the reason she did it was that I didn't want to go to the restaurant she wanted. [*Defense: rationalization.*]

> Th: That's the reason, but the reason she did it is not the feeling you have toward her. If we leave the reason off to the side, can we take a look at the feeling toward her for throwing the ring in the gutter? [*Point out the defense, differentiate the defense from the feeling, encourage the patient to turn against the defense, and then invite the feeling.*]

> Pt: I feel disappointed. [*Defense: confusing the stimulus with the feeling.*]

> Th: Of course! She disappointed you. That's what she did. What is the feeling toward her for doing that? [*Point out the stimulus, differentiate the stimulus from the feeling, and then invite the feeling.*]

> Pt: I feel uncomfortable about the whole situation, where to go, what to do, you know? [*Defense: vagueness.*]

> Th: *Uncomfortable* is vague. It doesn't tell us what the feeling is toward her for throwing the ring in the gutter. What is the feeling toward her? [*Point out the defense, differentiate the defense from the feeling, and then invite the feeling.*]

> Pt: I suppose I could be irritated. [*Defense: hypothetical speech.*]

> Th: You suppose? Either you are irritated or you're not. Which is it in your opinion? [*Point out and block the defense, and then invite the feeling.*]

> Pt: I don't feel anger. [*Defense: negation.*]

> Th: You say you don't feel anger. That tells us what you don't feel. But still we don't know what you do feel. What is the feeling toward her for throwing the ring in the gutter? [*Point out the negation, and then invite the feeling.*]

> Pt: [*Tears in his eyes.*] I feel sad. [*Defense: tears covering the anger toward her.*]

Th: Do you notice how these tears come in to cover your feeling toward her? If we put the tears to the side, could we take a look at the feeling toward her for throwing the engagement ring away? [*Point out the defense, encourage the patient to turn against the defense, and then invite the feeling.*]

Pt: I threw my glasses on the ground and they broke. [*Defense: displacement.*]

Th: But the glasses didn't do anything to you, did they?

Pt: No.

Th: If you don't put the feeling out onto your glasses, what is the feeling toward your fiancée? [*Point out the defense of displacement and invite the patient to turn against the defense and face his feeling instead.*]

Pt: I'm angry. [*The patient can describe his feeling, so we go to the next stage and ask, "How do you experience that anger physically in your body?*]

Each time, we address the patient's defense or anxiety and then focus on the feeling. Thus, inviting the feeling is not an indiscriminate intervention. Inviting the feeling allows us to assess the patient's responses so we know what to treat.

Let's review some common mistakes therapists make in this phase.

FAILURES TO INVITE FEELING

To keep a clear focus on the reactive feeling, ask, "What is the feeling toward her for throwing the ring?"

Notice how and why the following questions fail to keep an effective focus.

- "What are your feelings about that?" The therapist didn't focus on a specific feeling. The patient could say "sad" or "anxious." But the therapist cannot show the patient how sadness covers the reactive feeling of anger. The therapist becomes vague ("about that") rather than specific about the stimulus ("for throwing the ring in the gutter").
- "What's the feeling?" This question is not specific. The patient can say "anger," "sadness," or "anxiety," each of which would answer the therapist's question. Much better would be, "What's the

feeling *toward* her for throwing the ring in the gutter?" Focus on the reactive feeling.

- "Do you have a feeling about that?" The patient could say no. Of course, he has a feeling. Don't ask *if* he has a feeling. Ask, "*What is the feeling toward her for throwing the ring in the gutter?*"
- "What are your thoughts about that?" This question invites the patient to use the defense of intellectualization by sharing his thoughts, not his feelings.
- "Why did she do that?" The therapist invites the patient to speculate about someone else. This question invites the patient to project onto others rather than focus on his feelings.
- "What is that like?" This vague question invites thinking, not feeling.
- "How do you feel about that?" This question is vague. The patient could respond with a feeling, anxiety, or a defense, but you would not be able to help him face the feeling he avoids.
- "What was the feeling then?" This question invites the patient to detach from the present and think about the past. Focus on the patient's feeling in this moment. *Remind him of the stimulus* to trigger the feeling now: "What is the feeling toward her for throwing the ring in the gutter?"

INVITING FEELINGS

Do not be discouraged when the patient responds with anxiety and defenses. Those responses tell us what to treat: excessive anxiety or excessive defense. Each time, address the anxiety or defense, and then invite the feeling again. The patient comes to you suffering from presenting problems and symptoms caused by excessive anxiety or defenses. So their appearance in the therapy is wonderful! Now you can help the patient immediately overcome the causes of his problems.

Inviting the feeling has three stages, each of which can be blocked by anxiety or a defense. Always follow the sequence: help the patient (1) label the feeling, (2) experience the feeling, and (3) experience the impulse.

Stage One (labeling the feeling): "*What is the feeling toward him?*" The patient may use many defenses to avoid declaring his feeling.

Each time, address the defense, and then invite the feeling. After some defense work, the patient eventually says what he feels. Then we arrive at the next stage.

Stage Two (experiencing the feeling): *"How do you experience that anger (or other feeling) physically in your body?"* The patient may use many defenses to avoid declaring how he experiences anger physically in his body. Each time, point out the defense, and then invite the experience of his feeling: "How do you experience that rage physically in your body?" After more defense work, the patient eventually declares how he experiences his anger physically in his body. Then we arrive at the next stage.

Stage Three (experiencing the impulse): *"What is the impulse that goes with that rage?"* *"How do you experience that impulse physically in your body?"* The patient may ward off experiencing the impulse that goes with his feeling. Address each defense, and then ask, "How do you experience that impulse physically in your body?" Once the patient can experience his impulse physically in his body, he is ready for a breakthrough to the unconscious.

ANXIETY DURING THE PHASE OF INVITING FEELINGS

Addressing defenses is most of our work, but the topic of anxiety deserves a brief comment. Anxiety is a good sign, signaling that unconscious feelings are rising. All learning in therapy requires us to tolerate an optimal level of anxiety for the sake of our growth. If anxiety is too high, the brain cannot work properly, and new learning is impossible. When anxiety is at an ideal level for learning, the patient faces what he usually avoids and experiences anxiety in his striated muscles. (See chapter 2 on anxiety.)

When anxiety is too low, the patient is avoiding his feelings. He does not learn what triggers his anxiety. Therapists who avoid anxiety-provoking topics help patients avoid rather than master their difficulties.

Inviting feelings and addressing defenses mobilizes unconscious feelings, triggering unconscious anxiety in the voluntary (striated) muscles. Sighing and tensing of the muscles signal the rise of unconscious feelings the patient usually avoids. This rise of anxiety in the striated muscles is a sign of progress and no cause for concern. Treat the anxiety as a defense, and then invite the feeling.

Th: What is the feeling toward him for hitting you?

Pt: I feel tense. [*Anxiety in striated muscles.*]

Th: That's your anxiety. If we take that lid of anxiety off, could we take a look at the feeling underneath? [*Address anxiety as a defense, and then invite the feeling.*]

Each intervention triggering unconscious anxiety in the striated muscles is on the right track: toward feelings. We refer to a rise of anxiety after an intervention as *unconscious signaling*. If anxiety did not rise in the body, the intervention did not mobilize feelings. Perhaps the intervention did not focus on feelings, or it addressed the wrong defense. Every useful intervention should mobilize unconscious feelings and anxiety.

Patients who are willing to tolerate anxiety to achieve their goals will improve in therapy. Patients unwilling to tolerate anxiety will not improve. We must show them how avoiding their anxiety imprisons them and defeats their goals. Then they will turn against their defenses.

Pt: This is too uncomfortable.

Th: Obviously this anger makes you uncomfortable. Otherwise, you would have faced it years ago. But if you keep avoiding this anger that makes you uncomfortable, what will happen here?

Pt: I guess I won't get better.

Th: Right. We have this choice. You can avoid what makes you uncomfortable and have these symptoms, or you can face what makes you uncomfortable so you can achieve your goals. What do you think would be in your best interest?

Pt: I guess I have to look at this anger.

Th: You don't have to. It's a choice. You can keep avoiding this anger that makes you uncomfortable, and you have the right to do so.

Pt: But I can't keep going on like this.

Th: That's not true. You have been going on like this for twenty years, avoiding what makes you uncomfortable, and you can keep doing that if it is giving you the results you want.

Pt: That's just it. It's not working anymore.

Before we go to a transcript, let us review the goal and principles when inviting feelings. The goal of inviting feelings is to help the patient face and experience previously avoided feelings so that he does not have to use anxiety and defenses to avoid them. Once he no longer uses his defenses against feeling, his symptoms and presenting problems will go away. To achieve this goal, we follow three principles: (1) If the patient responds with feeling, explore feeling, (2) If the patient responds with excessive anxiety, regulate anxiety and then explore feeling, (3) If the patient responds with defense, help the patient see and let go of the defense and then explore feeling. Assess each patient response to see if it is a feeling, anxiety, or defense. This response will determine your next intervention.

Patients with low resistance respond with feelings. Explore their feelings.

Fragile patients respond with excessive anxiety. Regulate excessive anxiety, and then focus on their feelings. Moderately and highly resistant patients respond with defenses. Help these patients see and let go of their defenses and then focus on feelings. See figure 1.1 to understand the three basic choices when intervening.

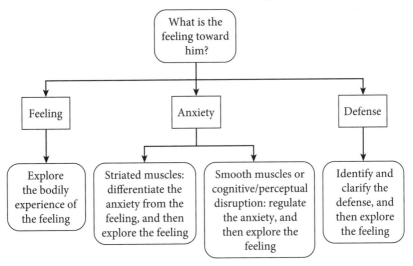

Figure 1.1   Decision tree: inviting the feeling

We invite feelings in three stages. First, we ask what feeling the patient has so he can label his feeling. Second, we ask how he experiences that feeling physically in his body. Third, we ask how he experiences the impulse that comes with that feeling. At each stage, anxiety or defenses may cause a detour. Regulate anxiety and help the patient see his defenses until he can go to the next stage. Then explore feelings at that level.

Table 1.1 illustrates the first two stages and sample responses of feeling, anxiety, and defense.

Table 1.1   Phases in inviting feeling

Intervention one: Inviting the feeling	"What is the feeling toward him?"	"What is the feeling toward him?"	"What is the feeling toward him?"
Response type	*Feeling*	*Anxiety*	*Defense*
Answer	"I feel angry."	"I feel tense."	"I feel detached."
Intervention two: The patient has identified his anger. So the therapist invites the experience of the feeling	"How do you experience that anger physically in your body?"	"How do you experience that anger physically in your body?"	"How do you experience that anger physically in your body?"
Response type	*Feeling*	*Anxiety*	*Defense*
Answer	"I feel heat coming up in my body."	"I feel nervous."	"I think he shouldn't have done that."

SESSION ILLUSTRATING HOW TO MAINTAIN A FOCUS ON FEELINGS

The following transcript is the initial session with a fifty-two-year-old man. He called for an appointment, suffering from various somatic complaints treated by his internist and a neurologist. He had been unable to sleep regularly for thirteen years. A recent examination at a local sleep clinic was inconclusive because the patient, without medications, slept twenty-six minutes during the entire evening! He also suffered from panic attacks, bowel complaints, headaches, shaking and trembling, and physical collapses at work and elsewhere. After a sudden physical collapse at his job, coworkers helped him into a car and took him home. His condition crippled him so much he could no longer go to work regularly and had to conduct office business by phone from his bed. Besides these conflicts, he took a caretaker role with his wife, who had been diagnosed with a bipolar mood disorder, and he feared sharing anything emotionally intimate with her.

The patient regarded all his somatic complaints as biological in origin and saw no psychological precipitants. Those became clear only through treatment. At the beginning of therapy he had no idea when his symptoms had dramatically worsened. However, after a few sessions he realized his symptoms first appeared after a beloved male boss left his organization and worsened further still when he and a mentally ill coworker were assigned the joint responsibility of managing his division. This worsening of physical symptoms led him to seek treatment.

Doctors had treated him for several years with a wide range of medications for anxiety, sleep, and seizure disorders. The doctors' inability to diagnose his condition and the possibility that he had Parkinson's disease left the patient fearing he was going to die soon because his condition had worsened. We spoke on the phone before our appointment and he told me of all his health issues. We agreed to meet, and his wife drove him to my office because he was no longer able to drive long distances.

The patient begins the interview by describing a recent meeting with his doctor. He told her he had made an appointment with me, a social worker. She suggested he see a psychiatrist instead and go on medications. The transcript begins about three minutes into the session.

Vignette One (minutes 3–5)

I start the interview by inviting the patient's feelings.

Th: When you say you felt unhappy, what was the emotion you felt toward her [the doctor]? [*Stage one: invite the patient to label his feeling.*]

Pt: Well, I think the emotion I felt toward her was the fact that it was like, "Well, a social worker's not good enough. You need a psychiatrist." [*Defense: Intellectualization. The patient does not differentiate between his feeling and a defense.*]

Th: That was your thought, presumably, but your feeling toward her? Your emotion toward her? [*Differentiate his defense of intellectualization from his feeling, and then invite the feeling.*]

Pt: I think my emotion toward her—a lot of that came down to the fact that I had not had as much contact with her as I would have liked during this process, you know? [*Defense: rationalization. The patient cannot differentiate his feeling from a defense.*]

Th: That's your thought. [*Identify the defense.*]

Pt: That's my thought. [*Begins to see the difference between his feeling and a thought.*]

Th: But your emotion toward her? Because you said it was a hot button. The emotion toward her? [*Invite the feeling.*]

Pt: I think the emotion toward her was that her questioning the fact that, well, you know, you need to see a psychiatrist. [*Defense: rationalization. Cannot differentiate his feeling from a defense.*]

Th: It sounds like that was the reason you had an emotion, but what was the emotion you had toward her? [*Differentiate feeling from the defense, and then ask about the feeling.*]

Pt: What was the emotion I had toward her? I think it was . . . it was frustration. [*Defense: confusing the stimulus (she frustrated him) with the feeling toward her for doing that.*] It was like, I have what I believe is a physical problem. You had raised this issue. The last time I had the last bad physical event and had gone home and had called her and talked with her, the first thing out from her was, "Do you need a psychiatrist?" [*Defense: rationalization.*]

Th: She was obviously frustrating you, right? [*Point out the stimulus.*]

Pt: Right.

Th: And your emotion toward her for frustrating you? [*Invite the feeling.*]

Pt: [*Sighs. Indication of access to striated muscle pathway of anxiety discharge.*] I was not—I don't think I was angry at her [*The defense of negation simultaneously represses and allows the anger to emerge.*], but I think it was a case of—I understood that she was— [hand opens up].

Vignette Two (minutes 6–14)

I continue to invite the patient's feeling.

Th: But the feeling toward her?

Pt: The emotion toward her was, "You're not believing what I'm saying. [*Defense: intellectualization.*]

Th: Well, that's certainly the thought you had. [*Identify the defense.*]

Pt: [*Switches leg position and becomes animated.*] That was the thought, you know.

Th: Yeah. But the emotion? [*Invite the feeling.*]

Pt: What's the emotion? I think, at that time— [*Sighs.*] Like I said, was I mad? Yeah, I was mad, sure. [*Emergence of the patient's anger.*]

Th: Uh-huh, so you were angry with her then.

Pt: I was angry with her. I had a perception that she could just close this off and say, "This is psychiatrist territory. I'm an internist. You need a psychiatrist."

Th: And that anger? How do you experience it even now? [*Stage two: invite the patient to describe how he experiences the anger in his body.*]

Pt: I'm in much more control, I think, of the situation. [*Defense.*]

Th: But if we don't control the anger now, if we let ourselves have a look at that right now, how do you experience that anger toward her right now? [*Identify the defense, invite the patient to turn against it, and then invite the experience of the feeling.*]

Pt: [*Sighs.*] How do I experience it now? [*Sighs.*] I really just didn't know exactly what to do at that point. I mean there was— [*Defense: rationalization.*]

Th: But the anger? How do you experience that right now? [*Block the defense, and then invite the experience of the feeling.*]

Pt: How do I feel about it right now? [*Defense: vagueness.*]

Th: How do you experience this anger toward her? [*Invite the experience of the feeling.*]

Pt: [*Sighs.*] How do I? [*Sighs.*] I'm going to go in a little bit different direction here. [*Defense.*]

The patient briefly describes how the doctor discusses his difficulties in a dismissive way. This is the defense of diversification. His anxiety drops because the therapist mistakenly follows the patient's defense rather than focuses on his feeling.

We return a minute later.

Th: But, if we come back—because you were obviously feeling quite angry with her for saying, you need to see a psychiatrist, for speaking to you in a clipped and dismissive manner. [*Return the focus to his feeling.*]

Pt: Right.

Th: How do you experience that anger toward her right now? [*Invite the experience of the feeling.*]

Pt: [*Sighs.*] I'm still frustrated, I mean— [*Defense: confusing the stimulus and his feeling. We could call* frustrated *a cover word.*]

Th: But the anger? How do you experience the anger physically? [*Invite the experience of the feeling.*]

Pt: [*Sighs.*] I have not made, you know—I go out. I walk. I try to let off steam. I just try to say, look, you know, she is who she is. She is trying to do her job, you know. [*Defenses: discharge, rationalization.*]

Th: Let's back up here. You feel angry with her. One of the ways you try to deal with anger is you try to walk it off. [*Identify and clarify the patient's defenses.*]

Pt: Yeah.

Th: And you say another way you try to deal with anger is to kind of steam it off.

Pt: Yeah.

Th: And another way you try to deal with anger is to come up with all kinds of rationalizations.

Pt: Yeah.

Th: And these are all mechanisms that you're using to deal with this very powerful emotion coming up inside you.

Pt: Right.

Th: If we don't rationalize away the anger, if we let ourselves have a more honest look at that emotion right now, how do you experience that emotion of anger toward her? [*Invite him to drop his defense of rationalization and describe the experience of his anger.*]

Pt: [*Sighs.*] How am I experiencing?

Th: Yeah, physically.

Pt: Physically? Physically, how am I experiencing that anger toward her? [*Sighs.*]

Th: Yeah.

Pt: [*Sighs.*] I have difficulty saying because I think I'm— As you said, I put up these mechanisms. I'm throwing it up here, I'm throwing it up here, and I'm saying— [*Becomes aware of the defenses he uses against anger.*]

Th: Yeah.

Pt: I'm not going to, you know, swear at the lady or go bananas and say— [*Defense: negation.*]

Th: In reality, obviously you're not.

Pt: In reality, I'm not.

Th: But physically, if we just look, in the privacy of this room, as we're trying to understand this emotion—this is a powerful emotion— how do you experience this emotion physically? [*Invite the experience of the feeling.*]

Pt: [*Sighs.*] I think I'd go back to this abandonment thing of, you know. [*Defense: cover word.*]

Th: Clearly she abandoned you in a certain sense, and this makes you feel very angry toward her. And the anger, how do you experience that physically? [*Differentiate the defense from his feeling and invite the experience of his feeling.*]

Pt: How do I physically?

Th: Yeah, how do you experience that direct anger? [*Invite the experience of the feeling.*]

Pt: [*Sighs.*] I hardly feel anything, and that's the truth. [*Defense.*]

Th: You hardly feel anything?

Pt: I hardly feel anything right now. I mean, it's just hard to—I just really, right now, between this whole process, I've just kind of cut all the emotional stuff off. [*He sees his defense of cutting off feelings.*]

Th: It's great you're so honest here because what this shows is with the tremendous anger that you feel toward this woman, one way you deal with the anger is you almost deaden your emotions. You try to deaden the rage. [*Point out the link between his defense and his collapses, i.e., his defenses are killing him.*]

Pt: Yes. [*Tears.*]

Th: And then we see that another way is that you're tempted to go to tears as a way to cover up this very heated emotion, right? [*Point out how the tears cover up his anger.*]

Pt: Yes.

Th: But obviously, you've not come here to deaden yourself or to be dead, right? [*Help the patient turn against his defenses, and remind him of his underlying wish to become well.*]

Pt: No.

Th: If we don't deaden this anger, and if we don't wash it away with tears. [*Encourage the patient to turn against his defenses.*]

Pt: Yes.

Th: If we have a more honest look at that anger, how do you experience this anger toward her? [*Invite the experience of the feeling.*]

Pt: [*Sighs.*] I'm trying. I guess it's hard to dig in here. [*Sighs.*] I just want to talk. Tell me if I'm not there. Ask questions please. [*Sighs.*] I think she's searching for the right answers. I'm just not confident that she's there. [*Defense: rationalization.*]

Th: That describes her, but if we take a look at the anger toward her? How do you experience that? [*Differentiate the defense from his feeling, and then invite the experience of his anger.*]

Pt: What am I feeling out of this? I guess . . . [*The phrase "I guess" is the beginning of the defense of hypothetical speech. Block that defense by asking about his feeling again.*]

Th: How do you experience this anger? [*Invite the experience of the feeling.*]

Pt: What I'm feeling out of this anger is that [*Sighs.*] . . . I feel . . . that I'm fighting to stay alive right now. [*The patient says he is fighting to stay alive: a rise in the therapeutic alliance. Unconsciously, he indicates that he has been killing himself.*]

Th: Hmm, fighting to stay alive. It sounds like you feel like you're alone in that fight. [*Mirror the patient's wish to stay alive.*]

The patient begins to cry and tries to say something but cannot. Grief emerges as he turns against the resistance. He continues to cry as he becomes aware of how he kills himself slowly. We return several minutes later to invite his experience of anger followed by a summary of his defenses against the experience of anger, especially his use of immobility (deadening his emotions and body).

Vignette Three (minutes 16–20)

I invite the patient to turn against his defenses.

Pt: [*Sighs.*] I think what's going on, like I said, is that [*Sighs.*] . . .

Th: The anger? [*Invite the feeling.*]

Pt: The anger, the anger is clearly, you know [*Sighs.*] I want to live. I don't want to die. I want something done now. I don't want to wait two weeks, four weeks, six weeks, you know . . . [*Rise in unconscious therapeutic alliance.*]

Th: And the anger? How do you experience it, physically, right now? [*Invite the experience of the feeling.*]

Pt: Physically, right now? I'm upset. There's no damn question I'm upset. [*Defense: cover word.*]

Th: Ah, but you're angry, right? [*Point out the cover word* upset.]

Pt: I am angry.

Th: And it's very important we help you with any of your conflict around anger because you need access to all the anger you've got in your body—right?—to fight for your life.

Pt: Absolutely.

Th: Because if you deaden your anger, you could be dead, right? It could be almost a form of suicide if you deaden your anger, right? [*Point out the price of his defenses, and mobilize the patient to let go of his defenses.*]

Pt: Right.

Th: Because you're in a position that you are having to really fight for your life. [*Mobilize the patient's will and help him engage in the therapeutic task.*]

Pt: I have to fight.

Th: If we don't deaden the anger, let's see if we can get to the bottom of what this is all about. [*Invite the feeling.*]

Pt: Yeah.

The first breakthrough of the patient's murderous rage occurred thirty-six minutes into the interview. The patient used the defenses of intellectualization, rationalization, negation, immobility, and displacement. Each time, I addressed the defense and then returned to the focus on feeling. First, I asked about the feeling toward the doctor. After a series of defenses, the patient could label his feeling as anger. When I asked how he experienced the anger physically in his body, the patient immobilized himself. When I addressed the patient's defense of immobilization and the patient turned against it, feeling and impulse rose in his body. Then the patient displaced his rage onto stuff instead of toward the doctor who had failed him. Once the patient turned against the defense of displacement, he experienced the impulse to grab in his hands and body.

Questions

Sometimes, therapists who read this transcript or see the video-taped case wonder, "Isn't there a danger the patient will fall apart if he experiences these feelings?" "Isn't it possible that these feelings will hurt the patient?" "Isn't there a danger I could hurt the patient?" One of the most important points to remember is this: feelings do not hurt the patient; defenses hurt the patient. Feelings do not cause the patient's suffering; his defenses do. Feelings do not make the patient fall apart, his anxiety and defenses can cause him to regress. If we regulate the patient's anxiety and address regressive defenses, we can help the patient face his feelings quickly or gradually, according to his capacity. His defenses were creating his suffering before he came to your office. You do not cause his suffering. He causes his suffering through defenses, which he does not see. Your task is to focus on his feelings and help him see and turn against his defenses. Lastly, in learning any treatment method, we make mistakes. Patients will nearly always forgive a mistake of the head, just not one of the heart.

Another question therapists ask is this: "If the patient does not know what he is feeling, why do you persist?" Due to defenses, the patient cannot know what he is feeling yet. He needs practice seeing his defenses and letting go of them before he will gain access to his feelings. If we use a neuroscience metaphor, his prefrontal cortex is not getting much information from his limbic system. So he won't know what his feelings are at first. We understand that the patient is giving the best answers he can. Yet if we keep asking for feelings, we keep building new neural connections between his prefrontal cortex and the subcortical regions of his brain. Think of learning to catch a ball when you were a child. You kept missing the ball or dropping it. But your father kept throwing the ball time after time while your brain kept forming new neural connections until you could catch that ball. The same principle is at work here. Through repetition we give the patient's brain a chance to form the neural connections so that he can recognize what he is feeling in his body.

SUMMARY

This case illustrates how to focus on feelings and identify defenses for patients with low and moderate resistance. From an evolutionary perspective, emotions allow us to react automatically to changes in the environment. From an interpersonal perspective, whenever we become close to others, nonconscious appraisal in the brain mobilizes feelings in the body. These feelings allow us to communicate with one another. They are the glue of our relationships. They "have healing power because they are . . . the primary mediators of social life" (Trevarthen 2009, 55). Feelings also strengthen our learning and memories. From a motivational perspective, feelings reveal which of our needs are met or unfulfilled. They propel us toward what we want. From the perspective of neuroscience (Damasio 1999), feelings provide us with our core consciousness. From the perspective of development, exchanging feelings is the basis of our intellectual and cultural development. And from an existential perspective, feelings reveal to us the value and meaning of our lives. Feelings "most profoundly shape our personhood and are most central to being human" (Gaylin 1990, 78).

We invite feelings to help the patient dare to become emotionally close again, after a life in which closeness led to pain. These feelings trigger anxiety and defenses. Defenses prevent the patient from being aware of his feelings, interfering with his sense of self, relationships, motivation, development, and even the meaning of his life. Thus, the therapist focuses on the feelings the patient avoids. When anxiety and defense arise, the therapist points out these "detours" and then invites the patient to face his feelings instead. How we do this varies according to the patient's strengths and weaknesses. This book contains numerous vignettes that illustrate how to handle those detours so the patient can face his feelings and channel them adaptively into action rather than suffer from anxiety and symptoms. Now we will explore the two major detours from feeling: anxiety and defenses.

RECOMMENDED READINGS

Malan, D. (1979). The dialogue of therapy and the two triangles. In *Individual psychotherapy and the science of psychodynamics* (pp. 74–94). London: Butterworths.

Malan, D., and Coughlin Della Selva, P. (2006). Introduction to the theory and technique of Davanloo's ISTDP. In *Lives transformed: A revolutionary method of dynamic psychotherapy* (pp. 10–33). London: Karnac.

RECOMMENDED MATERIALS

If you would like to learn how to address defenses and maintain an effective focus, you can receive a free audio skill-building course by subscribing at http://www.istdpinstitute.com.

CHAPTER TWO

Anxiety: The First Detour from Feelings

nxiety is a term that is widely used yet almost universally misunderstood. In the first part of this chapter we will define anxiety, its function, and its causes. Then we will differentiate anxiety from common misconceptions. And finally, we will describe the biological underpinnings of anxiety. In the second part of this chapter we will describe how to assess the discharge of anxiety into the patient's body, and how to assess when anxiety is too high, requiring regulation. Then we show a variety of techniques for regulating anxiety. In the third part of this chapter we show how to assess patients where anxiety regulation does not work. Here we show how to work with defenses that prevent anxiety regulation.

DEFINITIONS

What do we mean by the term *anxiety*? The affect of fear consists of the nonconscious detection of threat (Damasio 1999). The emotion of fear refers to the *unconscious activation of the body by the somatic and autonomic nervous systems* (Damasio 1999). These systems create the symptoms of the pounding heart and sweating palms. The *feeling of anxiety* refers to our conscious awareness of these bodily sensations (Damasio 1999).

We call these symptoms *fear* when they are triggered by objective threats or call them *anxiety* when they are triggered by our feelings (A. Freud 1936). Therapy focuses on anxiety triggered by feelings in a session. This emotional activation of the body supports defensive responses such as fight/flight and immobilization (Porges 1995). Thus, we must differentiate nonconscious threat detection (Panksepp 1998,

2009), nonconscious mobilization of emotion in the body (Damasio 1999; Panksepp 1998); and defensive responses (fight/flight and immobilization) (Porges 1995, 2001a, 2001b, 2011; Porges and Bazhenova 2006) from *conscious awareness of the feeling of anxiety in the body* (Damasio 1999).

Anxiety signals that feelings inside us are a threat. We cannot run away from them; we can only "hide" them by using defenses. Fear mobilizes the body to protect itself physically (Panksepp 1998), whereas anxiety mobilizes us to defend ourselves psychologically (S. Freud 1926/1961d).

The Function of Anxiety

Anxiety has a different function from other feelings: to signal and prepare the body to respond to danger. This involves four steps. First, a system prewired in the brain, inherited from the mammals (Panksepp 1998, 2012), nonconsciously assesses danger and sends a message to the amygdala. Second, the amygdala activates the somatic and autonomic nervous systems (Goldstein 2006), creating the emotion of fear in the body (Damasio 1999). Briefly, the somatic nervous system activates the voluntary muscles so we can run from, or fight with, an attacker. For those muscles to act externally, the autonomic nervous system must support them internally (LeDoux 1998). Third, now that the body has been activated, we can engage in defensive actions to fight with, flee from, or surrender to objective threats (Porges 1995, 2001a, 2001b, 2011; Porges and Bazhenova 2006; Kennard 1947). Fourth, we can become conscious of these bodily symptoms and label them as the feeling of anxiety (Damasio 1999).

How does anxiety prepare the body to act? When the amygdala mobilizes the somatic and autonomic nervous systems, the sympathetic branch of the ANS raises our pulse, breath rate, and blood pressure, withdrawing blood from the extremities and redirecting it to the large muscles so we can run or fight. That is why our hands and feet get cold. Other symptoms include dry mouth, dry eyes, constipation, and dilated pupils (Goldstein 2006; Hamill and Shapiro 2004).

The parasympathetic branch of the ANS lowers our pulse, breath rate, and blood pressure, resulting in a drop of blood flow to the brain. This creates symptoms of blurry vision, ringing in the ears, problems thinking, dizziness, nausea, diarrhea, and migraines. Other symptoms include increased salivation, teary eyes, constricted pupils, warm hands, cardiac arrhythmia, bodily anesthesia, and limpness (Goldstein 2006; Hamill and Shapiro 2004; McEwen, Bulloch, and Stewart 1999). This parasympathetic reaction enables animals to go limp when attacked by a predator and sometimes escape being eaten. The somatic and autonomic nervous systems create the symptoms of anxiety in our bodies (Goldstein 2006) in less than a second, before we consciously think about or see a threat (Ohman and Wiens 2003).

Yet if fear and anxiety allow us to survive, why are they such a problem? *Fear can be an adaptive response to an objective threat or a maladaptive reaction to a misperceived cue.* The emotion system designed for the jungle operates today in human relationships. However, we no longer have to fear dangers like saber-toothed tigers, just the occasional crazy driver.

To survive, animals must avoid predators; humans must avoid the loss of relationships. Many mammals live independently when only a few weeks old. We, however, cannot. Children rely on others to survive. Therefore, any feeling threatening the safety of our primary relationship endangers our survival (Bowlby 1969, 1973, 1980), triggering anxiety (Evans 1996; H. S. Sullivan 1953a, 1953b). Why does anxiety cause so many problems? A single experience is enough for a relationship-threatening feeling to trigger anxiety for a lifetime. Fear memories are permanent (Fanselow and Dale 2003).

The Causation of Anxiety

Milliseconds after anxiety symptoms are mobilized in the body, the amygdala sends a message to the prefrontal cortex, which is responsible for thinking and decision making, and can send corrective feedback. So conscious thought occurs *after* unconscious detection of a threat and mobilization of the body. According to LeDoux (1998), an unconscious cue triggers the amygdala and hypothalamus, which activate the autonomic nervous system, creating anxiety symptoms throughout the body. Then a message goes to the cortex, which provides feedback to the amygdala after it has already triggered the anxiety symptoms. Therefore, the body reacts *before* the prefrontal cortex can provide feedback regarding a visible cue: "Those stripes in the grass are just some sticks, not a tiger. You're safe."

In relationships, unconscious threats (such as emotions) are more difficult to evaluate because they are invisible. For instance, I ask a patient what feeling is triggering her anxiety. She thinks she is anxious because of a test she will take in three weeks. Her anxiety rises and falls in the session, yet the supposed cue (the exam) remains the same. Thus, the test cannot be the trigger. Then she remembers: her uncle just died. His death reminds her of her father's death, and her anxiety rises. Sadness is the trigger.

The threat-detection system we share with reptiles and mammals predates the evolution of the human prefrontal cortex and operates independently of it. We are anxious bodily before we know it cognitively. How adaptive! Imagine if one of our ancestors had seen a tiger and then thought, "Hmm. That looks like a furry quadruped running toward me. It certainly has large teeth." Crunch! He would have become dinner.

At the beginning of the session, the patient had forgotten her sadness. She was unable to scan her "internal savannah" for the feeling triggering her anxiety. As a result, she could only speculate about the trigger and decided it must be the test. This example shows how feelings, which are invisible, cause anxiety. Patients often do not recognize these invisible feelings because early in life they learned to ignore the feelings that made their caretakers anxious. ("My sadness makes Mom nervous. If I ignore it, she won't be upset, and our relationship will be secure.") Once ignoring feelings becomes an unconscious, automatic habit, we no longer know what triggers our anxiety. When a feeling enters the room, our bodies react as if it were a tiger, and we consciously do not know why. Let's look at the issue of causality.

- *Correct causality:* The patient experiences a feeling (sadness about her father's death) that triggers anxiety (racing heart, sweating palms, and tense muscles) that triggers a defense (rumination about the test) distracting her from her sadness.
- *Incorrect causality:* The patient thinks a test she will take in three weeks (defense of displacement) triggers her anxiety today.

The defense of displacement distracted her from her sadness, providing a reasonable explanation for her anxiety. As long as she avoided her grief, however, it pushed for expression, triggering her anxiety. Once she faced her sadness and grieved, her anxiety lessened, as her defense was no longer necessary. Sadness made her anxious because her abusive family condemned any expression of feelings.

The right hemisphere of the brain stores an internal working model of a child's relationships, determining how she handles her feelings (Schore 2002, 14). A securely attached person accepts her feelings and regulates her anxiety by paying careful attention to it. She regulates herself as others regulated her.

In contrast, an insecurely attached person reacts as if others will reject her feelings and anxiety. Feelings, perceived as dangerous, trigger unconscious memories of early relationships, which take the form of anxiety (Schore 2002, 21). The hippocampus, immature until the third or fourth year of life, remembers only the quality of early experiences—the somatic sensations and behaviors (De Rijk, Kitraki, and De Kloet 2010, 142; O'Keefe and Nadel 1978). Feelings trigger anxiety: bodily memories of an insecure attachment, sensations when anxiety was not regulated. These primordial representations of bodily states are the foundation on which all emotional growth and future experience proceeds.

Having clarified the concept of causality, let's clear up a few misconceptions about anxiety.

Anxiety Is Not a Stimulus

The literature on psychotherapy has described separation anxiety, related to losing a loved one; castration anxiety, related to damage to your body or genitals; moral anxiety, related to transgressing one's values; annihilation anxiety, related to being invaded and destroyed; fragmentation anxiety, related to self-disintegration; and persecutory anxiety, related to the belief that others want to hurt you (Waelder 1960). However, these are stimuli, not anxiety. If someone threatens to mutilate your genitals, you will feel anxiety in your body. However, castration is a stimulus or fantasy, not the resulting bodily state of anxiety.

Anxiety Is Not a Thought

A patient is angry with a professor who contemptuously criticized his paper in front of a class. Afterward he is afraid that the professor wants to attack him physically. Anger triggers his anxiety. Once he projects his rage onto the professor, he believes the professor makes him anxious, not his anger. This thought ("I fear him") results from projection. Anger causes his anxiety; projection creates his thought (table 2.1).

Table 2.1   The causality of anxiety

Sequence in time	Element of conflict	Description
1	Feeling	"I am angry with him."
2	Anxiety (bodily experience)	Blurry vision, ringing in the ears, and nausea.
3	Defense of projection (thought)	"I am not angry. My professor is angry with me."
4	Consequence (thought)	"I fear him." The patient fears the projection he has placed on the professor.

Anxiety Is an Unconscious Biophysiological Activation Pattern in the Body

Always differentiate thoughts in the mind (defense) from the feeling in the body (anxiety). To make this easier to see, table 2.2 lists the bodily symptoms of anxiety created by the somatic and autonomic (sympathetic and parasympathetic) nervous systems (Goldstein 2006; Hamill and Shapiro 2004).

Table 2.2.   Bodily symptoms of anxiety

Anxiety symptoms caused by the somatic nervous system	Clenched thumbs and hands Tension headaches Tense arms, shoulders, and neck. Sighing: tension in the intercostal muscles Tight stomach muscles, tension in feet and legs Fibromyalgia Chronic tensing of the pelvic muscles, resulting in painful sensations, painful menstruation, painful intercourse, menstrual irregularity, and vulvadynia

Anxiety symptoms caused by the sympathetic nervous system	Dry mouth Dry eyes Dilated pupils Cold hands Increased heart rate, blood pressure, and respiration Blushing Decreased motility of the gastrointestinal tract: constipation Constricted bladder sphincter: urinary retention) Shivering Piloerection (hair stands on end due to muscle contraction) Hyperventilation and fainting
Anxiety symptoms caused by the parasympathetic nervous system	Salivation Teary eyes Constricted pupils Warm hands Decreased heart rate, blood pressure, and respiration Increased motility of the gastrointestinal tract: nausea, vomiting, diarrhea Relaxed bladder sphincter: urge to urinate Migraines (due to vasodilation) Cardiac arrhythmia Dizziness Foggy thinking Bodily anesthesia Limpness

We'll refer to three patterns of unconscious anxiety discharge in the body (table 2.3): striated muscles, smooth muscles, and cognitive/perceptual disruption (H. Davanloo, supervision 2002–2004), each of which is created by the somatic and autonomic nervous systems.

Table 2.3   Pathways of unconscious anxiety discharge

Anxiety symptoms in the striated muscles	Hand clenching Tension in the intercostal muscles of the chest—sighing Tension in arms, shoulders, neck, legs, and feet Jaw clenching, biting Tension headaches
Anxiety symptoms in the smooth muscles	Bladder urgency and frequency Gastrointestinal spasm: irritable bowel syndrome, nausea, vomiting Vascular symptoms: migraine, hypertension Bronchi symptoms: asthma "Jelly legs": unsteady gait due to lack of tension (striated access)

Table 2.3 (continued)

Anxiety Symptoms in Cognitive/Perceptual Disruption	Drifting, dissociation, confusion, losing track of thoughts, poor memory
	Visual blurring, tunnel vision, blindness
	Anesthesia: sudden loss of feeling in areas of the body
	Fainting, freezing, fugue states, dizziness
	Hallucinations
	Ringing in the ears
	Projection, projective identification

In summary, nonconscious threat detection (affect) produces a biophysiological activation in the body (emotion) (Damasio 1999). Fear is the bodily reaction triggered by an objective danger. Anxiety is the bodily reaction triggered by a feeling (A. Freud 1936). Fear prepares the body to engage in defensive behaviors in response to external dangers. Anxiety triggers the mind to use psychological defenses to ward off internal feelings perceived as dangerous in a relationship.

ASSESSMENT OF THE PATHWAYS OF UNCONSCIOUS ANXIETY DISCHARGE

Every time you intervene during a session, you invite the patient to form a therapeutic alliance. This triggers feelings and anxiety based on past relationships. After each intervention, assess the following:

1. What is the pathway of unconscious anxiety discharge? If striated muscles, explore feelings and address defenses. If smooth muscles or cognitive/perceptual disruption, regulate the anxiety until it returns to the striated muscles, and then explore feelings.

2. How rapidly does the anxiety rise and fall? If a patient's anxiety rises slowly during the session when you explore feelings and drops quickly when you pay attention to it, the patient regulates her anxiety well. You can safely explore feelings. A rapid rise and slow fall of anxiety indicate poor anxiety regulation, possible regressive defenses, and lingering effects of neuroendocrine discharge. For instance, a patient may become sick to her stomach or project at the beginning of the session. These signs reveal a fast rise of anxiety. In such a case, regulate the anxiety until it returns to the striated muscles, and then explore feelings.

3. Can the patient observe and pay attention to her anxiety? If so, explore the feeling under the anxiety. If not, help her observe and regulate her anxiety.

4. Does anxiety regulation work? If not, identify the defenses preventing the patient from observing, paying attention to, and regulating her anxiety.

Assessment of Anxiety and Self-Observing Capacity

When anxiety regulation does not work, assess the patient's

1. Anxiety in her body
2. Ability to observe, pay attention to, and regulate it
3. Defenses, which prevent her from observing, paying attention to, and regulating her anxiety

When the patient cannot observe, pay attention, or regulate her anxiety, she uses defenses, which prevent her from doing so. Assessing these defenses is essential to make anxiety regulation possible.

How the Patient Walks In

We can begin assessing the patient's anxiety as soon as he enters the room by noticing his gait. A patient with striated muscle tension walks energetically, with an erect posture and an expressive or tense face. In contrast, a patient whose anxiety goes into his smooth muscles or cognitive/perceptual disruption enters slowly, perhaps a bit wobbly on his feet due to a lack of tension in his muscles ("jelly legs"). He sits in a slumped and tired posture, his face expressionless. When interventions evoke no tension or sighing, immediately assess his anxiety.

Response to Intervention

Now we will look at some transcripts that show how to assess the patient's pathway of unconscious anxiety discharge. The first transcript is a clinical example of striated muscle discharge created by the somatic nervous system.

Th: Could we look at an example of when this is a problem for you?

Pt: [Sighs.] Well, a couple days ago she told me she wanted to dump me.

Th: What is your feeling toward her for saying that?

Pt: [*Sighs. Shifts in chair.*] Well, I didn't like it. [*Defense: intellectualization.*]

Th: Of course, what is the feeling toward her for saying that?

Pt: [*Sighs. Wiggles fingers.*] I was angry.

Each time the therapist asks about emotional material, the patient becomes tense, sighs, and shifts in his chair. The patient's sighs and fidgeting indicate that his anxiety is discharged into the striated muscles. Patients whose unconscious anxiety is discharged only into striated muscles use isolation of affect as a defense. They can tell you what they feel but not how they experience the feeling. You can pursue high levels of feeling (H. Davanloo, supervision 2002–2004).

Unconscious Signaling

After the therapist intervenes, unconscious bodily signs of anxiety *signal a rise of unconscious feelings* (H. Davanloo, supervision 2002–2004) within one second. This unconscious signaling occurs when the patient's statement or the therapist's intervention triggers unconscious feelings. Now you know what topic to explore or which obstacle to focus on.

When interventions do not trigger unconscious signaling, you are not focusing effectively on feeling, anxiety is discharged into the smooth muscles or cognitive/perceptual disruption, or defenses are operating. If you shift the focus to the feeling and the patient sighs, you are back on track, getting closer to unconscious feelings. If anxiety goes into the smooth muscles or cognitive/perceptual disruption, regulate the anxiety until it returns to the striated muscles. When signaling stops due to defenses, help the patient see and let go of those defenses.

Suppose a patient is angry with his girlfriend, who cruelly dumped him for another man. As you ask about his anger, he covers it with thoughts. Signaling will drop if you listen to his defense of intellectualization, but it will rise if you point out his defense and invite him to feel his anger.

Another patient says he wants to face his grief over the loss of his wife. Is he being compliant? Assess his unconscious signaling. A sigh signaling anxiety shows that his genuine wish to grieve triggers feelings and anxiety. A lack of unconscious signaling shows that this defense of compliance represses rather than triggers feelings. Genuine feelings trigger unconscious anxiety; defenses such as compliance do not.

Unconscious signaling allows us to assess the pathways of unconscious anxiety discharge. Since anxiety can get too high, let's review the continuum of unconscious anxiety discharge.

How Anxiety Is Discharged in the Patient's Body

Since the pathway of anxiety discharge tells us what form of treatment to offer and where we should focus our work, we will now illustrate the range of responses patients offer so you can correctly assess a patient's pathway of unconscious anxiety discharge.

Patients with a High Capacity for Anxiety Tolerance: Striated Muscles

A patient with a high capacity for anxiety tolerance describes her presenting problem clearly with little anxiety. As you explore her difficulties, she will sigh, fidget with her hands, become tense, or shift positions in her chair—signs of anxiety in the striated muscles. She licks her lips, indicating a dry mouth (sympathetic nervous system). She intellectualizes and thinks clearly while her anxiety rises. Invite her to explore her problem and her feelings: "Could we take a look at a specific example of this problem?"

Patients Who Exceed the Threshold for Anxiety Tolerance: Smooth Muscles

A patient describes her problems clearly but with elevated anxiety. She first exhibits a dry mouth, some tension, and an elevated heart and breathing rate. As her feelings intensify, her anxiety shifts from the striated muscles into the smooth muscles. Now she exceeds the threshold for anxiety tolerance. She experiences nausea or the beginning of a migraine headache, her tension drops, her sighing stops, and she becomes limp.

When her tension drops and she becomes limp, she has just exceeded the threshold of anxiety tolerance. Now her repressive defenses of intellectualization and isolation of affect shift to regressive defenses such as projection and externalization. Rather than explore her problem, regulate her anxiety immediately to prevent a regression. To regulate the patient's anxiety, focus her attention on her bodily symptoms.

Describe the triangle of conflict (feeling, anxiety, and defense) several times. "Do you notice how your anxiety just shot up? So we see you were feeling angry with your boyfriend, you became anxious, and your anxiety caused a stomachache. Do you see that too?" Then invite her to repeat back what she heard. Once her anxiety returns to the striated muscles, explore feeling again.

Patients Who Enter the Session Already Exceeding the Threshold for Anxiety Tolerance: Smooth Muscles and Cognitive/Perceptual Disruption

A patient who enters a session already exceeding the threshold for anxiety tolerance sits slumped in the chair without tension in her body. She does not sigh or clench her hands. She describes her difficulties in a disorganized fashion, her vocal tone is flat, and her face is affectless. She has no access to striated muscle discharge of anxiety.

When asked whether she feels anxious, she may say no. She does not realize that her limpness, nausea, blurry vision, and cognitive confusion are symptoms of anxiety. The absence of tension (making her look superficially calm) is a sign of high anxiety discharged into the smooth muscles and cognitive/perceptual disruption. Regulate her anxiety immediately. Otherwise, she will begin to use regressive defenses such as projection, and her ability to differentiate you from her projection will disappear (Fonagy et al. 2002; Segal 1981).

The most severely anxious patients enter therapy already suffering from cognitive/perceptual disruption and projection. They equate the therapist with their projections, fearing (or feeling angry with) him.

They project their desire to understand themselves onto the therapist ("What are you trying to find out?"). They project their desire for the therapy ("Where is this therapy going?"). Or they project their will ("What do you want me to do?"). First, deactivate the projection to develop a therapeutic alliance. (See the example on pp. 53–56.) Once the projection has dropped, regulate the anxiety triggered by the underlying feeling. (See chapter 6.)

Some severely anxious patients are tense from head to toe. Tension *without* sighing or wringing of the hands is a freeze reaction, not striated muscle discharge of anxiety. These patients engage in thoracic rather than abdominal breathing and suffer from cognitive/perceptual disruption. They project a frightening image and then fear the therapist, freeze, or go limp (Scaer 2001). The patient's fearful look, shifting gaze, or angry glare are signs of projection.

Patients who dissociate usually experience a freeze response. They have symptoms of parasympathetic dominance (drop in blood pressure, slacking of tense muscles, and immobilization of the body) plus sympathetic activation (racing heart). High levels of endorphins cause numbness, dissociation, and amnesia and impair memory (Scaer 2001, 17, 2005). To regulate the anxiety, deactivate the projections (see pp. 75–77) and restructure time/space distortion (see "When Anxiety Regulation Does Not Work," pp. 78–82).

Once the patient can differentiate the therapist from the projection, the freeze response drops, and sighing respiration and hand clenching return. Then explore feelings. Just as reptiles become still when they cannot flee from a predator, some hypothesize that children freeze when they cannot escape from an abuser (Scaer 2001, 2005; Schulkin 2004). The same freeze response can occur when adults relive memories of traumas, losing the ability to differentiate the past from the present.

Why Does High Anxiety Create Cognitive/Perceptual Disruption?

The autonomic nervous system impairs cognitive functioning by decreasing blood flow to the brain while increasing the release of neurohormones.

- *Blood flow:* The parasympathetic nervous system causes a sudden drop in blood flow to the brainstem (Goldstein 2006), the frontal lobe (Arnsten 1997, 1998a, 1998b; Birnbaum et al. 1999), and Broca's area (Rauch et al. 1996). In response, the patient faints (Ziegler 2004), has trouble finding words to describe his experience, and loses consciousness and postural tone in sessions (Goldstein 2004, 103; Kaufmann 2004). Now the prefrontal cortex (Wehrenberg and Prinz 2007), no longer able to inhibit the amygdala (Grawe 2007) and the fear response, becomes less capable of executive functioning (Austin 2006).

- *Neuroendocrine discharge:* High levels of endorphins prevent explicit, declarative memory from forming (Newcomer et al. 1999) and consolidating (Scaer 2001). High cortisol levels damage the hippocampus (Sapolsky et al. 1990), reducing its size, which impairs learning (Lupien et al. 1998), executive functioning, and self-regulation (Blair, Granger, and Razza 2005). Stress hormones divert blood glucose away from the hippocampus to the striated muscles. This prevents the anxious patient from forming new memories or retrieving long-term memories in therapy.

- *Developmental physiology:* The repeated experience of severe anxiety during childhood causes cortisol releases to increase in frequency, further damaging the hippocampus. Physiologically, the hippocampus shrinks and the amygdala enlarges (Bremner et al. 1995, 2000; McEwen and Sapolsky 2000, 182; Sheline et al. 1996; Sheline, Gado, and Kraemer 2003), compromising brain development and creating the neurological basis for anxiety disorders. This altered development impairs the capacity for storing and retrieving new learning in therapy (Sapolsky 2004) and the ability to inhibit the amygdala. The patient's conditioned fear responses become stronger, and cognitive functioning decreases, making anxiety regulation more difficult.

In summary, symptoms of cognitive/perceptual disruption result from a drop in blood flow to the brain, a fall in the heart rate (the heart may even stop beating for a few seconds), and increased releases of adrenaline and other neurohormones (Goldstein 2004, 2006). Excessive anxiety impairs the patient's capacity to store, encode, and retrieve new information. All these causes explain why anxious patients suffer from cognitive difficulties. However, anxiety regulation can restore neurological functioning, reversing some brain deficits. That is why we begin regulating anxiety as soon as it goes over the threshold of anxiety tolerance.

The Threshold of Anxiety Tolerance

We help patients experience as much feeling as possible while anxiety is discharged into the striated muscles. That is the threshold of anxiety tolerance. When anxiety goes out of the striated muscles into the smooth muscles or cognitive/perceptual disruption, the patient has gone over that threshold and needs anxiety regulation. When patients experience their anxiety in the striated muscles, explore feelings and treat anxiety as a defense.

Th: What is the feeling toward him for hitting you?

Pt: I feel tense. [*The patient's anxiety is discharged into her striated muscles. She cannot differentiate her feeling from anxiety.*]

Th: Tension is your anxiety. [*Differentiate the feeling from anxiety.*] If you don't cover your feeling toward him with anxiety, what is the feeling toward him for hitting you?

Pt: I'm angry.

Sometimes the patient enters the session with anxiety triggered by feelings toward the therapist.

Pt: I feel anxious today.

Th: It's good you notice that. When did you start feeling anxious?

Pt: I felt fine when I woke up, but I started feeling anxious when I thought about coming here and as I was driving here. [*This suggests that feelings toward the therapist are triggering her anxiety.*]

Th: You became anxious when you were thinking about coming here today. I wonder what feelings you are having here toward me that could be making you anxious?

Pt: [*Sighs. Discharge of unconscious anxiety (sigh) indicates that feelings toward the therapist are triggering her anxiety.*] I feel fine, but there was something you said last time I didn't like.

Th: What was that?

Pt: You said I sabotaged my relationship with my boyfriend. [*After exploring what happened, explore the feelings.*]

Th: It sounds like you have a reaction to that. What is the feeling toward me?

Facing feelings toward the therapist is a corrective emotional experience. The patient learns to deal with her feelings adaptively in the here and now.

Events outside the therapy also trigger the patient's anxiety.

Th: You seem anxious. When did that begin? [*Find out the stimulus.*]

Pt: I think it started Thursday.

Th: What happened on Thursday that could have triggered your anxiety?

Pt: I don't know. It was a regular day. I got up. I visited my professor to talk about my dissertation because he had some reservations about it.

Th: Would you like to take a look at that?

Pt: He said the statistics were completely wrong, even though I had followed his instructions exactly. Then he said I have to do that section all over again.

Th: What is the feeling toward him for doing that?

Pt: [*Sighs.*] I'm really ticked off. [*Anxiety is in the striated muscles: explore the feeling.*]

Th: "Ticked off" is vague. If you don't cover the feeling with vagueness, what is the feeling toward him? [*Differentiate the feeling from the defense of vagueness.*]

Pt: I'm angry with him.

Th: You feel angry with him, and this anger makes you anxious. Then you deal with the anger by being a little vague. Do you notice that too? [*Triangle of conflict.*]

In this example, the patient's anxiety was in the striated muscles. However, when anxiety shifts from the striated muscles into the smooth muscles and cognitive/perceptual disruption, the patient goes over her threshold of anxiety tolerance (H. Davanloo, supervision 2002–2004). When this occurs, stop exploring feelings. Regulate the anxiety until it returns to the striated muscles. Then explore feelings again, gradually building the patient's affect tolerance. This method is called the *graded format* (Whittemore 1996).

Principle: *When anxiety goes into the smooth muscles or cognitive/perceptual disruption, stop exploring feelings and regulate the anxiety until it returns to the striated muscles. Then you can explore feelings again.*

The Graded Format

In the graded format, the therapist explores feelings until the patient's anxiety shifts into the smooth muscles or cognitive/perceptual disruption. The therapist regulates the anxiety until the patient's anxiety returns to striated muscles and then explores feelings again. By alternately exploring feelings and regulating anxiety, the therapist shifts the patient's anxiety into the striated muscles, builds the patient's feeling tolerance, and reduces the use of regressive defenses.

When the patient's anxiety goes into the smooth muscles or cognitive/perceptual disruption, follow these steps:

1. Stop exploring feelings.
2. Draw the patient's attention to her anxiety symptoms.
3. Help her see the sequence: stimulus, feeling, anxiety, and symptoms.
4. Describe the sequence until the patient's symptoms disappear.
5. Then explore feelings in a different relationship.

The Graded Format in Action

The following vignette shows how to assess when anxiety is too high, how to use the graded format to regulate the patient's anxiety, and how to explore feelings again. A depressed patient has described his conflicts with a verbally abusive daughter who lied about her drug use.

Th: What is the feeling toward her for doing that?

Pt: I'm getting a migraine. [*He has exceeded his threshold for anxiety tolerance. Stop exploring the feeling; regulate the anxiety.*]

Th: It's good you notice. This headache is a sign of anxiety. Are you aware of feeling anxious right now? [*Draw attention to the anxiety.*]

Pt: Not really. I'm just aware of feeling this headache. [*He is not aware of his anxiety.*]

Th: You notice the headache. What do you feel in your stomach right now? [*Help him see other anxiety symptoms.*]

Pt: A little queasy.

Th: That's another sign of anxiety. You've got this headache and a sick stomach, and those are two signs of anxiety. [*Draw his attention to his anxiety.*]

Pt: I didn't know that was anxiety. I feel that a lot.

Th: You have these symptoms of anxiety a lot. So it's important to notice that you had some feeling toward your daughter for lying to you. Then that feeling triggered this anxiety, which took the form of your headache and queasy stomach. Do you see that now? [*Draw his attention to causality: feeling triggers anxiety.*]

Pt: I see it now, but I didn't see it before.

Th: You just saw the headache, but now we see you felt something toward your daughter for lying to you, and that triggered anxiety, which went into your headache and in your stomach. [*Causality.*] How are your headache and stomach now? [*Assess if his anxiety has dropped.*]

Pt: The headache is gone and the stomach is okay. [*His anxiety has dropped quickly, so ask about the feeling again.*]

Th: Would you like to take a look at this feeling you had toward your daughter so we can help you feel your feeling instead of anxiety? [*Mobilize the patient to the task.*]

Pt: Yes.

Th: What is the feeling toward your daughter for lying to you?

Pt: Frustrated. [*He confuses the stimulus (what his daughter did) with his feeling toward her.*]

Th: Sure. She frustrated you by lying to you. What is your feeling toward her for doing that? [*Differentiate the stimulus from his reactive feeling.*]

Pt: I feel angry.

Explore feelings as deeply as possible while the anxiety goes into the striated muscles. As soon as the anxiety shifts into the smooth muscles or cognitive/perceptual disruption, regulate it. Once tension returns to the striated muscles, explore feelings again.

Some patients remain in a chronic state of free-floating anxiety during which the social engagement system (eye gaze, gesture, facial affect, vocal tone, control of the middle ear, orienting reflex) remains neurologically unavailable (Porges 2001a, 2001b, 2011). To regulate the patient's anxiety, focus on her body. Describe the triangle of conflict (feeling, anxiety, and defense) several times, and invite her to repeat back what she heard. Anxiety in the smooth muscles or cognitive/perceptual disruption drops slowly because the body needs time to metabolize the neurohormones that were just released (Franchini and Cowley 2004).

Assessing the Pathway of Unconscious Anxiety Discharge

We must assess each patient response to intervention to find out where his anxiety is discharged in the body. If anxiety is discharged in the striated muscles, explore feelings and help the patient see and turn against his defenses. However, as feeling and anxiety rise, the anxiety may shift into the smooth muscles or cognitive/perceptual disruption. At this point, we must shift to regulating the anxiety until it returns to the striated muscles. Then we will use the graded format. The following examples illustrate how to assess the pathways of unconscious anxiety discharge and how to recognize signs that you must use the graded format.

Vignette One: A Fragile Patient

Fragile patients suffer from anxiety in the form of cognitive/perceptual disruption and from regressive defenses. This example shows how to recognize signs of fragility so that you can work within the patient's capacity without triggering regressions. A middle-aged man slowly walks into the room without maintaining eye gaze, falls into the chair, and looks limp. [*No signs of striated muscle tension.*]

Th: What's the problem you would like me to help you with?

Pt: [*Pauses.*] Well, the first thing I should tell you . . . [*Pauses.*] I first entered psychoanalysis when I was thirteen years old. [*Patient doesn't answer the question. This is a defense against emotional closeness—not revealing his need to the therapist. However, it may also indicate a problem in thinking.*]

Th: I would like to hear more about your history later. [*Block the defense and then invite him to engage in the therapeutic task.*] But first, in order to be helpful to you, what's the problem you would like me to help you with?

Pt: I have problems with anxiety.

Th: Are you aware of feeling anxious right now? [*Immediately assess.*]

Pt: Yes. [*Ability to observe his anxiety.*]

Th: Where do you notice feeling anxious in your body? [*Assess the biophysiological discharge pattern.*]

Pt: All over. [*Vague generalization.*]

Th: But specifically where in your body?

Pt: I'm often sick in my stomach. [*Smooth muscles. He moves out of the present moment, a defense that prevents anxiety regulation now.*]

Th: Are you feeling sick in your stomach now? [*Block the defense of moving out of the present moment. Assess his anxiety in this moment.*]

Pt: Yes, I threw up before the session. [*Smooth muscles. Anxiety regulation is imperative. He moves out of the present moment, which shows he is unable to pay attention to his anxiety now.*]

Th: Are you feeling like throwing up now? [*Draw attention to this moment.*]

Pt: Yes, but not as much.

Th: You are feeling intense anxiety here today.

Pt: Not just today. I've been feeling this way for a couple of weeks. [*Since he called the therapist.*]

Th: You are feeling anxious here with me today, and you have been feeling intense anxiety ever since you made the call to my office.

Pt: Yes.

Th: We see that you have a problem with anxiety, and it is coming up here with me. Can we take a careful look at this anxiety in your body to help you with it? [*Invite him to observe and pay attention to his anxiety, to help regulate it and develop a therapeutic alliance.*]

Pt: Yes. [*Tears up.*]

Th: You mention feeling anxious in your stomach. Where else do you notice feeling anxiety in your body?

Pt: I have a migraine right now. [*Smooth muscles.*]

Th: That's another sign of anxiety. What's another sign of anxiety that you notice in your body?

Pt: What did you say? [*Problem with hearing. Possible sign of cognitive/perceptual disruption.*]

Th: I was wondering where else you notice this anxiety. Are you having some trouble with your hearing right now?

Pt: I don't think so.

Th: Is there any ringing in your ears?

Pt: Yes. [*Cognitive/perceptual disruption.*]

Th: That's another sign of anxiety. How is your vision? Is it clear or blurry?

Pt: I can see you, but it's a little blurry. [*Cognitive/perceptual disruption.*]

Th: That's another sign of anxiety. How is your thinking right now? Is it clear, or are you having trouble forming your thoughts?

Pt: I think it is clear, but people do tell me that I seem slow. [*His speech and thinking are slowed, although he doesn't notice. Cognitive/perceptual disruption.*]

Th: We see that you are very anxious. You have anxiety in your stomach, blurred vision, ringing ears, and difficulty forming your thoughts. All this is anxiety, and it has to do with coming here to see me today. So there must be a lot of feeling underneath that is triggering all this anxiety. [*Direct his attention to the feeling triggering his anxiety.*]

Pt: Yes. [*Wave of tears.*]

Th: I notice as these tears come up, there's another wave of anxiety. Do you notice that?

Pt: Yes. I'm afraid of what you want. [*Defense: projection—another sign of fragility. He wants to tell the therapist about his feelings, but through projection he assumes the therapist wants that. Deactivate his projection of will. Otherwise, he will ward off a "persecutory" therapist who "wants" something from him: a misalliance.*]

Th: Let's clarify something. Who called me for this meeting? [*Remind him of his desire for therapy, which he has "located" in the therapist. This deactivates his projection.*]

Pt: I did.

Th: And who thought he had a problem?

Pt: Me.

Th: And who asked me to help him with this problem?

Pt: Me.

Th: So who wants something out of this?

Pt: Me, but I'm wondering what you want. [*Projection still in place.*]

Th: But who wants something out of this?

Pt: Me.

Th: Right. Let me offer you something to think about. You are the one who wants something out of this. Right?

Pt: Yeah.

Th: And you are the one who wants to reveal something about himself to this therapist. Right?

Pt: Right.

Th: I wonder if you find it scary how much *you* want to reveal yourself here. [*Establish an internal focus. His anxiety is triggered by a feeling and desire inside him, not in the therapist.*]

Pt: That's true because I've been hurt before. [*He projects onto the therapist an image of someone who hurt him in the past. He cannot differentiate the therapist from this projection.*]

Th: As you and I sit here together, it's like there's an image of someone in the past that comes between you and me. And then when this image comes between you and me, you can lose touch with me and feel more in touch with this image instead? [*Address his projection.*]

Pt: Yes. [*Relaxes in his chair. Fear of the projection on the therapist evoked further anxiety. The drop in his anxiety signals that together the patient and therapist have cleared up the projection.*]

The patient's anxiety is discharged into the smooth muscles and cognitive/perceptual disruption. He observes it but cannot pay attention to or regulate it.

Once the patient lets go of his projection, remind him of his will to do therapy. Once he declares his desire to do therapy, ask him again what the problem is for which he wants help. With each new phase (e.g., revealing his problem, giving a specific example, declaring and experiencing his feeling in that situation), the fragile patient's anxiety will rise again, perhaps going into cognitive/perceptual disruption. Monitor and regulate his anxiety each time it exceeds his threshold for anxiety tolerance. If you intervene and regulate his anxiety as soon as it goes into the smooth muscles, you can often prevent it from going into cognitive/perceptual disruption. In this way, you build his capacities for feeling and anxiety tolerance.

Labeling each bodily symptom helps the patient observe his anxiety and what triggers it. These small-scale explanations orient the patient, make sense of his symptoms, lower his anxiety, and help him learn to self-regulate. Now he can see how feelings trigger anxiety in a predictable pattern. His bodily symptoms of anxiety become understandable reactions, which he can observe and regulate. Identifying and regulating anxiety is essential to co-create a therapeutic alliance with a fragile patient.

"Attack of the Adrenals"

When anxiety goes over the threshold of anxiety tolerance, one might imagine a loudspeaker announcement inside the brain: "Attention all parasympathetic forces. Urgent. Adrenal gland missile silos mounted atop kidneys have just released chemical cortisol weapons of brain destruction. Mobilize all internal defenses. Launch immediate counter-calm hormones before hippocampus is hammered by cortisol" (Franklin Institute 2004).

The continued discharge of norepinephrine by the adrenal gland sustains anxiety symptoms (Goldstein 2006; Rosen and Schulkin 2004, 176), making the patient hyperexcitable. The adrenaline impairs his short-term memory for several hours, so he cannot remember what you say in therapy (Joels and Karst 2010; Southwick et al. 2005). Once neuroendocrine discharge takes the prefrontal cortex "off-line," the patient acts inappropriately, is easily distractible, inattentive, disorganized, impulsive, and hyperactive (Arnsten 1998b; Porges and Bazhenova 2006, 4). His reasoning is less able to influence his behavior and thought.

Patients with depression, anxiety disorders, personality disorders, and autism suffer from disturbed autonomic nervous system functioning (Beauchaine 2001; Porges 2011; Prins, Kaloupek, and Keane 1995). High levels of neuroendocrine discharge make the brain malfunction, leading to problems of inattention, distractibility, impulsivity, intrusive aversive memories, and other symptoms of cognitive/perceptual disruption. Defenses emerge automatically, while the ability to reflect on them disappears.

Vignette Two: Going over the Threshold of Anxiety Tolerance

In this example, we show how to recognize when the patient's anxiety shifts over the threshold of anxiety tolerance, how to regulate the anxiety, and how to help the patient see causality in the moment. Earlier in the session the patient mentioned she suffers from irritable bowel syndrome.

> *Th:* You mentioned a family problem. Would you like to take a look at that?
>
> *Pt:* I've got a conflict with my son. He's been mentally ill for some years, and he's an alcoholic. This wouldn't be such a problem

except that he's living with me, and I told him he would have to leave if he kept drinking. He told me he stopped drinking, but then I keep finding empty bottles in the cabinets. [*She describes what her son does, not how this poses an emotional problem for her.*]

Th: How is that a problem for you?

Pt: I just don't know what to do about it. My friends say I should kick him out, but then I don't know where he would go. [*Clear statement of the problem. She realizes her friends have freer access to their anger ("kick him out"), but anger makes her anxious. Rather than feel angry toward her son, she worries and ruminates ("I don't know where he would go"). Worrying is a defense because it keeps her stuck, unable to channel her feelings into effective action.*]

Th: There's obviously some feeling you have toward your son, but then you seem paralyzed [*defense*], as if you don't know what to do with your feelings.

Pt: That's true. I don't know what to do.

Th: Would you like to take a look at these feelings regarding your son so we could help you get unstuck? [*Mobilize her will to the therapeutic task.*]

Pt: [*Sighs.*] Yes. [*Access to striated muscles. Clear wish to collaborate on the therapeutic task.*]

Th: What's the feeling toward your son who lied to you about his drinking?

Pt: [*Sighs. Clenched hands—striated muscles.*] I just feel he should have told me the truth. [*Defense: intellectualization.*]

Th: That says what you think [*describe defense*], but it doesn't tell us what you feel toward him. What is the feeling toward him? [*Separate the feeling from the defense, and then invite her to face her feeling.*]

Pt: Upset. [*Defense: vagueness.*]

Th: Clearly he upset you, but what's the emotion toward him for lying to you?

Pt: My stomach is starting to cramp. [*Smooth muscles. Her threshold for anxiety tolerance has just been crossed. Point out the triangle of conflict to bring her anxiety down.*]

Th: As soon as we touch on these feelings toward your son, do you notice how this anxiety comes in to attack you, as if it's against the law for you to have feelings toward him? [*Point out the function of the anxiety: to attack and punish her for her anger. Differentiate her from the anxiety.*]

Pt: I hadn't thought of it that way before. Do you think these cramps are related to my anxiety?

Th: What's the sequence we saw here? Feelings toward your son, then stomach cramps. [*Draw her attention to causality: anger triggers anxiety and defenses (intellectualization and turning on the self).*]

Pt: That's true.

In this example, the patient is able to tolerate a rise of her feelings briefly until her anxiety shifts out of the striated muscles into the smooth muscles. The therapist immediately begins to regulate the anxiety by pointing out the anxiety and the causal sequence: feelings trigger anxiety and symptoms.

When the patient's anxiety goes into the striated muscles, focus on the defenses to access the warded-off feeling. Interrupt each defense, one by one, as they arise. Often, highly resistant patients exhibit nonverbal defenses such as sitting in a slouched, uninvolved manner, and speaking with a detached voice and expressionless face without anxiety. These nonverbal behaviors should be addressed as defenses, not regarded as signs of cognitive/perceptual disruption.

In contrast, the fragile patient's anxiety is discharged into cognitive/perceptual disruption. When his repressive defenses fail, he becomes flooded with anxiety and projects his feelings onto the therapist. Then he becomes hypervigilant about the therapist's feelings rather than observant of his own.

Mobilizing Self-Observing Capacity in the Anxious Patient

Interestingly, many patients with high anxiety do not see it. As children, they learned to ignore their anxiety if it made their parents anxious (H. S. Sullivan 1953b). Ignoring feelings and anxiety was adaptive in the past but is maladaptive today. Ignoring anxiety ensures that it remains unregulated. Help the patient observe and regulate her anxiety so therapy can become useful. Focus on what the patient says and what her body does to provide moment-to-moment anxiety regulation. This regulation of her body is the precondition for a therapeutic alliance (Schore 2002) and any successful therapy.

In the following material, we distinguish observation from attention. A patient may not be able to observe that she is anxious. Another patient can observe her anxiety for a moment but not pay attention to it. Thus, she will not be able to regulate her anxiety. A third patient can observe and pay attention to her anxiety over an extended period of time so she can regulate it. Thus, first help the patient observe her anxiety. Then help her let go of defenses that distract her from paying attention to her anxiety. Then she can regulate it.

Defenses That Interfere with Anxiety Regulation

Helping patients observe and pay attention to their anxiety teaches them healthy self-regulation. When patients habitually ignore their anxiety (Ten Have de Labije 2006), it remains unregulated. Interrupt any defenses that prevent anxiety regulation in the moment. Always return the patient's attention to her bodily experience in the moment. Anxiety cannot be regulated in the past or the future, only now.

Vignette One: Ignoring—A Defense That Prevents Anxiety Regulation

This vignette shows how to interrupt defenses that prevent anxiety regulation and how to help the patient develop a capacity for compassionate attention to her anxiety—a precondition for co-creating any relationship for change.

Th: You appear anxious. Are you aware of feeling anxious?

Pt: No. [*No observing ability.*]

Th: Do you notice your foot tapping?

Pt: Yes.

Th: That's a sign of anxiety. Do you notice the tension in your shoulders?

Pt: Yes, but they're always like that. [*The patient observes a symptom of anxiety but ignores it and explains it away.*]

Th: You see this tension in your shoulders. It's there all the time you say, but you say that as if you consider that normal. [*The patient talks as if it is normal to ignore her anxiety. Address the syntonicity of her defense. If she thinks ignoring her anxiety helps her, she will see no reason to address it.*]

Pt: I don't know if it's normal, but I'm like this all the time.

Th: You see this isn't normal to be so anxious. It's just that you are anxious most of the time.

Pt: Right, but there's some other things I wanted to talk about. [*She ignores her anxiety now by talking about something else, but then she can neither regulate her anxiety nor access her feelings.*]

Th: Do you notice that you want to talk about something other than your anxiety right now? [*Draw attention to the defense of ignoring.*]

Pt: Yes, because I have other things I want to talk about. [*She knows she wants to talk about something else, but she does not see its defensive function or harmful effect.*]

Th: But if we talk about something else, we will ignore your anxiety. [*Clarify the defense of ignoring her anxiety.*] But if I ignored your anxiety, what kind of therapist would I be? [*Point out the cruel relationship she invites.*]

Pt: Not a very good one.

Th: Exactly. When you ignore your anxiety this way and try to talk away from it, is this a helpful or harmful way to treat yourself? [*Help her differentiate therapeutic from nontherapeutic activity.*]

Pt: It's not helpful, but it's what I do. [*She can see it is not helpful, but she has not differentiated from her defense. She is identified with it.*]

Th: Is that what you want to keep doing—ignoring your anxiety? [*Encourage her to turn against her defense.*]

Pt: No. It's just that I generally don't pay attention to it. [*She sees the defense now.*]

Th: That's important for us to notice. You've come here to get help with your anxiety, but to get help with it, both of us have to pay attention to it, see what's triggering it, and focus on that. If you ignore your anxiety, we won't be able to get to the bottom of your difficulties. [*Point out the task to the patient.*]

Vignette Two: Avoiding the Present Moment Prevents Anxiety Regulation

Regulating anxiety in the moment requires attention to experience in this moment. This vignette shows how to help the patient develop a capacity for moment-to-moment attention to her anxiety and inner life. This moment-to-moment focus on "now" reveals the intersection between this model of therapy and mindfulness.

Th: I notice you are anxious. Do you notice that?

Pt: Yes, I'm afraid of what we are going to get into here, and I'm afraid I'll feel worse. [*The patient ignores her anxiety now and focuses on a fantasy in the future instead. Ignoring her anxiety prevents her from regulating it.*]

Th: If we leave the future out of the picture for the moment [*block her defense of going off to the future, which will put her in a state of hyperarousal*], how do you experience this anxiety right now in your body? [*Mobilize attention to her anxiety in this moment.*]

Pt: I just feel really tense, but I don't see what good this will do. I remember in my past therapy one time— [*The patient focuses on a past event, preventing anxiety regulation now. By doing so, she treats other events as more important than her suffering in this moment: self-devaluation.*]

Th: We can get to that later [*block her defense of moving out of the present moment*], but right now, how do you experience this anxiety in your body?

Pt: Just really tense, like I said.

Th: We see you are feeling really tense right now here with me. Then we see that you are tempted to ignore your anxiety in this moment by going off to the future or the past. [*Point out her defenses.*] Do you see how you do that?

Pt: But those are important. [*She sees she ignores the present moment but not how that prevents anxiety regulation.*]

Th: Those other moments are important, and we'll get to them later, but right now you are anxious with me. If we go off to some other moment, we will be ignoring your anxiety in this moment. If we ignore your anxiety, will that help you or hurt you? [*Differentiate therapeutic from nontherapeutic behavior.*]

Pt: Not helpful.

Th: If we don't go off to the past or the future, can we keep our focus on how you experience this anxiety right now in your body? [*Orient her to the task: paying attention to her internal experience at this moment.*]

Principle: *To regulate anxiety, continually bring the patient back to the current moment. Fantasies of future dangers or memories of past traumas trigger increasing anxiety, preventing anxiety regulation. Focus on experience in this moment to calm the patient. Once you regulate her anxiety, explore her feelings again.*

Interventions to Mobilize Self-Observing Capacity

To regulate the patient's anxiety you must mobilize her ability to observe and pay attention to it. Then help her see the triangle of conflict and causality: feelings trigger her anxiety. Anxiety triggers her defenses. And defenses create her presenting problems. These are the self-observing capacities we must help the patient develop.

Principle: *If the patient is not aware of her anxiety, help her see and pay attention to it so it can become regulated before exploring feelings further.*

Intervene as follows:

1. Inquire into the presenting problem and feeling until the patient's anxiety goes over the threshold of anxiety tolerance into the smooth muscles or cognitive/perceptual disruption. Point out her anxiety: "Are you aware of feeling anxious right now?"

2. Help the patient observe and pay attention to her anxiety. Ask if she is aware of her anxiety. Inquiry into feeling while anxiety is unregulated will trigger worsened anxiety and regressive defenses. "Can we pay attention to your anxiety and see if we can help you bring it down?"

3. If she is not aware of her anxiety, point out the symptoms of anxiety in her body until she recognizes them. "The stomachache is a sign of anxiety." If she is aware of her anxiety but ignores it, address her defenses. "If you shift topics now, we will ignore your anxiety. Do you notice how you ignore your anxiety?" "Do you notice how you talk over your anxiety?" Once she turns against these defenses, she will learn to pay attention to and regulate her anxiety.

4. Once she observes and pays attention to her anxiety and her defenses against doing so, ask, "Would you like to take a look at the feeling underneath that is triggering your anxiety?"

5. When you ask the anxious patient about her feelings, she will almost always confuse her feeling with anxiety. Help her differentiate her feeling from anxiety. "That tension is your anxiety. How do you experience the sadness underneath that makes you so anxious?"

6. When the patient sees her feeling, point out the triangle of conflict: "This sadness [*feeling*] makes you anxious [*anxiety*], so you cover the sadness by explaining it away [*defense*]."

Principles for Anxiety Regulation

To regulate the patient's anxiety, differentiate her feeling from anxiety and from defense in the moment. To do so,

1. *Emphasize the present moment*: A feeling triggers anxiety now, not thoughts about the past or events in the future. Punitive thoughts may *perpetuate* anxiety, but an unconscious feeling triggers it. So find out what feeling triggers the patient's anxiety now. In an earlier example, a patient thought her test in three weeks caused her anxiety. In fact, her sadness triggered her anxiety. Ruminating about the test was a defense.

Principle: *Feelings in the present moment cause unconscious anxiety, not thoughts about the past or future.*

---

2. *Notice patterns of unconscious anxiety*: An unconscious feeling makes unconscious anxiety in the body rise. A defense makes anxiety fall. For instance, if a patient feels grief over the loss of a boyfriend who died but wards it off by devaluing him and voicing her anger, her anxiety will drop. However, when approaching her grief, unconscious anxiety will rise in her body.

Principle: *Unconscious feelings trigger unconscious anxiety in the body. Defenses do not.*

---

3. *Notice patterns of defense*: The feeling occurs first, then anxiety, and then a defense. A patient feels grief, her anxiety rises, and a moment later she distracts herself with a defense. Then her tension drops. When the patient faces a feeling, her anxiety will rise. When she uses a repressive defense, her anxiety will drop.

Principle: *Defenses occur after a rise of feelings and anxiety.*

4. *Pay attention to the process*:
    a. The therapist intervenes.
    b. The feeling rises immediately.
    c. Anxiety rises in a split second.
    d. A defense occurs in the next split second.

This sequence occurs repeatedly in every session. If not, the patient and therapist are not exploring feelings.

Principle: *Unconscious feelings trigger anxiety followed by a defense.*

5. *Help the patient see causality*: When the patient has a feeling, ask, "What triggered this feeling?" When the patient's anxiety rises, ask, "What are you feeling now that is triggering this anxiety?" When the patient experiences a symptom, draw her attention to the defense she just used, which is creating the symptom. "Do you notice how you became depressed just now after you turned the anger toward your teacher back onto yourself?"

Principle: *Draw the patient's attention to the stimulus triggering her feeling, the feeling triggering her anxiety in the body, and the defenses, which create her symptoms in the session. By seeing causality, she sees what causes her suffering at the moment she suffers.*

Psychodiagnosis of Anxiety: When No Signaling Occurs

Sometimes, no signaling of unconscious anxiety in the striated muscles results because the therapist is not focusing on the patient's feelings. However, if the therapist is focusing on the patient's feelings, the lack of unconscious signaling of anxiety can occur for other reasons (Abbass 2004; Abbass, Lovas, and Purdy 2008):

- *Involuntary referral:* The patient does not want to do therapy or share his feelings, so no feeling rises to trigger anxiety. *Solution:* Accept the patient's lack of desire. Point out that you have no right to do therapy with someone who does not want it. Leave the door open for him to return later when he is in a different stage of the change process (Miller and Rollnick 2002; Prochaska and Norcross 2007).

- *Ambivalence:* The patient has one foot in and one foot out. She does not want to be involved, so no feelings or anxiety will rise. *Solution:* Explore her ambivalence.
  - If she does not see how her defenses hurt her, she will not see how therapy could help her. Clarify causality to reach a consensus on what causes her presenting problems.
  - If she says she is doing therapy to obey someone else, this is a projection. Block this projection and clarify what is an internal problem for her until you reach a consensus on a problem she wants to work on.
  - If she projects her will onto the therapist, deactivate that projection until she owns her desire for therapy.
  - If she understands the task but does not believe she can do it, help her see the defense of underestimating herself.
- *No need for therapy:* The patient may have come to the wrong office while seeking a different professional. *Solution:* Refer the patient to the correct treatment or nontreatment. For example, a patient was referred to me for short-term therapy, but we learned he had suffered a severe head injury in a recent automobile accident. He did not need psychotherapy, but he did need physical therapy, neurofeedback, and psychoeducation about recovery from brain trauma.
- *Organic or brain factors:* The patient may experience genuine confusion about the therapeutic process due to brain injury, below-average intelligence, or physical illness and exhaustion. *Solution:* Explain the therapeutic task clearly and simply for patients with below-average intelligence to get a conscious therapeutic alliance. Do supportive psychotherapy while physically ill patients recover the strength to do an exploratory therapy.
- *Discharge of anxiety into the smooth muscles or cognitive/perceptual disruption:* The patient may look superficially calm because her anxiety is discharged into the smooth muscles and cognitive/perceptual disruption instead of tension. *Solution:* Regulate the patient's anxiety until it returns to the striated muscles.
- *Discharge of anxiety through subtle tensing or hiding the tension consciously:* The patient can get rid of his anxiety by chewing

gum so it does not show up elsewhere in the body. *Solution:* Ask the patient to take out the gum. Anxiety will appear in the body instead, becoming more obvious to the patient and more visible to the therapist. A patient who consciously hides anxiety will look stiff. His face will seem like a mask, lacking spontaneous expression. He immobilizes his body to avoid experiencing feelings in it.

- *Hiding of unconscious transference feelings through defenses:* These defenses include defiance, compliance, externalization, passivity, hopelessness, helplessness, high degrees of intellectualization, syntonic defenses, denial, and projection or projective identification. (See chapters 4, 9, and 12.) Rather than experience her anger, the patient can hide it under defenses. Unaware of her anger, she feels no anxiety. *Solution:* Help the patient see her defenses and turn against them. Feelings will rise, triggering anxiety in the body.

- *Repression of feelings:* The defense of turning anger on the self (repressing anger) makes the signaling of striated muscles drop. Someone who turns anger on himself will be depressed, perhaps revealing this defense of self-attack through his suicidal plans. In such a case, the defense of self-attack will prevent anxiety from rising. *Solution:* Help the patient see and turn against the defense. Feelings and anxiety will rise.

- *Errors in technique:* No unconscious anxiety will rise if the therapist does not focus on feelings consistently enough, focuses on defenses or on feelings that are not present, or challenges the defenses before the patient has differentiated himself from them. In this last instance, the patient will feel attacked. This misalliance will trigger conscious anger but not unconscious anxiety.

- *Activation of the transference resistance:* If a patient develops an oppositional transference resistance and the therapist argues with her, this interactional defense will repress feelings, and the patient will feel no anxiety. If the patient adopts a passive, helpless stance and the therapist acts out the active role of the "helper," the patient will feel no anxiety. When the therapist enacts the transference resistance, no unconscious anxiety will rise. *Solution:* Deactivate the transference resistance.

- *Overmedication:* Patients on many medications or illegal substances appear emotionally flat. These patients show no tension, fidgeting, or shifting in the chair. If a patient appears emotionally flat, ask if he is taking any psychotropic or pain medications. *Solution:* Consult with the psychiatrist to reduce the patient's medications. This sometimes helps the patient become aware of his anxiety and feelings.

Psychodiagnosis of Anxiety: Common Mistakes

Therapists unable to assess the discharge of anxiety in the body can make mistakes in assessment:

- When a patient exhibits some striated muscle tension, therapists sometimes fail to assess all the anxiety pathways. In fact, some patients will experience anxiety in both striated and smooth muscles or in all three pathways. Careful assessment of anxiety will help the therapist work within the patient's threshold of anxiety tolerance rather than go over it.

- When working with a patient who appears limp and calm, therapists sometimes assume the patient has no anxiety. As a result, they miss symptoms of smooth muscle discharge or cognitive/perceptual disruption, which are not visible.

- When working with a patient who appears limp and calm, therapists sometimes assume the patient has smooth muscle discharge or cognitive/perceptual disruption. If the therapist avoids focusing on unconscious feelings or relinquishing defenses, no unconscious anxiety will rise.

- When a patient is able to observe her anxiety, some therapists rush ahead without assessing whether the patient can pay attention to and regulate her anxiety. A patient may observe her anxiety but then ignore it, preventing anxiety regulation. Until the patient lets go of the defense of ignoring her feelings and anxiety, inviting feelings will fail. A patient cannot face and experience her feelings if she ignores her feelings and anxiety.

- Some therapists pursue feelings when anxiety goes into the smooth muscles or cognitive/perceptual disruption. This results in stomachaches, headaches, increasing depression, dissociation, and projection. Now the patient suffers from excessive anxiety. *The therapeutic goal is not to face one's feelings while paralyzed with anxiety but to experience one's feelings deeply while anxiety goes into the striated muscles.*

Some therapists mistake a freeze/immobilization response for striated muscle activation. A patient with this response has a hypervigilant or vacant stare, barely noticeable breathing in the upper chest, racing thoughts, or brain "fog" (Levine and Frederick 1997; P. Ogden, Minton, and Pain 2006; Scaer 2001, 2005). Do not assume the patient's anxiety is going into the striated muscles unless you observe clenched hands, abdominal breathing, and sighing.

When therapists avoid arousing anxiety by avoiding feelings and defenses, the patient will not gain the capacity to face and bear them, and her suffering will continue. When therapists explore rage based on a projection, a misalliance develops. Clear up the projection first. Then explore feelings.

The patient's trembling is often misinterpreted as a discharge of the patient's rage rather than as a sign of excessive anxiety requiring immediate regulation. Some therapists mistake fainting due to hyperventilation with fainting due to the parasympathetic discharge of anxiety. When patients hyperventilate, the blood becomes alkaline, leading blood vessels to constrict, which causes lightheadedness and sometimes fainting. Do not have the patient breathe into a paper bag. Instead, simply slow the patient's breathing by having her inhale for five seconds and exhale for five seconds over the course of a minute or two. Or invite her to hold her breath for fifteen seconds. The patient's carbon dioxide levels will return to normal, vasoconstriction will end, and dizziness will disappear. Then summarize the process for the patient to show causality and regulate the anxiety. Help her see that her feelings triggered anxiety, which triggered her symptoms.

Fainting due to the parasympathetic discharge of anxiety occurs after symptoms of nausea, jelly legs, and lightheadedness. With smooth muscle activation, blood vessels dilate, reducing blood pressure in the brain, leading to cerebral hypoperfusion. Regulate the patient's anxiety as soon as you see any signs of nausea to prevent lightheadedness and fainting from occurring at higher levels of anxiety. If faintness still occurs, summarize what has happened, describe the triangle of conflict, and encourage the patient to tense the muscles in her hands and arms (Gaynor and Egan 2011). Or you can encourage the patient to stand up slowly and then descend into a slightly squatting position with bent knees (Rothschild 2003). As she holds this position for a minute, her sympathetic nervous system will activate, balancing the parasympathetic activation. The symptoms of cognitive/perceptual disruption will disappear. Then you can summarize the process and begin to explore the patient's feelings again.

Some patients can experience anxiety going into several pathways at the same time. Traditionally, many believed the parasympathetic nervous system had a "braking" effect on the sympathetic nervous system (Gellhorn 1967; P. Ogden et al. 2006; Scaer 2001, 2005). However, recent research has shown this not to be true (Janig 2003, 142, 2007). Symptoms of anxiety vary because the sympathetic and parasympathetic branches can activate independently and antagonistically rather than in homeostatic balance (Berntson, Cacioppo, and Quigley 1991, 1994). This helps explain the spectrum of anxiety symptoms described by Abbass (2004, 2007) and Folkow (2000).

When regulating the patient's anxiety, first make sure the patient can see his symptom of anxiety, pay attention to it, and label it as anxiety. Then help the patient see causality: feelings trigger his anxiety. With these self-observing capacities in place, anxiety should return to the striated muscles. When it does not, we have to address defenses that prevent anxiety regulation.

Before we go to the next section, let us take a look at figure 2.1, which covers restructuring the pathway of unconscious anxiety discharge when it goes into smooth muscles and cognitive/perceptual disruption.

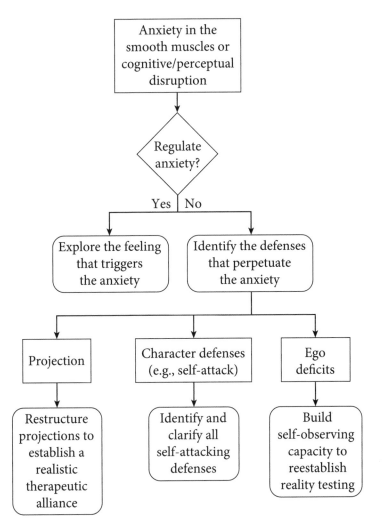

Figure 2.1   Restructuring the pathway of unconscious anxiety discharge when it goes into smooth muscles and cognitive/perceptual disruption

WHEN ANXIETY REGULATION DOES NOT WORK: THE CAUSES VERSUS THE PERPETUATORS OF ANXIETY

When the patient's anxiety goes into the smooth muscles or cognitive/perceptual disruption we first regulate it. However, under certain conditions anxiety regulation does not work. Then we must assess and differentiate the causes of anxiety from the perpetuators of anxiety in the patient.

Anxiety in the somatic and autonomic nervous systems is triggered by

- Objective dangers (A. Freud 1936)
- Unconscious cues (S. Freud 1926/1961d; A. Freud 1936), which are paired through conditioning with ANS arousal (H. Davanloo, supervision 2002–2004; LeDoux 1998, 2000, 2002; Panksepp and Biven 1998; 2012; Schore 1994, 2003a, 2003b)

Anxiety, once triggered by a feeling, can be perpetuated by ego deficits or regressive defenses. We must differentiate the causes of anxiety (unconscious cues) from the perpetuators (regressive defenses and ego deficits). When anxiety cannot be regulated, first identify and restructure the defenses and ego deficits perpetuating the anxiety. Then you can regulate the anxiety triggered by feelings.

Defenses That Perpetuate Anxiety

Some defenses do not repress but *perpetuate the anxiety*. Suppose a patient feels anger toward his critical father.

Th: How do you experience this anger toward your father?

Pt: [*Sighs.*] I think I wasn't a very good son to him. I was a stupid idiot. [*Identification with the critical father. Rather than be angry with his critical father, he identifies with his father and criticizes himself.*]

The defense represses the anger but at a price. The patient feels more anxious, not realizing he attacks himself (see table 2.4).

Table 2.4   Anxiety triggered by a feeling versus anxiety perpetuated by a defense

Unconscious feeling	Unconscious anxiety	Unconscious defense	Result
Rage at the critical father	Striated muscles (triggered by the feeling)	Self-attack, identification with the critical father	Anxiety in the face of an attack (perpetuated by the defense)

The anxiety in relation to these identifications has been called *superego anxiety* (A. Freud 1936, 55). For instance, rather than face his anger toward a critical father, a patient may identify with him and criticize himself. Thus, he enacts an identification with his father. When self-criticism and self-attack become a habit, the patient feels anxious, as if someone else is attacking him, but he does not see how he attacks himself. Anxiety regulation does not work when the defense of self-attack perpetuates the anxiety. Interrupt and point out self-attacking statements in a compassionate, nonjudgmental way.

Pt: I feel like a failure.

Th: Wow! Did you just see what happened? [*Interrupt the defense.*]

Pt: No. What?

Th: Do you notice how there's a critical mechanism in your mind that comes in here and puts you down? When this critical system in your mind comes up, does that get you down? Is it hurting you, do you think?

Interrupt the patient's self-attacks immediately. Once the patient can observe and stop his self-attacks, his anxiety will drop.

This examination of causality allows us to understand the steps in anxiety regulation. Cognitive therapy correctly points out a relationship between rumination and anxiety (Beck et al 1979; Beck and Emery 1985). However, it is not a causal relationship. In psychotherapy sessions, unconscious feelings trigger anxiety. Defenses arise in response to feelings and anxiety. Cognitive therapy addresses the defense of identification with the aggressor (rumination, self-attack, catastrophizing, etc.) that *perpetuates* the preexisting anxiety.

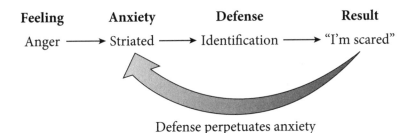

Feeling	Anxiety	Defense	Result
Anger ⟶	Striated ⟶	Identification ⟶	"I'm scared"

Defense perpetuates anxiety

Figure 2.2   Feedback loop to be broken for anxiety regulation

As shown in figure 2.2, the defense perpetuates the anxiety, creating a feedback loop that activates the autonomic nervous system indefinitely (McEwen and Lasley 2002).

Interrupt destructive cognitions resulting from identification with the aggressor to stop the feedback loop. Then explore the feeling triggering the patient's anxiety. Build the patient's capacity to bear the feeling. Then the risk of relapse will drop.

Principle: *When defenses perpetuate anxiety, help the patient see and let go of these defenses first so anxiety regulation can become possible.*

When Anxiety Regulation Fails: Ego Deficits, Regressive Defenses, and the Perpetuation of Anxiety

Focusing the patient's attention on his bodily symptoms will usually regulate anxiety caused by feelings. When it does not work, ego deficits, character defenses, or regressive defenses perpetuate the anxiety, preventing its regulation. In these cases, restructure that deficit or defense first. The following section will show how to address the most common regressive defenses and ego deficits that perpetuate anxiety.

Lack of Differentiation between the Observing Ego and the Experiencing Self

Some lower functioning patients become flooded with anxiety because they cannot distinguish themselves from their anxiety. They feel as if they "are" their anxiety, not that their anxiety is a symptom they can observe in the body. Help the patient differentiate himself from the anxiety he experiences: "Let's see if we can bring your head up above the anxiety water, so together we can look down and see what's going on down there." Motion with your hands, as if you are pushing the water down from above your head to below your shoulders to illustrate for the patient how to get his head above the anxiety (B. Winstanley, personal communication).

Use language that emphasizes observation to strengthen the patient's observing abilities: "Let's *step back* for a moment and see if we can *notice and observe* some bodily symptoms. If we take a moment to *look*, let's *see* where you *notice* symptoms of anxiety happening *in your body*." "Let's put the anxiety *out here* for a moment [gesturing with your hand from your chest out to the other side of the room] where we can take a *look* at it" (A. Sheldon, personal communication). This visual metaphor helps the patient observe his anxiety rather than be flooded by it.

Projective Anxiety

When the patient's feelings make her anxious, she may project any aspect of herself onto the therapist.

- *Projection of feeling:* An angry patient says, "I think you are angry at me."
- *Projection of the superego:* A patient who judges herself says, "I think you are judging me."
- *Projection of will:* A patient who wants to understand herself projects her wish onto the therapist and says, "I'm afraid of the questions you want to ask me."

The patient projects a part of herself onto the therapist and then fears the therapist rather than this internal aspect of herself. The fear of a projection is projective anxiety (H. Davanloo, supervision 2002–2004). We cannot regulate anxiety when projection perpetuates it. Deactivate the projection before attempting anxiety regulation.

Projection of Feeling

An angry patient says, "I think you are angry at me." When the patient projects his anger onto you and believes you are angry, he will fear you. This is projective anxiety. In this vignette, the therapist deactivates the patient's projective anxiety by helping him see the difference between the therapist and the projection.

Th: What's the evidence for that?

Pt: It's just the way I feel. ["*If I feel it, that makes it so.*" *Failure of reality testing.*]

Th: That's the way you feel. So we need to ask, "What is the evidence?"

Pt: I just think you are.

Th: Given you think and feel that, we need to check out whether that is really the case. I'm not aware of feeling angry, so I need to ask what the evidence is that you see.

Pt: I don't have any evidence. It's just a feeling. [*Progress in reality testing.*]

Th: It's just a feeling. I'm not aware of feeling angry toward you, and you mention you don't have any evidence that I am angry with you.

Pt: So what is your point?

Th: My point is this: you were talking about being angry with me for taking a vacation next month. Remember that?

Pt: Yes.

Th: As soon as you felt this anger toward me, you got anxious, and it's as if you asked me to hold your anger because it felt risky just to feel it toward me.

Pt: [*Relaxes in his chair: drop of projective anxiety.*] Yes, I think it did feel risky.

Th: Can we take a look at the anger toward me?

Projection of the Superego

A patient who judges herself says, "I think you are judging me." When the patient judges herself and projects this judgment onto you, she will fear you as a judge. This is projective anxiety. We must help her differentiate the therapist from a judge and then help her see her own internal judgment. Then we will have helped her develop an internal perspective on her problems.

Th: Do you notice how this punitive mechanism in your mind tries to place the image of a judge onto me? [*Differentiate the therapist from the projection.*]

Pt: I sense you are judging me.

Th: That's not my intent. You were just judging yourself, and then you put your internal judge onto me. [*Point out the projection of her superego.*]

Pt: And so now you are saying that I'm really pathological and sicko? [*Projection*]

Th: Wow! Do you see how cruel that punitive mechanism is to you right now? [*Point out the cruelty of the superego to help her turn against it.*]

Pt: [*Tears in her eyes.*]

Th: Do you see how the punitive mechanism takes my words of concern and twists them into something to torture you with?

Pt: But you are saying I am pathological. [*Projection.*]

Th: No. I am saying this punitive mechanism is treating you in an abusive manner, and I think it is very unfair to you. And I'm also saying that this punitive mechanism tries to twist my words of concern into something horrible, and then it abuses and accuses you.

Would you agree that this punitive mechanism is being unfair to you right now? [*Differentiate her from the punitive mechanism.*]

Pt: [*Relaxes. Drop in projective anxiety.*] Yes.

When she projects her conscience, she fears the judgment of others. Then she becomes blind to the ways she judges herself.

Projection of the Will

A patient who wants to understand himself projects his will onto the therapist and says, "I'm just afraid of the questions you want to ask me." To deactivate the projection, remind the patient of his will and desire to engage in therapy. When his anxiety drops, the projection has been deactivated. At that point, ask the patient what he feels so he notices the difference when he is connecting with his will rather than with his projection. Once the projective anxiety drops, regulate the anxiety caused by feeling (if this is necessary) or explore the underlying feeling. See the example on pp. 53–56.

Principle: *When the patient cannot differentiate you from the projection, deactivate the projection first before trying to regulate the anxiety. If the patient views you as an ogre, you will not be trusted to regulate the patient's anxiety.*

Symbolic Equation

The traumatized patient who equates a memory in the past with reality today relives the past rather than remembers it, retraumatizing himself. This problem is symbolic equation (Segal 1981). The patient equates a symbol (memory or fantasy) with reality. The patient may equate a feeling today with an experience in the past (reliving a memory, having a flashback) or equate the therapist with a projection. The patient becomes afraid of the therapist, unable to form a therapeutic alliance.

Vignette One: Equating a Memory of the Past with Reality in the Present

When the patient equates the therapy with a traumatic experience in the past, she loses contact with a helpful therapist and relives a trauma with a harmful figure. Our task is not to have the patient relive the past, which is traumatic, but to remember and work through the feelings of the past. To do that, we must help the patient differentiate the present from the past. In this vignette, the therapist has just asked the patient what the feeling is toward her abusive mother. The patient hides her hands, freezes, and braces herself.

Th: You seem to be bracing yourself. What is happening inside?

Pt: I feel anxious.

Th: I see that. How do you experience this anxiety in your body?

Pt: I'm just afraid because when I feel a feeling about my mother, it becomes real. [*She loses the distinction between reality in the present and a memory from the past.*]

Th: No wonder you are afraid. Even though we know it is today, Friday, in Washington, DC, once you have a feeling, your body can forget which day it is, and your body feels as if it is years ago, even though you and I know it is today. [*Differentiate the past from the present.*]

Pt: [*Relaxes.*] Yes, that is it exactly.

Th: It's important for us to remember that a feeling is just a memory. And our task here is to help you remember the past but not to relive it. Does that make sense? [*Clarify the therapeutic task to deactivate the projection. Sometimes the patient believes the therapist wants her to relive the trauma in therapy. Deactivating that projection brings down projective anxiety.*]

Pt: That makes sense. [*Relaxes more.*]

Vignette Two: Equating an Image from the Past with the Therapist

When the patient equates the therapist with a figure in the past, the patient can relive the past trauma and be overwhelmed with anxiety. To prevent this retraumatization, the therapist must help the patient differentiate him from the image from the past. A dissociative patient in his third session describes his reactions to learning that he dissociates in therapy. As he does so, his anxiety rises.

Th: What are you feeling right now?

Pt: Anxious.

Th: That's what I thought. Where do you notice that anxiety in your body right now?

Pt: In my chest and in my legs.

Th: What do you notice in your legs?

Pt: They're jumpy. [*The patient was experiencing an urge to run from the room, a topic that had been touched on before.*]

Th: They are jumpy. You have a connection with me in the present, and then we see anxiety come up. And we know we have been talking about how you and your wife can be even more connected, and we're trying to help you with anxiety because we saw last time that there's connection, anxiety, and then blip [*dissociation*] right?"

Pt: Yes.

Th: This is progress because you're present with me, and you are feeling anxiety without a blip.

Pt: Yes.

Th: That's progress. Right now you're feeling this anxiety as a jumpiness in your legs?

Pt: Yeah.

Th: How do you experience the jumpiness in your legs?

Pt: It's like a pressure in my legs. Yesterday I felt that same thing, and I had to keep moving my legs. I kept—they didn't feel comfortable in any position I put them.

Th: When you say the legs feel jumpy. What are your legs wanting to do?

Pt: Move.

Th: Are they wanting to jump? Are they wanting to run? If they just did what they wanted to do, what would they do?

Pt: If they were doing like last time I was here, they'd want to jump and then run.

Th: They'd want to jump. What do you notice feeling right now?

Pt: Tension.

Th: What do you notice feeling in your arms? Because you notice your arms are like this. [*Grabbing position.*] What's that? What are those arms wanting to do?"

Pt: Not sure. They're, they're kind of locked into position.

Th: They're locking into position. What are those arms wanting to do?

Pt: Well, the most comfortable position is like this. [*Places arms to his side at rest—defense.*]

Th: Yes, but they were doing something else, weren't they? There was this jumpiness in the legs and the arms. What do you notice in those arms?

Pt: They want to do something.

Th: What is that? What is it they want to do?

Pt: Protect myself. I felt comfortable protecting myself like this [*crosses arms across his chest*], and I think I was saying to myself, I don't want to protect myself. I want to move forward, and if I protect myself, I'm not going to be able to.

Th: But you know what? Your body is telling us at some point in your life you had to protect yourself, or you couldn't, right?

Pt: Mm-hmm.

Th: And it's telling me that right now. I want us to listen to your body because at some point you apparently had to not listen to it. I don't know when that was. Maybe you'll figure that out, but right now I'm seeing your body's having this reaction, as we have this connection because you know you're sitting here with me, mild-mannered therapist on Connecticut Avenue. But we're seeing your body is having a different experience. Your body's not here with me. Your body is with someone else. Your body is with somebody where you're feeling like you've got to jump and protect yourself or jump and run. [*Address time-space distortion. The present is not the past (Rothschild 2003). Differentiate the real relationship from the projection.*]

Pt: Okay.

Th: So it's sort of like we're having a relationship in stereo.

Pt: Okay.

Th: We've got two tracks right now. We've got a good connection. You're wanting to connect with me, and I'm wanting to connect with you in a psychotherapy relationship. And right now your body is telling me you're having a relationship with someone who's apparently dangerous, whom you want to protect yourself from or run away from. [*Distinguish the therapeutic alliance in the here and now from a projection based on the past (Bateman and Fonagy 2004; Fonagy et al. 2002).*]

Pt: Right.

Th: And that's getting in the way because you've been talking about how you and your wife have trouble making love. It's hard if this protecting and running and jumping urge is coming up in bed, right?

Pt: That's true.

Th: It's impossible, right? We're trying to help you with what your body does. I want us to really listen because you're here wanting to connect with me, but your body is doing something different. And we have to listen to what happens because in just connecting here with me, you got jumpy. [*His anxiety drops in his body.*]

Pt: Okay.

Th: Then there's this urge to jump and then the arms are wanting to protect you. How are the arms wanting to protect you?

Pt: More like, more like this. [*Crosses his arms in front of himself—defense.*]

Th: There's this and then there's this [*the therapist imitates the two defensive gestures*], but I also saw your hands are doing this [*the therapist imitates the impulse gesture*], and I want to pay attention. What's that? What are the arms wanting to do when they're like that [*in the grabbing position*]?

Pt: The thing that comes to mind that doesn't make any sense is that I want to put my hands around my father's neck and choke the life out of him. [*Emergence of the murderous impulse toward his father that evoked the unconscious anxiety. The patient holds his hands in front of his face as if strangling his father.*]

Th: Okay.

Pt: But that's with my hands in this position.

Th: Do I have your permission for us to go there?

Pt: [*Nods.*]

In this example, the patient's jumpy legs reveal his anxiety *and* his projection: he mistakes the therapist for his violently abusive father. He is not conscious of this projection, but his body reacts as if he is in danger with the therapist. To reduce the risk of his acting impulsively, the therapist invites the patient to pay attention to the urge to run, to notice, watch, and describe that urge. Next the therapist helps him see the difference between present and past, here and there, the therapist and someone else, the therapeutic alliance and a past relationship.

As those distinctions become clear to the patient, his anxiety drops, and his body relaxes. Suddenly, a murderous rage toward his father emerges.

Vignette Three: Equating Fantasy with Reality

Some patients, especially those with panic disorder, equate their fantasies with reality. Their conflicts often involve rage, which triggers anxiety, which becomes perpetuated because they lose sight of the difference between their fantasies and reality.

In this vignette, a patient has called the therapist's office crying hysterically, saying that she is lost but on her way. She arrives to her session twenty minutes late, hyperventilating, pouring out a story of how she got lost on her way to the appointment. Her daughter has recently gotten into legal trouble due to alcoholism, and the patient fears her daughter could lose her job.

> *Pt:* I'm just afraid she could die if she does not get into rehab. [*Speech races. Anxiety rises.*] Do you mind if I call her right now to find out if she is still alive? [*Failure to distinguish fantasy from reality.*]
>
> *Th:* You are obviously anxious right now. Would you agree? [*Interrupt her defense of rumination to draw her attention to her anxiety.*]
>
> *Pt:* Yes, do you mind if I call?
>
> *Th:* Before you do that, can we pay attention to this anxiety? You were so anxious before you got here that you said your eyes were blurry. Right?
>
> *Pt:* Yes.
>
> *Th:* That's a serious sign of anxiety. Then you got lost, which means your anxiety was so high, your mind wasn't working right. Would you agree?
>
> *Pt:* Yes, I was terribly anxious.
>
> *Th:* Let's pay attention to this anxiety that has been so torturous to you today. Where do you notice feeling tension in your body? [*Mobilize her attention to symptoms of anxiety in her body. Invite her to pay attention to one symptom until the symptom decreases or disappears. Then invite her to pay attention to another symptom. Five minutes later she is calmer.*] How is your vision now?
>
> *Pt:* My vision is fine now.
>
> *Th:* And how is your thinking?

Pt: Much better—it's not racing so much.

Th: That's another sign your anxiety has dropped. How is your breathing?

Pt: It's much better now. I was having trouble breathing, like I was choking.

Th: But now, in this moment?

Pt: Now the breathing is fine.

Th: We see that your anxiety was extremely high, your vision was blurry, your thinking was racing, your breathing was difficult, but now your vision is fine, your thinking is fine, and your breathing is easy. You are calm now. I assume you were not anxious when you began driving here today.

Pt: No, I was fine. I was looking forward to seeing you today.

Th: I wonder what happened on the way to my office that triggered so much anxiety?

Pt: Nothing. I talked to my husband, and he told me that my daughter did not follow the judge's instructions, so she could end up in jail.

Th: Even though the judge had told her, and you had told her.

Pt: Yes!

Th: What was your feeling toward your daughter for sabotaging herself like that?

Pt: I was angry.

Th: You were angry with your daughter. The anger made you anxious, and then you had a panic attack.

Pt: To punish myself.

Th: You were angry. You became anxious. Then you punished yourself with a panic attack, punishing yourself with a horrible fantasy that she would die.

Pt: But she could.

Th: That's not the point. The point is you have punished yourself many times for your anger by imagining her dead. [*Help the client see that real anger toward her daughter is triggering her imaginary fantasies, which lead to panic attacks.*]

Pt: I see. It's a way to hurt myself.

Th: Right. If a friend of yours had a problem with her daughter, would you torture her by whispering in her ear all day long, "Your daughter could die!"

Pt: Of course not.

Th: Why not?

Pt: Because it would be cruel and not true.

Th: And the same is true if you do it to yourself.

Pt: I see. [*Now she is much calmer because she can clearly distinguish fantasy from reality and no longer punishes herself in the session.*]

Regulate the patient's anxiety so her mind can function effectively. Then explore her feelings.

Vignette Four: Transient Delusion

In the face of rising feeling and anxiety, a fragile patient may suffer a transient delusion, which will heighten her anxiety unless you rapidly address it. In the following vignette, a patient suffered from panic attacks and frequent problems in reality testing. The therapist explores her anxiety after she becomes aware of feeling angry with her son.

Th: Where do you notice this anxiety in your belly? [*Explore her parasympathetic symptoms and mobilize her attention to her anxiety.*]

Pt: Right here, like acid in my stomach.

Th: Where else do you notice anxiety in your body?

Pt: [*Becomes weepy and more anxious.*] I feel like maybe I have my babies in my belly. Pregnant.

The feeling of rage triggers anxiety and the defense of a delusion. In effect, she is saying, "I am not the mother who feels rage toward my children; I am the mother who wants only to give birth to them." This breakdown of the boundary between reality and fantasy triggers more anxiety.

To increase the patient's orientation to reality, draw her attention to concrete facts that contradict the delusion. Then regulate her anxiety. Then point out causality: "You felt rage toward your son, and it made you anxious. So you tried to hide your rage toward your son by imagining that you only want to be pregnant with him."

Th: It's like your babies are in your belly.

Pt: Uh-huh, and I am trying to keep them from being— [*Rise in anxiety and weepiness. She does not distinguish between reality and her delusion.*]

Th: As you look at your belly, are you pregnant? [*Draw attention to reality.*]

Pt: [*Looks at her belly.*] No, but it feels that way. [*Cries.*]

Th: But are you pregnant, as you look there?

Pt: [*Looks at her belly.*] No. [*Cries.*]

Th: Are Jim and Jane [her children] in your belly right now?

Pt: But it reminds me of Jim. [*Still does not differentiate reality from fantasy.*]

Th: But are Jim and Jane in your belly?

Pt: No, they are not. [*Immediately calms down and takes off her coat. With the clear differentiation between reality and delusion, her anxiety drops quickly.*]

Th: They're not in your belly. What do you notice feeling in your belly now?

Pt: [*Sighs.*] A little better there. [*The return of sighing signals a drop in her anxiety from the high levels of moments before.*]

Th: Are you pregnant as you look there?

Pt: [*Calmly.*] No.

Th: Are Jim and Jane in your belly?

Pt: [*Calmly*] No. They are not here.

Th: Would you agree they are probably too big to be in your belly now?

Pt: [*Laughs and smiles.*] Yes. [*Her children are adults. Now able to differentiate reality from delusion, her anxiety drops further.*]

Th: How is your belly now?

Pt: The pain is still there, but it is smaller.

Transient delusions and losses of reality testing occur when anxiety goes into cognitive/perceptual disruption. Poor reality testing perpetuates anxiety. First, address the reality testing problems, then regulate anxiety, and then point out the causality of feeling, anxiety, and defense. Do not explore the content of delusions when the patient's anxiety is too high for her prefrontal cortex to function properly. She cannot distinguish between reality and fantasy, reflect on her delusion, think symbolically, or integrate information. She cannot look at the raging river because she is drowning in it.

The delusion's *content* is not as important as its *function*: to ward off feelings. Pay attention not to the delusion but to the person who is hidden underneath.

Principle: *To address reality testing problems, first try to regulate the anxiety. If this does not help, then address the ego deficits or projections, which perpetuate the anxiety.*

- *Remind the patient of reality to deactivate a delusion:* "As you look at your belly, are you pregnant?"
- *Remind the patient of reality to deactivate a projection:* "As you look at my eyes now, do these look like eyes of judgment? What do you see in these eyes?"
- *Remind the patient of contradictory realities to block splitting:* "You say you feel only angry with your husband and at the same time you remember nursing him lovingly before he died."

In response to these interventions, the patient may become dizzy. Regulate her anxiety and then show her causality: "Something about recognizing these complex feelings in you triggers some anxiety. You feel both angry with your dead husband and at the same time remember nursing him lovingly." If the patient regresses, becomes paranoid, and projects more violently, she is probably at a psychotic level of character structure and in need of a supportive form of therapy (Kernberg 1975).

Principle: *When unconscious feelings cause anxiety, regulate the anxiety, and then help the patient face the feelings. By facing and experiencing those feelings deeply, her anxiety and defenses will decrease.*

Following are some ways to address defenses or ego deficits, which prevent anxiety regulation: Restructure the defenses or ego deficits that perpetuate anxiety. Once projective anxiety or anxiety resulting from defenses drops, then regulate anxiety resulting from feelings. The following list summarizes how to do this:

- *Ego deficits:* Regulate the anxiety, show causality, and then explore feelings.
- *Self-attack:* Help the patient differentiate herself from and turn against this defense. Then explore the feelings she warded off by using this defense.
- *Projection:* Deactivate the projection and the resulting projective anxiety. Regulate anxiety due to feelings. Then explore feelings.

- *Splitting:* Draw the patient's attention to contradictory realities, building the capacity to bear these split-off feelings while anxiety is regulated.

For a summary of the decision tree for anxiety regulation, see figure 2.3.

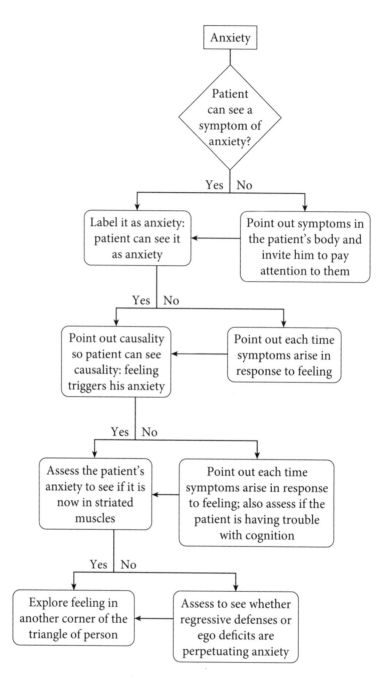

Figure 2.3   Decision tree for regulating anxiety

SUMMARY

Assess anxiety symptoms to find out the patient's threshold for anxiety tolerance. Once you regulate the patient's anxiety, build up his capacities for anxiety and feeling tolerance, so he can experience his feelings more deeply. If you cannot regulate the anxiety, address the regressive defenses, character defenses, or ego deficits that perpetuate it. Address them first to make regulating anxiety possible.

The ability to regulate a patient's anxiety depends in large part on how well you, as a therapist, regulate your own. Personal psychotherapy is essential for any practicing therapist: recognizing your anxiety will help you be sensitive to the anxiety of others. To develop your anxiety regulation to the highest levels, consider using a biofeedback device such as Healing Rhythms (http://www.wilddivine.com). It will help you monitor your heart rate variability and become better physiologically regulated. It will help you become more aware of subtle fluctuations of anxiety in your body so you can attune to yourself and your patients. Meditation and exercise are also recommended. To regulate others, you must be able to regulate yourself. To help others face their deepest feelings, you must be able to bear your own.

RECOMMENDED READINGS

Ten Have de Labije, J. (2006). When patients enter with anxiety in the forefront. In *The Collected Writings of Josette ten Have de Labije* (pp. 37–80). Del Mar, CA: Unlocking Press.

RECOMMENDED MATERIALS

If you would like to study a videotaped session that shows how to assess and regulate anxiety in a fragile patient, go to http://www.istdpinstitute.com/DVD and you will find a DVD of an actual session, a teaching DVD on fragility, and an analyzed transcript of the session on the DVD.

If you would like to review the basic points of anxiety assessment and regulation on videos by Jon Frederickson, you can visit the URLs below.

Anxiety assessment part 1 (May 24, 2012). http://www.youtube.com /watch?v=22yLR49VUeM.

Anxiety assessment part 2 (May 24, 2012). http://www.youtube.com /watch?v=FBZF-Ni4rNo.

Anxiety assessment part 3: Anxiety regulation (November 12, 2012). http://www.youtube.com/watch?v=Vo62ZMGl6ew.

CHAPTER THREE

Defenses: The Second Detour from Feelings

W hen we explore feelings, patients use defenses, which cause their presenting problems. Defenses automatically and unconsciously ward off aspects of reality and feelings that trigger anxiety. Since defenses prevent us from seeing reality accurately, we cannot respond adaptively. As a result, we fail to achieve our goals, and we experience increased negative feelings. In contrast, coping mechanisms are conscious strategies we use flexibly to solve an external problem. They decrease negative feelings, helping us function, so we can solve or manage our problem (Cramer 1991, 1997, 1998, 2003, 2006).

Defenses alter the way we feel by altering the way we see or interpret reality, but they do not change reality itself. For instance, an adolescent girl uses denial when she has unprotected sex. She tries to change her internal state of anxiety rather than face external reality: she could get pregnant. Denial avoids her anxiety internally, but it creates a new problem externally. Defenses distort our perception of reality, resulting in pathological functioning (Haan 1977).

Defenses also ward off unacceptable thoughts, impulses, and wishes (S. Freud 1894/1958). For example, if you ask a woman what she feels toward her boyfriend for hitting her, she might answer, "I think it was an immature thing he did." She intellectualizes to ward off the anger she cannot accept.

Defenses also function interpersonally to prevent emotional intimacy with others (Kernberg 1975; Kohut 1977, 1984; H. S. Sullivan 1953b; Winnicott 1965). A woman asks her boyfriend if he loves her. He replies, "Well, I'm not sure what you mean by the word *love*. I certainly have grown accustomed to your face." He intellectualizes to keep her and his feelings at a distance. Defenses can also maintain self-esteem and ward off negative feelings (Cooper 1998; Fenichel 1945; Kohut 1977). A medical student who flunks out of school says, "It's no big deal. I didn't want to be a doctor anyway." He uses denial to avoid a loss of self-esteem.

THE INTERPERSONAL ORIGIN OF DEFENSES

We learn as children to ignore any elements of reality (stimulus, feeling, anxiety, defenses, problems) that make our caretakers anxious so we can preserve our bond with them (Benjamin 1993; Bowlby 1973, 1980; Main 1995; H. S. Sullivan 1953b). The physically abusive father looks at his son and says, "Wipe that smile off your face, young man!" The boy hides his feelings to preserve an insecure attachment (Benjamin 1993, 1995; Cooper 1998).

This child learns not affect regulation but affect dissociation through ignoring his feelings like his father does. Avoiding feelings by using defenses explains the link between attachment style and psychopathology (Cassidy 1994; Dozier, Stovall, and Albus 1999; Main 1995; Sroufe 1989, 1996).

Having learned implicitly that feelings make a caretaker anxious, the child automatically uses defenses when feelings rise. The unconscious perception of threatening emotions triggers anxiety (see chapter 2) and defenses (Cramer 2006, 2008). These defenses, learned in childhood, become strengthened through countless repetitions (Grigsby and Stevens 2000), creating a rigid character structure by adulthood (Main 1995).

All of this occurs out of a person's awareness. Unconscious or implicit memory triggers defenses (Clyman 1992; Duffy 1997; Reber 1993), which occur automatically and habitually without awareness or effort. Patients do not use defenses consciously.

Imagine hopping on a bicycle to go for a ride. You would not consciously shift your balance to begin pedaling. It would just happen automatically. Bicycle riding is a set of motoric procedures never encoded in language. You are not conscious of cues telling you to shift your body for balance. This is unconscious procedural memory at work.

In fact, most of our everyday actions take place automatically through procedural memory (Bargh and Chartrand 1999). It is the most efficient way for the brain to work. Conscious awareness of a feeling is not necessary to activate a defense. This automaticity allows children to respond to emotions quickly and adaptively (Bradley 2000, 148). Defenses and resistances reveal how we learned to "ride a relationship."

Since nonconscious procedural memory triggers defenses from the beginning of life, the patient never sees them. That is why he assumes a defense is "how I am." You can concentrate on a phone conversation because you do not need to think about how to form words while you are talking. *Procedural memory runs automatically, precisely so your attention is free for other tasks.* You do not have to pay attention to the motoric procedures for scratching an itch or using a defense. They happen automatically.

Since defenses happen unconsciously, a patient cannot see them without the therapist's help. So first we help the patient observe and pay attention to his defenses. A patient who uses the defense of self-attack a thousand times a day will become depressed. If he doubts all of his decisions, he will become confused. Defenses create and maintain presenting problems. That is why it is an act of compassion to interrupt and identify the patient's defenses. They create symptoms.

But you may ask, "Isn't there a danger if you take away the patient's defenses?" The good news is, you cannot. You can take the wallet out of my pocket, but you cannot take away my ability to intellectualize. Defenses are behaviors (Wallerstein 1985). Once we bring defenses to the patient's awareness, they become choices the patient makes. She can face or avoid her feelings. We can point out how she avoids her feelings. We can point out the price: avoiding feelings causes her presenting problems. She will always have the choice to face her feelings or use a defense. No one can ever take that choice away from her.

Others may ask, "Aren't defenses essential for our functioning?" Healthy, mature defenses are essential for healthy functioning (Vaillant 1993). Maladaptive defenses are not. They create presenting problems and symptoms (Cramer 2006; Erickson, Feldman, and Steiner 1997; Gross and Levenson 1997). Children use defenses to adapt to their environment (Hartmann 1964). When generalized to other people, defenses become maladaptive, creating problems. We must help patients let go of destructive defenses, experience their feelings, and channel them into adaptive actions rather than maladaptive defenses.

Others may ask, "But without a defense, how can the patient defend herself?" Without a defense, a child could not defend herself from a parent disrupted by the child's feeling. However, an adult who uses denial, for instance, is unable to see reality clearly and respond to it. Thus, the defense that helped the child harms the adult, causing presenting problems and symptoms. We might say that the child's defenses become the adult's attackers.

When the patient uses defenses to avoid her feelings, we cannot engage in the therapeutic task. We must address them to co-create a healing, therapeutic alliance.

Table 3.1 shows typical defenses patients use to refuse an invitation to form a therapeutic alliance.

Table 3.1   Typical defenses

Intervention	Defense
"What is the problem you would like me to help you with?"	"I don't have a problem."
"Is there a specific example we could look at?"	"I can't think of one."
"What is the feeling toward him?"	"I don't have a feeling."
"Could we take a look at this?"	"Anything else but this."
"How do you experience this feeling physically in your body?"	"I don't."
"Is this a problem you would like to overcome?"	"No. This is not a problem for me."

Why does a patient respond in these ways? As a child, the patient used defenses to adapt to his caretakers and their fears. Every defense enacts this history (Gray 2005) of the need to adapt (Hartmann 1964). As an adult, the patient tries to fit with a listener whom he misperceives as someone risky in his past. For instance, the patient who criticizes herself perceives the therapist as someone who would criticize her. Thus, every defense originally had a self-affirming, positive effect. It reestablished a fit with someone in the past. However, defenses, which originated as adaptive regulators of relationships, become maladaptive perpetuators of the past.

DEFENSE WORK

Since defenses have always been unconscious as implicit, procedural memory, the patient is not aware of them. Thus, we must help the patient see them. Defense work has three stages: (1) identification; (2) clarification; and (3) confrontation. First, identify the defense so the patient can observe it. Second, clarify the defense by showing him its function and price. Once the patient sees the defense's function and price, make sure he recognizes that he is not the same as his defense ("That's just the way I am"). Then you can confront the defense. Now let us go to the first stage of defense work.

Defense Identification

As soon as a defense occurs, help the patient identify it. Point out the defense so he can see how he is avoiding feeling in the moment. Remember: if the patient cannot see his defense, he cannot let go of it. The following are examples of defense identification:

- "That's your thought, but your thought is not a feeling. Do you see how you cover your feeling with a thought?" [*Point out intellectualization.*]
- "Do you notice how you doubt yourself?" [*Point out self-doubt.*]
- "Do you notice how you distance yourself from your feelings right now?" [*Point out distancing.*]
- "It is not clear what the internal emotional problem is you would like me to help you with. Do you notice you are having trouble giving a clear example of what you want help with?" [*Point out vagueness.*]

Sometimes, to point out a defense, we must help the patient differentiate the defense from feelings. This is known as *differentiating the corners of the triangle of conflict.*

Th: What is the feeling toward him for slapping you?

Pt: I feel shut down. [*Patient does not differentiate the defense of shutting down from her feeling.*]

Th: Shut down is not your feeling. Shut down is how you deal with your feeling. You shut it down. [*Differentiate her feeling from her defense.*] If you don't shut down your feeling, what is the feeling toward him for slapping you?

A patient cannot turn against a defense she does not see. Anytime therapy is stuck, assess what defenses she uses that prevent a therapeutic alliance from forming.

Defense Clarification: The Price

The second step in defense work shows the patient the price and function of the defense. Help the patient see the price of the defense: it causes her symptoms and presenting problems. Always help the patient see *causality*: feelings trigger anxiety, which triggers defenses, which create presenting problems and symptoms.

The patient who does not see causality believes a defense helps her and will hold onto rather than let go of it. Thus, we have no consensus on the therapeutic task, so therapy cannot succeed. The patient must let go of her defenses to co-create a therapeutic alliance.

When the patient begins to see the defense, clarify its price. The following examples show how to clarify the price of the defense.

- "When you underestimate yourself like this, does that make you depressed?"
- "When you doubt yourself like this, could that be keeping you confused and directionless in life?"
- "When you distance yourself from your feelings now, that will prevent us from getting to the bottom of your difficulties. You say you want to get to the bottom of what is causing your depression, but now you are distancing yourself from your feelings, so we won't be able to get to the bottom of your difficulties. Do you see how you are working at cross-purposes with yourself?"
- "If you talk over your feelings, we won't find out what is going on underneath, and you'll keep feeling anxious rather than find out what feeling is underneath."
- "If we don't find out what the problem is you would like me to help you with, we won't be able to help you."

Defense Clarification: The Function

Once the patient sees the price of the defense, help her see its function. For example, you might show her that a defense wards off a feeling, denies reality, protects someone else, or punishes her.

Th: How do you experience this anger toward your father physically in your body?

Pt: I think he's right—maybe I don't have what it takes to go to college.

Th: When you underestimate yourself like this, do you see how you look at yourself through his eyes instead of your own? [*Identify the defense.*]

Pt: Oh, I criticize myself like he does?

Th: Yeah, do you see how you deal with your anger with him by criticizing yourself instead? [*Clarify the function of the defense.*]

Pt: I hadn't looked at it that way before.

Th: If we take a look at it that way, do you see how criticizing yourself is a way to cover up your anger toward him? [*Clarify the function of the defense.*]

Clarification of Character Defenses

We must clarify character defenses in a different way because character defenses have a different structure from other defenses. When a patient uses a character defense, she treats herself the way she was treated in the past. For instance, a patient who had a critical father criticizes herself. Thus, to clarify the price of character defenses, we must show the patient the price of how she relates to herself.

Th: What's the feeling toward him for slapping you?

Pt: I try not to make too much of it. [*Ignores and minimizes her feeling.*]

Th: You try not to make too much out of him slapping you. You try not to make too much out of him bruising you. You try not to make too much out of him hurting you. Do you notice how you ignore and dismiss yourself and your feelings? [*Identify the defense.*]

Pt: Yes, but I do it all the time.

Th: So let's check in on your goal. Is that what you want to keep doing—dismissing yourself and your feelings? [*Ask if the reason for the session is to engage in the therapeutic task or the antitherapeutic task.*]

Pt: No.

Th: After all, when you dismiss your feelings and say you don't want to make too much out of him slapping you, you invite me to dismiss you too and say it's no big deal. What kind of relationship would we have if we agreed to ignore your feelings when your boyfriend slaps you? [*Clarify the price.*]

Pt: Not a good one.

Th: If you ignore your feelings over being slapped, does that make you more or less likely to choose guys who will slap you? [*Clarify the price.*]

Point out the price of the defense today while empathizing with its value in the past. When the patient feels your empathy for the defense's origin, she can more easily let go of it today, feeling compassion for her past suffering.

Th: We can certainly understand why you laugh over your feelings. You've told me your father hit you and then laughed at your pain. How wonderful you found that solution to join him and avoid being hit more, but would you agree that what solved your problem with your father in the past invites your boyfriend to dismiss your feelings today?

Pt: When I laugh off my anger, he does too.

Th: Shall we take a stand against that self-dismissal?

Pt: Yes.

Confronting the Defense

If the patient sees the defense, its price, and its function and still uses it, we must address one more problem before confronting the defense. Often, patients cannot differentiate themselves from the defense: "That's just the way I am." When the patient identifies herself with her defense, do not confront it. She will believe you are attacking her as a person rather than confronting a behavior that hurts her. Identification with a defense is a central feature of syntonicity. (See chapter 8.)

To differentiate the patient from her defense, we must help her see the difference between herself as a person and the ways that she handles her feelings, between her as an agent and the choices she makes.

Th: Do you notice how you are detached now?

Pt: That's just the way I am. [*Identifies with the defense.*]

Th: No, it's not the way you are, but it is the way you deal with your feelings. [*Differentiate the patient from her defense of detaching.*] You detach from your feelings. It is what you do, but as long as you detach here with me, we will have the same kind of distant, detached relationship here you had with your ex-husband. [*Point out the price.*] Why do that to yourself?

Once the patient has differentiated herself from her defenses, the therapist can invite the patient to let go of the defense.

Pt: Yes, but I always detach from feelings. I've done it my whole life.

Th: The first question for us is this: what do you want to do about this detaching here with me? [*Point out her task: to progress, she must let go of her defense.*] As long as you remain detached here with me, this will be a detached relationship just like the one you had with your ex-husband. [*Point out the price.*] You said you want to have healthier relationships, and now we see how this habit could sabotage the healthy relationship here that you came to have. [*Point out how her defense obstructs her goal.*] As long as you detach, this will be a crippled therapy. What do you want to do about this destructive mechanism here with me? [*Confront the patient with her task: to let go of the defense.*]

When we confront the patient's defense, we challenge her not just to let go of her defense but, more importantly, to reach her full potential as a person. We encourage her to reveal who she really is, hidden underneath her defenses.

- "Is this the optimal level of functioning you aspire to?"
- "Is this an example of the kind of person you want to become?"
- "Is this behavior your goal, or is this what you want to overcome?"
- "Do you want self-doubt to win or you?"
- "Do you want to follow self-devaluation or your highest self?"
- "When you put yourself down, are you letting yourself reach your full potential?"

In this sense, confronting a defense is always encouraging a patient to face what she fears so she can resume the journey of self-creation that is personality itself. Every time she lets go of a defense, she makes the choice to explore her potentials that were hidden by the defense.

In response to defense identification, clarification, and confrontation, many patients let go of their defenses and face their feelings. However, some do not. Instead, they begin to distance themselves not just from feelings but also from *the therapist*. They resist emotional closeness. Now the patient enacts a past relationship, the transference, to avoid feelings toward the therapist. When this happens, shift from doing defense work to transference resistance work.

Shift from defense work to transference resistance work if the defenses persist, the patient becomes more distant, the defense work no longer triggers unconscious signaling of anxiety, or the patient becomes less collaborative.

TRANSFERENCE RESISTANCE WORK

As you draw attention to the patient's defenses, his feelings rise. In response, a highly resistant patient begins to resist emotional closeness by using nonverbal tactical defenses. The patient begins to avoid your eyes, assumes an uninvolved tone of voice, crosses his arms and legs, and takes a slouched position in the chair. He fails to answer your questions, fails to agree on the existence of a problem, or fails to declare his will to engage in the therapeutic task. He fails to give a specific example or declare a feeling. The patient's resistance triggers countertransference feelings in the therapist (T. Ogden 1982; Racker 1968). The therapist may become angry with the patient and his resistance. Or the therapist may ignore the resistance, working even harder.

Now the patient's defenses create a pathological relationship, keeping the therapist at a distance. So we shift from defense work to transference resistance work. Rather than address single defenses, focus on how the patient relates to the therapist. Transference resistance work has three stages: (1) identification, (2) clarification, and (3) confrontation. Confronting the transference resistance will go much more smoothly when you follow this sequence: (1) defense identification, (2) defense clarification, (3) defense confrontation, (4) transference resistance identification, (5) transference resistance clarification, and (6) confrontation of the transference resistance. The patient will see his transference resistance clearly and understand why you are confronting its destructive effects.

Principle: *When defense work yields little benefit, shift your focus from individual defenses to the therapeutic relationship. Focus on how the patient avoids you and the price: a crippled relationship and a failed therapy.*

Transference Resistance Identification

First identify the transference resistance so the patient can observe it. Then clarify its price and function. Then assess whether he recognizes he is not the same as his resistance: "That's just the way I am." Once he can see those elements, confront the transference resistance.

Start identifying the transference resistance by pointing out to the patient the defenses he uses to distance himself from the therapist.

- "Notice how you are looking away?"
- "Notice how you are going up in your head and having a conversation with yourself?"
- "Notice how you are pulling back from me right now?"
- "Notice how you are detaching again?"
- "Notice how you are sitting here? If one of your employees sat with you like this in an interview, how involved would you say he is?"

Identify defenses to point out the relationship the patient is creating. The following vignette shows how to help a patient see and reflect on the way he relates to the therapist.

Pt: I don't think I'm distancing.

Th: Do you notice how you are looking at the carpet instead of me? [*Point out the defense by which he resists emotional closeness with the therapist.*]

Pt: Yes.

Th: That's a sign of distancing. Do you see what I mean?

Pt: Yes.

Th: You see this wall of distancing that comes up between us. Do you notice how you are silent and go up in your head? [*Identify the resistance to emotional closeness.*]

Pt: Yes, but I'm thinking.

Th: You think by yourself rather than talk out loud here with me. That's becoming a barrier between you and me. First you form this wall of distancing, and now a wall of silence comes up between you and me. [*Identify the resistance to emotional closeness.*]

Pt: It's just easier for me that way.

Th: It's easier for you to put up this wall between you and me, just like the wall you say you have with your wife. What will happen here if you keep up the same wall of distancing and silence between you and me? [*Invite the patient to see the price of the resistance.*]

Pt: Nothing.

Th: And obviously you have not come here to achieve nothing.

Pt: No.

Th: You want to achieve your goals here, but your wall of silencing and distancing is defeating you. What do you think we can do about this wall coming up between us? [*Once the patient sees his transference resistance, invite him to turn against it.*]

A patient cannot turn against a transference resistance if he does not see it. Any time a therapy is stuck, assess your relationship with the patient. Is he active or passive? Does he join you or resist you? Is he involved or uninvolved? Describe each defense in terms of its relational impact: as a barrier to a collaborative relationship.

Transference Resistance Clarification

The second step is clarification, showing the patient the price and function of the transference resistance. Point out the destructive effects. Maintaining a pathological relationship with the therapist will result in the patient's continual suffering from symptoms, loneliness, defeat of the therapy, and failure to achieve his healthy goals.

The following interventions show how to clarify the price of the transference resistance:

- "You say this wall protects you, but hasn't it destroyed your three marriages and left you a lonely woman?"

- "You can keep this wall. After all, it is yours. And how wonderful that you can keep it, but as long as you keep up this wall with me, it will cause the therapy to end in failure just like your other therapies. Why set yourself up like that again? Haven't you suffered enough?"

- "You say you want me to help you, but at the same time you tell me to stop asking questions. I can do that. I have no right to ask you questions you don't want to answer, but as long as we don't ask the questions you came here to answer, what will happen?"

- "If you keep up this wall of devaluation, we will have only a crippled relationship that will be doomed to failure. No good can result if you keep this destructive wall here between you and me."

- "This wall of distancing will prevent us from getting to the bottom of your difficulties. There is no law that says you have to reveal yourself to me. You have every right to maintain this wall, but then I will remain another useless person in your life."
- "If you put up this wall of words, we won't find out who you are behind that wall, and you'll keep feeling anxious and depressed. Can we find out who you really are behind that wall?"

The following interventions show how to clarify the function of the transference resistance:

- "This wall keeps us at a distance."
- "As long as you maintain this wall, I will be on one side, you will be on the other, and I will be unable to help you."
- "Notice how you try to have a conversation with yourself in your head rather than talk to me? Notice how you put up this barrier to avoid relating here to me?"
- "You cover your feelings with thoughts, but these thoughts are a wall you put up here between you and me. As long as you put up this wall of thoughts, we won't find out who you really are behind this wall."
- "When you put up this wall of doubt between me and you, does this advance our therapy or is it a barrier to our working together?"

We no longer talk about a specific defense but the wall the defense creates. Letting go of one defense does nothing if the patient continues to relate to you pathologically. In the transference resistance, each defense is merely a brick in the wall. So address the wall as a whole: the relationship.

The patient must see causality clearly. Otherwise, we have no agreement on the therapeutic task. He will continue to enact a past relationship, and the therapy will fail. When the patient sees how his transference resistance creates his suffering, he can turn against it and face his feelings instead. Now he can co-create the therapeutic alliance with the therapist.

Use the following steps when identifying and clarifying the resistance:

1. *Point out a behavior several times so the patient can see it:* "Do you notice how you look away? Do you notice how you avoid my gaze? Do you notice how you look at the floor?"

2. *Point out the wall when the patient sees the behaviors:* "Do you notice how there is a wall of avoidance coming up here between you and me?"

3. *Point out his agency:* "Do you notice *you put up* a wall of avoidance here between you and me?"

4. *Point out the price:* "As long as you put up this wall of avoidance here between you and me, I will be on one side, and you will be on the other side of the wall, and I won't be able to help you."

5. *Invite the patient to let go of the resistance:* "What do you think we can do about this wall?"

When the patient sees the transference resistance and its function and price, confront it. (See chapter 13.)

Transference Resistance and Inviting Feelings Toward the Therapist

To reduce the resistance and increase the rise of feelings, the therapist needs to (1) identify, clarify, and confront the transference resistance and (2) invite feelings toward the therapist, which the transference wards off: "Notice how you put up this wall of words and stories between us? This wall creates distance between us. As long as it's here, we can't get a clear look at your difficulties. What is the feeling toward me that leads you to put up this wall?"

This is one of the most important points we can make. When the patient resists closeness with you, it is because he experiences feelings toward you based on his past relational experience. The transference (his behavior) is a resistance against experiencing the feelings toward you. Thus, when we address the transference resistance (the behavior by which he avoids feelings toward you), we always follow up by asking what feelings he has toward the therapist that make him put up this wall. And we will continue asking about the feelings toward the therapist until he can experience them as deeply as possible, which will lead to a breakthrough to the unconscious.

The patient is in conflict. He wants to face his feelings, and he resists them. Mobilize his will to become well (inviting feeling, mobilize him to the task), point out the cost and suffering inflicted by the transference resistance, and then ask about the feelings toward the therapist. In this way, you will decrease his resistance and mobilize his unconscious feelings, preparing the way for a breakthrough to unconscious feelings.

Although we have just been talking about the transference resistance, in fact, patients resist feelings with different kinds of defenses. Thus, we can talk about levels of resistance.

- Moderately resistant patients use repressive and tactical defenses. Identify and clarify the defenses to access their feelings.

- Fragile patients may use repressive, tactical, and character defenses, but with a rise of feeling and anxiety, repressive defenses eventually fail. In response, the patient resorts to regressive defenses. Help the patient observe and let go of these defenses to tolerate higher levels of feeling (see chapters 7 and 9).

- Highly resistant patients, however, do not benefit from defense identification and clarification alone. These patients use defenses to form a wall (enacting a past relationship) to distance themselves from the therapist. Point out the ways the patient distances himself in therapy. Once the patient sees and begins to turn against the wall, ask about his feeling toward you. Address each defense as a wall between the therapist and patient. Continue inviting feelings and addressing the transference resistance until a breakthrough to the unconscious occurs. Either the patient will experience grief and guilt over the suffering he has inflicted on himself through his defenses or he will experience a breakthrough of complex feelings toward the therapist. This ushers in the breakthrough to the unconscious.

SUMMARY

First identify the defense. If the defense persists, clarify its function and price. If the defense still persists, confront the defense. If the defense persists, most likely the patient is enacting a character defense or a transference resistance. Identify the character defense or transference resistance, and then clarify its function and price. If it persists, confront the character defense or transference resistance. Then a breakthrough to feeling will occur.

In summary, all patients use defenses to avoid feelings and anxiety. Help them see and let go of the defenses that create their presenting problems and symptoms. Address defenses moment by moment in the here and now so the patient's suffering can end as soon as possible.

Principle: *Address the patient's defense as soon as she uses it. That promotes experiential learning.*

When helping the patient see and let go of his defenses, his capacity for self-observation should be mobilized in a stepwise fashion. Figure 3.1 shows the steps for mobilizing the patient's self-observing capacities and the order in which they should be mobilized.

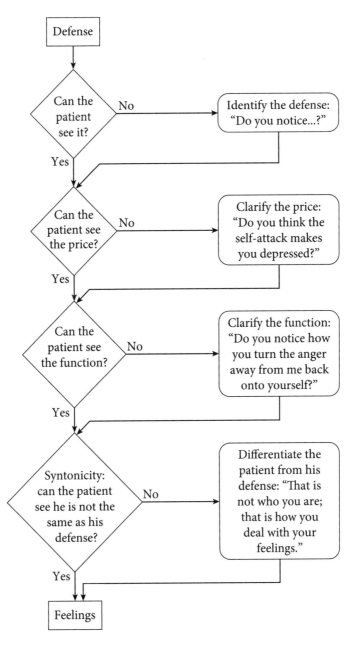

Figure 3.1   Decision tree for defense work

RECOMMENDED READINGS

Blackman, J. (2004). *101 defenses: How the mind shields itself.* New York: Taylor and Francis.

Coughlin Della Selva, P. (1996). Working with defenses. In *Intensive short-term dynamic psychotherapy: Theory and technique* (pp. 53–78). New York: Wiley.

Cramer, P. (2006). *Protecting the self: Defense mechanisms in action.* New York: Guilford Press.

Cramer, P. (2008). Seven pillars of defense mechanism theory. *Social and Personality Psychology Compass, 2*, 1963–1981. This article summarizes all the current research supporting the concept of defense.

Frederickson, J. (1999). Theory of defense analysis and defense analysis studies. In *Psychodynamic psychotherapy: Learning to listen from multiple perspectives* (pp. 165–204). New York: Taylor and Francis. These chapters will teach you how to recognize when a patient uses a defense.

CHAPTER FOUR

Tactical and Repressive Defenses

Patients can use tactical, repressive, character, and regressive defenses (Davanloo 2000, 111–181). Since these defenses have different purposes and structures, they require different types of intervention. Thus, we devote separate chapters to these defense groups.

Repressive defenses keep feelings out of awareness. Tactical defenses (Davanloo 1990, 2000) also repress feelings, but function primarily as a tactic to keep the therapist at a distance. They reveal a resistance to emotional closeness. Moderately resistant patients let go of repressive defenses easily to face their feelings. Highly resistant patients continue to use tactical and character defenses to distance themselves from the therapist. Address these defenses or the patient will remain distant and fail to form a therapeutic alliance.

Since repressive defenses can be used to keep the therapist at a distance, it can be difficult to differentiate them from tactical defenses. Here, we focus on tactical defenses that avoid feelings *and* increase the distance from the therapist. The later examples of repressive defenses show patients who try to connect to the therapist but avoid their feelings.

TACTICAL DEFENSES

Tactical defenses function as tactics to keep the therapist at a distance. Among the most common tactical defenses are cover words, distancing, diversification, evasiveness, generalization, indirect or hypothetical speech, retraction, rumination, and vagueness. In the following vignettes, the principle of intervention will remain the same:

help the patient see the defense and its price so he can let go of his defense and face his problems and feelings.

Cover Words

When we invite the patient to describe what he feels, he may offer a watered-down word rather than the feeling. For instance, rather than say he feels angry with the boss who publicly humiliated him, he may say he feels frustrated, upset, irritated, or uncomfortable. These words cover his true feeling, anger. Here we look at a different example.

Pt: As you know from the phone call I left, my wife died yesterday.

Th: I'm so sorry. What feeling are you having over your wife's death?

Pt: I feel upset. [*Defense: cover word.*]

Th: Obviously, her death upset your entire world. What is your feeling over losing her?

Pt: I'm still in shock.

Th: Of course, it came as a shock since you didn't know she had cancer. What is the feeling over losing her?

Pt: It's terrible. [*Defense: Cover word.*]

Th: I agree. What are you feeling over her loss?

Pt: I feel lost without her. [*Defense: Cover word.*]

Th: You are without her. You lost her, and obviously this triggers a lot of feelings over losing her, holding her hand while she died, and making the funeral arrangements.

Pt: [*Tears form in his eyes.*]

Th: What are you feeling now?

Pt: I'm sad.

Point out and block tactical defenses so feelings can rise to the surface.

Distancing

Some patients will use gestures, tone of voice, and words to maintain interpersonal distance from the therapist. As an analogy, imagine knocking on someone's door (J. Ten Have de Labije, personal communication). He talks to you through the door, but does not open it to let you in the house. Thus, the therapist must address this defense of distancing to have any genuine contact with the patient.

Th: You want me to help you with this powerful anger you feel toward this doctor whose malpractice left you in pain?

Pt: Sure. [*Defense: Said in a diffident tone of voice.*]

Th: You don't sound sure. [*Point out the nonverbal distancing.*]

Pt: No, I'm sure. [*Defense: Looks away.*]

Th: Do you notice how you turn away right now and look out the window? [*Point out the behavior.*]

Pt: Yeah, what of it?

Th: Do you notice how you are distancing yourself from me right now? [*Point out the defense.*]

Pt: [*Looks back at the therapist.*] Yeah, I notice that.

Th: If you distance yourself, that's going to get in our way here. What do you think we can do about this tendency to distance yourself from me? [*The patient must see and let go of the defense to get better.*]

Diversification

The patient may change topics to avoid feelings. This is not free association *to* the feeling. Rather, it is associating *away from* the feeling. Block the defense and return to the focus.

Th: You mention that you have conflicts with your husband. Can we take a look at a specific example where you were in conflict with him?

Pt: First I should probably tell you about my aunt. [*Defense: diversification.*]

Th: Before we get to that, could we look at a specific example where you have a conflict with your husband? [*Block the diversification.*]

Pt: He and I were going to the mall to go shopping. I really like shopping at Macy's, but then there was this sale at Filene's. [*Defense: diversification.*]

Th: [*Interrupts.*] You are doing a beautiful job telling me about your shopping trip, but can we hear a specific example of a conflict you had with your husband? [*Block the diversification.*]

Pt: I'm getting there. It's just that I wanted to get some shoes at the store after I bought a dress I had seen in the window. [*Defense: diversification.*]

Th: [*Interrupts.*] Do you notice that when I ask you to give me a specific example of a conflict with your husband, you go off to shopping, to Filene's, and then to your shoes? Do you notice how you avoid this conflict with your husband by going off to other topics instead? [*Point out the pattern of diversification.*]

Pt: I know. My husband always tells me how I talk all over the place.

Th: Do you see how right now you change topics to move away from talking about the conflict with your husband? [*Point out the defense and clarify its function.*]

Pt: I do now that you point it out.

Th: This is very important. You have asked for my help in dealing with your conflicts with your husband, right?

Pt: Yes.

Th: It's important because you want to get help with these conflicts, but then we see that changing topics deprives you of the help you want. You ignore your problems here by talking about Filene's and shoes. Then you invite me to pay attention to Filene's instead of your problems. It's as if your problems are the last thing to which we should pay attention. Do you see what I mean? [*Point out the defense of diversification and its destructive effects.*]

Pt: [*Tears.*] I hadn't thought about it like that.

Th: Could this be a way you put yourself at the end of the line? You invite me to give more attention to shoes and Filene's department store than to you? Do you think that might be a way you deprive yourself of our attention to you? [*Point out the price of diversification: she ignores her inner life and invites others to do the same.*]

Pt: I do put myself last. [*Sees the defense.*]

Evasiveness

Some patients avoid giving clear, concise answers, so the therapist cannot get a clear picture of their difficulties. Help the patient by pointing out the defense of evasiveness.

Th: You mentioned that you had a conflict at work.

Pt: I don't know if I would say it was a conflict—maybe more of a disagreement or a discussion. [*Defense: evasiveness.*]

Th: First you said it was a conflict, then you said it's a disagreement, and now you say it's a discussion. Do you notice how you avoid giving a clear answer? [*Point out the defense.*]

Pt: It's a complicated situation. I don't know how to describe it. [*Defense: evasiveness.*]

Th: Actually, you have described it in three ways, but you keep shifting. Do you notice how you avoid saying what happened at work? [*Point out the defense.*]

Pt: I'm trying to.

Th: You describe what happened at work but not in a clear way. [*Point out the defense.*]

Pt: My boss says I'm not clear. [*Rise in self-awareness.*]

Th: And now we see here how you avoid giving a clear answer about this problem at work. If we don't get a clear picture, we won't be able to help you with this problem at work. [*Point out the price of the defense.*]

Pt: Okay, it was a conflict I had with my boss.

Generalization

A patient may describe himself in general terms with the therapist. Point out and block this defense and help the patient become more specific.

Th: What is the problem you would like me to help you with?

Pt: It's not a specific problem. More of a general problem. Perhaps it's an emotional problem. I don't know. [*Defense: generalization.*]

Th: But specifically, what is the emotional problem you would like me to help you with? [*Block the defense: encourage the patient to be specific.*]

Pt: Like I said, it's not a specific problem. My previous therapist called it a *personality disorder.* [*Defense: generalization.*]

Th: If we leave your previous therapist out of this, what is the emotional problem you would like me to help you with? [*Block the defense, and return the focus to an internal emotional problem.*]

Pt: There is a behavioral problem. [*Defense: generalization.*]

Th: What is the behavioral problem you would like me to help you with?

Pt: There's a tendency in certain situations to avoid intimacy. [*Defense: generalization.*]

Th: Do you notice how you speak in generalities: "certain situations"? Do you notice how you are vague here with me? [*Point out the defense.*]

Pt: Vague? Yes, I'm vague.

Th: As long as we talk in these vague generalities, we won't get a clear idea of your internal difficulties, and this will just be another failed therapy. What do you think we can do about this tendency to speak in vague generalities here? [*Point out the price of the defense, and encourage the patient to let go of it.*]

Pt: I guess I need to try not to be vague.

Th: If you don't go off to these generalities, what's the problem you would like me to help you with?

Pt: My girlfriend said I should come because of something that happened between us.

Although we still don't know the internal emotional problem, the defense work has helped him shift to a clearer description of his problem. We would continue our inquiry about the incident with his girlfriend and work on his tactical defenses.

Indirect or Hypothetical Speech

Rather than make a clear statement about an anxiety-laden topic, patients qualify it. They say "probably," "maybe," "could be," "I suppose," "I guess so," "you may be right," "sort of," or "I must be feeling sad." Through these terms they turn a fact into a mere hypothesis.

Th: You mention you have problems of intimacy with your wife. Is this the problem you would like me to help you with?

Pt: I suppose. [*Defense: hypothetical speech.*]

Th: You suppose? Either it is or it isn't. [*Block the defense.*]

Pt: It could be. [*Defense: hypothetical speech.*]

Th: Again you say "could be." Either it is the problem you want me to help you with or it isn't. [*Block the defense.*]

Pt: Maybe it is, and maybe it isn't. [*Defense: hypothetical speech.*]

Th: Again you sit on the fence. You notice how you say "suppose," "could be," and "maybe"? Do you notice how you leave things in the air? [*Point out and block the defense.*]

Pt: It's sort of a problem in my opinion. [*Defense: hypothetical speech.*]

Th: You say "sort of." Do you notice how you water things down? [*Point out and block the defense.*]

Pt: I guess so. [*Defense: hypothetical speech.*]

Th: You guess so? Either you see that you are indefinite or you don't. Which is it? [*Block the defense.*]

Pt: I guess you could say I leave things indefinite. [*Defenses: hypothetical speech and projection onto the therapist.*]

Th: But in your opinion? [*Block the defense of projection since it is the more pathological of the two defenses the patient uses in this moment.*]

Pt: I leave things indefinite. I think that's a possibility. [*Defense: hypothetical speech.*]

Th: A possibility? Do you notice how you keep both feet firmly on the fence? Do you see how you leave everything indefinite and vague? How you refuse to say clearly where you stand? [*Point out and block the defense.*]

Pt: Now that you mention it.

Block indefinite speech, point it out to the patient, and call into question his stance of never declaring himself clearly.

Retraction

Retraction is a form of undoing. The patient says something and then takes it back.

Th: What is the feeling toward him for saying that?

Pt: I was angry.

Th: How do you experience that anger physically in your body?

Pt: I don't know that it was anger, more irritation. [*Defense: retraction.*]

Th: Do you notice how you move away from your anger? [*Point out the defense.*]

Pt: I wouldn't say I was angry. [*Defense: retraction.*]

Th: You said you were angry. Now you try to unsay it. Do you see what I mean? [*Point out the defense.*]

Pt: Maybe I wasn't angry. [*Defense: retraction.*]

Th: But you said you were. As soon as you say you were angry, you try to take it back. Do you see what I mean? [*Point out the defense.*]

Pt: Maybe I didn't feel angry at all. [*Defense: retraction.*]

Th: Now you try to erase your anger. First you say you were angry, then you try to take it back, and then you try to erase it. Do you see how you avoid your anger? [*Point out the defense.*]

Pt: I do now.

Rumination

Wondering, speculating, and ruminating can look like collaboration, but they are defenses. The patient ends up in a state of confusion to avoid the experience of his feelings. Interrupt rumination. Help the patient see and turn against it.

Pt: Other therapists have said that I have a tendency to be passive-aggressive. [*Defenses: rumination and projection onto other therapists.*]

Th: And you? Is it your opinion that you are passive-aggressive? [*Block the projection.*]

Pt: I guess, given that a number of previous therapists have indicated— [*Defenses: rumination and projection.*]

Th: [*Interrupts the rumination.*] But in your opinion? [*Block the projection.*]

Pt: Uh, yes, I would say I am passive-aggressive. Of course, that could be due to neurotransmitters, my psychiatrist said— [*Defense: rumination.*]

Th: [*Interrupts the rumination.*] But if we don't go off to neurotransmitters, you say you are passive-aggressive?

Pt: Yes, I suppose that is an area of my psychotherapy that has not been resolved, so I am disappointed about that. [*Defense: rumination.*]

Several other forms of rumination deserve mention. When patients ruminate about what others might feel or think, block it.

Pt: I think the reason he did that was because the stock market fell that day.

Th: We can only speculate about what he feels, but we could get absolutely clear about what you feel. Can we take a look at what the feeling is toward him for firing you?

Some patients ruminate about the past. When this happens, block the rumination.

Pt: I wonder what would have happened if—

Th: [*Interrupts.*] We can only speculate about what never happened. If we don't go off to fantasy, can we take a look at the feeling toward him for firing you?

Patients may ruminate about the future.

Pt: If that happens again, I can imagine taking him to the top of the tower—

Th: Do you notice you go off to a fantasy of the future to avoid your feelings right now? If we leave the fantasy to the side, what is the feeling toward him for firing you?

A patient may ruminate rather than declare his will to engage in therapy. Do not explore the rumination. Block it and focus on the patient's will to engage in the task.

Pt: I'm afraid I will find out something about myself that I won't like.

Th: You probably will. Are you willing to face that?

If the patient says he "dreads" what he will find out about himself in the therapy, rather than ask about his rumination, you can say, "You are afraid of what you will discover. You can avoid this fear and never find out what is going on underneath your symptoms. Or we can face this fear *together* and find out what has been causing your difficulties. Which way do you think will be best for you?"

Vagueness

When patients remain vague about the problem for which they seek your help or about an example of it, they make it impossible for the two of you to get a clear picture of the problem. Always help the patient see and let go of the defense of vagueness so you can get a clear understanding of the triangle of conflict.

Th: What is the problem you would like me to help you with?

Pt: It's a relationship problem of sorts. [*Defense: vagueness.*]

Th: Do you notice how you become vague when I ask about your problem? [*Point out the defense.*]

Pt: It is kind of vague. I'm not really sure there is a specific problem really. [*Defense: vagueness.*]

Th: Do you notice though that you are being vague? [*Point out the defense.*]

Pt: I'm vague, but the problem is vague I think. [*Defense: vagueness.*]

Th: But the problem is that as long as you are vague, we won't get a clear picture of your difficulties. And if we don't get a clear picture of your difficulties, I won't be able to help you. [*Point out the defense and the price: therapy won't help him.*]

Pt: I see what you mean. The problem is I got fired at my workplace after getting into an argument with my boss. [*Now the problem emerges more clearly.*]

For more extensive commentary on tactical defenses, see Davanloo 2000, 111–181.

REPRESSIVE DEFENSES

Tactical defenses have an interpersonal function: to keep the therapist at a distance. Repressive defenses have an intrapsychic function: to keep feelings at a distance. Among the most common repressive defenses are avoidance, denial, displacement, identification with the aggressor, identification with the object of one's rage, instant repression, intellectualization, isolation of affect, minimization, rationalization, reaction formation, and suppression. The principle in these vignettes is always the same, help the patient see and let go of his defense, so he can face his warded-off feeling.

Avoidance

All defenses serve to avoid feelings. In the following example, the patient admits she avoids her feelings. The therapist must remind the patient that avoiding feelings is the antitherapeutic task. Facing the feelings we usually avoid is the task that accomplishes the goals of therapy.

Th: How do you experience this sadness over your husband's death?

Pt: I try to avoid any reminders of it. [*Defense: avoidance.*]

Th: To avoid your sadness. Do you notice how you are trying to avoid your sadness right now here with me? [*Point out the defense in the here and now.*]

Pt: I don't want to face it. [*The defense of avoidance is syntonic, so the therapist must help the patient let go of the defense.*]

Th: You don't have to face this sadness. You have been able to avoid it for the past two years since he died, and you can avoid it for the rest of your life if you want. [*Deactivate the projection of her healthy desire to face her feelings.*] But as long as you avoid your sadness, we won't be able to help you mourn his death and put an end to this depression. As long as you avoid these feelings about him, your suffering will continue. [*Point out the price of the defense.*] Why do that to yourself?

Pt: I don't want to suffer anymore. It's just that I'm scared of feeling the sadness.

Th: We can face that fear and master it so that you can overcome this depression, or you can avoid this sadness and remain depressed. But obviously you have not come here to continue your suffering.

Pt: No. I remember the day I heard he died. I shut down completely. [*With this memory, she signals her willingness to explore her sadness and grief.*]

Denial

Denial is a way to ignore reality. Anna Freud (1936) proposed the following four ways to deny the existence of reality:

- *Denial per se:* Saying that something in reality does not exist
- *Denial in fantasy:* Paying attention to a fantasy rather than reality
- *Denial in words:* Paying attention to false words rather than reality
- *Denial in deed:* Behaving as if something in reality does not exist

All of us use denial at one time or another, so we must assess it. Is the patient's denial due to an inability to test reality? That would be a sign of psychotic illness. Or does the patient see reality but deny it to avoid internal emotional conflict? That is a sign of neurotic illness (Blackman 2004).

Defenses That Deny Reality

Many defenses can be enlisted for the purpose of denying reality, including the following:

- *Withdrawal of attention:* When a patient uses denial, she withdraws her attention from external stimuli or internal feelings that would cause pain and anxiety. The patient sees neither the stimulus nor her feeling because she does not look at them.

- *Negative hallucination:* The patient sees what is not there to avoid what is there in reality. She may say, "He asked me to set the wedding date," when in fact, her fiancé had just ended the engagement.
- *Ignoring:* This is a less extreme form of denial because reality can be brought back into focus. When patients ignore the stimulus to feeling or their feelings, they fail to see essential aspects of reality and misperceive the meaning of events.
- *Negation:* The patient perceives her feeling but negates its meaning. For example, a patient who has just been cruelly rejected by her ex-fiancé may say, "I do not feel angry."
- *Minimization:* The patient perceives the stimulus (the rejection) but minimizes her emotional reaction to it. For example, she may say, "I feel maybe a little bothered."
- *Overexaggeration:* The patient not only denies reality but exaggerates the opposite feeling. She believes this exaggerated fantasy to avoid facing the reality of his rejection. For example, she may say, "I am even more in love with him than ever. I can hardly wait to make love to him again."
- *Reversal:* The patient changes her experience of anger into its opposite. She may say, "I feel quite happy."
- *Ridicule:* The patient perceives the stimulus (the rejection) but denies its importance and, thus, the reality of any feeling response. She may say, "Oh that? That was nothing. I've had many men before. I'll have many men in the future."
- *Fantasy:* The patient acknowledges her perception of reality but changes it into a less threatening fantasy. She relates only to those portions of reality consistent with her fantasy. Her fantasy about reality takes precedence over her perception of it (see Cramer 2006, 44–46). She may say, "I know he'll get over it. He really loves me. It's just a phase he is going through."

All forms of denial interfere with the perception of reality. The patient does not see, avoids, or distorts what she perceives. Reality is not threatening because she does not perceive it.

Denial Per Se

With *denial per se*, the patient denies reality despite overwhelming evidence to the contrary. Remind the patient of his denial and the reality he denies. Do not argue with the patient. Let the reminders of reality do the work for you.

A patient mourning the recent death of his wife reports that he plans to visit a woman who enjoys bondage and discipline, a form of sadomasochistic enactment.

> *Pt:* I know when I go to see her that either I'll feel guilty for going or she'll make me feel shitty.
>
> *Th:* I want to go visit a woman who makes me feel guilty and shitty. [*Mirror the contradiction.*]
>
> *Pt:* I find her very interesting. [*Defense: denial of who he is meeting and why.*]
>
> *Th:* I am very interested in a woman who makes me feel guilty and shitty. [*Mirror the contradiction.*]
>
> *Pt:* I know I'll feel worse about myself.
>
> *Th:* I want to meet a woman who will make me feel worse about myself. [*Mirror the contradiction.*]
>
> *Pt:* [*Laughs.*] I know it sounds crazy. I know she will either reject me or run away from me.
>
> *Th:* I want a woman to reject me or run away from me. [*Mirror the contradiction.*]
>
> *Pt:* Hmm. It is a distraction from all this sadness over Anne's death.
>
> *Th:* I want a woman to reject me so I don't have to face the sadness over Anne's leaving me through death. [*Point out the function of the denial: to avoid the grief over his wife's death.*]
>
> *Pt:* It's so painful. [*Face contorted in pain and grief as he cries.*]

Denial in Fantasy

With *denial in fantasy*, the patient denies reality by paying attention to a fantasy. Help the patient see the contrast between reality and her fantasy.

A patient's son has recently been arrested and has a history of lying to her.

> *Pt:* He said he was not drinking anymore, so I was shocked to learn that he was drinking again. [*Defense: denial in fantasy.*]

Th: I expect my son who lies to tell me the truth. [*Point out the defense: she pays attention to the fantasy son she wishes she had rather than her real son.*]

Pt: But I was shocked! [*Defense: denial in fantasy.*]

Th: Of course, you were. If you see the truth and then deny it, you will be shocked when the truth shows up again. [*"Shocked" is the result when the patient denies reality and reality shows up anyway.*]

Pt: I see. If I deny the truth, then I am surprised when he lies again. [*Improved reality testing.*]

Th: You see the truth. You deny it. Then you are shocked. The denial hurts you. When you deny it again, you set up the whole cycle of self-harm.

Pt: But he really hurts me. [*Projection: she hurts herself when she uses denial.*]

Th: May I offer another perspective?

Pt: Yes.

Th: The first time he hurt you by lying to you. But if you had faced the truth that first time, he could never have hurt you again because you would have been prepared to deal with a liar. Instead, each time you denied the reality that he lies, you set yourself up to be shocked and hurt. I would propose that he hurt you once, but your denial has hurt you hundreds of times. Would you agree? [*Point out the externalization: she punishes herself by denying his lying, but she blames him for the way her denial hurts her.*]

Denial in Words

With *denial in words*, the patient denies reality by paying attention to someone's words, not his deeds. Reminding the patient of the difference between what someone says and does may not help because the intervention does not address her denial. Point out that she *listens* to the other person's words and *ignores* his deeds. This denial through words or selective inattention is the key.

A patient in an abusive marriage says her husband hit her.

Th: What are you feeling toward him for hitting you in the face this week?

Pt: We talked about it, and he said he's sorry, and he won't do it again. [*Defense: denial in words.*]

Th: You pay attention to his words rather than his deeds. [*Point out the denial.*]

Pt: But he said he wouldn't do it again. [*Defense: denial in words.*]

Th: That is what he said. Do you notice you pay attention to what he said but not what he did? [*Point out the denial in words.*]

Pt: But he said he was sorry. [*Defense: denial in words.*]

Th: But do you notice that you pay attention to what he says and ignore what he does?

Pt: My mom says that too. [*Defense: projection—"That's not what I think; that's what my mom thinks."*]

Th: What's your opinion? Do you notice you believe his words and try not to believe his fists? [*Point out the denial.*]

Pt: Hmm. I hadn't thought of it that way.

Denial in Deed

With *denial in deed*, the patient denies reality by acting on the basis of his fantasy. Remind the patient of the difference between reality and the fantasy upon which his actions are based.

Pt: I talked to Jennifer on the phone and told her I thought we could still work things out between us. I asked her if I could come over to her place and talk things out, but she said, "Don't even think of it. I don't ever want to see you again." But I figured, "Hey, if we don't talk this through, we can't ever work this out." So I drove over to her place and went up to the door and pushed the doorbell. She comes to the front door, opens it, curses at me, throws a glass of water on me, and then tells me to get the hell out of her life. Can you believe that?" [*Defense: denial in deed. Rather than face this sad reality, the patient acts as if this is not reality.*]

Th: You visited a woman who said she didn't want to see you again. [*Point out the denial in fantasy.*]

Pt: But how are we going to work this out? [*Denial per se.*]

Th: I want to work things out with a woman who doesn't want to work things out with me. [*Point out the denial in fantasy.*]

Pt: But shouldn't we be able to work things out? [*Defense: denial in fantasy.*]

Th: Shouldn't reality be different from what reality is? [*Mirror the patient's denial in fantasy.*]

Pt: Shouldn't it? [*Defense: denial in fantasy.*]

Th: No. Reality is what it is, but you act as if Jennifer wants to work things out when in reality she doesn't want to. And when you act as if you can ignore reality, you get hurt and set yourself up for more punishment. Don't get me wrong. You can keep on acting as if reality doesn't exist, but we shouldn't be surprised when reality shows up.

Pt: [*Chuckles.*] That's true.

Displacement

Displacement involves expressing a feeling toward someone or something else rather than toward the person where the feeling belongs. A patient describes how his boss humiliated him in front of colleagues during a business meeting.

Pt: And then I went back to the office and sat down. I was so furious, I slammed my fist on the desk. [*Defense: he displaces the rage he felt toward his boss onto his desk instead.*]

Th: But the desk didn't do anything to you, did it?

Pt: No.

Th: Obviously this anger wasn't intended for the desk, was it?

Pt: No, I was furious toward Alex.

Th: You felt the rage toward Alex, but it came out toward your desk instead.

Identification with the Aggressor

The patient may identify with the person who hurt her to avoid feeling anger toward him. The patient may take the point of view of the other person and agree with his criticisms, for instance. Help her differentiate herself from the aggressor.

Th: What's the feeling toward your professor who ridiculed your paper and then threw it into the trash can right in front of you?

Pt: I think he was right. It probably was a dumb paper. [*Defense: identification with the aggressor. She adopts her professor's point of view.*]

Th: Do you notice you put yourself down now? [*Point out the defense.*]

Pt: What?

Th: Do you notice how you put yourself down now and call your paper *dumb*? Do you notice that? [*Point out her defense.*]

Pt: Yes, but—

Th: [*Interrupts the patient's likely continuation of self-attack.*] Do you
notice how you put yourself down now just like your professor
did? [*Point out the defense.*]

Pt: I didn't see that before. But what if he is right? [*Defense: identification with the aggressor.*]

Th: Do you think it is right to put yourself down and call yourself
dumb? Do you think that is the optimal way to treat yourself?
[*Point out how she treats herself.*]

Pt: No.

Th: Do you notice how you began to put yourself down just after you
described how your professor did that?

Pt: I see what you mean, but why is that important?

Th: Because putting yourself down makes you depressed. If you don't
put yourself down, what is the feeling toward the professor for
disrespecting you?

Pt: I was angry.

Th: You felt angry with him for criticizing you unfairly. Then you
turned your anger toward him back onto yourself by criticizing
yourself. In effect, you did to yourself what he had done to you.
Do you see what I mean?

Identification with the Object of One's Rage

Sometimes patients ward off their rage by identifying with the person with whom they are enraged. One moment they experience anger
toward someone, and the next moment they say, "But I do the same
thing." They identify with the other person, no longer aware of their
rage toward him.

Pt: I feel like you weren't so helpful in the last session.

Th: And it sounds like you have some feeling about it.

Pt: Yes.

Th: So what's the feeling toward me for not helping you more?

Pt: I'm angry.

Th: How do you experience this anger toward me for not helping you more?

Pt: I'm just angry.

Th: And how do you experience this anger toward me in your body?

Pt: I'm hardly one to talk. I have been holding feelings back. [*Defense: identifying with the object of his rage. First he said that the therapist did not help him. Now he turns the roles around and says he is not helping himself.*]

Th: Do you notice you are describing your behavior now? A moment ago you were freer to talk about the fact that I didn't help you last time. If we don't turn the camera back onto you, how do you experience this anger toward me?

Pt: I'm not being fair. After all, you have been really helpful. [*Defense.*]

Th: And yet we see you feel angry because I didn't help you last time. If we don't turn the criticism back onto you, can we take a look at this anger toward me? [*Point out the defense of identifying with the person he criticizes.*]

Pt: I didn't see that.

Th: If you don't turn the criticism and anger back onto yourself, let's see how you experience this anger toward me. [*Point out the defense and then encourage him to face his feeling toward the therapist.*]

Instant Repression

Defenses can immediately repress awareness of a stimulus or the resulting feeling (Davanloo 1990, 2000). This occurs in patients suffering from depressive, functional, and psychosomatic disorders. A patient describes an argument with his wife while clenching his fists, then he drops his hands, which become limp: instant repression of the angry impulse. If asked what his impulse was, he won't know. If asked what his feeling is toward his wife, he won't know, or he will say he is anxious. Without an awareness of his feeling, the patient cannot differentiate his feeling from anxiety.

Address the defenses that create instant repression. Otherwise, each time you ask about rage, the patient will use instant repression and suffer symptoms of depression or somatic complaints. (See Ten Have de Labije and Neborsky 2005, Ten Have de Labije 2005, and

Neborsky 2005 for a detailed study of instant repression. The following material on instant repression summarizes their articles.)

Instant Repression of the Stimulus

Suppose you ask about the stimulus: "What happened that triggered these feelings and symptoms?" A patient who uses defenses that create instant repression of the stimulus will respond in one of the following ways:

Denial: "Nothing happened."

Ignoring: "We broke up, but I don't think that's what is bothering me."

Making one's head empty: "Gosh! I have no idea."

Selective memory loss: "We went to a restaurant, but I don't remember anything happening there that would account for this."

Instant Repression of the Feeling

Suppose you ask about the feeling: "What do you feel toward him for breaking up with you that way?" A patient who uses defenses that create instant repression of the feeling will respond in one of the following ways:

Denial: "I don't feel anything about it."

Ignoring: "I'm not happy about it, but it's no big deal. After all, I haven't been so pleased with him myself."

Making one's head empty: "I don't know what to say." "Nothing occurs to me." "I'm empty." "Maybe I don't have any feelings."

Selective memory loss: "I remember he said he wanted to break up, and we talked about it. I tried to get him to rethink his position, but I don't remember feeling anything about it at the time."

Motoric retardation/immobility: The patient's body movements slow down or stop. The patient has not declared her anger at her boyfriend in the session, but her arms rise in frustration as she talks about him. Then her arms suddenly drop and remain immobile on her lap. Immobilization instantly represses the impulse.

Each of these defenses prevents the patient from seeing the stimulus or feeling or how she experiences her feeling. As a result, she cannot recognize the triangle of conflict or causality. To establish an intrapsychic perspective, help her see the stimulus, feeling, anxiety, defense, and causality. The defenses that create instant repression prevent the patient from becoming aware and attentive to her inner life. Thus, the therapist must help her see and let go of her defenses, which create instant repression before exploratory therapy will be possible.

Ten Have de Labije and Neborsky (2005) outline how to awaken the patient's observing capacities:

1. Explore current situations in which the patient experiences her problems. When doing so, the patient will use defenses.

2. Each time, identify the defense and help the patient see its function, and then continue to explore the current situation.

3. Each time the patient uses this defense in the therapeutic relationship identify the defense, help the patient see its impact on the therapy, and then continue to explore the current situation.

4. Once the patient can see the defense, which interferes with her ability to see the stimulus, encourage her to picture the stimulus in detail (what the other person did or said that triggered her feelings).

5. When the patient pictures what that person did, she will have a feeling for a split second and then instantly repress it. Intervene immediately to help the patient notice her split-second experience of the feeling, and then differentiate that feeling from her anxiety, and differentiate the feeling from the defense in this moment that creates the instant repression.

6. When the patient uses instant repression, do steps 2, 3, 4, and 5 again until she can describe the stimuli that triggered her feelings, can bear her feelings for longer periods of time before she uses her defenses, can distinguish her feelings from anxiety and defense, and can see causality (feeling triggers anxiety, which evokes defenses, which cause her presenting problems). Then go to the next step.

7. Invite the patient to label her feeling correctly and give words to what the feeling is about. This will mobilize complex transference feelings and defenses.

8. Encourage the patient to turn against her defenses so she can face her feeling and get to the bottom of her difficulties. Help her see how her defenses perpetuate her suffering and prevent her from forming a healing therapeutic alliance. As she turns

against her defenses, she will experience, explore, and understand her complex feelings.

Instant repression can be hard to recognize. When a patient says she "feels nothing," the therapist might view this as a fact: "She feels nothing." Research shows we feel all the time, but defenses limit self-awareness by distracting our attention away from our feelings. When a patient denies, ignores, or forgets her feeling, empties her head, or immobilizes herself, the result will be "I don't feel anything," "Nothing occurs to me," "I'm empty," or "I don't remember feeling anything." The statement "I don't have a feeling" means "Defenses keep me from knowing what I feel." Therefore, assess which defenses she uses.

Identifying the Defenses That Create Instant Repression

This vignette will show how to assess the defenses the patient uses that prevent him from being aware of his anxiety. The patient describes a situation where he was angry with his girlfriend.

Th: Are you aware of feeling anxious?

Pt: No. [*Defense: denial. The patient is tense head to toe and looks terrified.*]

Th: Do you notice tension in your shoulders?

Pt: Yes.

Th: That's a sign of anxiety. [*Continue to point out symptoms of anxiety in the patient's body for a minute.*]

Pt: I'm like this most of the time, but it's no big deal. [*Defense: ignoring.*]

Th: So you ignore your anxiety most of the time. [*Identify the defense.*]

Pt: There's no sense making a big deal of it. [*Defense: rationalizes using the defense of ignoring.*]

Th: Now you try to justify ignoring your anxiety. [*Identify the defense.*] But if we ignore your anxiety, it will get worse. Shall we pay attention to your anxiety? [*Invite the patient to let go of the defense of ignoring.*]

Pt: I have no idea. [*Defense: empties his head.*]

Th: We've got a problem here. A part of you wants to get to the bottom of this anxiety and find out what's been driving this terrible anxiety. [*Healthy wish.*] Another part of you doesn't want to look at this, wants to tune out, and is dominating our work right now. [*Point out the conflict.*]

Pt: What do you mean? [*Does not see how emptying his mind blocks the therapeutic task.*]

Th: You want to get to the bottom of the anxiety, right?

Pt: That's why I'm here.

Th: We can ignore your anxiety, or we can face it and find out what is driving this anxiety. But when I ask you which way you want to go, you say you have no idea. That's a problem. If you have no idea what you want to do, we have no idea what to do. Do you see how that is an obstacle? [*Point out his choice: engage in the therapeutic task or use his defenses? Point out the price of the defense.*]

Pt: I want to address this anxiety. [*Turns against his defense.*]

Th: Where do you notice feeling this anxiety in your body?

Pt: I don't know. [*Defense: does not pay attention to his anxiety.*]

Th: Of course, because you ignore your feelings and anxiety. [*Not knowing is the result of defenses.*] So could we pay attention to your body instead and help you with this crippling anxiety? [*Point out his choice: engage in defenses or the therapeutic task?*]

Pt: I want to do whatever it takes to get rid of this anxiety.

Th: Is our goal the same: to rid you of these anxiety problems?

Pt: Yes.

Th: Where else do you notice feeling this anxiety and tension in your body?

Pt: In my chest and my stomach. [*Now he pays attention. Anxiety in the striated muscles.*]

Th: What's the feeling underneath that is driving this anxiety?

Pt: [*Silence.*]

Th: What's happening?

Pt: My mind wandered away. [*Defense: ignoring—instant repression as soon as we explore his feeling.*]

Th: It's great you can see that. You want to get to the bottom of these feelings, but then you wander away as soon as we look at them. [*Outline his internal conflict.*] What's going to happen here if you wander away from your feelings? [*Help him turn against the defense by helping him see how it will defeat his goal.*]

Pt: I won't get anywhere. [*Recognizes the price of the defense.*]

Th: Exactly. Why do that to yourself? We can wander away, or we can find out what the feeling is that is driving your anxiety. [*Point *out his choice: defense or therapeutic task?]* What is your choice? *[Invite the patient to turn against the defense.]*

Pt: I don't want to wander. *[Turns against the defense but not toward the therapeutic task.]*

Th: But what is your choice?

Pt: I want to find out what the feeling is that makes me so anxious. *[Turns toward the therapeutic task.]*

The defenses of denial, ignoring, rationalizing, and emptying his head have distracted the patient's attention away from his feelings, so he is not aware of them.

Intellectualization

When the patient intellectualizes, she uses thoughts to cover up feelings. Help the patient see that thoughts are not feelings, and then help her face her feelings instead.

Th: What was the feeling as you saw your father dying in the hospice?

Pt: I realized that it was all for the best. He was a religious man, and he was looking forward to meeting his maker. *[Defense: intellectualization.]*

Th: That tells me your thought, but it doesn't tell me what you felt toward him. *[Point out the defense.]* If you don't cover your feelings with thoughts, what do you feel now as you remember him dying?

Pt: It was the fact that he would no longer be suffering from cancer. *[Defense: intellectualization.]*

Th: Do you notice you offer thoughts instead of your feeling? Obviously, there is some feeling about your father's death, yet you cover your feeling with all these thoughts. Do you notice how you offer thoughts instead of your feeling? *[Point out the defense.]*

Pt: Now that you mention it.

Th: Can we find out who you are underneath all these thoughts? What's the feeling as you remember your father dying in the hospice?

Pt: I feel sad.

Isolation of Affect

The patient may be able to tell you what he feels ("I feel angry"), but not how he experiences that feeling in his body ("I don't feel anything in my body"). How does that happen? The patient ignores the physical experience of anger in his body through repressive defenses. Some regard isolation of affect as a defense. I regard it as the result of defenses. The question becomes, which defenses does he use to "isolate" himself from his feeling?

Pt: I was angry when she threw my resume in the trash.

Th: How do you experience that anger toward her?

Pt: I don't. [*Defense: isolation of affect.*]

Th: You know you are angry, but you don't feel it.

Pt: Oh, I'm angry. [*Nonverbally shows no signs of the feeling.*]

Th: You say you are angry, but you don't sound angry, and you don't look angry. [*Draw attention to the patient's defense. His nonverbal defenses do not match his verbal statement.*]

Pt: [*Fidgets in chair. Sighs.*] Maybe I'm not angry. [*Defense: retraction.*]

Th: But you just said you are. Do you notice how you ignore your anger as soon as you say it? [*Point out the defense of ignoring.*]

Pt: [*Sighs.*] If I don't feel angry, maybe I'm not angry. [*Defense: denial.*]

Th: But you said you are angry that she threw your resume in the trash. How do you experience that anger now as you remember her throwing the resume in the trash? [*Encourage the patient to face his feeling by reminding him of the stimulus.*]

Pt: [*A fist forms. Unconscious rise of feeling.*]

Th: Do you notice that fist? How do you feel your anger right there?

Pt: I feel I'm getting hot. [*Experiences his rage.*]

Minimization

Some patients will admit a feeling but minimize its impact. When they do, however, they get incorrect information about how important the feeling was. Point out the patient's use of minimization so she can feel her feeling and receive the information it offers.

Th: What is the feeling toward him for throwing you out of the car?

Pt: A little peeved. [*Defense: minimization.*]

Th: A little peeved?

Pt: Yes.

Th: Do you notice how you minimize your feelings? He threw you out of his car and left you stranded in the snow, and then you say you feel a little peeved. Do you see how you water down your feelings? [*Point out the defense of minimization.*]

Pt: That's true. He did throw me out of the car.

Th: If we don't water down your feelings, can we have an uncensored look at them?

Pt: I was angry!

Rationalization

When rationalizing, the patient describes the reasons for his feelings rather than the feelings themselves. Help the patient differentiate reasons from feelings, and then help him face his feelings instead.

Th: You had a strong feeling when your employee tried to steal from your firm.

Pt: Right because she— [*"Because" signals that the patient is beginning to rationalize.*]

Th: If we don't go to *because*, what is the feeling toward her? [*Interrupt the rationalization.*]

Pt: If she hadn't done it— [*Defense: denial in fantasy. He relates to what he wish had happened rather than what happened in reality.*]

Th: But she did. And now you move to thoughts, but that won't help you. What is the feeling toward her? [*Interrupt and identify the defense, then ask for the feeling.*]

Pt: I think my anger is due to her similarities to my mother. [*Defense: rationalization.*]

Th: Now you try to analyze your anger. But how do you feel it physically in your body? [*Identify the defense and then ask about the feeling.*]

Pt: But it's true. She is like my mother. [*Defense: rationalization.*]

Th: I'm sure it is. However, you bring this truth in to cover another truth: your anger. If you don't cover your anger with reasons, how do you experience this anger toward your employee?

Pt: How can I feel angry when the company has already punished her? [*Defense: rationalization.*]

Th: That's not your anger. That's how you explain it away and rationalize it away, but these explanations do not tell us how you experience your anger. [*Point out the defense.*]

Pt: I'm just trying to explain to you why I felt what I felt. [*Defense: rationalization.*]

Th: Rather than tell me how you experience your feeling physically in your body, you tell me all the reasons why you feel your anger and why you shouldn't. Still, we don't know how you experience this anger physically in your body. How do you experience this anger physically in your body? [*Point out the defense and invite the feeling.*]

Pt: [*Sighs. Pounds his fist on the chair.*] I tell you I think it's because— [*Rise of feeling (fist) followed by rationalization.*]

Th: If we don't go off to *because*, how do you experience this anger right now in your fist? [*Block the defense and invite the feeling.*]

Pt: [*Looks at his fist.*] My fists are tense.

Patients use *because* to rationalize. Point out that reasons are not feelings.

Reaction Formation

Reaction formation is acting the opposite of what one feels. Help the patient see and let go of this defense, and then invite her to face her warded-off feeling.

Th: Your boyfriend slapped you and called you names. What do you feel toward him for doing that?

Pt: I understand why he did that. He had a bad relationship with his mother. So I decided to pay for his mortgage. [*Defense: reaction formation. She acts the opposite of an adaptive feeling.*]

Th: That's your understanding, but what's the feeling toward him for slapping you and calling you names? [*Point out the defense.*]

Pt: At the time I was angry.

Th: Rather than feel your anger, you acted the opposite instead. [*Point out the defense of reaction formation.*]

Pt: What do you mean?

Th: Rather than feel your anger toward him, you covered it up with understanding. Then you acted the opposite of your anger. An angry woman doesn't go out and pay his mortgage. [*Point out the defense of reaction formation.*]

Pt: You've got a point there.

Th: If we don't act the opposite of your anger, can we have an honest look at this anger?

Suppression

Suppression involves the conscious avoidance of a feeling. Help the patient see and let go of the defense so she can face the feeling she has been avoiding.

Pt: It's painful that he has just left me for another woman, but I just try not to think about it. Eventually, I just forget about it. [*Defense: suppression.*]

Th: I hear that, but if forgetting your feelings worked, would you be here? [*Point out the price of the defense.*]

Pt: [*Smiles.*] No.

Th: No matter where you go, there you are. Your feelings are inside you. It's important we notice that when you forget your feelings and refuse to think about them, you treat yourself like your husband has treated you. Why do his dirty work? Why walk away from your feelings like he did to you? [*Point out how suppression is a way to ignore herself like her husband ignored her; it's a form of self-neglect.*]

Pt: [*Tears.*]

SUMMARY

Moderately and highly resistant patients use repressive and tactical defenses. Repressive defenses push feelings out of awareness. Tactical defenses push the therapist away.

Principle: *Address repressive defenses by focusing on how the patient avoids feelings. Address tactical defenses by focusing on how the patient avoids closeness with the therapist.*

RECOMMENDED READINGS

Davanloo, H. (2000). Management of tactical defenses in intensive short-term dynamic psychotherapy, part I: Overview, tactical defenses of cover words and indirect speech. In *Intensive short-term dynamic psychotherapy* (pp. 111–134). New York: Wiley.

Davanloo, H. (2000). Management of tactical defenses in intensive short-term dynamic psychotherapy, part II: Spectrum of tactical defenses. In *Intensive short-term dynamic psychotherapy* (pp. 135–182). New York: Wiley.

RECOMMENDED MATERIALS

To increase your skills at defense identification and intervention, you may want to download the audio files for defense skill-building exercises at http://www.istdpinstitute.com/resources/20-skills-to-overcome defenses/. These five hours of training will help you learn to identify and intervene effectively with over twenty different defenses that prevent the establishment of a therapeutic alliance.

CHAPTER FIVE

Psychodiagnosis: Co-Creating an Effective Focus

T o know what to say, we need to know what is going on. To know what is going on, we need to assess each patient's response moment by moment. That assessment, known as *psychodiagnosis* (H. Davanloo, supervision 2002–2004), determines every intervention by the therapist.

In theory, the therapeutic process appears simple:

- You ask what internal emotional problem the patient wants help with, and he gives you a clear answer.
- You ask if he would like to explore a specific example, and he gives you one and explores it.
- You ask if he would like to take a look at his feelings, and he says he would.
- You ask, "What is your feeling toward X?" He answers you with a feeling.
- You ask, "How do you experience that anger/sadness in your body? He tells you.
- You ask, "What is the impulse with that feeling?" He tells you and faces his feelings deeply, achieving insights along the way.

But therapy never goes this way. Why? Instead of offering a problem, a specific example, or a feeling, the patient responds with anxiety and defenses. Perhaps the patient claims he has no emotional problem (defense). He describes his problem but is "unable" to come up with a specific example of it (defense). He offers an example, but when you ask what he feels, he says he has "no feeling" (defense). Rather than exploring his problems and feelings (the therapeutic task), he uses the detours of anxiety and defense.

That is not a problem but an opportunity to help the patient. If the patient responds with anxiety that is too high, regulate his anxiety, and then explore his feeling. If the patient responds with a defense, help him see and let go of the defense, and then explore his feeling. When the patient goes off to a detour, help him see it so he can return to the therapeutic task: facing the feelings he usually avoids.

PSYCHODIAGNOSIS

Therapists sometimes become frustrated with a patient's responses of anxiety or defense. They want to see feelings right away. But remember: all patients' responses—even anxiety and defense—are good because they tell you the problem to treat in this moment. To assess that problem and intervene, follow these three principles:

1. Assess each patient's response (Is it a feeling, anxiety, or a defense?)
2. Assess the patient's capacity for self-observation in this moment.
3. Intervene to help the patient with that specific problem.

This process of assessment we call *psychodiagnosis*. Diagnosis in psychotherapy usually refers to phenomenology: assessing the patient's directly observable symptoms. A phenomenological diagnosis tells us what symptoms the patient has but not what causes them or how to treat them. For instance, suppose we had four depressed patients. Their depressions could have been triggered by a heart surgery, a recent loss, longstanding pathological mourning, or chronic self-attack. These patients would need four different treatments for the same diagnosis.

Psychodiagnosis assesses the patient's responses to discover the cause of the symptoms (Coughlin Della Selva 2001). Moment to moment, the therapist assesses the patient's responses of feeling, anxiety, and defense. Through this assessment, the therapist discovers the feelings with which the patient struggles, the anxiety discharge pattern in the body, the defenses that create the symptoms, and his self-observing capacity. Now the therapist knows what feelings to focus on, how to address the anxiety, what defenses to restructure, and which self-observing capacities to strengthen so the patient can recover. Psychodiagnosis tells us what causes the symptoms, what to focus on, what to treat, and how to treat—moment by moment. To know how to analyze each patient's response, we must first understand the triangle of conflict.

Psychodiagnosis of the Triangle of Conflict

Whenever a stimulus occurs, we feel a reactive feeling. This triggers anxiety. Anxiety triggers defenses. And defenses cause symptoms and presenting problems. Feeling, anxiety, and defense together comprise the *triangle of conflict*. Anytime a patient has a presenting problem or symptom, we try to find out what triangle of conflict causes that problem or symptom. To do that, we examine each patient response in therapy.

Each time you intervene, the patient can respond in only three ways:

- Feeling (or a clear answer to your question), which deepens the alliance.
- Anxiety, which weakens the alliance.
- Defense, which weakens the alliance.

If the patient responds with feeling, we can explore the feeling. However, the patient usually responds with anxiety or defense. Now the therapist must psychodiagnose the pathway of anxiety discharge, the defense, and the patient's self-observing capacity to assess the patient's need and intervene effectively.

Psychodiagnosis of Anxiety

Each time the patient responds to an intervention, watch the patient's body to assess the pathways of unconscious anxiety discharge.

- Striated muscles
- Smooth muscles
- Cognitive/perceptual disruption

The patient's pathway of unconscious anxiety discharge tells us his capacity to bear feelings and his threshold of anxiety tolerance, that is, when his anxiety shifts from the striated muscles into the smooth muscles or cognitive/perceptual disruption. Anxiety is a good sign. It means the patient is facing feelings he previously avoided. If we avoid conflictual feelings, the patient's anxiety will remain low, but he will not learn to face the feelings and issues he usually avoids. On the other hand, if his anxiety becomes too high, the patient cannot integrate new learning and will begin to regress. Work at the highest level of feeling the patient can bear while his anxiety is discharged into the striated muscles.

Psychodiagnosis of Defense

To learn what causes the patient's symptoms and presenting problems we must identify the defenses he uses. We assess defenses to find out the patient's character structure, ability to observe and let go of defenses, and capacity to bear feeling.

Character Structure

The types of defenses the patient uses correlate with character structure. Moderately resistant patients use repressive and tactical defenses. Highly resistant patients use tactical, repressive, and character defenses, as well as the transference resistance (a pathological relationship enacted to keep the therapist at a distance). Fragile, depressed, and somatizing patients use repressive, character, and regressive defenses. The following list shows the types of defenses that fall under each category. Later in the book you will learn the psychodiagnostic implications those defenses have for choice of treatment.

- *Nonverbal tactical defenses:* Laughter, mimicry, dismissive sighing, bodily posture (such as crossed legs and arms), avoidance of eye contact, and gestures
- *Verbal tactical defenses:* Vagueness, generalization, cover words, arguing, forgetting, minimizing, rumination, hypothetical speech, evasiveness, rambling, indecision, and racing speech
- *Repressive defenses:* Isolation of affect, denial, repression, negation, intellectualization, rationalization, slowing down, and reaction formation
- *Regressive defenses:* Helplessness, passivity, weepiness, compliance, somatization, turning on the self, depression, projection, splitting, externalization, dissociation, hallucinations, and delusions
- *Character defenses:* Ignoring, neglecting, forgetting, dismissal of oneself as the patient was dismissed by others in the past

- *Transference resistance:* Enacting of a past relationship to resist experiencing feelings toward the therapist

Ability to Observe and Let Go of Defenses

With the therapist's help, moderately resistant patients can usually see their defenses and let go of them fairly quickly. Highly resistant patients do not see their defenses, mistakenly believing their defenses are who they are as people. These patients require much help to see and let go of their defenses to face their feelings. Fragile, depressed, and somatizing patients do not see their character and regressive defenses. Regressive defenses lead to a loss in reality testing, and some patients cannot differentiate the therapist from a projection. These patients need to let go of their regressive defenses to establish an intrapsychic focus in therapy. Then they will see that defenses, not other people, create their symptoms.

Capacity to Bear Feelings

Moderately and highly resistant patients can bear high levels of feeling because their anxiety is discharged into the striated muscles. Fragile, depressed, and somatizing patients can bear only low levels of feeling before their anxiety shifts into the smooth muscles or cognitive/perceptual disruption. Some can bear only low levels of feeling and conflict before they try to get rid of their feelings through regressive defenses such as projection and externalization.

The Psychodiagnosis of Self-Observing Capacity

To feel her feelings deeply, a patient must be able to observe and pay attention to them. To regulate her anxiety, a patient must be able to observe and pay attention to it. To see and turn against her defenses, a patient must be able to observe and pay attention to them and the suffering they cause. The patient must be able to observe and pay attention to feelings, anxiety, and defenses moment by moment to get well. The following is a list of the self-observing capacities we need to mobilize in patients in the following order:

- Ability to observe
  - Feelings
  - Unconscious anxiety in the body

- Defenses
- The difference between the observing ego and experiencing self
- The difference between other people and projections
- Ability to pay attention to
  - Feelings
  - Anxiety
  - Defenses
  - The relations among feeling, anxiety, and defenses
  - The therapeutic relationship
- Ability to differentiate
  - Stimuli from feelings
  - Feelings from anxiety
  - Feelings from defenses
- Ability to see causality
  - Process in which a stimulus triggers a feeling, the feeling triggers anxiety, and anxiety triggers defenses, which create the presenting problems
- Dystonicity
  - Ability to differentiate oneself from the defenses one uses
  - Ability to see the price of the defenses
  - Ability to experience grief/guilt over the price paid for the defenses

ASSESSING THE PATIENT'S RESPONSE TO INTERVENTION

After each patient response, ask yourself: "Is this a feeling, anxiety, or a defense?" If the patient expresses a feeling, explore it. If the patient responds with anxiety in the smooth muscles or cognitive/perceptual disruption, regulate it, and then focus on the feeling. If the patient responds with anxiety in the striated muscles, keep exploring feeling. If the patient responds with a defense, help the patient see and let go of the defense, and then invite the feeling. These are the three basic interventions. Now let us review the sequence of assessment and intervention that guides our work.

THE CYCLE OF PSYCHODIAGNOSIS

To intervene, the therapist must know what problem the patient needs help with in this moment. To learn this, the therapist assesses the patient's response to intervention. The patient's response will be a feeling (which the therapist will explore), excessive anxiety (which the therapist will regulate so they can explore the patient's feeling), or a defense (which the therapist will help the patient see and let go of so they can explore the patient's feeling). Thus, the therapist assesses each patient response to develop an intervention

1. The patient's response to intervention.
2. Psychodiagnosis by the therapist. Where is the patient's response on the triangle of conflict? Should you explore a feeling, regulate anxiety, or address a defense? What problem of self-observation prevents the patient from seeing a feeling, regulating anxiety, or letting go of a defense?
3. Intervention by the therapist to address the specific psychodiagnostic problem in this moment.
4. The patient's response to intervention.
5. Psychodiagnosis by the therapist.

This cycle of intervention, response, assessment of the response, and intervention determines the progression of the session.

OUTLINE OF TYPICAL DETOURS

Now we will review some of the most common responses by patients, their psychodiagnostic implications, and interventions to address them. Each time, help the patient regulate his anxiety and let go of his defenses so he can face his warded-off feelings.

The patient can answer any question with a feeling, or with a detour to anxiety or a defense. When he answers the therapist's question or offers a feeling, continue exploring. If he responds with a detour to anxiety or defense, help him see the detour and return to an effective therapeutic focus.

Interventions for Detours When Asking for a Problem to Work On

To co-create a therapeutic alliance, we need to know what problem motivates the patient to seek therapy. Thus, we always begin by asking the patient about the problem for which he seeks our help. Since many of our patients have been hurt in previous relationships, they fear depending on us. Thus, rather than offer a clear example of a problem, the patient may offer a detour.

> *Intervention:* "What is the problem with which you would like me to help you?"
>
> **Response:** "There are a lot of situations in which I am in conflict with my fiancée, and I don't know how to deal with her."
>
> *Psychodiagnosis:* The patient gives a clear answer to your question.
>
> *Intervention:* "Could we look at a specific example where this problem comes up?"

Anxiety Detours

Sometimes the patient, rather than offer a presenting problem, will present with anxiety instead. This section will show common detours to anxiety, how to assess them, and how to intervene.

> *Intervention:* "What is the problem with which you would like me to help you?"
>
> **Response One:** "I'm nervous." [*The patient shows muscle tension and begins talking rapidly.*]
>
> *Psychodiagnosis:* The patient experiences a fast rise of anxiety in the striated muscles and uses a regressive defense.
>
> *Intervention:* Mobilize attention to the anxiety, assess it, and point out the destructive consequences of talking over and ignoring the anxiety.
>
> *Th:* This nervousness is a sign of anxiety. I notice you are talking rapidly over your anxiety. Do you notice that too?
>
> *Pt:* [*Defense: rushing speech.*] I always do.
>
> *Th:* When you talk over your anxiety, that's a way to ignore it. [*Identify the defense.*]
>
> *Pt:* If I ignore my anxiety, it will go away. [*Defense: rationalization and denial.*]

Th: But has it ever gone away? [*Confront the denial.*]

Pt: No.

Th: Ignoring the anxiety may make you less aware of it, but your body is still anxious.

Pt: Yes.

Th: Ignoring your anxiety actually isn't helping you. Could we pay attention to your anxiety and see if we can bring it down? [*Help the patient let go of the defense.*]

Response Two: "I'm feeling a pain in my stomach."

Psychodiagnosis: The patient experiences a fast rise of anxiety in the smooth muscles.

Intervention: Stop the inquiry into the problem and mobilize attention to the anxiety immediately to regulate it, and then invite feeling. "You are aware of pain in your stomach. That's a sign of anxiety. Are you aware of feeling anxious right now? What else do you notice in your body right now that is a sign of anxiety?" [*Go through the complete list of symptoms to assess her pathways of unconscious anxiety discharge.*]

Intervention: Once the patient can observe her symptoms of anxiety, regulate it by promoting higher-level defenses, such as isolation of affect and intellectualization. "You have come here of your own free will to tell me about your problem. You want help; this makes you anxious, and the anxiety goes to your gut. Do you see that sequence?" [*Once anxiety is no longer in the smooth muscles and is in the striated muscles instead, ask about her feeling again.*]

Response Three: "I'm sorry. What did you say?"

Psychodiagnosis: The patient exhibits no tension anywhere in her body. Assessment reveals that she is experiencing cognitive/perceptual disruption; she is unable to think or remember what you said.

Intervention: Regulate the anxiety immediately by mobilizing attention to the experience of anxiety. "Before we get into that, how is your thinking right now? Is it a little cloudy? Are you feeling a little confused? How is your vision? Are your ears ringing? Okay. I noticed that as soon as I asked what you would like me to help you with, your anxiety went straight up, and your mind blanked out. Did you notice that? How is your thinking now? [*Talk about the triangle of conflict and mobilize attention to the body until the symptoms of cognitive/perceptual disruption disappear.*] "Is this problem of anxiety and your mind blanking out something you would like me to help you with?"

Defense Detours

Sometimes the patient, rather than offer a presenting problem, will present with a defense instead. This section will show common detours to defense, how to assess them, and how to intervene.

Intervention: "What is the problem with which you would like me to help you?"

Response One: "Let me first tell you my history."

Psychodiagnosis: Rather than answer the question directly, the patient uses diversification as a defense. We have no agreement to do therapy yet, so we cannot interpret the defense.

Intervention: Block the defense and restate the question. "I look forward to hearing your history, but first, can you tell me the problem you would like me to help you with?"

Response Two: "Probably a lot of things. I can't think of anything specific right now."

Psychodiagnosis: The patient uses the tactical defense of vagueness to keep the therapist at a distance.

Intervention: Block the defense and invite the patient to declare an internal problem. "That's a bit vague. Could you be more specific about the problem you would like me to help you with?"

Response Three: "I'm not sure I have a problem."

Psychodiagnosis: The patient exhibits high resistance. She denies she has a problem rather than share one.

Intervention: Stop the inquiry. Since the patient says he has no problem, you have no agreement to do therapy. You have no permission to interpret. Instead, make noninterpretive interventions to address her denial. Point out the contradiction between what she says (she has no problem) and does (she is sitting in a therapist's office). "And yet I'm sure you wouldn't come here for no reason at all" or "So although *you* say you have no problem, your *feet* brought you here anyway."

Response Four: "I thought you could tell me what my problem is."

Psychodiagnosis: The patient projects her responsibility onto the therapist and then becomes passive.

Intervention: Deactivate this projection of responsibility. "Only you can know for sure what your problem might be."

Response Five: "The problem is my husband and the way he handles our money." The patient is fidgeting.

Psychodiagnosis: The patient experiences anxiety in the striated muscles accompanied by externalization and projection. If we agree that her husband is the problem, we just help her blame others for her problems. We would fail to establish an intrapsychic focus.

Intervention: Block the projection and ask for an internal focus. "Since he's not here, I can't help him. So I wonder with what internal problem you would like me to help you?"

Response Six: "I don't know what you are looking for."

Psychodiagnosis: The patient projects her will to reveal herself onto you: "I don't want to reveal myself. You want that." If no anxiety goes into the striated muscles, cognitive/perceptual disruption is the pathway of unconscious anxiety discharge.

Intervention: Deactivate the projection of her will to avoid a misalliance. Remind her of her will to look inside herself, which she has forgotten.

Th: Was it your will to come here today?

Pt: Yes.

Th: Was there a problem you wanted me to help you with?

Pt: Yes.

Th: Did you come of your own free will, or were you forced to come here?

Pt: No one forced me.

Th: So who is looking for help? Who is actually looking for something out of this?

Keep asking about her will until she stops projecting it onto you. Do not explore anything until her projection drops. Then her projective anxiety will drop and you can explore.

To regulate anxiety accompanied by projection, we must understand the causality of anxiety: (1) rise of feeling, (2) rise of anxiety, (3) defense of projection, and (4) projective anxiety due to fear of the projection on the therapist. Feelings trigger anxiety, but projection perpetuates it. Only by deactivating the projection will anxiety regulation be possible. Thus, we need to use the following steps in this order:

Step One: Deactivate the projection until the projective anxiety drops.

Step Two: Regulate the anxiety until it returns to the striated muscles and cognition becomes clear.

Step Three: Explore feelings in another relationship.

Response Seven: "I don't want to talk about it because I don't want you to get into my stuff."

Psychodiagnosis: The patient's anxiety is in the striated muscles, and she uses the tactical nonverbal defense of speaking in a detached, uninvolved tone of voice. This defense is part of a transference resistance: "I want you to help me even though I don't reveal myself to you."

Intervention: Deactivate her projection and her defiance. Point out the therapeutic task and her choice, but leave the choice up to her. "The good news is, it is impossible for me to get into your issues. [*Deactivate the projection.*] You can reveal your emotions or conceal them. The control is yours. So the only question is whether you want to go into your issues and listen to yourself. [*Point out the therapeutic task.*] And that is entirely under your control. If you pay close attention to your feelings and the bodily sensations that accompany them, those feelings will allow you to know yourself. But only you can choose to look at your stuff."

Focus first on how she relates to herself before focusing on the relationship with the therapist. To have a good therapeutic alliance, she first must have a good relationship with herself, paying attention to her inner life.

Interventions for Detours When Inviting a Specific Example of the Problem

Once the patient describes the problems for which he seeks help, we ask for a specific example of the problem. By exploring that specific example, we can find out what the triangle of conflict is that creates the patient's problems and symptoms.

Intervention: "Can we take a look at a specific example?"

Response: "I asked her to marry me, but then she suddenly turned, spit on me, and said she would never marry me. She said she found me despicable and worthless. Then she took the ring and threw it into the street."

Psychodiagnosis: The patient gives a clear answer. He exhibits no resistance yet.

Anxiety Detours

When the therapist asks for a specific example of the problem, the patient may offer a detour of anxiety that requires anxiety regulation before exploring a specific example.

Intervention: "Can we take a look at a specific example?"

Response: "I'm getting sick to my stomach just thinking about it."

Psychodiagnosis: The patient's anxiety is discharged in the smooth muscles.

Intervention: The therapist must regulate the patient's anxiety before exploring a specific example of the problem.

Th: That's a sign of anxiety. Are you aware of feeling anxious right now? [*Identify and label the symptom as anxiety.*]

Pt: Yes.

Th: As soon as I invited you to look at a specific example of this conflict, you became anxious, and the anxiety gave you a stomachache. Do you see that too? [*Point out causality: stimulus, anxiety, and symptom.*]

Pt: Yes. It feels scary to look at this.

Th: I'm sure it does. Would you like to face this conflict so we can help you overcome your anxiety?

Pt: [*Sighs.*] Yes. I have to get rid of this anxiety. [*The patient's anxiety is back in the striated muscles now so it is safe to resume the exploration of a specific example of the problem.*]

Th: Can we take a look at a specific example of where you and she were in conflict?

Defense Detours

When the therapist asks for a specific example of the problem, the patient may experience anxiety over the increased closeness and dependency that will result. As a result, some patients offer defenses rather than a specific example of their problem. The therapist must address those defenses until the patient offers a specific example of the problem.

Intervention: "Can we take a look at a specific example?"

Response One: "I can't remember one."

Psychodiagnosis: The patient uses the defense of forgetting, repression. This tactical defense keeps the therapist at a distance.

Intervention: Point out the price of the defense to help the patient turn against it. "If we don't have a specific example, we won't be able to get a clear picture of your problem, and we won't be able to help you with it. So could we look at a specific example of where this problem comes up for you?"

Response Two: "It's more of a general problem. I can't think of anything specific."

Psychodiagnosis: The patient uses the tactical defense of vagueness.

Intervention: Block the defense and then invite a specific example. Ask for a specific example until the patient presents one. "A 'general problem' is vague. As long as this remains vague, we won't get a clear picture of your problem, and we won't be able to help you with it. Could we look at a specific example of where this problem comes up for you?"

Response Three: "There are so many, I can't think of a place to start."

Psychodiagnosis: The patient uses the tactical defense of avoidance.

Intervention: Block the defense, draw the patient's attention to the price of the defense, and then invite a specific example. "Notice how you are having a hard time coming up with a specific example? That's going to be a problem because if we don't have a specific example, we won't be able to get a clear picture of your difficulties. What can we do about that?"

Response Four: "My fiancée likes to bring up difficult topics lots of times."

Psychodiagnosis: The patient generalizes to avoid giving a specific example.

Intervention: Block the defense, and then invite the patient to share a specific example. "That is a bit general. Could we look at a specific example in which this is a problem for you?"

Interventions for Detours When Inviting Feelings

Once the patient offers a specific example of the problem, we explore his feelings in that example to find out the triangle of conflict that causes his problems. However, the patient usually offers detours of anxiety and defense, rather than describe his feeling.

Intervention: "She yelled and spit at you, called you names, and threw the ring into the street. What is your feeling toward her for doing that?"

Response: "I was angry."

Psychodiagnosis: The patient gives a clear answer to the question.

Intervention: Explore how the patient experiences his feeling in his body. "How do you experience that anger right now, physically in your body?"

Anxiety Detours

When the therapist invites the patient to label his feeling, anxiety will be aroused. The pathway of anxiety discharge will determine the therapist's interventions as illustrated in the following examples.

Intervention: "She yelled and spit at you, called you names, and threw the ring into the street. What is your feeling toward her for doing that?"

Response One: "I feel tense."

Psychodiagnosis: The patient's anxiety goes into the striated muscles. Since the patient cannot distinguish his feeling from anxiety, he cannot observe the feeling, only symptoms of anxiety.

Intervention: Differentiate anxiety from the feeling. "The tension is your anxiety. If you don't cover your feeling with anxiety, what is the feeling that makes you so anxious?"

Response Two: "I feel sick to my stomach."

Psychodiagnosis: The patient's anxiety is discharged into the smooth muscles. Since the patient cannot distinguish his feeling from anxiety, he is unable to observe the feeling, only symptoms of anxiety.

Intervention: Regulate the anxiety by mobilizing self-observation, and then point out causality. "Where do you notice that symptom in your stomach? Do you notice any other symptoms of anxiety in your body right now? So we notice that when I asked about your feeling, you became anxious and then got sick to your stomach."

Differentiate his feeling from anxiety and point out causality: "As you looked at your feeling toward Melanie, this anxiety comes in and attacks your gut. Do you see that?"

After drawing the patient's attention to causality, you can also regulate the anxiety by switching the focus to the patient's feeling in another relationship. "Does anxiety attack you as soon as you face your anger in other relationships? Could we look at an example?"

Defense Detours

When the therapist invites the patient to label his feeling, anxiety and defenses are triggered. Thus, the therapist must identify, point out, and help the patient see the defenses he uses. Once the patient sees the defenses he uses, he can make a different choice and face the feelings he has previously avoided.

Intervention: "She yelled and spit at you, called you names, and threw the ring into the street. What is your feeling toward her for doing that?"

Response One: "I feel hurt."

Psychodiagnosis: The patient confuses his feeling with what the other person did (the stimulus). That is why he cannot see his feeling of anger.

Intervention: Help the patient differentiate the stimulus from the feeling. "Absolutely! She hurt you! [*Point out the stimulus.*] That's what she did. What is your feeling toward her for doing that?" [*Differentiate the stimulus from the feeling.*]

Response Two: "I feel sad."

Psychodiagnosis: The patient cannot distinguish his feeling from a defensive affect. That is, sadness comes in to cover his anger. If someone has hurt the patient, the patient will feel sad. But what function does the sadness serve now? Does sadness mobilize or paralyze the patient? Does his sadness help him face or avoid his complex emotions? Here, the patient's sadness has a defensive function. It covers his anger.

Intervention: Differentiate the feeling from a defensive affect. "Right. You feel sadness. This sadness is between you and you, but I'm asking you something different: what is the feeling toward her for hurting you?"

Response Three: "I think she was wrong to do that."

Psychodiagnosis: The patient does not distinguish his feeling from the defense of intellectualization.

Intervention: Help the patient distinguish between the feeling and the defense, and then invite the feeling. "That's your thought, but your thought is not the same as a feeling. If you don't cover it with a thought, what's your feeling toward her for doing that?"

Response Four: "I wonder why she did that?"

Psychodiagnosis: The patient does not distinguish his feeling from the defense of rumination.

Intervention: Help the patient distinguish between his feeling and the defense, and then invite the feeling. "We can only speculate about why she did it, but we could get absolutely clear about how you feel. What's the feeling toward her for doing that?"

Response Five: "I was so stupid to trust her."

Psychodiagnosis: The patient uses the defense of self-attack. Address this defense immediately. Otherwise, his self-attack will make him depressed in the session.

Intervention for a depressed patient with low observing capacity: Help the patient see the defense of self-attack. "Let's pause for a moment and look at what happened here. I asked you what you feel toward her, and instead, this critical system in your mind began to criticize you. Do you see that? So that criticism must be doing a number on you. As soon as you pay attention to your feeling, it's like this critic comes into the room to interrupt you. Does that make sense?"

Continue until the patient sees the difference between his feeling and the defense of self-attack. The defense of self-attack must become dystonic before he can fully access his rage.

Response Six: [*Sighs.*] "I feel confused."

Psychodiagnosis: The patient's anxiety goes into the striated muscles, so this is a repressive defense.

Intervention: Differentiate the feeling from the defense. "Confusion is a thought. If we don't cover the feeling with a thought, what's the feeling toward her?"

Response Seven: [*The patient's body goes limp.*] "What did you say? I feel confused."

Psychodiagnosis: The patient's anxiety is discharged into cognitive/perceptual disruption. The patient's anxiety has become too high.

Intervention: Regulate the anxiety and show the causality of feeling, anxiety, and symptoms.

Th: You are confused? How is your thinking now?

Pt: Not good.

Th: Is it cloudy?

Pt: Yes.

Th: That's a sign of anxiety. Did you just blank out?

Pt: It's like my mind emptied.

Th: That's another sign of anxiety. How is your vision and hearing?

Pt: My vision is a bit blurry.

Th: That's another sign of anxiety. Are you feeling faint or dizzy?

Pt: No.

Th: When I ask about your feeling, your anxiety goes up rapidly, your mind starts not working right, and you become confused. Do you see that sequence?

Response Eight: [*The patient sighs.*] "I don't feel anything."

Psychodiagnosis One: The patient's anxiety is in the striated muscles, so this is the defense of denial.

Intervention: Identify the defense, encourage the patient to turn against it, and then invite the feeling. "The only time you don't have a feeling is when you are six feet under the ground, and you're not dead yet. If you don't deaden your feelings, what is the feeling toward her?"

Psychodiagnosis Two: If the patient denied his feelings right away, this is the defense of instant repression.

Intervention: Point out the defense. "Do you notice you said that right away, before you even looked inside to see what you feel?" To better understand this defense, imagine that you asked a friend if she had any flour in her pantry and she replied, "I don't know." You would be a bit perturbed because she said she didn't know rather than open the door to her pantry to see what was in there.

Response Nine: "I'm embarrassed. I feel so bad."

Psychodiagnosis: Rather than describe a feeling toward his fiancée who hurt him, the patient describes a feeling toward himself. In effect, he "borrows" her shame (Nathanson 1992), identifying with her, rather than face his feeling toward her. Here, shame functions as a defensive affect to hide his anger.

Intervention: Point out the defensive function of shame. Differentiate the patient and his feeling from the defensive affect of shame. "Do you see how this embarrassment attacks you just when I ask you what you feel toward her? It's like the shame police come in to Taser you before you tell me how you feel toward her. Do you see that? Could we take a look at the feeling underneath, the feeling the shame has been covering?"

Interventions for Detours When Inviting the Physical Experience of Feeling

Once the patient has correctly labeled his feeling, ask him how he experiences that feeling physically in his body. In response, the patient may use detours of anxiety and defense. The following vignettes show how to address these detours and maintain an effective therapeutic focus.

Intervention: "You felt angry with her. How do you experience this anger physically in your body right now?"

Response: "I feel some heat coming up from my belly, and my hands want to grab something."

Psychodiagnosis: The patient is aware of the experience of his feeling.

Intervention: Explore how he experiences that impulse physically in his body. "If you let that heat come up through your body, what impulse comes up with that rage?"

Anxiety Detours

Rather than describe how he experiences the anger in his body, the patient may report the experience of anxiety instead. The therapist must differentiate the patient's feeling from anxiety, regulate the anxiety if it is too high, and then invite the patient to face the feeling that triggered his anxiety.

Intervention: "You felt angry with her. How do you experience this anger physically in your body right now?"

Response: [*Sighs.*] "I feel fear."

Psychodiagnosis: The patient fails to differentiate his anger from his anxiety, which is discharged into the striated muscles.

Intervention: Differentiate the anxiety from the feeling, and encourage the patient to face his anger. "That's your anxiety, but fear is not your anger. If we don't cover this anger with fear, can we have an uncensored look at how you experience this anger in your body?"

Defense Detours

Rather than describe how he experiences his anger physically in his body, the patient may use defenses. The therapist must help the patient see and let go of his defenses so he can face the warded-off feeling.

Intervention: "You felt angry with her. How do you experience this anger physically in your body right now?"

Response: "I feel like walking away from her."

Psychodiagnosis: The patient does not differentiate his feeling of anger from his defense against it. He wants to walk away from her and his feelings.

Intervention: Differentiate the feeling from the defense and then invite the feeling. "You want to walk away from her and your anger. If you don't walk away from your anger, how do you experience this anger toward her?"

PSYCHODIAGNOSIS: PHASE OF INQUIRY

Tables 5.1 through 5.3 show how different patient groups respond at each phase of developing a therapeutic alliance (declaring an internal problem, offering a specific example, and declaring a feeling). These different responses (access to feeling, pathway of anxiety discharge, and types of defense) allow the therapist to psychodiagnose the patient's character structure (low, moderate, or high resistance; or fragile spectrum).

Table 5.1 Declaring a problem

"What is the problem with which you would like me to help you?"

Character	Low resistance	Moderate resistance	High resistance	Fragile spectrum
Answer	Clear	Vague	"No problem."	Disorganized
Anxiety	Striated muscles	Striated muscles	Striated muscles	Smooth muscles and cognitive/perceptual disruption
Defense	Few defenses	Repressive and tactical defenses	Tactical, repressive, and character defenses and transference resistance	Repressive defenses, which fail, followed by character and regressive defenses

Table 5.2 Phase of inviting a specific example

"Can we look at a specific example?"

Character	Low resistance	Moderate resistance	High resistance	Fragile spectrum
Answer	Clear example	Moderately clear example	"I can't think of one."	Disorganized by anxiety, pressured speech, or projection

Table 5.3 Phase of inviting feeling

Therapist's intervention: "What's the feeling toward her?"

Character	Low resistance	Moderate resistance	High resistance	Fragile spectrum
Answer	"Anger."	"I'm frustrated."	"I don't have a feeling."	Floods with anxiety and then projects or becomes depressed

SUMMARY

Each patient's response to intervention will be a feeling, anxiety, or a defense. Psychodiagnosis allows us to assess the patient's responses so we can offer targeted interventions moment by moment. Next, we will take the concepts of feeling, anxiety, defense, and psychodiagnosis and show you different ways to co-create a therapeutic alliance with a broad range of patients.

Principle: *Assess each patient response, so your intervention will address the patient's need in this moment.*

RECOMMENDED READINGS

Frederickson, J. (1999). The theory of the analysis of conflict and conflict analysis studies. In *Psychodynamic psychotherapy: Learning to listen from multiple perspectives* (pp. 51–110). New York: Taylor and Francis. These readings will help you listen to a session in terms of the triangle of conflict.

Frederickson, J. (2012). Maintaining an effective focus on feeling. http://www.istdpinstitute.com/Maintaininganeffectivefocus/. This is a private download only for purchasers of this book.

RECOMMENDED MATERIALS

For three videos on psychodiagnosis presented by Jon Frederickson, you can visit the URLs below.

Intensive short-term dynamic psychotherapy part 1 (October 5, 2011). http://www.youtube.com/watch?v=cKzmk2-xnzY.

Intensive short-term dynamic psychotherapy part 2 (October 5, 2011). http://www.youtube.com/watch?v=dK2x906ptWA.

Intensive short-term dynamic psychotherapy part 3 (January 18, 2012). http://www.youtube.com/watch?v=sDmVgoKPVkw.

CHAPTER SIX

Inquiry: Co-Creating a Conscious Therapeutic Alliance

The first task in therapy is to co-create a relationship for change. Sometimes people assume one exists if the patient shows up for therapy and says what comes to mind and the therapist listens. Yet none of these elements constitutes a therapeutic alliance. Let us clarify the task and the purpose of psychotherapy. The term *psychotherapy* derives from a Greek word meaning "healing of the soul (*psyche*) within the person (*intrapsyche*)." Hence, focusing inside oneself is the *intrapsychic* perspective. A psychodynamic therapy tries to cure psychological symptoms resulting from the dynamic conflict among the feelings, anxiety, and defenses within a person.

To establish this internal focus, the therapist asks about the problems and symptoms for which the patient seeks help. Next, the therapist asks for a specific example of where those problems occur. By exploring that example, the therapist and patient discover the conflicts at work in her life. Now the therapist helps the patient engage in the therapeutic task: let go of her defenses, face her fears, and experience the feelings she has avoided. As she does so, the patient experiences a rise in emotions and memories, so she can experience the unconscious forces driving her suffering. These experiential insights lead to long-lasting change.

To co-create a therapeutic alliance, we mobilize ingredients in a specific order.

1. Establish an internal emotional problem to work on.
2. Establish that it is the patient's will to work on the problem.
3. Look at a specific example of the problem to discern and get consensus on the triangle of conflict.
4. Get consensus on the therapeutic task.

FIRST INGREDIENT: A DECLARED INTERNAL EMOTIONAL PROBLEM

We begin by asking, "What is the problem you would like me to help you with?" Choose your wording carefully to show that therapy focuses on *her* problem, not someone else's.

Th: What's the problem you would like me to help you with?

Pt: I've been feeling depressed ever since my fiancé broke up with me two months ago. [*Clear declaration of an internal problem.*]

The therapist assesses the severity of the patient's symptoms, vegetative signs, and previous depressive episodes. The depression was not severe, there were no vegetative signs, and she had no previous episodes. He continues with the inquiry.

Th: One problem you would like me to help you with is your depression. Are there any other problems you would like me to help you with?

Pt: I think I have a problem in relationships because I didn't see this coming at all. I was shocked that my fiancé broke off the engagement. He said we had problems in our relationship, but I just wrote that off as a little anxiety. I don't know what I was missing.

Th: It sounds like you just told us what you were missing. He felt you had problems in your relationship, but when you wrote it off as anxiety, you missed the importance of what he was saying. He told you. You wrote it off. Then you suffered the consequences. Does that fit? [*Point out how her defenses of denial and ignoring blinded her—the cost.*]

Pt: I hate to say it, but, yes, that does fit. I hadn't seen that before.

Th: Seen what?

Pt: That when I ignored a problem, it happened anyway, and I paid the price.

Th: It sounds like ignoring him might have alleviated your anxiety in the short term, but it set you up horribly for this breakup. [*The price of the defense.*]

Pt: Right.

Th: You want me to help you with this depression. Would you like me to help you deal better with the feelings in your relationships so your denial doesn't set you up for another heartbreak? [*Get consensus on the presenting problems for which she seeks help.*]

Pt: Yes.

SECOND INGREDIENT: THE PATIENT'S WILL TO DO THERAPY

Once the patient declares an internal emotional problem, ask if it is her will to seek therapy. Often, patients have been referred against their will or under a threat by a spouse, boss, or even court authorities. We have no right to do therapy without the patient's desire and permission. If the patient expresses verbally or nonverbally any reluctance in the opening minutes, ask, "Is it your will to be here?" "Did you come here of your own free will?" "Are you required to come here, or was this your decision?"

If a patient does not declare an internal emotional problem or her will to do therapy, you have no right to work with her. If she does not want to do therapy, do not explore further. Instead, find out what prevents her from seeking help to achieve *her* goals for *her* benefit.

THIRD INGREDIENT: CONSENSUS ON THE INTRAPSYCHIC CONFLICT

Once the patient declares an internal problem and her desire for the therapist's help, ask, "Can we look at a specific example of where this problem occurs?" The problem the patient declares motivates her to seek help. Patients never say, "Give me deeper insight into my intrapsychic conflicts." They come because they suffer. If you can show a patient how her defenses create her suffering, she will let go of them and engage in the therapeutic task. Explore a specific example of her problem to find out which defenses create her symptoms and presenting problems.

Explore that specific example by asking, "What is the feeling toward him?" The patient will respond in one of three ways: a feeling, anxiety, or a defense. Moment by moment, help the patient pay attention to these reactions. When the patient can see the feelings, anxiety, and defenses operating in the session, she will understand the conflict causing her problems.

Th: I notice when we talk about your anger, you get a little vague and criticize yourself instead. Do you notice that too? [*Point out the triangle of feeling, anxiety, and defense.*]

Pt: Now that you point it out, yes.

Th: I wonder if that happened with your boyfriend too. You mention you were angry with him, but you became vague rather than reveal your feelings directly. Then you blamed yourself rather than hold him responsible for his outburst when visiting your parents. Do you think this tendency to blame yourself and turn the anger on yourself might be making you depressed? [*Link the conflicts in therapy and other relationships. Show how her defenses create her presenting problems.*]

Pt: I hadn't seen that connection before, but yes, that makes sense.

With consensus on the intrapsychic conflict causing her difficulties, we can take the next step.

FOURTH INGREDIENT: CONSENSUS ON THE THERAPEUTIC TASK

In relationships, the patient's feeling triggers anxiety and defenses that create her presenting problems and symptoms. So the patient must (1) turn against the defenses that create her presenting problems and symptoms, (2) face what she fears rather than avoid it, and (3) feel her feelings as deeply as possible. By doing so, she will learn to experience her feelings and channel them into adaptive actions, not into maladaptive defenses and symptoms.

Th: There's a conflict here. When you feel angry in relationships, you become vague and turn the anger on yourself, which makes you depressed. When you don't express your feelings or concerns, you become more distant and lose the emotional closeness you want. Is that a fair summary? [*Get consensus on the internal conflict.*]

Pt: Yes, that makes sense.

Th: If you like, our task here would be to help you turn against these mechanisms of self-blame and turning anger on yourself because they make you depressed. Does that fit? [*Get agreement on the therapeutic task.*]

Pt: Yes.

Th: And once we turn against those mechanisms, our task is to face this anger, get to the bottom of your feelings, and find out what has been driving this pattern of self-punishment. Is that something you would like to do?

Pt: Yes, but I'm afraid of my anger. [*Obstacle to engaging in therapy. Point out the patient's choice and mobilize her will to the task.*]

Th: Of course, you are. Otherwise, you wouldn't be here, but if you continue to avoid your anger, what will be the result? [*Help her see the price of the defense.*]

Pt: I'll probably just stay the same. [*She begins to see how her defense creates her symptoms.*]

Th: Do you want your fear of anger to be in control, or would you like to master your fear so you are in control? [*Mobilize her awareness of her positive goal.*]

Pt: I'd like to master my fear, but I don't know how. [*We must clarify the therapeutic task.*]

Th: We have two choices. You can avoid your anger and remain anxious and out of control. [*Unhealthy choice based on maladaptive defenses.*] Or together, we could face this anger and feel it as deeply as possible so you can feel powerful and in charge rather than anxious and out of control. [*The therapeutic task.*] Instead of turning the anger onto yourself, you could channel it into healthy assertion. Instead of being vague, you could be clear about what you want. Instead of criticizing yourself, you could have a healthy sense of self-esteem. And instead of hiding your feelings, you could express them and have more emotionally intimate relationships. [*Results of the defenses versus the therapeutic alliance.*] What choice would you like us to make today? Shall we avoid this anger, or would you like to overcome this fear so you can be in charge? [*Point out the choice and invite the patient to declare her choice.*]

Pt: When you put it that way, I'd be silly not to try to look at my anger. [*"When you put it that way" is a possible indication of projection. She does not entirely own that this is her desire.*]

Th: But is that what you want for yourself, for your goals, for your purposes? [*The therapeutic task is not designed to achieve the therapist's but the patient's goals.*]

Pt: Yes, that's what I want. [*Now she wants us to explore her feelings and conflicts together.*]

Defenses defeat her goals. The therapeutic task will help her achieve them. Remind the patient of her goals so she can see when she is on or off task. Experiencing and sharing feelings allows us to build emotionally secure relationships. In contrast, defenses ward off feelings, creating insecure attachments. Defenses cheat us of the intimacy we long for. Out of compassion, the therapist interrupts and blocks defenses so patients can share their feelings and co-create a relationship for change.

THE THERAPEUTIC TASK

Dag Hammarskjöld, secretary-general of the United Nations, once said, "Life only demands from you the strength that you possess. Only one feat is possible: not to run away." And the therapeutic task is to help the patient not run away from his feelings that make him anxious.

Yet if we do not spell out the task, the patient does not know what to do in therapy: "I'm here. I'm talking. I'm telling you what is happening in my life. Why am I not getting better?" No psychotherapy can succeed with those ingredients alone. Passivity does not work. The patient must demonstrate some emotional courage by (1) letting go of defenses, (2) facing what she fears, and (3) experiencing her feelings. Talking, logging hours, and showing up are not enough.

A patient usually suffers from relationship problems because her defenses prevent emotional closeness. If she adopts a passive, defiant, or uninvolved stance in other relationships, she will do so in therapy as well. However, that kind of behavior results in failure. Remind her of her goals. Help her see defenses and relational patterns that sabotage her goals. Then invite her to let go of self-defeating defenses, and face what she has previously avoided so she can achieve her goals.

First, offer an invitation to the therapeutic task. "I'm going to invite you to pay careful attention to the feelings in your body, any anxiety you feel in your body, and any shifts in our connection so we can understand what is going on underneath to create these problems that are bothering you. Does that sound like something you would be willing to do?"

Next, mobilize the patient's will to face what she fears.

Pt: I'm afraid of those feelings.

Th: Of course, but our task here is to face what you are afraid of so you can master your anxiety rather than remain its slave. As long as you avoid these feelings, you'll have symptoms instead. Why do that to yourself? You can run away from your feelings and have the same problems, or we can face those feelings and help you become free of these symptoms. What would you like us to do?

Next, mobilize the patient's will to pay attention to her anxiety. "If you ignore your anxiety, it just builds, and then you end up suffering from these terrible stomach cramps and anxiety. If you ignore your anxiety, the therapy will be a painful experience for you, and I don't want that to happen. Could we pay careful attention to your anxiety so we can get rid of these symptoms and find out what is causing them? Does that make sense to you?"

Finally, mobilize the patient's will to turn against the defenses and face her feelings.

Pt: I don't want to take a look at those feelings. [*Defense.*]

Th: That's going to be a problem.

Pt: How come? I never look at those feelings.

Th: Of course, but has that been working? You've been avoiding your grief over the loss of your husband. You became depressed, and this has been going on for how many years?

Pt: Five.

Th: By avoiding the grief, you have become depressed instead [*price of the defense*]. You don't have to face this grief if you don't want to. After all, no one can make you. But as long as you don't, your depression will continue and the therapy will fail [*price of the defense*]. You can avoid this grief and continue to suffer [*anti-therapeutic task*], or we can face these feelings and get rid of this depression [*therapeutic task*]. What shall we do?

The following list outlines the purposes of the therapeutic task:

- *Understanding:* Together the patient and therapist pay attention moment to moment to observe the sequence of feelings, anxiety, and defenses creating the patient's difficulties.

- *Anxiety regulation:* The patient and therapist must pay attention moment to moment to decrease the patient's anxiety and discover what feelings trigger it. This close, mutual attention regulates the patient's anxiety, providing a background of dyadic affect regulation (Schore 1994, 2002). This regulates her body and restores her cognitive functioning: the preconditions for an effective treatment.

- *Secure attachment:* The patient who uses defenses to ignore her inner experience invites the therapist to do the same, thereby creating an insecure attachment. The therapist blocks the patient's defenses and encourages mutual attention to feelings, anxiety, and defenses to establish a secure autonomous attachment.

- *Achievement of a positive goal:* Psychotherapy tries to help the patient achieve her healthy goals. Since defenses sabotage her goals, creating her difficulties, the therapist encourages the patient to let go of her defenses so she can get what she wants.

INGREDIENTS FOR A CONSCIOUS THERAPEUTIC ALLIANCE

The therapist and patient must create the ingredients for a conscious therapeutic alliance in the following steps. If the therapist skips a single step, the conscious therapeutic alliance will not be strong enough to achieve the patient's goals.

1. The patient describes an inner problem.
2. The patient declares her will to seek therapy.
3. The patient offers a specific example.
4. The patient and therapist agree on the patient's internal conflict.
5. The patient and therapist agree on the therapeutic task to achieve the patient's positive goals.
   a. The patient is willing to turn against her defenses.
   b. The patient is willing to face what she fears.
   c. The patient is willing to experience her feelings as deeply as possible.

A patient with low resistance forms a therapeutic alliance quickly. A moderately resistant patient's defenses may emerge only after step five. A highly resistant patient often puts up a barrier at steps one or two. A fragile patient can flood with anxiety at steps one through four. Wherever obstacles occur, resolve them before going further.

DECISION TREE

The decision tree in figure 6.1 illustrates the sequence of steps in developing a therapeutic alliance as well as the most common detours. On the left-hand side you will find the steps. On the right-hand side you will find the most common detours that prevent the establishment of that ingredient for the therapeutic alliance. When you are stuck with a patient, see which ingredient is missing. Then look to the right-hand side to see which defense is preventing you from forming the therapeutic alliance.

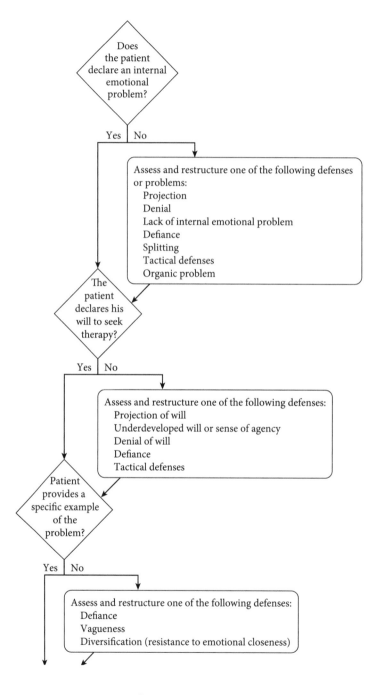

Figure 6.1   Decision tree for a conscious therapeutic alliance

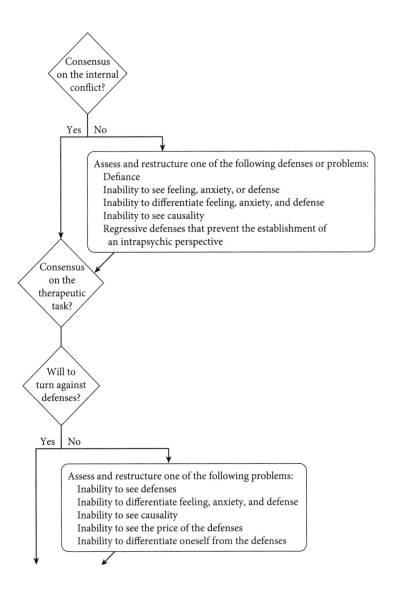

Figure 6.1   Decision tree for a conscious therapeutic alliance (continued)

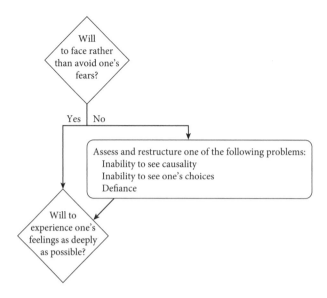

OBSTACLES TO FORMING A CONSCIOUS THERAPEUTIC ALLIANCE

Obstacles to forming a conscious therapeutic alliance can occur at any stage in the process: resistance to declaring an internal emotional problem, resistance to declaring one's will to work on that problem, resistance to offering a specific example of the problem, or resistance to labeling a feeling. We will now review a series of vignettes that illustrate these resistances at each stage of developing a therapeutic alliance.

Resistance to Declaring an Internal Emotional Problem

Inquiry invites a close relationship, triggering feelings, anxiety, and defenses. The pathway of anxiety discharge and type of defenses tell us where the patient is on the spectrum of neurotic disorders. In fact, the patient's responses to the first questions during the phase of inquiry can let us know if the patient has low, moderate, or high resistance or is fragile.

Th: What is the problem you would like me to help you with?

Low resistance patient: I've been feeling depressed ever since my mother died. For some reason I haven't been able to cry about her death, even though I know I miss her terribly. [*Clear answer without defenses.*]

Moderately resistant patient: I'm not sure really. [*Defense: vagueness.*] Just a little down [*Defense: minimization*] for the last six months. I'm not sure why. [*Defense: vagueness.*] Maybe it's due to my mom's death. I just haven't been the same since." [*Moderately clear answer with some defenses.*]

Highly resistant patient: I don't have a problem. [*Defense: denial.*] My wife thought I should be here. [*Defense: projection. Defenses arise immediately with no clear presenting problem and no will to explore one.*]

Fragile patient: I'm just really anxious. [*Initial declaration of a problem.*] But I'm mostly afraid of the questions you want to ask. [*Defense: projection. Anxiety rises rapidly, leading to regressive defenses. A fragmentary or disorganized answer reveals how the rapid rise of anxiety interferes with her thinking. She forgets her desire to tell the therapist about her difficulties. Rather than tolerate her internal conflict of both wanting and not wanting to talk, she projects her wish to talk onto the therapist and fears him.*]

Patients' responses allow us to assess the specific weaknesses and defenses we need to treat. To illustrate this process of psychodiagnosis and intervention, we will study a series of responses to our initial question in the first session.

We ask, "*What is the problem you would like me to help you with?*"

The patient will respond in one of three ways by presenting

- The problem for which he seeks treatment
- High anxiety and symptoms
- Defenses against declaring a problem

Vignette One: Low Resistance Patient

Notice in this example that the low resistance patient uses very few defenses. We can begin exploring his problem right away.

Th: What's the problem you would like me to help you with?

Pt: I've been feeling depressed lately, and I'm having trouble in my relationship with my wife. [*Describes his problem clearly.*]

Intervention: Explore the patient's problems to find out what conflicts create his problems. "How long have you felt depressed?" "What symptoms have you noticed?" "How severe has it been?" "You say it started three months ago. What was going on in your life then?" Once you have explored the depression, investigate other problems: "Can you tell me what troubles you in the relationship with your wife?"

Principle: *Once the patient declares his problems clearly, explore them to formulate the triangle of conflict (feeling, anxiety, and defense) to learn which defenses create his symptoms (depression and the poor relationship with his wife).*

Vignette Two: Fragile Patient

Notice in this example that the fragile patient, rather than respond with her problem, floods with anxiety. Thus, the therapist's first task is to regulate the patient's anxiety so that exploring feelings can be done safely.

Th: What's the problem you would like me to help you with?

Pt: There are so many things. I don't know where to start. [*Defense: vagueness. Patient fidgets in her chair, and her eyes dart back and forth rapidly as she avoids the therapist's gaze: signs of anxiety and projection.*]

Th: How are you feeling right now? [*Assess her anxiety.*]

Pt: I'm anxious.

Th: Where do you notice feeling the anxiety in your body? [*Assess her anxiety.*]

Pt: All over. [*The rapid rise of anxiety shows she cannot regulate it. Regulate the anxiety immediately.*]

Th: Let's notice in your body where the anxiety is. Do you notice any anxiety in your stomach? [*Draw attention to the anxiety first to regulate it.*]

Pt: I feel nauseous, like I'll throw up. [*Anxiety discharged into the smooth muscles.*]

The therapist's invitation to a relationship immediately triggered feelings and overwhelming anxiety.

Principle: *Regulate overwhelming anxiety before focusing on the patient's declared internal problem. Then show the patient what triggered the anxiety. "Do you notice that your anxiety went up as soon as you said you want to open up? It's as if an alarm bell went off as soon as you declared that this is your will. You want*

to open up in order to get to know yourself better, so you have
better information about yourself and that feels a little risky."

Let's continue with this patient further.

Th: You're feeling nauseous. It's good you notice. That's another sign of anxiety. So isn't it sad that as soon as you want to tell me what you want me to help you with, this anxiety comes in to attack and strangle you? As if it's against the law for you to tell me what you want help with. [*Differentiate her wish to talk from the anxiety. Describing something that attacks her helps her differentiate herself from her anxiety.*]

Pt: [*Body relaxes.*] That's it. It's like it's against the law for me to talk about me. [*Now that she has differentiated herself from the experience of anxiety, her anxiety drops.*]

Th: As if it's against the law for you to talk about you. So let me ask you a question that may seem a bit odd: Is it *your* will to talk about you? Is that what *you* want? [*Mobilize her awareness of her will to deactivate the projection of it onto the therapist.*]

Pt: Yes, I want to talk about me. It's just I get scared. [*Now she sees causality: talking about herself to the therapist triggers anxiety.*]

Th: This is what you want? [*Mobilize her awareness of her will to do therapy.*]

Pt: Yes. [*With her will on-line, we can explore a sample problem.*]

Inviting the fragile patient to describe her problems triggers feelings and overwhelming anxiety. Identify her anxiety and the trigger: revealing herself. Ask if she wants to talk about herself. Mobilize *her* will to engage in the therapeutic task. Otherwise, a fragile patient projects her will onto you and experiences *your* wish to do psychotherapy as if you are persecuting her. Once she projects onto you, she will defy and oppose you. Mobilize her awareness of her will to deactivate the projection onto you. Then the two of you can join forces to pursue her goal together.

Whenever the patient experiences anxiety while expressing her will, help her observe that sequence. Moment by moment, attend to her anxiety and the triggers. Help her declare her internal problem and her wish for therapy until they no longer trigger anxiety.

> **Principle:** *Do not inquire into the highly anxious patient's inner world until she declares an internal problem and her desire to explore it with you. In the absence of a stated problem and her wish for your help, you do not have her permission to do therapy. By proceeding without the patient's desire, you will "create" a resistant patient. (To see how to develop an alliance with a fragile patient, go to http://istdpinstitute.com/dvds/ to purchase a psychotherapy video of an initial session with a fragile patient.)*

Vignette Three: Highly Resistant Patient

The highly resistant patient responds primarily with defenses. As a result, the therapist must address the patient's defenses against revealing a problem.

Th: What's the problem you would like me to help you with?

Pt: I don't have a problem." [*Defense: denial.*]

> **Principle:** *Without a declared internal emotional problem, you have no permission to explore one. Confine yourself to mirroring back contradictions in what he says or contradictions between what he says and does.*

Th: And yet you are here. [*Point out the contradiction: a man without psychological problems is in a psychologist's office.*]

Pt: That's true, but it was my wife's idea. [*Defense: projection. He attributes his desire for therapy to his wife. Patients who don't want to come to therapy won't.*]

Th: Although it was your wife's idea, you came instead. [*Point out the contradiction between what he says and does.*]

Pt: Because she thought it was a good idea. [*Defense: projection—"My wife had this thought, not I."*]

Th: In your opinion, you don't have an internal emotional problem. This was your wife's idea, but you ended up following her idea instead of your own. How does that come to pass? Is this something that happens in your life? Do you find yourself doing one thing when you want something else? [*Point out the contradiction.*]

Pt: I hadn't thought of that. I do go along with what she says a lot of the time. [*Implicit admission of an internal problem.*]

Th: A lot of the time you go along with her ideas instead of your own? [*Reflect his problem.*]

Pt: Yeah. [*Fidgets. Unconscious feelings trigger anxiety in the striated muscles. Anxiety in the striated muscles needs no regulation.*]

Th: As you said, that may not be a problem for you. [*Mirror his resistance to deactivate his defiance.*] After all, you may have come to regard this as normal and acceptable to go along with her ideas instead of your own.

Pt: I don't think it's normal, so to speak [*Slight turn against the defense*], but I have accepted it for quite a while. [*Syntonicity: he is willing to accept this problem.*]

Th: Although, in your opinion, this doesn't seem normal [*reflect back his awareness*], you're aware that you have accepted her ideas and gone along with them but then have ignored your own. [*Clarify his defense of ignoring himself.*]

Pt: I hadn't thought of it that way, but it's true [*rise in awareness*]. It's easier just to go along with her. [*Rationalizes his defense of ignoring himself.*]

Th: In your opinion, this is not normal, but it has become the norm. It has been easier for you to go along with her ideas than to stand up for your own.

Pt: Now that you put it that way. It has been easier for me to go along with her than to stand up for my own ideas. [*He still has not said this is a problem for him. We have no right to explore it yet.*]

Th: It's been easier for you to go along with her ideas than to stand up for your own ideas. And that may be acceptable to you, to let go of your ideas to keep the peace. [*Mirror a resistant belief to deactivate it.*]

Pt: I don't know that it's really acceptable. It's just that's how I've handled the situation. [*Ignoring his point of view is becoming less acceptable.*]

Th: It's not really acceptable to you. It's just that over time not standing up for yourself has become a habit.

Pt: Right. It's been a habit.

Th: To act on her ideas but not act on yours.

Pt: That doesn't sound too good. [*The defense is becoming less syntonic.*]

Th: How so? [*If the therapist agreed, the patient might argue. Instead, invite the patient to describe his own dawning awareness of his self-neglect.*]

Pt: It doesn't sound good that I don't act on my ideas. I mean I know that's not right.

Th: You know it's not right not to stand up for yourself. [*Reinforce his healthy awareness.*] You know that. It's just that you have gotten in the habit of doing something that's not right for you. [*Show how his defense of ignoring himself hurts him. This helps differentiate himself from his defenses—how he treats himself.*]

Pt: Yes. There have been some things I wanted to do and I didn't do them because my wife thought it wasn't a good idea. [*He reveals how his defense creates problems for him. We are closer to a consensus on his internal conflict.*]

Th: Ignoring what you want may please your wife. But it doesn't always please you. [*Point out the price of this defense: he is not pleased.*]

Pt: That's for sure. There are all kinds of things I haven't done. [*More aware of the defense's price.*]

Th: Ignoring what you want has led to some disappointment. [*Point out the price of his defense.*]

Pt: Yeah. That's been a problem [*finally declares an internal problem: he ignores his feelings and desires*] because I end up arguing with my wife about this.

Th: It sounds like ignoring your feelings and desires is a problem. [*Reinforce his healthy awareness.*] And that leads you into arguments with your wife. But it sounds like, in spite of the arguments, you find you don't listen to your desires or act on them. [*Point out how the defense of arguing does not solve his problem. He blames his wife for what he does: ignoring what he wants.*]

Pt: That's true. No matter how much I argue with her, I don't get what I want. [*He doesn't yet connect this result to ignoring what he wants.*]

Th: When she ignores what you want, you do too. And when you ignore your desires, you don't get the results you want. [*His defense, not his wife, causes his problems.*]

Pt: I hadn't thought of that before. If I ignore what I want, I won't get what I want. [*An intrapsychic focus: his actions create his problems.*]

Th: Is that something you would like to change so you get more of what you want? [*Invite him to turn against the defenses and engage in the therapeutic task.*]

Pt: Yeah, because I'm really frustrated.

Typical of many highly resistant patients, this man responded with defenses rather than describe an internal problem. Since this type of patient can irritate the therapist, therapists often make the mistake of confronting the patient prematurely before the patient can see and differentiate himself from his defenses. As a result, the therapist should abide by the following principles when working with a highly resistant patient who does not yet see his defenses.

- *Principle One:* Do not explore a problem with the patient until he declares one that he wants to explore with you.
- *Principle Two:* Address splitting and projection by noting contradictions within the patient's statements or contradictions between what he says and does.
- *Principle Three:* Acknowledge any healthy shifts the patient makes toward collaboration.
- *Principle Four:* Mirror the patient's level of resistance. Do not challenge defenses he does not see. When you challenge the patient prematurely or assume he is willing to explore a problem before he is, you are relating to the patient in your mind, not the one who is before you. Your resistance to dealing with the patient you have will make him more resistant to you.

Obstacle to Declaring an Internal Emotional Problem: Externalization

Sometimes patients believe other people, not their defenses, cause their suffering. This external focus prevents an internal focus in therapy. For example, the patient may say, "I don't have a problem. My wife is the problem."

The patient who does not see the defenses creating his problems believes other people create them. He invites you to engage in "sociology," observing other people, rather than psychology, looking into himself. The patient asks you to do psychotherapy "by proxy": "Don't treat me. Treat my wife, who is not here." Therapy with a patient who is in the room can be difficult, but treating an invisible patient is impossible!

When patients externalize, first help them develop an internal focus. Without looking at a patient's inner life, we cannot do psychotherapy. Let's look at some examples that show how to help the externalizing patient shift from blaming others for his problems so he can recognize how he causes his own suffering.

Th: What's the problem you would like me to help you with?

Pt: I'm hoping you can help me with my wife because she is my biggest problem. [*The patient believes his problem is his wife, not how he deals with his feelings. He invites you to treat her.*]

Th: Since she's not here, I can't help her. [*Note the reality. Then invite an internal focus.*] I wonder what the *internal* problem is you would like me to help you with?

Pt: That's the thing. I don't think I have a problem. It's my wife that's the problem. And I'm hoping you can help me deal with her.

Th: You are having trouble dealing with your wife. [*Implicit statement of a problem.*]

Pt: Yes.

Th: Can you give me an example of where you are having a problem in dealing with your wife? [*Explore his problem to develop an intrapsychic focus.*]

Pt: Like today, I was going to come here on time. She was hung over and asked me to wait for her. She wanted a lift to the hairdresser, but then she made me wait for her. She made me late, and we got into an argument. [*He chose to wait, be late, and suffer, but he blames his wife for his choices. He does not see his defenses of externalization and blaming.*]

Th: She was late. [*Mirror back the reality so the patient can see how he made himself late.*]

Pt: Yes.

Th: And she asked you to wait and make yourself late.

Pt: Yes, and I hate when she does that.

Th: So when she asked you to wait, you decided to wait. [*Reflect the facts we can agree on, and include the element of choice: how he made himself late.*]

Pt: Right.

Th: You decided to wait, and by doing so, you made yourself late. [*Show causality. His choice to wait made him late, not his wife. As long as he blames her for his choice, we will not establish an intrapsychic focus. He punishes himself and makes himself late to deal*] *with feelings he has when his wife is late. Addressing externaliza-tion helps the patient regain an internal locus of control and hope that he can solve his problems.*]

Pt: She asked me to!

Th: That makes sense. She wanted you to wait. So you decided to wait and made yourself late, but then you blamed her for your de-cision to make yourself late. [*Differentiate her request from his choice to hurt himself by making himself late.*]

Pt: But she asked me to!

Th: Of course! That's what she wanted. Then you had two options: to say no to yourself and make yourself late or to say yes to yourself and come on time. You chose to say no to yourself, but then you blamed her for the choice you made. [*Point out his defense: "I didn't punish myself; my wife punished me."*]

Pt: I hadn't seen that before. [*Now he can see his defense rather than blame his wife.*]

Th: Is that a pattern for you, to say no to yourself, to deprive yourself in that way? [*Invite the patient to see the price of his defenses.*]

Pt: I do blame her a lot for when we are late. [*He sees his behavior but not its defensive function: "If I can blame her, I don't have to face how I cause my suffering."*]

Th: You blame her a lot when you decide to be late together with her. [*Clarify the defense of externalization.*]

Pt: Yes.

Th: Would you like to know what's driving that pattern of self-deprivation? [*Invite him to focus on the feelings, anxiety, and de-fenses that create his presenting problems—arguments and a poor relationship with himself and his wife.*]

Pt: Yes. [*Intrapsychic focus: the patient sees that his defenses, not his wife, create his suffering.*]

Undo the patient's externalization to establish an internal focus. The patient who externalizes creates an external locus of control: "My wife controls my life and creates my problems." Thus, he believes ther-apy cannot help him. "If my wife creates my problems, my therapy won't change her, so I have no hope for therapy." Help him see the in-ternal locus of control: "It's not my wife but my defenses that create my problems." Now therapy makes sense: "I can take a stand against these defenses to make different choices." Hope is reborn when he realizes he can see and let go of the defenses that create his suffering.

Obstacle to Declaring an Internal Emotional Problem: Vagueness

In this example, you will see why it is important to address vagueness as a defense against describing a presenting problem. Do not explore any problem if the problem or example is vague. When the problem is vague, you cannot find out what the triangle of conflict is.

Th: What's the problem you would like me to help you with?

Pt: I've just been feeling in a bad mood. [*Defense: vagueness.*]

Th: Can you be more specific?

Pt: Not really, I just don't feel so hot. [*Defense: vagueness.*]

Th: What is going on in your life to trigger that?

Pt: I don't know. I think it's just my life in general. [*Defense: vagueness.*]

Th: I hear you have a bad mood, and you think it's your life in general, but this is vague. Could you be more specific? [*Point out the defense.*]

Pt: Yesterday I had a crying jag when I got home from work.

Th: What was going on at work that could have triggered that?

Pt: I don't know if it was anything at work. I just feel tired when I get home. [*Defense: vagueness.*]

Th: You had a crying jag at home yesterday and were tired. What happened earlier that could have triggered that crying jag?

Pt: I talked to my boss, but I don't think it was that. [*Defense: denial.*]

Th: What did you and your boss talk about?

Pt: He said he was going to have to let me go because they are downsizing. [*Stimulus.*]

Th: What is your feeling toward him for saying that?

Pt: I just feel down. [*Defense: vagueness.*]

Th: Feeling "down" is vague. If you don't cover the feeling with vagueness, what is the feeling toward him for firing you? [*Point out the defense and focus on the warded-off feeling.*]

Pt: I was angry. Well, not angry exactly. [*Defense: undoing.*]

Th: You just said "angry." Do you notice how you start to take it back?

Pt: Well, I'm not sure. [*Defense: indecision.*]

Th: You say angry; then you take it back and cover the anger with indecision. Do you notice how you cover the anger toward your boss by getting a bit indecisive? [*Point out defenses.*]

Pt: Yes, but now I don't have a job! [*Starts to tear up.*]

Th: Do you notice how these tears come in to cover up your anger?

Pt: But I feel sad.

Th: And you feel angry, but we can see now you feel angry with your boss. Then you cover the anger with indecision and sadness. I wonder if the crying jag was a way to cover up your anger at your boss. [*Clarify the function of the defense.*]

Pt: I think I do that a lot.

The patient presents her problem in such a vague way we cannot get a clear idea of her problem or its trigger. Focus on the defense of vagueness until a clear picture of the problem emerges. To explore the "down" feeling would not make sense until we know where it fits on the triangle of conflict.

Obstacle to Declaring an Internal Emotional Problem: Projection

The highly resistant patient often uses projection to avoid declaring a problem to work on in therapy. This vignette illustrates how to block projections to maintain a consistent focus on the presenting problem.

Th: What's the problem you would like me to help you with?

Pt: My husband and I are having lots of arguments, and my psychiatrist suggested I see you to deal with my issues. [*Defense: projection onto the psychiatrist.*]

Th: I understand that was your psychiatrist's idea, but what is the *internal* emotional problem with which you would like me to help you? [*Block the projection.*]

Pt: The arguments with my husband. [*Defense: said diffidently.*]

Th: How are the arguments a problem for you? [*Assess whether this is a problem for her.*]

Pt: He is always going on about wanting more sex, and I'm not interested.

Th: You are not interested in more sex, but I'm not sure how this is a problem for you.

Pt: I thought you would think it is a problem. [*Defense: projection.*]

Th: If it's not a problem for you, I have no right to explore it. [*Block the projection.*] That's why I'm wondering what the problem is you want me to help you with.

Pt: I don't know. I mean I would like it if we didn't argue so much.

Th: How is that a problem for you?

Pt: I just wish he would just leave me alone. [*This is an externalizing focus. "The problem is him, not how I deal with my feelings."*]

Th: That's what you want him to do, but it's still not clear how the arguments are a problem for you.

Pt: I get so angry.

Th: How is that a problem for you?

Pt: When I get really angry, I throw things.

Th: Mm-hmm.

Pt: And sometimes I yell at our four-year-old son.

Th: Sometimes this rage at your husband is directed at your four-year-old son instead.

Pt: Yes.

Th: And is that something you want to get a handle on?

Pt: Yes, because he doesn't deserve it. [*First declaration of an internal problem.*]

Th: So something happens with your husband that triggers a lot of rage. One way you deal with it is to yell at your son. And you would like some help in figuring out what is going on underneath this rage so your son doesn't have to suffer the results. [*Summarize the triangle of conflict to see if we have consensus on the conflict and the task.*]

Pt: Yes.

In this case, the patient presents something that troubles others but not her. So we have no right to explore the disputes. Clarify how the presenting difficulty is a problem for her. Otherwise, we cannot establish a therapeutic alliance.

COMMON NONPROBLEMS

When the therapist asks the patient what the problem is he wants help for in therapy, the patient may claim he has no problem, as we have seen. But sometimes the patient may offer something that is not a problem or is not a problem for the patient. If the therapist does not recognize a nonproblem, he may explore it only to run into a dead end.

Vignette One: Nonpsychological Problem

Patients can avoid revealing an internal emotional problem by revealing something that is either not a problem for the patient or a problem outside the therapist's expertise. This vignette reveals how to block this defense and maintain an effective therapeutic focus on an internal emotional problem. Remember: without the patient's declaration of an internal emotional problem, we have no right to attempt therapy.

Th: What is the problem you would like me to help you with?

Pt: My wife wants a divorce.

Th: How is that a problem for you?

Pt: I'm not sure that it is, to be honest. I've been fed up with her.

Th: It's not clear if this divorce is really a problem for you.

Pt: It is.

Th: How so?

Pt: It's going to cost me a lot of money. [*Nonproblem psychologically speaking.*]

Th: Of course, but as a therapist, I can't help you with the financial problem. [*Point out the reality.*] I wonder what the emotional problem is you would like me to help you with.

Pt: Emotional problem? Well, I have been yelling at my daughter quite a bit. [*For the first time, he indicates that something he does creates a problem for him.*]

Th: How is that a problem for you?

Pt: I think it's making her afraid of me, and I don't want that to happen because my wife is moving out of town and she'll have custody of my daughter. [*He declares an internal emotional problem.*]

Vignette Two: People Pleasing by Not Having a Problem

Sometimes patients are afraid to depend on others for help. As a result, they may try to please the therapist by presenting as if they do not have a problem. Block this defense as quickly as possible so the patient can begin to see her need to depend and her fear of doing so.

Th: What's the problem with which you would like me to help you?

Pt: I'm doing really well this week. Everything's going well. I haven't had any upsets this week. Everything has been fine since my boss is out of town on a business trip. And my boyfriend has been on his best behavior. So I'm actually feeling just fine. [*Racing speech and gaze avoidance indicate anxiety and defense.*]

The patient says she is fine to avoid revealing a desire for help. After the patient's second sentence, the therapist could say, "I'm glad things are going so well. Yet since you are here, what is the problem you would like me to help you with?" Here, the therapist could block her defense and return the focus to the problem. Or the therapist could focus on the patient's racing speech: "I'm glad everything is going well. I notice your speech is racing, which is often a sign of anxiety. Are you aware of feeling anxious right now?" In this case, the therapist might focus on regulating the anxiety if it appeared to be too high.

RESISTANCE TO DECLARING ONE'S WILL TO WORK ON THE PROBLEM

Often a patient becomes hesitant or passive as soon as you explore the problem he wants to resolve in therapy. You are exploring, but he is not. Mobilize his will to the task to co-create the therapeutic alliance.

Asking him to declare his will to engage in therapy invites greater emotional intimacy. This invitation, based on his relational history, triggers unconscious feelings, anxiety, and defenses against emotional closeness.

Address those defenses until the patient can own his desire for treatment rather than project it onto others. He must become aware sequentially of (1) his will to engage in therapy, (2) how he experiences his will, and (3) the feelings, anxiety, and defenses triggered by his will to engage in the task. He must acknowledge his wish for treatment and his goals (Kenny 1998), so he can achieve them (Ainslie 2001). This gives him enhanced self-control (Elster 1999, 2000).

Some neuroscientists propose that our experience of will is illusory because neural activation occurs before consciousness (Wegner 2002). Yet illusions about perception do not lead us to discard the concept of perception. So these illusions should not lead us to dismiss the concept of free will (Schulkin 2007; Sternberg 2010). Will has both conscious and unconscious dimensions, like all aspects of our inner life. Obviously, nonconscious brain activation precedes any conscious activity. As Grawe (2007, 106) pointed out, "If I regard the preparatory, unconscious processes as a part of myself, just as much as my conscious experience, then it is still me that makes decisions. My Self—my personality—consists of implicit (unconscious) and explicit (conscious) aspects. My volitional decisions are not forced upon me by some external agent."

Our emphasis on will is similar to that in Buddhist mindfulness practice. According to the Buddha, you "own" your will. You are free to use it and to receive the results of your efforts (Schwartz and Begley 2002, 303). In therapy and Buddhism, the quality of the patient's attention determines her awareness and what she wills. The choice to pay attention is "the essential phenomenon of will" (W. James quoted by Schwartz and Begley 2002, 317).

The choice to pay attention to feelings rewires and changes the brain. "Moment by moment we choose and sculpt how our ever-changing minds will work, we choose who we will be . . . , and these choices are left embossed in physical form on our material selves" (Merzenich and deCharms 1996, 77).

Vignette One: A Patient Who Has Already Declared a Problem

In this vignette, we will see how to help a patient who has declared a problem but does not want to work on it. The therapist must be alert to any signs that the patient is reluctant, and then mobilize the patient's will to engage in the therapeutic task.

Th: Can you tell me more about this problem with your wife?

Pt: I'm not sure how important it is. [*Defense: minimization. Lack of will to explore his declared problem with the therapist.*]

Th: You mentioned this problem with your wife. Is it your will to look at this problem? [*Invite the patient to declare his will.*]

Pt: I think so. [*Defense: hypothetical speech and a detached voice.*]

Th: You seem uncertain. Do you notice that? [*Point out the defense.*] Are you sure you want to look at this problem? [*Invite the patient's will until he declares it without anxiety or defenses.*]

Pt: I know I'm supposed to. [*Defense: projection of will onto others.*]

Th: But do you *want* to? [*Block the projection of will.*]

Pt: That's the thing. I'm not sure I really want to look at it. [*Defense: defiance. The patient projects his will onto the therapist, and then defies the therapist as the repository of the patient's will.*]

Th: That's okay. I have no right to help you with this problem with your wife if you don't want to look at it. I'm here to help you with what *you* want. And if you don't want me to help you with that problem, I have no right to try. [*Deactivating the projection of will onto the therapist deactivates the defiance that the projection creates.*]

Pt: Hmm. I thought you would pursue this because I thought you would think it was important. [*He sees how he projects his will onto the therapist.*]

Th: I have no right to pursue this if it's not important to you and if you don't want to. So do you want to explore this conflict with your wife? [*Deactivate the projection of will and then ask about his will to engage in the therapeutic task.*]

Pt: Well, it is important. [*He still does not declare his will.*]

Th: Although it is important to you, it still may not be something you want to explore. [*Reflect the conflict between his wish to explore and his resistance to doing so.*]

Pt: I'd like to resolve this problem with my wife. [*Defense: detached voice. Verbally, he moves forward, but nonverbally he resists.*]

Th: Are you sure? [*Invite him to declare his will.*]

Pt: Yes. [*Defense: said in a detached voice.*]

Th: You don't sound sure. How do you experience that inside—that you know you want this? That this isn't simply someone else's idea but yours? How do you experience inside that you know this is what *you* want? [*As long as he does not experience his desire, he projects it onto someone else.*]

Pt: [*Sits up, looks more alert and involved.*] I can't go on this way. [*Defense. We see him experience his will nonverbally, but we don't hear it yet verbally.*]

Th: How do you experience inside that you want to explore this here with me? [*Invite him to declare his will.*]

Pt: [*Facial expression becomes more serious.*] I want to get to the bottom of this once and for all.

Principle: *Focus on the patient's will until he is emotionally committed to engaging in therapy. Then we can explore his conflict collaboratively.*

Vignette Two: A Fragile Patient Who Has Declared a Problem

Often, fragile patients become anxious when they reveal a problem and suffer from cognitive/perceptual disruption. They can forget that it was their will to look inside themselves in therapy. Instead, they project their will onto the therapist and fear the therapist. In this example, you will learn how to identify and deactivate the projection of will so the patient owns her will to engage in therapy.

Th: Would you like to take a look at this conflict with your husband? [*Mobilize the patient's will to the task.*]

Pt: I'm not sure. [*Defense: indecision.*]

Th: Some hesitance is here. Do you notice? [*Point out the patient's defense.*]

Pt: [*Nods.*]

Th: Was it your will to come here today? [*Invite her to declare her will.*]

Pt: Yes.

Th: Was there a problem that you wanted help with?

Pt: Yes.

Th: And do you want help for that problem? [*Invite her to declare her will.*]

Pt: Yes, I just am afraid of what we'll get into. [*Her speech races and she fidgets: signs of a sharp rise in anxiety. Declaring her will triggers anxiety.*]

Th: You seem anxious. Are you aware of feeling anxious? [*Mobilize her attention to the anxiety to regulate it and head off regressive defenses that arise in response to a sharp rise of anxiety.*]

Pt: Yes.

Th: Where do you notice feeling this anxiety?

Pt: In my head, in my arms. I have some trouble breathing, and my stomach doesn't feel too good. [*Signs of anxiety in the striated and smooth muscles.*]

Th: On the one hand, there's this anxiety that comes up in your body, and on the other hand, there's your will to explore. Do you notice how just telling me what you want triggers this anxiety, as if it's against the law for you to say what you want? [*Differentiate her will (trigger) from the anxiety, help her observe herself.*]

Pt: [*Settles down into her chair, less anxious. Nods.*]

Th: It's as if it's against the law for you to say what you want, as if the police come in and Taser you with anxiety just for saying what you want out of this therapy.

Pt: That's it.

Th: If we put that anxiety off to the side, is this what you want—to explore this conflict with your husband? Do you want to know what you are feeling under the anxiety so you have better information about you? [*Mobilize her will to her goal.*]

Pt: Yes, I want to. [*Becomes anxious.*]

Th: What do you notice happening in you right now? [*Mobilize her attention to her anxiety and causality: her will to reveal herself triggers anxiety.*]

Pt: I'm getting anxious.

Th: Isn't that interesting? You got anxious as soon as you said, "Yes, that's what I want to do." Then this anxiety comes in to inhibit you as soon as you express what you want. Do you notice that? [*Show causality.*]

Pt: I have a hard time saying what I want. [*She can observe this sequence without flooding with anxiety or resorting automatically to defense.*]

Th: Isn't that interesting? Saying what you want triggers this anxiety that inhibits you. What's that like to step back and observe these two elements: your will and this anxiety? [*Mobilize her awareness of two things at once: build her capacity to observe and tolerate internal conflict.*]

Pt: It's weird.

Th: It really is, isn't it? It's weird to begin to notice how expressing what you want is one thing, and this anxiety is another. If we go back, how do you experience this want as yours? How do you feel that in your body? [*Separate her will from her anxiety, and then invite her to pay attention to her will and how she experiences it.*]

Pt: I know I should talk about it. My doctor told me to. [*Defense: projection of will. Block the projection and focus on the patient's experience of her will.*]

Th: That's what he thinks, but how do you, in your opinion, feel this inside as your desire? [*Block the projection of will and invite her experience of her will.*]

Pt: [*Sits up and looks at the therapist.*] Because I want a better relationship than my parents had. I don't want my daughter to suffer like I did. [*With this implicit rise of will in her body and her verbal declaration, we can explore her conflicts. Each later declaration of will to reveal herself more deeply may trigger feelings and anxiety, leading to cognitive/perceptual disruption. If so, show causality and regulate the anxiety before going further.*]

RESISTANCE TO EXPLORING A SPECIFIC EXAMPLE OF AN INTERNAL EMOTIONAL PROBLEM

Once the patient has declared his will to explore an internal emotional problem, ask, "Can we look at a specific example of where this depression is a problem for you?"

Often, patients use defenses to avoid declaring a specific example of the problem they want to explore. The types of defense and pathway of anxiety discharge tell us what type of character structure the patient has.

Low Resistance Patient

A low resistance patient usually reveals a specific example readily without using defenses.

Pt: Yes. It's had a terrible impact on my marriage. I haven't wanted to go out with my wife, and I can tell she is resenting me for wanting to stay at home and not go out. It happened just last night.

Psychodiagnosis: The patient gives a clear answer without anxiety or defense.

Intervention: Explore a specific example of where his depression affects his marriage.

Moderately Resistant Patient

A moderately resistant patient will use repressive and tactical defenses. Once we point out those defenses, however, the patient will readily offer a specific example of his problem.

Pt: I get depressed a lot.

Psychodiagnosis: The patient does not give a clear example but acknowledges he has a problem.

Intervention: Block the defense of vagueness and maintain a focus on a specific example.

Th: Can we take a look at a specific example that triggered your depression?

Pt: It started after my boss fired me on my last job. [*Blocking the defense allowed the patient to present a clear example.*]

Highly Resistant Patient

A highly resistant patient responds with a defense rather than with a specific example of the problem. We must help the patient see the defense and its price so he will let go of the defense and offer a specific example of his problem instead. Remember: without a specific example of the problem, we cannot explore the triangle of conflict to get consensus on what causes the patient's problem.

Pt: I can't think of a specific example.

Psychodiagnosis: The patient does not give an example of his problem. He does not see his defense.

Intervention: Help the patient see his defense.

Th: Do you notice you have a hard time giving me a specific example? [*Point out the defense.*]

Pt: That's just it. When people ask me things, I just come up with nothing. [*He invites the therapist to have a relationship where the therapist asks for information and the patient withholds what is necessary to do therapy.*]

Th: I understand. It's just that as long as we don't have a specific example of this problem, then obviously I wouldn't be able to help you with it. [*Point out the price of the defense.*]

Pt: But I really can't come up with a specific example. [*Defense.*]

Th: If you can't come up with a specific example though, we won't be able to get a clear picture of your difficulty. Then I won't be able to help you. [*Point out the price of his defense.*]

Pt: It happens all the time. [*Defense: vagueness.*]

Th: But a specific example?

Pt: It's something that goes on a lot. [*Defense: vagueness.*]

Th: "Goes on a lot" is vague. Can we look at a specific example?

Pt: Like with my mother, it happens every time I visit. [*Defense: generalization.*]

Th: Can we take a look at a specific example where you become depressed when you visit your mother?

Pt: It happened just yesterday. [*Patient begins to describe a specific example.*]

Principle: *Keep your focus, blocking and labeling defenses, until the patient gives a specific example.*

Fragile Patient

The fragile patient will use repressive defenses until her anxiety rises over the threshold of anxiety tolerance. At that point, the patient begins to suffer from cognitive/perceptual disruption. The therapist must regulate the patient's anxiety first, and then ask again for a specific example.

Pt: It happens all the time. I don't think there's a specific trigger. [*Sign that the patient is unaware of the stimulus, the feeling that is triggered, her anxiety, or her defense.*]

Th: Can we take a look at an example where you remember becoming depressed so we can see what is triggering this crippling depression?

Pt: I was very depressed yesterday.

Th: When did it start?

Pt: I think it started as soon as I woke up.

Th: Could we look at what happened the day before?

Pt: Nothing much really. [*Defense: denial and ignoring of stimuli.*]

Th: What happened?

Pt: I got up as usual and did some last-minute revision of my presentation. I went to the art school and gave my presentation as a form of performance art. The professor said in front of the group that it was the worst presentation he had ever seen. Other students were shocked by what he said and talked to me afterward. Then after school I went to my part-time job. [*She presents the stimulus and then ignores its importance and her reactive feelings.*]

Th: You mention that the professor said it was the worst presentation he had ever seen. What's the feeling toward him for saying that?

Pt: [*Blank look.*] I'm sorry. What did you say?

Th: Did your mind blank out just now?

Pt: Yeah, that happens a lot.

Th: That's a sign of anxiety. As soon as I ask what the feeling is toward your professor, you get anxious, and your mind conks out. Do you see that now?

Pt: Now that you point it out.

Th: It sounds like there is some feeling toward the professor that makes you anxious.

Pt: My friends said they were angry. [*Defense: projection.*]

Th: And you? Do you share that reaction with them? [*Block the projection.*]

Pt: I mean he's a really arrogant guy. [*Defense: rationalization.*]

Th: Are you aware of feeling angry with him?

Pt: Yes, I can see that now. [*Progress: she feels her anger without suffering cognitive/perceptual disruption.*]

We would explore this example so she could see how she turned her anger toward the professor onto herself and became depressed. Fragile and highly resistant patients often ignore events that trigger their feelings. As a result, they don't know what causes their symptoms. Explore events preceding a rise in symptoms to discover the stimulus to the feelings.

RESISTANCE TO DECLARING A POSITIVE GOAL

There is a saying that if you do not know where you want to go, you will probably get there. Likewise, in therapy we need to know the positive goals the patient wants to achieve through therapy. Without the patient's positive goals, he will have no motivation to engage in the therapeutic task. Thus, before exploring feelings and conflicts deeply with the patient, make sure you and the patient have agreed on the positive goals the therapy is designed to achieve.

However, the patient may have difficulty declaring a positive goal for therapy. If so, the therapist must assess what prevents the patient from declaring a positive goal and help the patient overcome that barrier. Otherwise, the therapist and patient will not be able to develop a therapeutic alliance.

Patients can have trouble declaring a positive goal due to a transference resistance, a failure to see causality, or long-term depression that has left the patient feeling depleted or hopeless. The following examples show how to help these patients declare a positive goal.

Transference Resistance

Some patients may resist presenting positive goals as part of a transference resistance. The patient, by not providing a positive goal, may be inviting the therapist to present the positive goals. Then the patient reluctantly goes along at best or opposes the therapist at worst.

In this example, the patient has just described a situation in which he gives people what they want, even though by doing so, he cheats himself. Afterward, he becomes angry with them for "exploiting" him, blaming them for his choice to abandon his own interests.

> *Th:* You see that you sacrificed yourself but blamed them for your choice. Would you like us to take a look at that so we can help you give up this pattern of exploiting yourself? [*Mobilize the patient to the therapeutic task.*]
>
> *Pt:* I'm sixty-two years old. It's too late for me to change. Maybe I should give up. [*Invitation to a passive transference resistance: "I will give up and ask you, the therapist, to take responsibility for my therapy by breathing hope into me."*]
>
> *Th:* Shall we give up now? [*Block the transference resistance.*]
>
> *Pt:* [*Looks up surprised.*] Are you saying I should give up? [*Defense: projection.*]
>
> *Th:* You said you should give up. I'm just asking if we should stop now so you can give up.
>
> *Pt:* No, I've got to turn this around. If I give up now, things won't change.

Failure to See Causality

When patients do not see how their defenses create their presenting problems, they assume something else does: spouses, other people, life, or fate. "Why do bad things keep happening to me?" "It's just one damned thing after another." "I think it's just my fate." "Life sucks, what can I say?" "I think it's my karma to suffer in this lifetime."

Since they attribute their suffering to external forces, they feel hopeless. If they do not see causality, do not confront their hopelessness as a defense. If they believe other people or fate cause their problems, they should feel hopeless. Help patients see causality. Once they recognize how things they do (defenses) create their problems, they regain an internal locus of control and can feel hope again.

> *Th:* You see that you sacrificed yourself but blamed them for your choice. Would you like us to take a look at that so we can help you give up this pattern of exploiting yourself?
>
> *Pt:* It feels so hopeless. They will never care about what I want. [*Defense: projection. He does not care enough about what he wants.*]
>
> *Th:* They should care about what you want. Is that true?
>
> *Pt:* Yes. They should. [*Defense: denial in fantasy. Rather than relate to reality (they do not care more about what he wants than what they want), he relates to his fantasy of how reality "should" be.*]
>
> *Th:* Is that true?
>
> *Pt:* Yes. Are you saying they shouldn't care about what I want?
>
> *Th:* People who don't care about what you want should care about what you want. Is that true? [*Identify the defense of denial in fantasy.*]
>
> *Pt:* Yes. Don't you agree?
>
> *Th:* Reality should be what reality is not. Is that true? [*Mirror his denial.*]
>
> *Pt:* It should! [*Defense: denial in fantasy.*]
>
> *Th:* You say reality should be your way, but then reality keeps on being what it is. It must be hard to be having this fight with reality.
>
> *Pt:* It is.
>
> *Th:* Do you notice how when you fight reality, reality always wins? [*Point out the price of denial.*]
>
> *Pt:* Yes, but shouldn't they care about my needs? [*Defense: denial in fantasy.*]

Th: No. That's not their job. They should care about their needs.

Pt: I think they should also care about mine.

Th: That's your job. You should care about your needs, but you ask other people to do your job.

Pt: But they should!

Th: If you don't care about your needs, if you don't pay attention to them, why should they?

Pt: But they ask me to ignore my needs.

Th: And you can say, "No, I will pay attention to my needs" or "Yes. I will ignore my needs." And you let me know you ignore your needs but blame others for your choice.

Pt: I hadn't thought of it this way before.

A patient who uses the defenses of externalization and denial in fantasy feels hopeless about the possibility for personal change. Once he sees his defenses, he can turn against them and create a better life.

Depression

A depressed patient often presents with negative rather than positive goals for therapy. Do not proceed until the patient has declared some positive goals for the therapy. This vignette shows how to persist with a depressed patient, blocking defenses until the patient can declare a positive goal.

Th: What would you like me to help you with?

Pt: I don't want to feel depressed. [*Negative goal.*]

Th: What do you want to feel instead? [*Mobilize the patient's awareness of a positive goal.*]

Pt: I just don't want to feel like a constant failure. [*Negative goal.*]

Th: If this therapy is successful, what do you want to feel instead? [*Mobilize the patient's awareness of a positive goal.*]

Pt: I don't know. I've always felt depressed. [*No one has ever felt depressed every single second of his life. This statement reveals that the patient cannot remember any experiences right now that are incongruent with his depressed state. This illustrates how memory can be state dependent: a depressed patient remembers only depressing memories.*]

Th: But it sounds like you want to feel something different.

Pt: Yeah.

Th: How do you want to be different? How will we know we have succeeded?

Pt: I won't be depressed. [*Negative goal.*]

Th: What will you feel instead?

Pt: I'll feel like getting up in the morning.

Th: You'll feel like getting up in the morning. How else will you feel?

Pt: I won't feel sad. [*Negative goal.*]

Th: What will you feel instead?

Pt: I wouldn't say happy but maybe content.

Some chronically depressed patients cannot formulate a positive goal for the therapy. Instead, they ruminate about negative goals (things they want to avoid). Negative goals mobilize their avoidance system (Grawe 2007), triggering anxiety, defenses, and resistance. Negative goals cannot be the basis for a therapeutic alliance. Interrupt depressive rumination to prevent depression in a session. Then focus on the positive goals the patient wants to achieve.

To do so, ask questions such as these:

- "When this therapy succeeds, how will you know? How will you be different?"
- "You mention feeling depressed, detached, and unengaged in relationships now as we begin the therapy. How do you want to be different when we end? For instance, instead of being detached in relationships, what's the healthy alternative you want to be instead?"
- "You said you don't want to feel depressed. That tells us what you don't want to feel. What do you want to feel instead?"

When you ask the patient for his positive goals, he can respond with

1. Positive goals
2. Anxiety and symptoms
3. Defenses

Response One: Patient makes a declaration of a positive goal.

Pt: I want to feel happy instead of depressed. I want to respect myself instead of being down on myself, and I want to have more intimacy in my relationships.

Intervention: Reflect back the patient's positive goal to ensure mutual understanding and to mobilize the approach system. With the patient's will and goal mobilized, explore a specific example.

Th: You want to feel happy instead of depressed. You want to respect yourself instead of being down on yourself, and to be more intimate in relationships instead of detached.

Pt: Yes.

Th: You've told me that when you have feelings in a relationship, you get anxious and then deal with feelings and intimacy by detaching and avoiding. If you like, we could help you face those feelings and get to the bottom of them so that instead of detaching from your feelings and from your partners you could be intimate, and instead of avoiding emotional connections and becoming lonely you could form closer relationships. [*Outline the therapeutic task: face feelings and turn against defenses to overcome her symptoms and achieve her goals.*] Is that something you would like to do? [*Enlist the patient's will to engage in the therapeutic task.*]

Pt: Yes.

Th: Can we take a look at a specific example where this conflict around intimacy came up for you? [*Invite her to focus on a specific example of the conflict.*]

Response Two: Patient immediately is flooded with anxiety or symptoms occur.

Pt: I want to feel happy instead of depressed. [*Tension goes out of the patient's muscles as she becomes limp, a sign of rising anxiety.*]

Th: What do you notice feeling right now?

Pt: Tired.

Th: Does it feel like a good tired like after exercising, or does it feel like a sick tired?

Pt: Like a sick tired.

Th: That's a sign of anxiety. Are you aware of feeling anxious right now?

Pt: I feel sick to my stomach, but I have stomach problems.

Th: Being sick to your stomach is a sign of very high anxiety. Did you notice what triggered your anxiety just now?

Pt: No.

Th: You mentioned that you want to feel happy and then suddenly became anxious. [*Point out causality.*] Does it feel a little scary to declare a positive goal here with me? [*Invite her to observe causality.*]

Pt: [*Becomes tense. Shifts in chair.*] Yes, it does feel scary.

Th: It feels a little scary to form a positive goal for you, to take your side. [*Point out causality.*]

Pt: Yes, a lot scary.

Th: Now that you can observe that sequence and you can observe the anxiety in your body, how is your stomach?

Pt: It feels better now, not so jumpy. [*Pointing out causality regulates the patient's anxiety.*]

The patient's expression of positive goals or desires often triggers anxiety or defenses. Identify the anxiety when it is in the forefront, and help the patient pay attention to it for self-regulation. Then help the patient see causality: declaring a positive goal or her will triggers anxiety. Many fragile patients were punished as children for expressing what they wanted. Thus, expressing their will and desire triggers unconscious anxiety.

Response Three: Patient uses defenses.

Pt: I just don't want to feel depressed and anxious anymore, and I sure don't want to have any more crappy boyfriends [*negative goals*], but I don't know if that is possible for me. [*Defense.*]

Th: I notice you underestimate yourself right now. When you underestimate yourself, does this make you happy, or does it make you depressed? [*Identify and clarify the defense.*]

Pt: Depressed.

Th: Is this habit of underestimating yourself something you would like to overcome in therapy?

Pt: If it's possible. [*Defense: self-doubt.*]

Th: I notice you doubt whether progress is possible for you. Does your mind have a tendency to doubt you and your potential? [*Point out the defense.*]

Pt: [*Tears.*] Yes.

Th: Do you think that habit of self-doubt might be hurting you? [*Point out the price of the defense.*]

Pt: I think it hurts me a lot.

Th: As soon as you declare that you would like to feel better, it's as if a policeman comes into the room to doubt you. It's as if it is against the law to have faith in you and believe in your potential. Does that fit? [*Point out causality.*]

Pt: Yes. I think I doubt myself a lot.

Th: It sounds like you doubt yourself as soon as you express your desire for a better life here. Do you see now how that happened?

Pt: I do now.

We can work productively only if the patient wants to achieve a positive goal. If the patient has no positive goals for the therapy, you should probably not try to treat the problem (Grawe 2007, 41).

ESTABLISHING CONSENSUS ON THE TRIANGLE OF CONFLICT

We explore a specific example to develop a consensus with the patient on his feelings, anxiety, and defenses (the triangle of conflict). This consensus on what causes the patient's problems is essential to get a consensus on the therapeutic task.

In the following vignette, notice how the therapist checks in constantly to make sure the patient sees his feeling, anxiety, and defenses. That way, the therapist and patient jointly co-create a consensus on what causes the patient's problems.

Th: What's the internal emotional problem you would like me to help you with?

Pt: My doctor said I should come to see you. [*Defense: projection onto the doctor.*]

Th: That's what he said, but in your opinion, what's the internal emotional problem you would like me to help you with? [*Block the projection, and then return to the question.*]

Pt: You should ask my doctor. [*Defense: projection.*]

Th: Since he's not here, I have to ask you. [*Point out the reality.*]

Pt: I don't know.

Th: Yet you are here. And I'm sure you wouldn't come here for no reason at all. [*Point out the contradiction between what he says ("I have no psychological problems") and what he does (he comes to a psychologist's office).*]

Pt: That's true.

Th: What's the internal emotional problem you would like me to help you with?

Pt: I've been a little down lately. [*Begins to declare an internal emotional problem.*]

Th: A little down?

Pt: Yeah. Trouble sleeping, not eating much, not much desire for much of anything.

Th: These are some symptoms you have: trouble sleeping, not eating much, not much desire for anything. Have you always been this way, or is this a more recent change?

Pt: No, I haven't always been this way.

Th: When did it start? [*Find out what triggered the onset of his symptoms.*]

Pt: Oh, about two years ago.

Th: What was happening around that time?

Pt: Not much that I can think of. Oh. I lost my job and was unemployed for a while.

Th: Can you tell me more about that?

Pt: I was a vice president with XYZ Company. I'd been there for twenty years and had done really well, but it turned out that an accountant under me was embezzling funds. The company accused me of embezzlement and fired me on the spot. Later, the auditors discovered it was the accountant and not me, but by then it was too late. I'd been fired. There was new management in the company, so no one was going to ask me back.

Th: These symptoms started when you were fired from this job, although you had been a vice president after twenty years of excellent service. You were fired through no cause of your own but because you were wrongly blamed for the crime of a subordinate. You must have some feelings about that. [*Asking about feelings will trigger feelings, anxiety, or defenses.*]

Pt: Yeah. I got over them. [*Defenses: denial and detaching.*]

Th: "Getting over them" tells us how you detached from your emotions. [*Identify his defense.*] Would you like to take a look at these emotions so we can see what triggered all these symptoms? [*Invitation to the task.*]

Pt: I was not pleased when the boss called me in. [*Defense: minimization.*]

Th: "Not pleased" tells me what you didn't feel. What is the feeling toward him? [*Identify his defense, and then ask about the feeling.*]

Pt: No feeling really. [*Defense: denial.*] I just thought he didn't handle it well. [*Defense: intellectualization.*]

Th: That's what you thought, but what's the feeling toward him if you don't cover it with thoughts? [*Label the defense, invite him to turn against it, and then ask for the feeling that the defense has been hiding.*]

Pt: I thought the fact that— [*Defense: intellectualization.*]

Th: [*Interrupts the defense.*] That's your thought, but if you don't cover your feeling with thoughts [*differentiate his defense from his feeling*], what's the feeling toward the boss for firing you, disbelieving you, and blaming you for someone else's crime? [*Invite the feeling.*]

Pt: Disbelieved. [*Defense: the patient confuses the stimulus with his feeling. The boss did not believe him (stimulus), and this triggered a feeling in the patient, probably anger.*]

Th: He disbelieved you. That's what *he did*, but what do *you feel* toward him for doing that? [*Differentiate the stimulus from the feeling, and then invite the feeling.*]

Pt: I felt I was wrong because I should have known what that accountant was doing. [*Defense: he turns anger onto himself rather than feel it toward his boss. This would cause depression.*]

Th: You notice I'm asking you about the feeling toward your boss?

Pt: Yes.

Th: And do you notice how a critical part of your brain takes the feeling toward your boss and turns it into criticism on you now? [*Show how he turns the anger on himself rather than feel it toward his boss.*]

Pt: I didn't see that, but I can see how you see that.

Th: Do you think that turning this feeling toward your boss into criticism of yourself might be hurting you? [*Help him see how the defense makes him depressed.*]

Pt: Yes I think it is hurting me because I have been getting really depressed, and my wife tells me I am too hard on myself. [*Patient can see causality: turning anger on himself makes him depressed.*]

Th: Could we take a look at the feeling toward your boss without turning it into criticism of yourself, so we can see what is driving this depression? [*Mobilize his will to the task.*]

Pt: Sure.

Th: So what's the feeling toward your boss? [*Invite the feeling.*]

Pt: Anger.

Th: Your boss blamed you for the accountant's crime [*stimulus*]. You felt angry with your boss [*feeling*], and that's not a problem. The problem is the way you handle your anger. When you get angry, you cover it up with thoughts [*defense*]. Or you distance yourself from your anger and other emotions so that you are out of touch with what you feel. Or you deny that you are angry and get more out of touch with what you feel and want, and that leads you to feel unmotivated. Then you showed us how you turn anger into self-criticism, and that makes you depressed [*problems caused by his defenses*] or you turn the anger at him onto yourself, and that also gets you depressed. Do you see what I mean? [*Outline the triangle of conflict so he can see what causes his problems.*]

ESTABLISHING CONSENSUS ON THE THERAPEUTIC TASK

Having explored the patient's conflicts and established a consensus on what creates the patient's difficulties, we can get consensus on the therapeutic task. Following are the structures for the interventions you can use to help the patient formulate the therapeutic task:

1. "We see that when you have x feeling, you use a, b, and c defenses."

2. "When you use a defense, do you think that might create this presenting problem?"

3. "Our task, if you want to pursue it, is to let go of those defenses and face the feelings."

4. "Our goal is for you to have an adaptive capacity instead of a symptom. For example, instead of feeling timid, you could experience your power; instead of feeling depressed, you could feel happy; instead of feeling anxious, you could feel confident;

and instead of feeling like a victim, you could assert yourself effectively."

5. "Does that sound like something you would like to do?"

Therapeutic Task: Help the patient let go of his defenses and face his feelings. This task achieves his therapeutic goal.

Therapeutic Goal: Help the patient replace his defenses that cause symptoms with adaptive channeling of his feelings that create healthy functioning.

The following vignette shows how to establish a consensus on the task during the phase of inquiry. The patient suffers from depression, anxiety, and conflicts with colleagues.

Th: Can we look at an example of a situation where you have trouble with conflicts?

Pt: Sure. There was a situation in which a person misperceived me in a way I thought was unfair. [*She presents the problem but in such a vague and generalized manner we can't explore it.*]

Th: Can you be more specific? [*Invite specificity.*]

Pt: It was the new bookkeeper. I needed a paper from a drawer in her office, and we have had access to that drawer for years, but when I came in there she started yelling and accused me of violating company policy.

Th: What was the feeling toward her when she yelled at you? [*Invite the feeling.*]

Pt: I felt like a little girl. [*Defense: she takes a little girl position rather than face her feelings toward the bookkeeper.*]

Th: I understand you began to take the position of a little girl, even though you are obviously a competent adult. [*Point out the defense.*] But from your perspective as a competent adult, what is your feeling toward her?

Pt: I felt timid. [*Defense.*]

Th: When she started yelling at you, you took a timid, little girl position. Do you think that little girl position helped you deal with her, or did it get in the way? [*Help her see the price of the defense.*]

Pt: It definitely gets in the way. [*She sees her defense is maladaptive.*]

Th: If we don't go to timidity or the little girl position [*invite her to turn against the defense*], can we see what the feeling is underneath, the feeling you have toward her?

Pt: I was angry. [*Feeling.*]

Th: You felt angry with her, and then covered your anger with timidity and with a little girl façade, but what you really felt was anger.

Pt: That's true, but I feel timid right now. [*Defense.*]

Th: As soon as this anger comes up between us, you are tempted to cover your anger now with timidity [*point out the defense*] rather than have us face the anger together. [*Distinguish the defense from the therapeutic task.*] Do you see what I mean?

Pt: Yes.

Th: What impact will that have on our work if you cover your anger with timidity rather than face it in therapy? [*Draw her attention to the price of the defense. Point out the difference between using a defense and the therapeutic task: turning against defenses.*]

Pt: I guess I wouldn't get to the anger.

Th: When you hide your anger under timidity, do you think that is helping you, or is that causing the work problems you mentioned? [*Invite her to see how the defense creates her presenting problem. Turn her against the defense.*]

Pt: It could be causing my work problems. [*The patient does not see clearly how her defenses create her problems.*]

Th: When you hide your anger under this little girl façade, does this make you feel powerful and strong, or does it make you weak and anxious?

Pt: It definitely makes me anxious.

Th: When you hold back your anger under the timidity and take more of this yelling without standing your ground, does that make you feel good or depressed?

Pt: I haven't thought about this before, but I can see how this has made me depressed.

Th: We can see how hiding your anger under timidity and the little girl façade has made you anxious and depressed and has prevented you from being able to deal with work conflicts in the powerful adult manner you would like. Our task, if you want to pursue it, is to let go of this timidity and little girl façade here so we can face your anger completely and get to the bottom of what has been driving this submissive pattern of behavior. That way we can help you feel your anger and power rather than cover your power with this façade of timidity. We can help you assert yourself effectively so you don't have to feel depressed; and we can help you show your adult capacities so you don't have to hide in the anxious façade of the little girl. Does that sound like something you would like to do? [*Outline the patient's task in therapy.*]

Remind the patient of her goals and her task. Each time she uses a defense, point out her choice: she can use her defenses and continue to suffer, or she can turn against her defenses and achieve her positive goals.

During the phase of inquiry, we establish a conscious therapeutic alliance based on the patient's willingness to explore the conflicts creating his presenting problems. Moderately resistant patients collaborate easily. Fragile patients become overwhelmed with anxiety. Highly resistant patients use defenses instead of exploring.

We do not take an extensive history initially for several reasons. First of all, we have no right to take the patient's history until he says he has a problem he wants to resolve in therapy. Second, it is not safe to take the patient's history until we know where his anxiety is discharged. As he describes traumas in his past, anxiety can become discharged into cognitive/perceptual disruption. The patient, rather than remember his history, begins to relive it in the therapy, retraumatizing himself. Do not take a full history until you have assessed the patient's anxiety and helped him regulate it. We do not take a history initially with highly resistant patients because presenting the history in a defensive, detached manner is not healing or integrative. Instead, we work on defenses until the history emerges with deep feeling and insight, leading to an integrative experience.

We take a history not just to gain information but to form a healing relationship. Getting information without regulating the fragile patient's anxiety would be harmful, not healing. Getting information while defenses are high creates an avoidant, detached nontherapeutic relationship. Help the patient's feelings come out with regulated anxiety. Address any defenses so the past can emerge in an emotionally integrative fashion while anxiety is regulated.

First, get an intrapsychic focus by asking for an internal problem to work on. Then assess each response to intervention. If the patient floods with anxiety, regulate the anxiety and then explore feelings. If he presents with numerous defenses, help him turn against them and then explore feelings. Through this exploration you will learn the conflicts that cause his problems.

As the patient reveals his feelings, anxiety, and defenses to you, he is simultaneously revealing his history. Every time we invite him to form a closer alliance, unconscious feelings related to past relationships emerge in the here and now. These unconscious feelings trigger unconscious anxiety in his body, revealing his history of affect regulation. The defenses he uses reveal how he learned to avoid his feelings with others. These moment-to-moment fluctuations of feeling, anxiety, and defense present his relational history, or the "present unconscious" (Fonagy et al. 2002). The procedural memory of his relationships reveals not only his defenses but the history of his suffering.

Once he relinquishes his defenses, his history will emerge spontaneously, and he will experience breakthroughs to unconscious feelings. Then he will emotionally experience the connections between his past and present in a new way.

THE UNCONSCIOUS THERAPEUTIC ALLIANCE

Establishing a conscious therapeutic alliance triggers feelings and anxiety in the patient because the therapist invites the patient to reveal her inner life. The invitation to an emotionally intimate relationship evokes two kinds of reactions. On the one hand, the patient unconsciously resorts to defenses based on her past suffering. "How dare you tempt me to be close to you after what was done to me!" In spite of the patient's resistance and anger, the therapist gently yet firmly persists, demonstrating to the patient that he wants to know her deeply and is willing to face her feelings.

This dedicated focus on her inner life mobilizes the patient's longings for love and freedom from suffering, accompanied by positive feelings toward the therapist who persists in spite of her resistance. This inner wish for emotional freedom, to know herself deeply and to love, and the deeply positive feelings for the therapist together constitute signs of the unconscious therapeutic alliance (Davanloo 1987). Why unconscious?

Sometimes patients are so resistant that we see almost no conscious therapeutic alliance, but the bodily signs of feeling and anxiety reveal to us that there is a part of the patient, albeit unconscious, that longs for inner freedom. Unconscious anxiety and feeling are signals telling us that a part of the patient longs for health and wholeness, even if the patient's words deny this. Through our dedication to her inner freedom, we can mobilize her desire to relinquish her defenses and reveal who she truly is underneath.

All our interventions are designed to increase the conscious and unconscious therapeutic alliance. Never mistake the resistance for the patient. The resistance is merely the tragic façade with which the patient has covered herself. As one patient said to me, "I always realized that you saw that person wasn't me. You saw who I could be underneath before I could see it myself." That person underneath is our ally.

One can think of the unconscious therapeutic alliance as the patient's inherent wish to become at one with the Truth of her existence. Bion refers to our epistemophilia, our love of the truth, as a Truth instinct (Bion 1970). He suggests that we have an inherent instinct to become transformed by becoming at one with the emotional truth in this moment. We help the patient face the truth so she can lead a life in the truth rather than remain imprisoned in her false self. Through our focus on the patient's feelings, we form a partnership with her unconscious longing for union with the truth. In this sense, the unconscious therapeutic alliance is relational. In our work, *both* the therapist and the patient long to become at one with the emotional truth in this moment. In fact, it is the therapist's courage to face and experience the truth of this moment that gives the patient the courage to do the same. And sometimes, it is the patient's courage that gives us the faith to go forward.

SUMMARY

During the phase of inquiry, the patient and therapist co-create a relationship for change. To develop a therapeutic alliance, the therapist and patient must explore and discover the following ingredients in this order:

1. An internal emotional problem he has (the intrapsychic focus)
2. His will to seek therapy for this problem
3. A specific example of the problem
4. A positive goal the therapy is designed to achieve

Through exploring the problem, the therapist and patient develop a consensus on

1. The conflicts creating the patient's presenting problems
2. The therapeutic task

We co-create this relationship for change step by step. Anytime you run into problems, refer to this list of ingredients to find out which element of the therapeutic alliance is missing. Often, the two missing ingredients are a presenting problem and a specific example. Figures 6.2 and 6.3 show the decision trees for those two steps in developing an alliance.

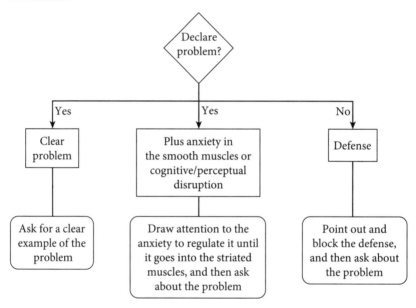

Figure 6.2   Inquiry: Declaring an internal emotional problem

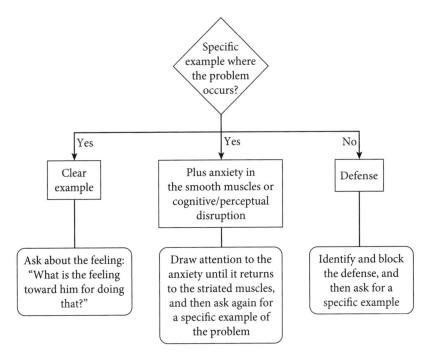

Figure 6.3 Inquiry: Getting a specific example of the problem

RECOMMENDED READINGS

Coughlin Della Selva, P. (1996). The trial therapy. In *Intensive short-term dynamic psychotherapy: Theory and technique*. (pp. 26–57). New York: Wiley.

Lebeaux, D. (2000). The role of the conscious therapeutic alliance in Davanloo's intensive short-term dynamic psychotherapy. *International Journal of Intensive Short-Term Dynamic Psychotherapy, 14*(1), 39–48.

RECOMMENDED MATERIALS

If you want to view some video presentatons by Patricia Coughlin on forming a therapeutic alliance, visit the URLs below.

Intensive short-term dynamic psychotheapy part 4 (May 5, 2012). http://www.youtube.com/watch?v=eVOgXhq49ek.

Intensive short-term dynamic psychotheapy part 5 (June 27, 2012). http://www.youtube.com/watch?v=DDKEGwXiNsY.

PART TWO

Building Capacity in Fragile Patients

CHAPTER SEVEN

Treating Fragility, Depression, and Somatization

One day a traumatized patient described how her mother tried to smother her to death. Just before she flooded with anxiety, I interrupted and asked her to slow down. When she asked why, I replied that a garden needs only a little rain to grow well. If there is too much rain, the garden's soil can be washed away. She said, "Well, in my previous therapy I think I got eroded."

The spectrum of fragility refers to patients who suffer from anxiety discharged into cognitive/perceptual disruption, low self-observing capacity, and regressive defenses (H. Davanloo, supervision 2002–2004). These patients can tolerate only a little feeling before they flood with anxiety, which shifts out of the striated muscles.

Patients with mild fragility use repressive defenses during the phase of inquiry. Their anxiety rises until it shifts out of the striated muscles into cognitive/perceptual disruption. They blank out, they experience blurry vision and ringing in the ears, but they do not necessarily project. Moderately fragile patients shift to cognitive/perceptual disruption and begin to use regressive defenses such as weepiness, self-attack, and somatization.

Severely fragile patients experience cognitive/perceptual disruption and use regressive defenses even before the session begins. Their self-observing capacity is very low. Most important, they equate others with their projections. The loss of reality testing means the therapist must restructure projections to form a therapeutic alliance.

Fragile patients with depression begin to use regressive defenses such as weepiness, self-attack, and projection of the superego before they shift into cognitive/perceptual disruption. Fragile patients with somatic symptoms often use the defense of somatization. Impulsive patients use projection, verbal discharge, and acting out to get rid of their internal feelings. Severely fragile patients resort to projection, splitting, and projective identification.

Before pursuing a breakthrough to unconscious feelings with fragile patients, the therapist must restructure the pathway of unconscious anxiety discharge, the regressive defenses, and self-observing capacity (Gottwik et al. 1998a, 1998b, 1998c). First, restructure the patient's pathway of anxiety discharge so it goes in the striated muscles at high levels of feeling. Otherwise, the patient will be overwhelmed with physical symptoms, and her brain will not function properly. Then restructure her regressive defenses, which cause panic states, depression, somatization, acting out, and a loss of reality testing. While restructuring anxiety and defenses, build the patient's self-observing capacity. Otherwise, no intrapsychic focus will be possible.

ASSESSMENT OF FRAGILITY: ANXIETY

The symptoms of cognitive/perceptual disruption are blurry vision, tunnel vision, ringing in the ears, falling asleep, thought blocking, genuine inability to think, dissociation, projective identification, passing out, and equating the therapist with a projection. For instance, when inviting feeling, "What is the feeling toward your wife?" the following answers reveal fragility.

Blank stare. [*Cognitive/perceptual disruption.*]

"What did you say?" [*Cognitive/perceptual disruption.*]

"I think you are angry at me." [*Projection: the patient looks frightened, as if he believes you are the same as his projection.*]

A man argues with his wife and stomps out of the house but cannot remember what he said to her. [*Possible cognitive/perceptual disruption.*]

A woman speaks about her sadistic mother, suddenly feels murderous rage, and jumps out of her chair. [*Cognitive/perceptual disruption, loss of orientation to time and place.*]

As a result of cognitive/perceptual disruption, severely fragile patients often cannot give a clear account of recent events, or they present as hypotonic, speaking lifelessly.

Fragile patients often use impulsive masturbation, compulsive sex, or drugs to anesthetize rather than regulate their anxiety. Having outlined the anxiety symptoms, let us look at the fragile patient's self-observing capacity and regressive defenses, and how to treat them.

Principle: *Regulate anxiety as soon as it goes into the smooth muscles or cognitive/perceptual disruption. Do not resume exploration of the feeling until anxiety goes in the striated muscles. (See chapter 2.)*

ASSESSMENT OF FRAGILITY: LOW SELF-OBSERVING ADAPTIVE CAPACITY

Even before arriving at the first session, severely fragile patients may suffer from cognitive/perceptual disruption. They project onto and fear the therapist, whom they equate with their projection. They may get lost on their way to the session or call several times to confirm the appointment hour because anxiety impairs their memory.

The severely fragile patient ignores his anxiety as soon as he observes it. Therefore, he cannot regulate it. Instead, he resorts to regressive defenses such as talking over the therapist, pressured speech, or projection to ignore his anxiety.

He ignores his anxiety, the stimulus, and his feelings. As a result, he cannot see the triangle of conflict causing his difficulties. Projection prevents him from seeing causality correctly. He thinks other people, not his feelings, make him anxious.

We must help the fragile patient: (1) observe and pay attention to his feeling, anxiety, and defense in the moment; (2) distinguish the feeling from anxiety and defense; (3) see causality: a stimulus triggers feelings that evoke anxiety that trigger defenses that cause the presenting problems; (4) tolerate the feeling while anxiety is discharged in the striated muscles; (5) see and let go of regressive defenses; (6) differentiate himself from his defenses; and (7) differentiate the therapist from projections.

Principle: *Strengthen the fragile patient's observing capacities first, so he can regulate his anxiety and let go of his defenses. Do not encourage any pathological regression, transference neurosis, or psychosis.*

ASSESSMENT OF FRAGILITY: REGRESSIVE DEFENSES

Severely fragile patients habitually use splitting, which is the basis of other defenses they use.

Projection: I split off a feeling or desire as "not me" and project it onto you.

Projective identification: I split off a feeling or desire of mine and make you feel it instead (Grotstein 1985; T. Ogden 1982).

Dissociation: I split off a feeling or desire as "not me" and no longer experience it as part of me.

The feelings of severely fragile patients are not repressed out of awareness by defenses, but separated in consciousness by splitting. For instance, a moderately resistant patient may intellectualize and be unaware of anger toward his boss. In contrast, a fragile patient splits anger off from himself. "I never feel anger." Then he projects: "My boss is angry at me." Or he may split off love, so he feels only rage toward a formerly loved one. Then the split-off rage can rise rapidly without other mixed feelings (Reller 2005, quoted by Troendle 2005). A woman claims she feels only rage toward her dead husband but no grief, love, or guilt. She splits off her rage from the complex mixed feelings typical of any human relationship. Exploring her split-off rage is destructive, encouraging splitting and devaluation.

Principle: *Restructure regressive defenses as soon as they occur. Restore reality testing by restructuring projection. Eliminate physical symptoms by restructuring somatization. Increase feeling tolerance by restructuring discharge and acting out. Then explore the feeling again. (See chapter 9.)*

Symptoms Created by Regressive Defenses in Fragile Patients

Chronic projection results in diffuse, free-floating anxiety that covers split-apart or incompatible feelings. For instance, a woman struggling with rage toward a former guru covered it up with idealized love for him. Momentarily aware of her criticism, she blanked out, her anxiety covering her rage. She idealized her guru again but claimed I was critical of him. By projecting her anger onto me, she did not have to experience the conflict between her anger and love for the guru.

Chronic projection can also create social phobias. A patient judges herself for a moment and then imagines others judge her. Now afraid of people whom she believes are judging her, she does not see that she projects. Such patients can lose their reality testing for several hours or days. They do not suffer from social anxiety: fear of other people. They suffer from and *fear the projections they place on others*. Constant projection makes them constantly anxious. Their anxiety is not repressed by defenses or character traits. It is chronically perpetuated by projection, which must be restructured.

Splitting keeps "good" and "bad" feelings separate. To avoid complex emotions, the patient relies on splitting, viewing people as all good or all bad. By doing so, his cognitive functioning and reality testing become impaired, leaving him prone to further panic reactions. As a result, the patient has a partial, shifting, and distorted view of himself and others. He cannot differentiate fantasy from reality.

A patient, angry with the therapist for having been on vacation, splits off the anger as "not me." The second step is projection, attributing her anger to someone else. If she projects her anger onto the therapist, she becomes afraid of him. If she judges herself, she projects, accuses the therapist of judging her, and fears him as if he were a judge. If she splits off her desire to look at her feelings, she projects, accuses him of wanting to look at her feelings, then either fears or defies "his" desire. "What do you want from me?" The patient's defiance serves as an imaginary boundary between herself and her denied desire, now projected onto the therapist. Through projection, she can deny the existence of feelings, judgments, and desires within herself.

Splitting can also create multiple, bizarre, chronic bodily symptoms in somatizing patients. One patient had somatic symptoms in his wrist with no apparent medical cause for many years. Doctors had done so many surgeries that his wrist no longer functioned. He entered the office with a leg in a splint and his arm in a sling due to unspecified pain symptoms, which defied the diagnostic skills of his physicians. Following a breakthrough to his feelings, the patient's symptoms disappeared.

Fragile patients often suffer from dissociative reactions, fugues, and amnesia, leading to conditions such as chronic depersonalization. A woman sought treatment for ADHD. Instead of ADHD, we discovered that frequent experiences of dissociation interfered with her memory, concentration, and thinking. As a result, her academic performance plummeted until she began therapy. Severe suicidality often involves splitting. A woman telephoned me to say she had hundreds of pills in her apartment and intended to kill herself. After I had her hospitalized, she threatened to sue me for having called the police. Her call revealed that she wanted to live. But once I acted on her healthy wish, she could split off and project her wish onto me. Then she raged at me (her projected wish to live) for having saved her life. Perverse behavior and fantasies also involve regressive defenses. A patient claimed his photographs of nude children were not illegal (omnipotent denial). He said he was comfortable with child pornography but was convinced I judged him for it (projection of the superego). Rather than tolerate his own judgment, he projected it onto me.

Impulsivity in fragile patients often results from acting out of rage, split apart from complex feelings. For instance, a man sent a hate-filled letter to his son and proudly read it to me. Until we discussed his letter and feelings in detail, he felt only split-off rage, but no guilt or grief about his acting out. Nor did he see how the acting out punished him by killing off the love his son could have felt for him.

THE GRADED FORMAT: THE TREATMENT FOR THE SPECTRUM OF FRAGILITY

We use the graded format for patients who suffer from regressive defenses, low self-observing capacity, and anxiety discharged into the smooth muscles and cognitive/perceptual disruption (H. Davanloo, supervision 2002–2004; Whittemore 1996). The following conditions require the graded approach:

- Depression with episodes of major clinical depression
- Chronic depression
- Depressed patients with high resistance and functional disturbances, such as migraine headaches, stomachaches, and diarrhea
- Panic disorder
- Severe psychosomatic disorders
- Fragile character structure

- Problems of impulse control
- Highly syntonic character pathology

Use the graded format when you see the following responses or symptoms:

- Anxiety discharged into cognitive/perceptual disruption or the smooth muscles
- Regressive defenses (e.g., self-attack, weepiness, conversion, ego syntonic self-hatred, somatization, projection, and suicidal ideation)
- Low self-observing capacity

When patients suffer from the symptoms listed above, the therapist needs to shift from a purely exploratory approach to one that builds structure within the patient. That is, the therapist must change the pathway of anxiety discharge in the patient's body, build the patient's capacity to bear feelings internally without projecting them onto others, and build the patient's capacity to observe his feelings, anxiety, and defenses internally. To do this, the therapist uses the graded format, a process whereby the therapist gradually invites feeling until the patient's problems with anxiety, regressive defenses, or self-observing capacity arise. The therapist builds the patient's capacity at that moment and then gradually invites feeling again. Step by step the therapist builds the patient's capacities. The following steps outline the sequence of interventions for the graded format:

1. Invite feeling until the patient goes over the threshold for anxiety tolerance or uses a regressive defense.
2. Stop inviting feeling and offer a cognitive summary of what just happened so the patient can see the sequence of feeling, anxiety, and symptom or defense.
3. When anxiety returns to the striated muscles, and the patient's thinking clears up, invite feeling again in a different relationship.

Keep repeating that cycle, building the patient's capacity to bear the feeling at higher levels while anxiety remains in the striated muscles. Even low-level breakthroughs of feeling increase the fragile patient's capacity. The more feeling the patient can bear while anxiety goes into the striated muscles, the fewer symptoms she will have. Eventually, she will be able to bear her feelings while anxiety goes into the striated muscles and without using regressive defenses.

The Threshold of Anxiety Tolerance

When anxiety moves into smooth muscles or cognitive/perceptual disruption, regulate anxiety until it returns to the striated muscles. However, the anxiety of fragile patients decreases slowly because the body must metabolize the released neurohormones. Be patient until anxiety returns to the striated muscles and cognitive functioning improves.

Patients with mild fragility can pay attention to their anxiety quickly with the therapist's help. Moderately fragile patients need help to see and let go of defenses of ignoring, neglecting, and denying anxiety so they can pay attention to and regulate it. (See chapters 2 and 9.) Restructure the projections of severely fragile patients first, before regulating their anxiety. (See chapters 2 and 9.)

Restructuring Anxiety

As soon as anxiety moves out of the striated muscles, invite the patient to pay attention to her anxiety. Then help him see causality: the feeling triggers anxiety symptoms. In this excerpt, notice how the therapist regulates the patient's anxiety, helps him see causality, and then shifts to a different example.

Th: What is the feeling toward your wife for walking out on you?

Pt: I feel like she let me down. [*Defense: confuses the stimulus (what she did) with his feeling toward her.*]

Th: Yes, she did. What is the feeling toward her for doing that?

Pt: Irritated. [*Defense: vagueness.*]

Th: "*Irritated*" is a bit vague. Could we get a clearer picture of this feeling toward her?

Pt: [*Patient's face goes blank and his muscles go slack.*] What did you say?

Th: How is your thinking right now?

Pt: My mind kind of blanked out.

Th: That's a sign of anxiety. Are you aware of feeling anxious right now?

Pt: Yes.

Th: As soon as you mentioned feeling irritated at your wife, you got anxious, and then your mind blanked out. Do you see how that sequence just happened?

Pt: I do now.

Th: It sounds like we should help you with this irritation so you could just feel it and channel it in a healthy manner instead of having your mind conk out on you when you need it the most. [*Point out the therapeutic task.*]

Pt: That's what happens. My mind conks out.

Th: Wouldn't it be nice to be able to feel your irritation without your mind giving out on you?

Pt: [*Sighs.*] Yes, it would.

Th: Can we take a look at another situation where this irritation comes up? [*Move to another example to explore his feelings.*]

Restructuring: The Cognitive Recapitulation

Once the patient's anxiety has crossed the threshold of anxiety tolerance, the therapist will cognitively summarize the process to help the patient regulate her anxiety. In this cognitive recapitulation, the therapist will go through the following steps to regulate the patient's anxiety before exploring feeling again in a different example of the problem.

Step One: Point out the symptom. [*"Do you notice how your mind blanked out?"*]

Step Two: Identify that symptom as a sign of anxiety. [*"That's a sign of anxiety."*]

Step Three: Point out the triangle of conflict and causality. [*"You felt this irritation toward your wife, you got anxious, and then your mind blanked out. Do you see that?"*]

Step Four: Check to see if the symptoms have stopped. If not, repeat steps one through three until the symptoms disappear. [*"How is your thinking now?"*]

Step Five: Explore the feeling in an example with a different person. [*"Would you like to take a look at another example in which this anger comes up for you so we can help your mind no longer conk out on you?"*]

Whenever the patient experiences cognitive/perceptual disruption, cognitively summarize what has just happened until the patient's anxiety returns to the striated muscles. Encourage intellectualization, a more mature defense, when the patient's anxiety becomes too high. Since the patient's anxiety went over the threshold of anxiety tolerance, we assume the patient has gone as far as she can in this example of her problem. Thus, we offer the defense of displacement by encouraging her to explore her feelings in a different relationship so we can continue to build her capacity.

Restructuring Regressive Defenses

Moderately and highly resistant patients use repressive defenses to keep feelings out of their awareness. Fragile patients use regressive defenses, which lead to a regression in reality testing and worsened physical symptoms. Address regressive defenses immediately.

Once anxiety shifts into the smooth muscles, repressive defenses fail to keep anxiety from rising so cognitive/perceptual disruption results. Moderately fragile patients shift to regressive defenses such as weepiness. If anxiety rises even more, regressive defenses such as splitting and projection emerge. Severely fragile patients use regressive defenses such as splitting and projecting at the beginning of the session. They do not see the feeling triggering their anxiety because they either project it onto others or anxiety clouds their awareness. You can ask the obsessive patient to put anxiety to the side and examine his feelings, but not the fragile patient. He cannot differentiate himself from the anxiety that floods him. Address ego deficits and regressive defenses first to form a therapeutic alliance.

Often, the first regressive defense we must address is projection. Everyone uses projection at one time or another (Willick 1985). However, fragile patients lose the ability to differentiate reality from fantasy. When they project their internal judgments, they imagine the therapist is judging them. In response, they fear or become angry with this supposed judge. Help the patient see the difference between the therapist and the projection. Otherwise, the loss of reality testing will create a misalliance.

Gently invite the fragile patient to face his feelings until regressive defenses (projection, primitive idealization, splitting, etc.) emerge.

Then stop inviting the feeling. Restructure regressive defenses. First, help him observe and pay attention to his defenses. Then help him see causality: his defenses create his presenting problems. Only when he sees how his defenses hurt him will he understand the therapeutic task: letting go of his defenses. (See chapter 9.)

Once a fragile patient sees how he has hurt himself, he will feel anxiety, grief, and guilt. If these feelings trigger cognitive/perceptual disruption, he may use splitting and projection to get rid of those feelings. To avoid his internal judgment, he may project this internal judge: "I feel you are criticizing me." Now he fears or is angry toward the supposedly "critical" therapist. He is in conflict between his wish to get well and his defenses, which sabotage his wish. To avoid this conflict within himself, he imagines the conflict is outside himself, that is, between him and the therapist. To address his defense, remind him of a contradiction within himself, which he avoids through splitting.

In the following example, an actively alcoholic man has just told me that he does his best professional work after having drunk one and a half bottles of wine. Notice how I mirror his irrationality so he can see it more readily and reflect on it.

> Th: You say this drinking is a problem, but at the same time you think you do your best work when you have a bottle and half of wine in you. [*Mirror the contradiction he avoids through splitting.*]
>
> Pt: I know you don't think that's a good idea. [*I never said that. He projects his healthy awareness onto me.*]
>
> Th: But in the end only you can know what is good for you, and if drinking a bottle and a half of wine allows you to do your best work, who am I to get in the way? If it works for you, why do anything different? [*Mirror his denial and block the projection of his awareness.*]
>
> Pt: I'm not sure it is working. [*Rise in awareness.*]

Responses to Integrating Splitting and Projections

When the patient takes back what he projected onto others, he will experience a rise of anxiety. He may sigh (anxiety returns to the striated muscles) and reflect on how he has projected. If he experiences transient cognitive/perceptual disruption, point out causality. Cognitively summarize what has just happened until his anxiety returns to the striated muscles. This builds his capacity to bear conflictual feelings without using splitting or projection.

Pt: I feel dizzy.

Th: As soon as you feel your anger, you get anxious, and then you get dizzy. You said he was angry with you, but now we see you are angry with him, and your anger makes you anxious, then you get dizzy. Do you see that? [*Cognitive recapitulation.*]

Pt: I didn't, but I do now.

In response to this work, some patients become more disorganized, project more, and develop a psychotic transference (Kernberg 1975). Unable to tolerate becoming aware of their splitting and projection, they suffer from a psychotic level of character structure. They are candidates for supportive but not exploratory therapy (Kernberg 1975).

Implications for Technique

Since fragile patients have such a low level of anxiety regulation and affect tolerance, we must tailor our techniques to their capacity. In contrast to the ways we can work with low, moderately, and highly resistant patients, fragile patients require a careful stepwise mobilization of their capacities as outlined in the following recommendations.

Do Not Challenge Defenses in Fragile Patients

Premature confrontation triggers a rapid rise of feeling and anxiety, causing cognitive/perceptual disruption, projection, and a misalliance. Instead, rely on inviting the feeling, defense identification, and defense clarification to help the fragile patient let go of his defenses. Confrontation is not usually necessary. He resists because his anxiety is too high or he equates his projections (of anger, will, or superego) with reality. Premature confrontation confirms his projections.

Differentiate Unconscious Feelings from Conscious Defensive Affects

Unconscious feelings emerge in the highly resistant patient when you invite the feeling and point out defenses. Eventually, he feels angry with you, even though he does not understand why. This anger, transferred to you, belongs to an earlier figure in the patient's life.

In contrast, the fragile patient's feelings trigger cognitive/perceptual disruption. Unable to tolerate the anger rising within himself, he projects his internal judgment onto the therapist. Now the patient can be angry with the supposedly judgmental therapist. This anger is not an unconscious feeling toward the therapist. It is a conscious feeling *in reaction to an unconscious* defense, his projection of a judge.

His conscious anger is a defensive affect, a feeling that results from, or functions as, a defense. We do not explore defensive affects, for that would only strengthen the patient's projection. Instead, we deactivate the projection, which generates the defensive affect. (See chapter 10.)

Do Not Explore Feelings Resulting from the Defense of Projection

Fragile patients can tolerate only a small amount of feelings before their anxiety goes into cognitive/perceptual disruption. Then they resort to projection. They may project their will to explore onto the therapist and become defiant, as if the therapist is persecuting them. Or they may project their anger, imagining the therapist is angry with them. In each case, the patient is not angry with you, but at a projection, and cannot distinguish you from it. (See chapter 9.)

Therefore, restructure the fragile patient's projection first so he can experience that aspect of himself without projecting it onto you. Then you can safely explore his feelings toward you.

Th: What are you afraid I will think?

Pt: Oh, I know you aren't angry with me.

Th: Sure. In your head and in my head we both know that, but in your gut, your feelings, something else is going on. Inside, what are you afraid I will think?

Reinforce the patient's reality orientation first, and then label the projection. Distinguish reality from fantasy. Assess his anxiety when you address his splitting and projection.

Pt: I'm a little dizzy right now.

Th: You know I'm not angry with you. At the same time, you have this other reaction. Notice how you get dizzy when we see these two reactions inside you?

Pt: Yeah.

Th: You see I'm not angry, and yet your gut tells you something different. Just noticing that contradiction, you got a little anxious and dizzy. How is your head now?

Pt: It's fine now. I know you're not angry, but it's like my gut was saying you want to attack me.

Remind the patient of the split-apart experiences within himself that triggered his anxiety. In response to the cognitive summary, he calms down, and his reality testing improves.

Differentiate Anxiety Caused by Feelings from Projective Anxiety Caused by Projection

When the patient projects his will to explore on you, he will fear you as a persecuting therapist. His projections create projective anxiety. Clarify projections until the projective anxiety drops. Then assess the remaining anxiety triggered by feeling. (See chapter 2.)

Invite Feeling Gradually to Build Capacity

Carefully dose any questions that evoke feeling. Too rapid a rise of feeling can trigger projections and overwhelming anxiety. Inviting feeling with the fragile patient may consist merely of questions to get a clear picture of the conflict.

Build Observing and Attentive Capacities

Experiencing feelings while flooded with anxiety does not heal the patient. As soon as these patients experience a feeling, encourage them to pause, observe, and then pay attention to the feeling. Once they can do so without cognitive/perceptual disruption, encourage them to feel the feeling more deeply.

Managing Regressive Transferences

In a neurotic transference, the patient can differentiate you from the projection. In a regressive transference, the fragile patient cannot. Help the patient differentiate you from his projection. Then regulate his anxiety and build his self-observing capacity so he can bear his feelings and inner judgment without projecting these onto others. Do not allow regressive transferences to become entrenched. As long as he is afraid of a projection he places on you, he will have a fearful misalliance with a projection, not a therapeutic alliance with you.

To deactivate a projection, invite the patient to talk about what he is afraid of or what he believes you think or want. Be patient and deliberate so he can see his projection. Always show him causality: "This relationship triggers feelings that make you anxious. You deal with your feelings and anxiety by putting this part of yourself onto me." These interventions reestablish a therapeutic alliance and prevent regression. (See "When Anxiety Regulation Does Not Work" in chapter 2 and the section on "Projection" in chapter 9.)

The Emergence of Complex Feelings

An emotionally close therapeutic alliance triggers powerful unconscious feelings toward the therapist based on the patient's past experience. These feelings trigger overwhelming anxiety. In response, the fragile patient can either become overwhelmed with anxiety that covers the mixed feelings or split off some part of her internal experience and deny its existence or project it onto others. Once she denies or projects a part of herself onto someone else, she no longer feels internal conflict. Thus, we can see a layering of conflicts in the fragile patient, as illustrated in table 7.1.

Table 7.1.   The sequence of causality and layers of experience in the fragile patient

Surface to depth	Expression of the conflict	Experience
Layer four	Projective anxiety triggers feedback loop.	"As a result, I am now flooded with projective anxiety."
Layer three	Regressive transference creates projective anxiety.	"I am afraid of you and what you might do to me [regressive transference]."
Layer two	Defenses of splitting and projection create the regressive transference.	"I am not angry at you [denial and splitting], you are angry at me [projection]."
Layer one	Complex feelings from the past trigger anxiety and regressive defenses.	"I feel anger toward you related to the relationship with my father. This triggers anxiety in me, so I use a regressive defense."

Maintaining a Therapeutic Focus with the Fragile Patient

Keep a steady focus on (1) the patient's problem, then (2) his will to explore it, then (3) a specific example of the problem, and then (4) his feeling in that situation. Ask about feelings when he avoids them. Always focus on his experience of the feeling, anxiety, or defense active in this moment. The following are good examples of maintaining a therapeutic focus:

"What is the problem with which you would like me to help you?"

"How is that a problem for you?"

"Is it your will to look at this here with me?"

"Can we take a look at a specific example where this problem occurs?"

"What is the feeling toward him for doing that?"

"How do you feel here with me?"

"How do you experience this feeling right now, physically in your body?

"What is the feeling you have now as you remember that incident?"

The following are poor examples of maintaining a therapeutic focus:

"What is that like?" [*Too vague and invites thinking rather than feelings.*]

"What are your feelings about that?" [*Too vague. Better:* "What is the feeling toward *him for doing that?*"]

"How did you feel about that?" [*Too vague.*]

"What were your thoughts about that?" [*Invites thoughts rather than feelings.*]

"Why did you feel that?" [*Invites the patient to speculate about rather than experience his feelings.*]

"Why do you think he did that?" [*Invites the patient to speculate about others, that is, to project. If we strengthen the defense of projection, we make the patient worse.*]

"Why did you turn the criticism back onto yourself?" [*Invites the patient to speculate about his defense rather than face the feeling that triggers it. The depressed patient will feel criticized and flatten out.*]

"Was there some feeling about that?" [*We always feel. Better:* "What is the feeling toward him for doing that?*"]

"What were the feelings you had when he hit you?" [*The patient always has a feeling, anxiety, and sometimes, a defensive affect. Responses such as "I felt anxious" or "I felt sad" would be accurate but would get you no closer to the reactive anger. That is why the question must focus on the feeling the patient avoids: "What is the feeling toward him for doing that?"*]

Maintain a Focus on the Patient's Will

If the patient is passive or is projecting his will to do therapy upon the therapist, deactivate the projection of will by asking the following questions:

"Is that something you want to look into?"

"Is that a problem with which you want my help?"

"Is that your wish?"

"Is that something you want to examine?"

"Did you come of your free will?"

"Were you brought here against your will?"

"Is this your idea?"

"Would you like to get to the bottom of this problem?"

"Would you like to see the feeling underneath this anxiety?"

"Would you like to find out who you really are underneath this self-attack?"

"Would you like to overcome this problem?"

"Do you want to reveal yourself so you have better information about yourself to help you make better decisions on your behalf?"

Some patients reveal their projection of will by taking a passive stance. Rather than support the patient's passivity by being active, help the patient become active.

"What do you make of it?"

"What do you think we ought to do?"

"Let's see what we will do."

"How do you suggest we proceed?"

"We could face this problem or avoid it. Which way do you think would be most helpful to you?"

The fragile patient's defenses create chaotic, wandering, unfocused sessions that yield little benefit. Patients may relate to you in a disorganized, inattentive, dismissive, and noncollaborative manner. Why? They are unaware of the therapeutic task: to pay continuous, kind, and loving attention to the bodily experience of their feelings and anxiety, and shifts in the degree of our collaboration (defenses). When you inform the fragile patient of this task, find out if he understands and is willing to do it. Knowing what to do in therapy orients the patient, reducing his anxiety.

The following statement is longer than what I usually offer, so you can break it up into parts. But these are all elements of the therapeutic task the patient should know. If the patient is not engaging in the therapeutic task, ask yourself, "Did I tell him what the therapeutic task is?"

Th: You have let me know what you want me to help you with. To do that, we need to pay careful and kind attention to what you are feeling in your body, notice where you feel anxiety in your body, and note any shifts in your feelings and anxiety. We need to become aware of these internal shifts so we can understand what is creating the problems you have. We also need to pay close attention to our collaboration. Sometimes your attention goes out of the room or to another subject. When that happens, both of us need to come back to our focus, and see what derailed you. Whatever distracts you from your goals in here will prevent you from achieving them. We need to pay attention to these shifts so we can achieve your goals. Does that make sense to you?

If the patient hesitates, he may be projecting his will to do therapy onto the therapist. In response, mobilize his will to engage in the therapeutic task.

"Are you willing to pay attention to your feelings, anxiety, and these shifts so we can find out what's going on?"

"Do you want to know what is driving your problems so you could be more in charge of your life?"

"Is this a problem you want to explore so you can get free of it?"

Once the patient has agreed on his goals for therapy, we can help him see when his defenses sabotage his goals.

Th: I notice you are starting to describe your ex-wife's difficulties again. If we talk about her problems instead of yours, will we be helping her or helping you?

Pt: Her.

Th: Could this be an example of how you put her needs before your own?

Pt: Yeah, I guess so. I hadn't thought about it that way.

Th: If we talked about her instead of you, who would get the most attention here, her or you?

Pt: Her.

Th: Does that sound fair to you?

Pt: No, it doesn't.

Th: Shall we focus on her goals or yours right now?

Pt: Mine.

STRUCTURE OF THE SESSION: INVITING FEELINGS IN THE GRADED FORMAT

For severely fragile patients, asking about the feeling toward someone can activate too much anxiety too quickly. Rather than ask, "What is the feeling toward him?" you may use a gradual approach. Start with the past tense. "What did you think?" [*This helps the severely fragile patient become aware of her reaction as a preliminary step toward awareness of feeling. Do not do this with higher capacity patients since it encourages them to intellectualize.*] "What was your reaction to him?" "How did you feel toward him?" Then shift to the present tense. "How do you feel toward him now?" A sequence of interventions like this allows you to build the dosage of feeling the patient faces so her affect tolerance can increase.

Build the patient's capacity by using a graded invitation to feeling.

1. *Invitation to be aware of the stimulus to feeling*: Before inviting feeling, you can ask the patient about the stimulus to feeling. Asking about the stimulus builds the patient's capacity to bear feeling before labeling it.
   - "Something I said caused a response. What did I say?"
   - "I said something about you and your mother. What did I say just now that is triggering you?"
   - "You're right. I said that. What's that like to notice that and let it sit here between us?" [*Build her capacity to tolerate awareness of the stimulus to the feeling.*]

2. *Invitation to be aware of her reaction*: Asking about the patient's reaction allows her to become aware of her feeling before labeling it. This also builds her capacity to tolerate feeling.

- "It sounds like you had a reaction to what I said. Do you notice that?"
- "You are noticing this reaction. Let yourself notice this reaction to what I said. How do you notice this reaction? What is it like to let yourself notice that reaction and sense it?"
- "It sounds like you had a thought about what I said. What is your thought about what I said?"
- "What is your reaction to what I said?"

3. *Invitation to link her reaction to feeling*: After having explored the stimulus and the reaction (an intellectualized way of talking about the feeling), we have built the severely fragile patient's capacity enough that we can ask more directly about feelings.

- "It sounds like there is a feeling that goes with this reaction. What is that feeling?"
- "What do you notice feeling in reaction to what I said?"
- "What do you notice feeling in reaction to my saying you are close to your mother?"
- "What is the feeling toward me?"
- "What do you feel toward me?"

This sequence of interventions allows feeling to rise gradually, building the patient's capacity without running the risk of going over the threshold of anxiety tolerance too rapidly. Use this extremely graded approach only with severely fragile patients. Support the severely fragile patient when feelings overwhelm the capacity for self-observation:

- "Let's step back and notice this feeling and observe it."
- "What's it like to see that feeling and notice it?"
- "Let's pause. When you step back to notice this feeling, what are the sensations in your body that you are aware of?"
- "If you don't dive into the feeling, what happens as you just let your toe be in the water for a minute?"

Help her bear as much feeling as she can while her anxiety remains in the striated muscles and her thinking capacities are intact. Continue building her capacity step by step until she can bear the full force of her feelings.

When to Decrease the Invitation to Explore Feelings

We explore feelings to help build the patient's capacity for affect tolerance and to restructure her pathway of unconscious anxiety discharge, regressive defenses, and self-observing capacity. However, it is also important to know when to shift from exploring feelings to restructuring. Begin restructuring as soon as you see the following responses:

1. Unconscious signaling of anxiety in striated muscles stops. The patient experiences difficulty breathing because the intercostal muscles are not operating automatically. The patient becomes suddenly limp and slumps in the chair, feeling weak. Isolation of affect disappears;
2. Anxiety shifts into smooth muscles producing physical pain;
3. Anxiety shifts into cognitive/perceptual disruption: the patient becomes confused or angry with you, equating you with a projection;
4. Defenses become regressive: splitting, projection, dissociation, and acting out occur in session.

These signs indicate that the patient has gone over the threshold of anxiety tolerance. If you continue to invite feeling, the patient will react with uncontrolled anxiety, rage, depression, somatization, or other forms of severe regression.

Instead of inviting feeling, regulate the patient's anxiety.

1. Stop inviting feeling.
2. Offer a cognitive summary of what just happened.
3. Invite the patient to describe the bodily symptoms of anxiety; ground her in her body.
4. Help the patient intellectualize about other topics.
5. If these anxiety-regulation techniques do not work, address ego deficits and defenses, which perpetuate anxiety (see chapter 2).
6. Invite the patient to explore feelings in another corner of the triangle of person.

As a reminder, the triangle of conflict refers to the feeling, the anxiety it triggers, and the defense used to avoid the feeling. The triangle of person refers to three kinds of relationships where conflict can occur: a relationship in the past, the present, or with the therapist. If the patient explored a relationship with his boss and his anxiety became too high, regulate the anxiety and help him see the triangle of conflict. Then invite the patient to explore feelings again, not with the boss, but in a relationship in the past or with the therapist. Extended invitation to feeling in the transference, confronting defenses, and breakthroughs to unconscious feelings are possible only when the patient's anxiety goes into the striated muscles.

When to Resume Invitation to Feeling

Invite feeling when anxiety goes into the striated muscles or the patient uses isolation of affect. When the patient suggests we explore an issue or asks, "Why does that happen?" he is intellectualizing and ready to explore feeling. The gentle invitation to reveal himself stirs up feelings toward the therapist. A small rise of these feelings often decreases his anxiety, mobilizing his hope, energy, and motivation. Stop exploring feeling when it doesn't help, is too uncomfortable, or triggers anxiety over the threshold for anxiety tolerance.

Restructuring the Pathway of Unconscious Anxiety Discharge

When anxiety goes over the threshold of anxiety tolerance, regulate it. If it does not come down, try the following steps:

1. If the patient floods with anxiety, differentiate the observing ego and the experiencing self (see chapter 2). Encourage him to step back and take a look at the symptoms in the body. Help him *see* rather than *be* the anxiety. Mutual attention to the physical experience of anxiety forms a partnership for regulation. "When alone in the forest at night we are afraid, but holding hands with another person makes our anxiety go away. Anxiety is not overcome by force alone, but through a regulating relationship" where both of us pay close, careful, kind attention to the patient's inner life. This partnership is the necessary precondition for building the patient's capacity (Troendle 2005, my translation).

2. If he does not pay attention to his anxiety so it can get regulated, address the character defenses by which he ignores his anxiety.

3. If he is barely breathing or has jumpy legs, address projections perpetuating the anxiety (see chapter 2).

BREAKTHROUGH TO THE UNCONSCIOUS FOR THE FRAGILE PATIENT

The first breakthrough to feeling will last for a second, involving merely a tear or a flicker of sadness in the face. The patient can experience only a tiny bit of his complex feelings without experiencing cognitive/perceptual disruption. Work for multiple small, unremarkable breakthroughs to build capacity gradually. As you do so, the therapy may look quite cognitive. The first visualizations of the impulse may involve little experience of the rage. The breakthroughs increase isolation of affect and bring anxiety over time into the striated muscles.

Once the murderous rage has emerged, guilt and grief begin to pass. In response, fragile patients may somatize, become depressed, project, or have conversion symptoms. When this occurs, summarize what happened, and modulate the affective experience to bring the patient's anxiety back into the striated muscles.

Premature breakthroughs to the unconscious lead to dissociation, projection, and loss of reality testing (patients with cognitive/perceptual disruption), depression and suicidality (depressed patients), somatization (somatizing patients), panic attacks (panic patients), acting out (impulsive patients), and increased resistance or premature termination. Always assess the pathways of anxiety discharge and defense structure before pursuing a breakthrough to unconscious feelings.

Limits of Self-Observing Capacity in the Fragile Patient

Always assess impulsivity with a fragile patient. A low self-observing capacity means a low affect tolerance, which means low impulse control, which means increased acting out. For instance, a patient was hesitant to explore her rage. When the therapist asked if she had ever lost control of her anger, she replied she had once stabbed someone! Assess the patient's impulse control inside and outside of the session. Signs of poor impulse control include talking over you or interrupting you before you finish a sentence, a raised voice, yelling, or cursing. Other signs include actions to get rid of feeling experience such as moving arms around wildly, standing up, or getting out of the chair to show you something.

In summary, restructure anxiety until it goes into the striated muscles. Help patients see and let go of regressive defenses. Build the patient's self-observing capacity to get a consensus on the triangle of conflict and the therapeutic task. Once you build these capacities, you can help the fragile patient face her feelings as deeply as possible.

DEPRESSION

Depressed patients can face unconscious feelings quickly when anxiety goes into the striated muscles, and they use repressive and tactical defenses. Shift to the graded approach when anxiety goes into smooth muscles or cognitive/perceptual disruption, or regressive defenses occur (Trunnell 1987). Help the patient regulate her anxiety and see the regressive defense. Then show her causality (anger triggers these defenses, which make her depressed). When anxiety returns to the striated muscles and she lets go of the regressive defense, explore feeling again.

In the following excerpt, the therapist must help the patient first see the defense, and then its price and function. Until the patient sees those three things, she will not be able to let go of the defense to face the underlying feelings.

> *Th:* We see you feel this anger toward your boss, and as we explored this anger toward your boss, do you notice how the anger goes back onto you? [*Defense: self-attack.*]
>
> *Pt:* But maybe I really am a terrible employee. [*Defense: self-attack.*]
>
> *Th:* Notice how you are describing yourself right now? A moment ago, you were feeling angry with your boss [*point out the defense*], and then the next minute, do you see how the telescope shifts from him back onto you? How you turn the focus onto you rather than let it stay on him a minute longer?
>
> *Pt:* I see what you mean now.

Th: When you shift this focus back onto yourself, could that be a way of protecting him in this room from your anger? [*Clarify the function of the defense.*]

Pt: Maybe.

Th: We see you feel this anger toward your boss. As we explored this anger toward your boss, do you notice how your body suddenly went weak on you? [*Defense: conversion.*] Notice how you dropped your power there?

Pt: I do feel real tired now.

Th: You felt this anger toward him. It went back onto you. Then you got tired. [*Point out causality.*] Would you be willing to power back up so we could take a look at your power? [*Encourage the patient to turn against the defense and face her feeling instead.*]

The patient must let go of defenses, which turn rage on the self. Otherwise, each time the patient focuses on her rage, she will turn it against herself, becoming more depressed and symptomatic. We use the graded format to keep the fragile patient from flooding with anxiety and the depressed patient from becoming overwhelmed by depression caused by regressive defenses. Build her capacity to tolerate anger without turning it on herself. At the slightest sign of a depression-causing defense, intervene immediately to help her see and let go of it.

Depressed patients usually have trouble differentiating feeling from anxiety and feeling from defense. Suppose the therapist asks, "What is the feeling toward him for slapping you?"

Pt: I feel anxious. [*Inability to differentiate feeling from anxiety.*]

Th: That's your anxiety. What is the feeling toward him that makes you anxious?

Pt: I feel shut down. [*Inability to differentiate feeling from defense.*]

Th: Shutting down is not your feeling. [*Differentiate defense from feeling.*] Shutting down is how you deal with your feeling. You shut down. If you don't shut down on your feeling, what is the feeling toward him for slapping you? [*Invite the patient to turn against her defense and face her feeling.*]

Pt: [*Weepiness.*] Angry. I wish I had him back. [*Regressive defense: weepiness.*]

Th: Tears are not anger, are they? [*Differentiate defense from feeling.*] Notice how the tears come in to cover your anger? [*Clarify the function of the defense.*] If we don't cover your anger with tears and longing, can we take a look at the anger underneath? [*Invite the patient to turn against the defense and face her feeling.*]

Carefully differentiate the patient's feeling from defenses. Otherwise, each time the therapist asks about feeling, the patient will respond with a defense, becoming more depressed and symptomatic.

Each time you invite a feeling, the depressed patient will either become anxious or use a defense that causes depression. Regulate the anxiety, restructure the regressive defense, or build self-observing capacity. Then invite the feeling again. Repeat until the patient can bear the full extent of her feelings without anxiety going into the smooth muscles or cognitive/perceptual disruption, or using regressive defenses.

Invite the Feeling

Continue inviting the feeling and building capacity until the patient can bear the full extent of her feeling without getting depressed. Then a breakthrough to the unconscious will be possible. Imagine turning the hose on in your front yard only to discover it has so many leaks that water cannot get to the nozzle. So you turn the water on briefly, see a leak, and turn off the faucet. You patch the hose and then turn on the water again to find the next leak. You keep turning the faucet on and off to identify and patch leaks one by one. Eventually, it is safe to turn the water on all the way because it will get to the end of the hose. Inviting feeling and building capacity are the two basic interventions to use with depressed patients.

Depressed patients can have a moderately resistant, highly resistant, fragile, or borderline level of character pathology. So assess the patient's capacities to develop a treatment plan that addresses the patient's specific problems of anxiety regulation, regressive defenses, and self-observing capacity. In all cases of depression, regulate anxiety, build self-observing capacity, address regressive defenses, and help the patient disidentify with defenses.

The Graded Format: An Example

In the following vignette, a severely depressed woman has just described an incident when her boyfriend insulted her in front of her friends. Without even labeling her feeling, she begins to cry. Notice how the therapist must help the patient see the regressive defense of weepiness and let go of it before her anger can rise.

Th: As we step back for a moment, it sounds like you have a reaction to him for talking that way. [*Graded inviting of feeling.*]

Pt: I just feel bad.

Th: A bad thing happened. What is your reaction to that? [*Differentiate the stimulus (what he did) from her feeling.*]

Pt: I didn't like it.

Th: Of course, what's your thought about that? [*Invite her to describe her thought about the stimulus before we ask about her feeling.*]

Pt: [*Weepiness. Tears in her eyes.*]

Th: Notice how these tears come in now as soon as we look at your thought? Notice how these tears come in to wash away your thought? [*Point out causality.*] Let's take a few breaths to firm up and take a look at this thought.

Pt: I think he shouldn't have done it. [*Weepiness: tears in her eyes.*]

Th: So tears come in to wash away this thought. [*Clarify the function of the tears as defense.*] Let's see if we can put the tears to the side so we can look at your thought. [*Invite her to turn against the defense.*] This thought, "He shouldn't have done it," is that an approving thought or a critical thought?

Pt: A critical thought.

Th: What do you notice sensing in your body as you let this critical thought be in your mind?

Pt: I feel tightness in my chest.

Th: Just notice that sensation in your body as you let yourself hold a critical thought. How would you label that sensation?

Pt: Irritated. [*In a highly resistant patient, this is a tactical defense: a cover word. In a severely depressed patient, this is a successive approximation toward anger, so we support it.*]

Th: You feel irritated toward him. What do you find irritating? [*Asking her to elaborate on the stimulus evokes feeling gradually, making it easier for her to sense and label it correctly.*]

Pt: It irritates me that he doesn't listen to me and that he told me one thing and did another.

Th: How do you experience that irritation in your body? [*Invite the feeling.*]

Pt: [*Her hands suddenly rise as if to strangle someone and then drop.*] I don't know.

Th: I notice something in your hands there. [*I mimic what her hands did.*] What do you notice?

Pt: [*Smiles.*] I don't know. I feel irritated.

Th: How do you experience that irritation? [*Invite the feeling.*]

Pt: Anger?

In contrast to patients with a higher capacity, we might ask the depressed patient to intellectualize about her irritation or the stimulus to build her capacity to bear her feeling. Always work at the highest level of feeling she can tolerate to build her capacity. When you work beneath her capacity, no new learning will take place.

Depressed patients who face rage in the session may punish themselves afterward, becoming depressed. To prevent destructive acting out after sessions (1) turn the patient against self-attack before exploring rage; (2) clarify causality; and (3) predict self-attack to prevent relapse.

Th: We have learned today that one way you deal with your anger is that you turn it on yourself in the form of self-criticism. And we have learned that another way you deal with your anger is to dismiss it as if your feelings are no big deal. And we have noticed that turning the anger onto yourself and dismissing your feelings make you depressed. Given that you have faced a lot of rage today, how might you be tempted to punish yourself after the session? [*Invite the patient to think about her defenses in advance to prevent relapse.*]

Pt: In the past I would binge on food, or I would call a guy up to have sex.

Th: And how would we understand that now?

Pt: That would be a way to punish myself.

Th: For what?

Pt: For this rage I just felt toward my dad? But why?

Th: You just said he called you a whore. If you go out and have sex, it's as if you say, "I would rather pretend to be a whore like you said, Dad, rather than feel this rage toward you."

Pt: Oh my God! That is so true. I would be doing what he said I was.

Th: That would be a way to punish yourself rather than feel the rage toward him. If you don't punish yourself now, how would you like to handle your anger instead this week?

Pt: I have to stop treating myself like a whore and face my rage toward my dad instead.

To prevent relapse, help the patient anticipate and plan for a relapse, that is, the temptation to use a regressive defense. If the patient does not see and turn against the defense of self-attack, she will attack herself after the session and become more depressed. For instance, a therapist explored a patient's anger toward her mother but did not help her see and let go of her self-attack. After the session, the patient cut herself.

As soon as the patient turns rage against herself, pause, and stop the self-attack. Help her see the defense, then explore anger again. Repeat this sequence until she can experience her rage deeply without anxiety and defenses.

Depressed patients almost always use character defenses, that is, they treat themselves as others did in the past. For instance, a young woman dismissed herself just as her molesting father did. Rather than feel rage toward him, she identified with him and turned the rage onto herself through self-dismissal. By dismissing herself, she enacted her identification with her dismissive father. (See chapter 12.)

As soon as the patient uses a character defense, help her see and let go of the identification with the abuser so she can face her rage toward him instead. She must let go of this defense before rage will be easily available.

Th: What is the feeling toward him for raping you?

Pt: I hate him. [*Defense: said with a detached voice.*]

Th: You say that with a detached voice. Do you notice that? [*Defense identification.*]

Pt: It's behind me. [*Character defense: dismissing herself and her feelings as her molesting father did to her.*]

Th: You say the rape is behind you. You say the molestation of a thirteen-year-old girl is behind you. You say your feelings are behind you. Do you notice how you ignore, dismiss, and detach from your feelings? [*Point out the character defense. A molester ignores, dismisses, and detaches from the feelings of his daughter.*]

Pt: I didn't do it on purpose.

Th: No, of course, you didn't do it on purpose, but do you see how you ignore, dismiss, and detach from your feelings?

Pt: Yes.

Th: Is that how you want to treat your feelings? Do you want to imitate your father who ignored, dismissed, and detached from your feelings? [*Help her turn against the defense of identification.*]

Pt: I sure don't want to imitate him!

Th: If we don't ignore your feelings or detach from them, can we have an honest look at your feeling toward your father for robbing you of your innocence? [*Invite the patient to let go of the defense and face her underlying feelings.*]

If the patient continues to use character defenses, point them out. Often, these patients will defend the people who abused them.

Pt: He had a bad childhood.

Th: Do you notice how you take his side instead of your own?

Or these patients judge themselves.

Pt: Maybe I was just a slut.

Th: Would you like to look at yourself through the eyes of his judgment or through the lens of self-compassion?

Or these patients minimize what the abuser did, an identification with the abuser.

Pt: It wasn't that bad.

Th: Is that what you felt when he was raping you, or is that what he said afterward?

Address each character defense until the patient can feel the full extent of her rage toward the abuser without turning it against herself. When these defenses are not addressed, the therapy remains stuck, or the patient attacks herself after exploring her rage.

Another problem can occur if the therapist does not summarize what the patient learned in the session. If the patient does not see her defense in the moment or its price, she will keep using it and become depressed after the session.

Th: As we faced this rage you feel toward your father, you dealt with it by turning it on yourself. You are angry with him. Then we saw how you got angry with yourself. You criticized him. Then you began to criticize yourself. You judged his behavior. Then you began to judge yourself. Do you see that sequence now as we look back on it?

Pt: Yes, I do now. I just didn't see it before.

Th: That's why we need to take care to see what has been going on outside your awareness. Once you can see this self-attack, you can make a different choice about how to deal with your feelings.

Pt: That makes sense.

Th: Then we saw how this self-attack, self-criticism, and self-judgment started to make you depressed here in the session. Do you see that too?

Pt: Now I do.

Th: Based on what we've learned today, how might you deal with your anger toward your father before I see you next time?

Pt: If the past is any indication, I might attack myself again.

Th: When that happens, what would be the healthy alternative to self-attack?

Pt: To just feel the rage toward my father?

Th: What do you think?

At the end of the session, summarize what you have learned and make sure the patient sees her regressive defenses, their price, and causality: "You punish yourself for the rage you feel toward your father. When you do that, you abuse yourself as he did rather than feel the rage where it belongs." This understanding helps the patient let go of her self-destructive defenses, preventing relapse.

Hopelessness

Depressed patients' hopelessness can be the result of a defense, a realistic assessment of a situation for which there is no hope, a transference resistance in which the therapist is expected to hold the hope for the relationship, or the result of not seeing causality.

In the following example, the patient's hopelessness is due to a defense: he engages in a hopeless strategy of denying reality. His girlfriend ended their relationship, but rather than face his loss, he contacts her repeatedly. Each time, she angrily tells him to leave her alone. The issue is not that the relationship is hopeless. The patient's strategy of denial is hopeless. The patient feels rage toward the woman who dumped him, but rather than face his rage and loss, he calls her up, inviting her to punish him. He complains about how badly she treats him. All the while, he ignores how he perpetuates his suffering by calling her repeatedly.

In another example, a patient's hopelessness about her illness is a realistic assessment. The patient has stage four cancer, which has metastasized and is not responding to treatment. She faces a hopeless prognosis. Her hopelessness is a realistic assessment of a medical condition over which she has no control. The therapist can help her grieve the loss, prepare for death, say goodbye to loved ones, and find meaning in her life.

Another patient declares that therapy is hopeless, asking the therapist to prove to him why he should have hope. This is a transference resistance. [Metacommunication: "I will take a passive/hopeless position. Breathe life into me."]

Defenses can create a hopeless situation. For instance, a woman is angry with colleagues whom she accuses of using her. They made unreasonable requests of her. Rather than face her anger, she covers it up by giving them what they ask (*reaction formation*) and overextending herself (*self-punishment*).

When the therapist asked about this pattern, the patient said she tried to trust everyone. This is denial. Not all people can or should be trusted. After many betrayals she said she felt hopeless about life. Her life was not hopeless. Trusting untrustworthy people and hoping they will become trustworthy is hopeless. Channeling anger into self-punishment creates a hopeless result. Giving others what they want (while hoping they will give you what you want) is a hopeless venture. When she could see that her defenses created a hopeless situation, she could channel her anger more adaptively.

Principle: *Assess whether the patient's hopelessness is a rational response to a loss in reality or an irrational result of her defenses.*

In summary, depressed patients tolerate a low level of feeling before they use regressive defenses that cause depression, such as turning on the self, identifying with the object of one's anger, conversion, weepiness, cutting, and suicidal ideation. As soon as a patient uses a regressive defense, stop exploring feeling. Offer a cognitive summary of what just happened so he can see the defense, let go of it, and stop the slide into depression in the moment. Once he can see the defense and turn against it, invite him to face the feeling. Each time, he will be able to face increasing amounts of feeling until he can bear the full amount of his rage without any self-attack.

SOMATIZATION

Somatization refers to conditions where patients suffer from physical symptoms without any identifiable medical cause. Understanding of this condition has been hampered by three main problems. First, some have assumed that patients are malingering when they suffer from genuine, undiagnosed medical conditions. Second, therapists have failed to recognize the precise relationships between bodily symptoms and the activation of the somatic and autonomic nervous systems. Third, clinicians have failed to differentiate bodily symptoms resulting from anxiety from those resulting from the defense of somatization.

We will assume the patient has received a thorough evaluation, which has found no medical cause for the symptoms. We will show the relations between bodily symptoms and the somatic and autonomic nervous systems. We will also show how to differentiate psychogenic from medically caused symptoms. Finally, we will discuss how to treat symptoms resulting from the defense of somatization. These contributions have allowed this treatment model to treat psychosomatic problems effectively in a short-term therapy format (Abbass 2005, 2007; Abbass et al. 2008; Abbass et al. 2009; Frederickson 2005).

Patients who suffer from somatization disorder incur nine times the health care expenses of the average American (Smith, Monson, and Ray 1986). They report being bedridden for two to seven days per month (Katon et al. 1991). In one longitudinal study (Coryell and Norten 1981), only 31 percent recovered after fifteen years. They suffer side effects from medication and stop using it. There is no effective pharmacological treatment for somatizing disorders.

The diagnosis of somatization dates from the ancient Egyptians (see Woolfolk and Allen 2007, for a brief review). The term *somatization* first appears in the work of Stekel (1924, 341), referring to "the conversion of psychological states into physical symptoms." S. Freud and Breuer (1883–1895/1974) thought that somatic symptoms resulted from traumatic experiences hidden from consciousness. Freud believed that once patients felt these unexpressed emotions, symptoms would disappear. Later, F. Alexander (1950) differentiated between psychosomatic symptoms that symbolically communicate or represent a psychological conflict and those resulting from emotional arousal.

Symptoms Due to Unconscious Discharge of Anxiety

There are three patterns of somatic symptoms that result from anxiety discharged through the somatic and autonomic nervous systems:

- *Striated muscle tension:* Unconscious anxiety manifests in symptoms of hand clenching, sighing, and hyperventilation. The chronic tensing of the skeletal muscles can result in tension headaches (due to muscle tension around the c1, c2, and c3 vertebrae), and pain in the abdominal wall, chest, back, joints, limbs, and extremities (Abbass et al. 2008). Chronic tensing of the pelvic muscles results in painful sensations, painful menstruation, painful intercourse, menstrual irregularity, and is a cause for vulvadynia. Muscle tension can lead to a lump in the throat and difficulties in swallowing. Psychosomatic fits or convulsions result when the patient experiences an unconscious impulse combined with tension and unconsciously holds back the impulse.

- *Excessive sympathetic nervous system activation:* Symptoms include urinary retention, constipation, dry eyes, and sensitivity to light due to dilated pupils. Fainting, loss of consciousness, dizziness, and heart palpitations can occur in response to excessive heart rate and hyperventilation.

- *Excessive parasympathetic nervous system activation:* Localized weakness results from the loss of striated tension. The patient, weak and unsteady on his feet ("jelly legs"), has trouble walking. Deafness, ringing in the ears, blindness, blurry vision, and tunnel vision are symptoms of cognitive/perceptual disruption. Fainting, loss of consciousness, memory loss, amnesia, or dizziness can occur due to hypoperfusion in the brain. Anesthesia or loss of sensation can also occur. Nausea, vomiting, diarrhea, abdominal bloating, and gas result from anxiety discharged into the gastrointestinal tract. These forms of dysfunction can cause food intolerances. Abdominal pain can result from the activation of the somatic nervous system (tension in the abdominal wall) or parasympathetic nervous system (nausea in the stomach). Always differentiate these two pathways of anxiety discharge when assessing abdominal pain. Migraine headaches take several forms, some of which can be triggered by the discharge of anxiety into the parasympathetic nervous system. Parasympathetic activation will cause symptoms of frequent and sudden urges to urinate or defecate, difficulty breathing, and sick tiredness. When asked, the patient will report that she doesn't feel a healthy tired sensation like after exercise but rather a sick tired sensation (J. Ten Have de Labije, personal communication).

The chronic use of repressive defenses is associated with compromised immune system function (Jamner, Schwartz, and Leigh 1988), elevated blood pressure (King et al. 1990), pain severity for chronic pain patients (Deschields et al. 1995), and irritable bowel symptoms (Toner et al. 1992). Elevated sympathetic and parasympathetic discharge decreases immune function (Schulkin 2004). Increased somatic nervous activation increases pain sensitivity. Elevated sympathetic activation raises blood pressure. Elevated parasympathetic activation causes irritable bowel symptoms. Chronically elevated anxiety leads to functional symptoms as well as dysfunction in multiple organ systems (Schulkin 2004). Many patients who assume they have a chronic medical condition suffer from chronically dysregulated anxiety.

Patients who use repressive defenses discharge their anxiety primarily in the somatic and sympathetic nervous systems. They suffer from tension headaches, back pain, and elevated blood pressure. Patients who use repressive and some regressive defenses discharge their anxiety into the somatic and parasympathetic nervous systems. They suffer from gastrointestinal complaints, irritable bowel syndrome, and migraine headaches. Patients who use regressive defenses and whose anxiety is discharged into cognitive/perceptual disruption suffer from chronic fatigue, dizziness, and problems in walking. They complain of negative feelings, most of which result from regressive defenses such as externalization and projection.

We can reduce anxiety symptoms through regulating anxiety and inviting the underlying feeling. We can reduce somatizing symptoms by helping the patient see and let go of his defense and then face his feelings. The symptoms of classical somatization can be identified through two clues. First, they often do not look like anxiety symptoms discharged through the somatic and autonomic nervous systems. Second, they symbolically express the identification with the body of the person toward whom the patient experiences murderous rage.

Symptoms Due to Expression of Unconscious Conflict

Up to this point we have looked at somatic symptoms that result from the discharge of anxiety through the somatic and autonomic nervous systems. However, somatic symptoms can also occur due to the defense of somatization—identifying with the body of the person toward whom the patient feels rage. The following symptom pictures are consistent with the defense of somatization.

Paralysis: Feeling rage toward the police, the patient becomes paralyzed.

Anesthesia: Anesthesia can also result from an unconscious identification. For instance, a patient reports no feeling in his arms. Once he feels his murderous rage toward his ex-wife, in his fantasy he imagines chopping her arms off. Afterwards he regains sensation in his arms, and the therapist points out the identification with the murdered figure. The patient identified with the wife as a punishment for feeling rage toward her.

Abdominal pain: The patient imagines being angry with someone and then reports a pain in his stomach. Later he imagines hitting his father in the stomach. He wanted to hit his father but identified with him and took the blow to the stomach himself.

Headache: A headache can also express a psychological conflict. A patient expresses rage toward her ex-fiancé and then gets a headache. Later she imagines murdering him by hitting him on the head with a shovel. At that moment, her headache disappears. When a headache symptom does not fit the form for a tension or migraine headache, consider the possibility of the defense of somatization. The patient reports unusual symptoms: "I feel like something has cut straight through my head." "I feel this stabbing pain like a knife just went into the back of my head."

Principle: *If somatic symptoms result from anxiety in the striated muscles, explore the feeling and address defenses. When somatic symptoms result from anxiety in the smooth muscles or cognitive/ perceptual disruption, use the graded format and restructure the pathway of anxiety discharge, and then explore the feeling. When somatic symptoms result from the defense of somatization, restructure that defense, and then explore the feeling (table 7.2).*

Table 7.2   How to eliminate somatic symptoms in patients

Cause of somatic symptoms	*Anxiety in the striated muscles*	*Anxiety in the smooth muscles or cognitive/ perceptual disruption*	*Defense of somatization*
Treatment	Invite feeling until breakthrough occurs. Then striated symptoms will cease.	Restructure the pathway of anxiety discharge, and then invite feeling.	Restructure the defense of somatization, and then invite feeling.

How to Assess Whether a Somatic Symptom Is Psychogenic or Medically Caused

Current self-report measures cannot differentiate organic from functional symptoms. In the past, if clinicians found no medical cause for a symptom, they assumed it had a psychological cause. Rather than assume, we can assess.

Watch the patient's body to observe where anxiety is discharged. If somatic symptoms rise and fall when feelings rise and fall, the symptoms are psychosomatic. They are caused by anxiety or the defense of somatization. If the symptoms do not shift in response to anxiety and feeling, psychological causes do not play a role in symptom creation. Most patients with somatic symptoms in a therapist's office suffer from symptoms resulting from unconscious anxiety (Abbass 2005, 2007; Abbass et al. 2008) or the defense of somatization.

The following excerpt illustrates how somatic symptoms emerge in response to a rise of unconscious feeling and anxiety in the body.

Vignette One: Migraine Headache

The patient's anxiety went into her striated and smooth muscles for the first few minutes of the initial session (she felt sick to her stomach). After an hour into the session, we explore anger toward a past boyfriend who abused her daughter.

Th: What is the feeling toward him?

Pt: I should have been there. [*Defense: self-blame.*]

Th: But the feeling toward him?

Pt: [*Puts hand on her head.*]

Th: What is happening?

Pt: I'm getting a migraine headache.

Th: Notice how this feeling comes up toward your boyfriend, and you start to get a headache? [*Point out causality.*]

Pt: I get headaches a lot when there's stress.

Th: And right now we see the stress is this feeling toward your boyfriend, right?

Pt: Nods.

Th: And then when you feel this anger, notice how you get a headache instead?

Vignette Two: Cognitive/Perceptual Disruption

In this vignette, the patient quickly experiences somatic symptoms due to cognitive/perceptual disruption.

Th: You had invested all this time developing the school program. You put several years of your life into this and then all of a sudden they kicked you out. What is the feeling toward them for doing that to you?

Pt: [*Patient's eyes go blank.*]

Th: What is happening?

Pt: I feel really dizzy.

Th: That's a sign of anxiety. Notice when we look at your feeling that you get anxious and dizzy? [*Point out causality.*]

Pt: I don't feel anxious, just dizzy.

Th: Do you notice how you get dizzy as soon as you look at the feeling toward these people?

Pt: I do now. I don't know what it means.

Th: Let's find out. If it happens again, we'll know that you get dizzy when you have a feeling. Are you aware of your vision being blurry right now?

Pt: Yes.

Th: That's another sign of anxiety.

Pt: I must be anxious a lot because I always get blurry vision.

Explore the patient's difficulties until anxiety goes into the smooth muscles or cognitive/perceptual disruption. Then help her see causality: feeling triggers anxiety symptoms. In the here and now, the therapist and patient can assess the psychological significance of the patient's symptoms. If the patient disagrees, the therapist can say, "You may be right. I may be wrong. Let's just flag this, and, if it happens again, we'll find out together if this is a pattern." With each rise of feeling, the patient's symptoms rise again. Show causality so she can recognize how feeling triggers her bodily symptoms. This mobilizes her to face her feelings.

Patients who somatize as an expression of psychological conflict need a different approach. The defense of somatization often involves rage toward someone who hurt the patient. In response to a rise of feeling, the patient identifies with the body of the person toward whom she feels rage. A patient wants to cut off her father's arms and then feels as if her arms are not attached to her body. The patient unconsciously identifies with the body of the person she wanted to attack. The conscious painful symptom in her body corresponds to the unconscious attack on the other person's body. The patient unconsciously protects the other person by turning the attack on her own body. Help her face this rage as deeply as possible without somatizing so she can access the unconscious mixed feelings toward the hated figure. By experiencing those feelings, she will no longer need to use the defense of somatization.

Somatization can also be a defense against loss. A woman whose mother died of lung cancer coughed whenever she began to grieve. By "becoming" her mother through her health problem, she could avoid saying goodbye.

To assess somatization, notice causality. In what context does the symptom occur? For instance, a woman felt nauseous and dizzy around dinnertime. Medical assessment found nothing unusual. When asked what happened at dinner, she said nothing happened. On further inquiry, however, she reported that just before dinner her angry husband came home and verbally abused her. One man reported constant tension headaches. His wife raged at him constantly. When she left home to go on a trip, his headaches stopped.

Principle: *Ask what the feeling is toward the other person and observe feelings, anxiety, and defense. If somatization is an issue, somatic symptoms will rise when feelings rise in the session.*

Vignette One: The Defense of Somatization

The patient is feeling murderous rage toward his physically abusive father. Notice how the patient identifies with the object of his rage and suffers a somatic symptom as a result.

Th: How does this rage go out onto him?

Pt: I punch him right in the face just like he used to do to me.

Th: Mhmm. And then?

Pt: I hit him again, and he falls over.

Th: Mhmm.

Pt: And then I see an ax, and I pick it up and chop him right down the middle of his skull.

Th: Mhmm, and what does he look like now?

Pt: Ooof. I've really got a splitting headache right now. [*Defense: somatization.*]

Th: Isn't that interesting? You just chopped him in the head, but who gets the headache? [*Point out causality.*]

Pt: What?

Th: You just chopped him in the head, but who got the headache?

Pt: I did.

Th: See how you chopped him in the head, but then you turn the rage onto your head instead so it's your head that's split instead of his? [*Point out the defense of somatization.*]

Pt: Oh, wow! I didn't see that.

Th: If we don't put the rage on your head, how else does this rage need to go out onto him? [*Invite him to turn against the defense and face his feeling instead.*]

Pt: I need to finish chopping him up.

Th: How do you picture that?

Vignette Two: The Defense of Somatization

The patient struggles with rage toward her son who has jeopardized his career through an illegal act, which has drawn the attention of the police. Again, we see someone who identifies with the object of her rage and suffers a somatic symptom as a result.

Th: What is the feeling toward him for doing that?

Pt: I'm angry.

Th: How do you experience that anger physically in your body?

Pt: I just feel limp. It's as if I cannot move my arms or legs. I'm so tired. [*Defense: somatization.*]

Th: But tired is not anger, is it? [*Differentiate the defense from her feeling.*]

Pt: No.

Th: Tired is a way to cover your anger. [*Clarify the function of the defense.*] If we don't cover your anger with tired, how do you experience this anger toward him?

I continue focusing on her anger and addressing her defenses until she describes her rageful impulse.

Th: And how does this rage go out onto him?

Pt: I don't know why, but I want to take an ax to him and chop his arms and legs off so he can't do anything wrong again.

Th: And then?

Pt: I feel so tired all of a sudden. It's like I can't move. [*Defense: somatization.*]

Th: Isn't that interesting? As soon as you chop off his arms and legs so he can't move, who can't move now? [*Point out the defense of somatization.*]

Pt: I can't move.

Th: As soon as you chop off his hands and arms, you chop off your own, and you become the chopped-up body, the exhausted body, and the body that can't move. You put all the rage onto your body instead of feeling it toward him. Do you see what I mean?

Pt: [*She sits up in the chair.*]

Th: It's important we face this rage toward him in fantasy because you have been chopping yourself up in reality, becoming the dead woman. If you don't turn the rage onto your body, how does the rest of your rage want to go out on him?

Pt: [*Her fists rise.*] I want to hit him for everything he did to me.

Th: How do you picture that in your mind?

After the breakthrough to her rage, I pointed out how she became the woman without arms and legs as soon as she said she felt angry with her son. Help the patient see the links between her conscious symptom and unconscious rage, guilt, and grief so she can overcome her defense of somatization.

Tension Headaches

Although headaches are usually listed as a form of somatization, we must differentiate three different types according to their cause: anxiety, somatization, and medical conditions.

Tension headaches result from anxiety discharged into the somatic nervous system, creating tension affecting the c1, c2, or c3 vertebrae. These patients have difficulty moving the head and neck. When anxious, they become tense in the neck, face, scalp, and jaw, and they feel pressure on the forehead, the neck, the sides of the head, or a tightening around the head. They are often sensitive to light, due to pupils dilated by the sympathetic nervous system.

Tension headaches result from anxiety, not the defense of somatization. Help the patient experience his rage; his anxiety will drop, and the headache will disappear. Always ask about the event that occurred just before the headache. Explore the feelings in the conflictual situation. As you do so, the patient will become tense. If a tension headache occurs during the session, point out causality and invite feeling until feelings come out and the patient's headache stops.

Migraine Headaches

Many migraine headaches are purely medical in origin. We will explore only those that arise in response to emotional triggers. Migraine headaches are vascular headaches. In the brain, blood vessels traveling within the meninges start to throb with pain when their nerve fibers are activated. The blood vessels narrow, decreasing the flow of blood and oxygen to the brain. To compensate, other blood vessels open wider, increasing blood flow.

Patients who suffer from smooth muscle discharge of unconscious anxiety often have migraines in response to a rise of feeling. As soon as a migraine appears, summarize the conflict in the here and now. "You are feeling angry toward your boss, and this makes you anxious. Is there anywhere else that you notice this anxiety in your body? Can you describe those sensations in your body?" Keep the patient's attention on anxiety until the migraine disappears. Then point out causality. "You were feeling anger toward your boss. The anger made you anxious, and the anxiety triggered the migraine. Shall we take another look at this anger? Wouldn't it be nice just to feel your anger so you wouldn't have to have a headache instead? How else do you experience this anger toward your boss?"

Always regulate anxiety and point out causality at the slightest sign of a migraine so it does not worsen. Gentle invitation to the feeling raises the amount of feeling and anxiety the patient can tolerate before anxiety shifts into the smooth muscles. Boost the patient's capacity for affect tolerance to reduce the frequency of migraines.

Explore feelings in the session to differentiate psychogenic from medically caused migraines. Psychogenic migraines appear in response to a rise of feeling and anxiety. In any case, patients suffering from migraines should be thoroughly evaluated by a medical professional.

Somatization Headaches

These headaches usually occur as soon as the patient's rage or impulse rises. Point out how she experienced her rage just before the headache. When we see the impulse toward the head of the other person, make the cognitive link.

> *Th:* You wanted to chop him in the head, but then you gave yourself this splitting headache instead. Do you see how you turned the rage toward him onto your head instead?

Principle: *Point out how her guilt over her rage led her to identify with the body of the person she wanted to attack. This cognitive summary helps her see causality and turns her against the defense of somatization.*

SUMMARY

Psychosomatic symptoms result from the discharge of anxiety in the body or the defense of somatization. To assess a symptom, explore a conflictual situation and ask about the patient's feeling. When symptoms increase in response to a rise of anxiety, they are psychogenic. If no change occurs in response to a rise of feeling and anxiety, physical symptoms are most likely medically caused.

Principle: *Ask about feelings until the patient starts to have a somatic symptom. Pause and summarize the triangle of conflict so the patient can see causality. This intervention allows anxiety to drop and symptoms to decrease.*

Th: You were feeling angry toward your boss. Then you became anxious and got sick to your stomach. So we see a link between feeling angry and getting anxious in your stomach. Do you see that too?

When somatic symptoms result from the defense of somatization, invite feeling until the defense of somatization occurs. Immediately restructure the defense. Otherwise, more severe symptoms will result. Once the patient sees the defense and the symptoms drop, invite feeling within that example, so the patient can bear more intense feeling without the defense of somatization. A breakthrough allows the patient to experience the link between her unconscious feelings and her defense of identifying with the person toward whom she felt rage. Understanding this link enables the patient to overcome the defense of somatization.

Once the patient can see causality and the symptom disappears, explore the feeling again, each time increasing the patient's ability to tolerate her feeling until her anxiety is no longer discharged into bodily symptoms. For patients whose symptoms result from the defense of somatization, the cognitive summary explains how the defense works. When the patient can see that sequence and her symptom disappears, invite the feeling so the patient can tolerate her rage without using the defense of somatization. When anxiety goes into the striated muscles, explore the feeling and restructure defenses until the patient experiences a breakthrough to the feeling, at which point the symptoms will drop.

The fragile spectrum includes fragile, depressed, somatizing, and impulsive patients. These patients need the graded approach to restructure the pathway of unconscious anxiety discharge, so anxiety goes into the striated muscles. They use regressive defenses, which the therapist must restructure to establish an intrapsychic focus. All of these patients have problems in self-observing capacity, which we will examine in the next chapter.

RECOMMENDED READINGS

Abbass, A. (2005). Somatization: Diagnosing it sooner through emotion-focused interviewing. *Journal of Family Practice, 54*(3), 215–224.

Abbass, A., Kisely, S., and Kroenke, K. (2009). Short-term psychodynamic psychotherapy for somatic disorders. *Psychotherapy and Psychosomatics, 78*, 265–274.

Abbass, A., Lovas, D., and Purdy, A. (2008). Direct diagnosis and management of emotional factors in chronic headache patients. *Cephalagia, 28*(12), 1305–1314.

Davis, D. (1988). Transformation of pathological mourning into acute grief with intensive short-term dynamic psychotherapy. *International Journal of Short-Term Psychotherapy, 3*, 79–97.

Davis, D. (1988). Transformation of pathological mourning into acute grief with intensive short-term dynamic psychotherapy, part II. *International Journal of Short-Term Psychotherapy, 3*, 279–298.

Frederickson, J. (2007). The man who awoke from a coma: Treatment of a dissociative patient. http://www.istdpinstitute.com /resources/.

Trunnell, T. (1987). The management of the mechanisms of depression in intensive short-term dynamic psychotherapy. *International Journal of Short-Term Psychotherapy, 2*, 1–15.

Whittemore, J. (1996). Paving the royal road: An overview of conceptual and technical features in the graded format of Davanloo's ISTDP. *International Journal of Short-Term Dynamic Psychotherapy, 11*, 21–39.

RECOMMENDED MATERIALS

You may want to view the following videos to better understand how to work with fragile patients.

Working with the fragile patient. A set of DVDs including the initial session, a teaching DVD, and an analyzed transcript of the session at http://www.istdpinstitute.com/DVD/.

Restructuring projection with a borderline patient. A set of DVDs including the initial session, a teaching video on projection, and an analyzed transcript of the session at http://www.istdpinstitute .com/DVD/.

CHAPTER EIGHT

Building Self-Observing Capacity

T he triangle of conflict tells us where to focus: feeling, anxiety, or
defense. Self-observing capacity tells us the extent to which the
patient can bear his feeling, regulate his anxiety, and let go of his
defenses.

Moderately resistant patients can observe their feelings, anxiety,
and defenses with some help from the therapist. However, patients in
the fragile spectrum and highly resistant patients often cannot observe
or pay attention to their feelings, anxiety, or defenses.

If a patient cannot observe his feelings, he can't experience them. If
he cannot observe or pay attention to his anxiety, he cannot regulate
it. If he cannot differentiate his feelings from anxiety, he will become
more anxious when you ask about feelings. If he cannot differentiate
his feelings from defenses, he will become more defensive when you
ask about feelings. If he cannot see how his defenses create his presenting problem, he will see no reason to let go of them. Therefore, we have
to mobilize all of these capacities before the patient can experience
a breakthrough to his unconscious feelings (S. Freud 1923/1961c; A.
Freud 1936). The patient is unaware of his feelings because defenses
prevent him from observing and paying attention to them.

During the phases of inquiry and invitation to feeling, assess each
patient response for his self-observing capacities (A. Freud 1936) in
this order (Ten Have de Labije 2006):

1. *Observation*: Can the patient observe his feeling, anxiety, and
   defenses in the moment?
2. *Attention*: Can the patient pay attention to his feelings, anxiety,
   and defenses in the moment?

3. *Differentiation*: Can the patient differentiate his feelings from anxiety and defense?

4. *Causality*: Can the patient see that his feeling triggers anxiety which triggers defense in the moment? Can he see how his defenses create his presenting problems?

5. *Syntonicity*: Does he identify with his defenses, or does he see that his defenses are how he avoids his feelings? Does he feel sadness or guilt over the suffering he has inflicted on himself through his defenses so he can turn against them?

Psychodiagnosis of each patient response determines the next intervention. If the patient cannot declare an internal problem or express his will to explore it, assess the anxiety and defenses that prevent him from doing so. If he cannot label his feeling or experience it, assess the anxiety and defenses that prevent him from doing so. Assess his capacity to observe and pay attention to the defenses that prevent him from labeling and experiencing his feeling. Also assess his ability to differentiate feeling from anxiety and defense. Before confronting the resistance, assess his awareness of causality, and the syntonicity of his defenses. After each patient response, assess his self-observing capacity. Intervene, and then assess his next response to intervention.

ELEMENTS OF SELF-OBSERVING CAPACITY

Many patients cannot observe, pay attention to, or experience their feelings without excessive anxiety. First strengthen patients' capacity for observation and attention so they can turn against the defenses. This process of building capacity in patients is called *restructuring* (Davanloo 1990).

Davanloo (1990, 2000) described restructuring in terms of separating the ego and superego, differentiating the corners of the triangle, and separating the patient from the resistance. Ten Have de Labije (1999, 2005) described restructuring as the development of specific self-observing capacities. Neuroscientists and psychoanalysts understand this in terms of differentiating the patient from defenses (procedural memory) (Grigsby and Stevens 2000).

Today nearly all models of psychotherapy agree on the central role of the patient's attention and awareness. How do we understand the *observing ego* (S. Freud 1923/1961c) today? From the perspective of neuroscience (Grawe 2007; Grigsby and Stevens 2000) and complexity theory (Palombo 1999), there is not a thing in the brain called the *ego*. Instead, the capacities we put under the rubric of ego are emergent properties of complex interactions between different parts of the brain. Thus, the perspectives of neuroscience and complexity theory allow us to understand the emergence of self-observing capacities without a reified concept of the ego.

The following case vignettes show how to mobilize self-observing capacities. They must be mobilized in sequence because each capacity builds on the previous ones.

Principle: *After each response of the patient assess the problem of self-observing capacity in that moment. Intervene to address that problem and listen to the patient's response to intervention. Assess the next problem of self-observing capacity. Continue to assess and build the patient's self-observing capacities until she can tolerate a breakthrough to unconscious feelings without out excessive anxiety.*

Observation

Can the patient observe her feeling, anxiety, and defense in the present moment?

Vignette One: Lack of the Ability to Observe Anxiety

In this excerpt you will see how the therapist assesses the patient's responses and sees her inability to observe her anxiety. The therapist mobilizes this capacity before doing anything else in therapy. Without the ability to observe and regulate anxiety, the highly anxious patient will not be able to co-create an effective therapeutic alliance.

> *Th:* What's the internal emotional problem you would like me to help you with?
>
> *Pt:* [*Racing speech.*] There are a lot of things. I don't know if you read my chart, and then there's more than that since I met with the doctor.
>
> *Th:* [*Interrupt her racing speech.*] Do you mind if I interrupt you for a moment?

Pt: No. What?

Th: [*Speak very slowly to slow the patient down.*] Do you notice that you are talking really quickly right now? [*Identify her defense of racing speech.*]

Pt: I talk rapidly all the time. People are always telling me to slow down. [*She observes the defense, but it is syntonic.*]

Th: [*Interrupt the racing speech again.*] And we see that racing speech right now. You see, racing speech is often a way to run over feelings and anxiety. [*Show its defensive function.*] But if you race over and ignore your anxiety, it will just get worse. Our task here is to pay close attention to feelings in your body, anxiety in your body, and any shifts in our connection so we can see what is causing your difficulties. [*Mobilize her to the therapeutic task.*] I'm going to invite you to slow down. If you don't race and don't cover your feelings with words, what do you notice feeling inside?

Pt: My head is full of thoughts wanting to come out. [*Her speech races again as she uses the defense of verbal discharge to avoid feelings in her body.*]

Th: What do you notice feeling in your body now, if we don't race over it? [*Help her observe her anxiety.*]

Pt: Real anxious. [*Now she can observe her anxiety. The therapist intervenes before the patient's next defense.*]

Th: Where do you notice this anxiety in your body right now? [*Help the patient keep observing her anxiety.*]

Pt: I'm feeling sick to my stomach.

Racing speech prevents patients from seeing or regulating their anxiety. This results in worsening symptoms. Immediately interrupt this defense and mobilize attention to anxiety. Racing speech is not free association. It is a sign of unregulated anxiety, which makes the patient unable to observe or pay attention to her anxiety or engage in true self-reflection in that moment. Any time patients present with unregulated anxiety in the session, (1) block defenses that prevent anxiety regulation; (2) present the therapeutic task (attention to her feelings, anxiety, and defenses); (3) draw attention to the anxiety until it is regulated; (4) point out the feeling that triggers the anxiety; (5) differentiate feeling from anxiety; and then (6) invite the feeling.

Vignette Two: Lack of an Ability to Observe a Defense

In this example, the therapist assesses the patient's response and sees the patient's inability to observe a defense. The therapist will help the patient observe the defense before doing anything else. As long as the patient does not observe the defense, he will keep using it and become depressed in session.

Th: How do you experience this anger toward Jim for insulting you?

Pt: I was a stupid jerk to go to that bar in the first place. [*Rather than describe his anger, the patient uses the defense of self-attack.*]

Th: Do you notice you put yourself down right now? [*Draw attention to his defense.*]

Pt: No. [*The patient has no ability to observe his defense of turning anger on himself.*]

Th: Do you notice you are calling yourself a name now?

Pt: Yes, but I think it's true. [*He cannot observe the defense. He can see he calls himself a name, but he does not see the function that serves: to turn anger toward Jim back onto himself.*]

Th: Do you notice when this anger comes up toward Jim, there's a critical part of your mind that turns the anger toward him back onto you instead?

Pt: I don't understand. [*He cannot observe his defense.*]

Th: Do you notice how when this anger comes up toward Jim, a critical part of your mind turns the criticism back onto you instead of onto him? [*Help him observe the defense of turning anger on himself.*]

Pt: You mean I criticize me instead of him? [*Now he sees the defense.*]

Th: Yes, you criticize yourself instead of him. Do you think that might hurt you, get you feeling down? [*See if he can observe causality: defenses create his depression.*]

Pt: I think it definitely hurts me.

In this example, the patient initially does not observe his defense of self-attack. Point out this defense from different vantage points until he sees it. Otherwise, it will make him depressed, and he will be unable to face his rage toward Jim.

Spectrum of the Ability to Observe a Defense in Depressed Patients

The capacity to observe a defense exists on a spectrum from complete awareness of the defense to none. If you are aware of where the patient is on the spectrum of syntonicity, you can target your interventions to the patient's level of awareness and meet her where she is.

- "I hate myself." *Psychodiagnosis:* Self-attack with an implicit awareness of the feeling involved and where she directs it. The patient is not aware of her rage toward her boyfriend, her anxiety, or defense.

- "I'm upset with him, but I'm angry at myself." *Psychodiagnosis:* She has a muted awareness of her feeling, but not of her anxiety or defense.

- "I feel he shouldn't have done that." *Psychodiagnosis:* No self-attack. *Defense:* intellectualization. The patient is not aware of her feeling, anxiety, or defense.

- "I'm miffed." *Psychodiagnosis:* No self-attack. *Defense:* minimization. Patient has a muted awareness of her feeling, but not of her anxiety or defense.

- "I'm angry, but I don't notice feeling anything." *Psychodiagnosis:* No self-attack. *Defense:* isolation of affect (she is aware of her feeling without experiencing it). The patient is aware of her feeling but not her anxiety or defense.

- "I'm angry and I feel a heat rising up within me." [*Fists clenched.*] *Psychodiagnosis*: The patient is aware of her feeling, feels her rage physiologically without any defenses, and experiences the impulse in her fists.

Diagnosis tells us about the depression created by defenses. Psychodiagnosis tells which defenses create the depression.

Vignette Three: Lack of the Ability to Observe a Feeling

In this excerpt, notice how the therapist assesses the patient's responses and sees her inability to observe a feeling due to defenses. The therapist will help the patient see and let go of each defense so she can become aware of the feeling underneath.

Th: What is your feeling toward him for pushing you out of the car?

Pt: I don't know. [*Lack of the ability to observe feeling.*]

Th: Would you like to know what you are feeling so we can find out what's driving this anxiety? [*Mobilize the will to observe her feelings.*]

Pt: Yes.

Th: What's the feeling toward him for pushing you out of the car? [*Invite the feeling.*]

Pt: I didn't like it. [*Defense: intellectualization.*]

Th: That's your thought. [*Identify the defense.*] If we don't cover the feeling with a thought, what's the feeling toward him for pushing you out of the car? [*Invite the feeling.*]

Pt: I thought he was wrong to do that. [*Defense: intellectualization.*]

Th: That's your thought [*identify defense*], but if you don't cover your feeling with a thought, what's the feeling toward him for pushing you out of the car? [*Differentiate the feeling from the defense, and then invite the feeling.*]

Pt: I guess I'm angry. [*She is finally able to observe her feeling, but she uses the defense of vagueness.*]

Th: You guess? [*Point out the defense of vagueness.*] Either you are or you aren't. It doesn't make a difference to me. [*Block the defense.*]

Pt: No, it's true. I'm angry with him for doing that. [*Now she can observe her feeling. Next ask, "How do you experience this anger physically in your body?"*]

Attention

First mobilize observation and then attention to feeling, anxiety, or defense in this moment.

Vignette One: Lack of Ability to Pay Attention to Feeling

Notice how the therapist assesses the patient's responses and sees that the patient is unable to pay attention to her feelings for more than a second before using a defense. Thus, the therapist will focus on the defenses that prevent the patient from paying attention to her feelings.

Th: What did you feel toward him when he pushed you out of the car?

Pt: I was angry, but the thing I want to talk about is this test next week. [*She observes her feeling for one second and then ignores it. No ability to pay attention to her feeling.*]

Th: Do you notice you avoid this feeling of anger? [*Point out the defense of diversification.*]

Pt: No. [*She does not observe her defense.*]

Th: Do you notice you said you feel angry with him? [*Point out the sequence of feeling and defense.*]

Pt: Yes.

Th: As soon as you said you feel angry, you talked about the test instead. You moved away from your anger. Do you see that? [*Point out, and then see if she can observe, the sequence of feeling and defense.*]

Pt: Now that you point it out, but I did want to talk about the test. [*She sees the sequence, but not the defensive function of talking about the test: to avoid her anger.*]

Th: But do you see how talking about the test is a way to move away from your anger? [*Point out the defensive function.*]

Pt: Yes. [*The patient sees the function of talking about the test: to avoid her anger. The defense is syntonic since she still wants to talk about the test and ignore her feeling.*]

Th: Is this a habit you have of distracting yourself from your anger and ignoring it? [*Point out the defense of ignoring her feeling.*]

Pt: Yes.

Th: Does that help you channel your anger in a healthy direction or is it getting in your way? [*Separate the patient from her defenses.*]

Pt: I can see how it gets in my way. [*She sees the destructive effect of ignoring her feelings.*]

Th: If we don't ignore your feelings, how do you experience this anger toward him for pushing you out of the car? [*Invite her to turn against the defense and pay attention to her feeling.*]

Vignette Two: Lack of Ability to Pay Attention to Anxiety

If the patient cannot pay attention to her anxiety, she will be unable to regulate it or recognize the triggering feeling. Notice how the therapist assesses the patient's responses and sees that the patient is unable to pay attention to her anxiety due to defenses, which distract her attention. Thus, the therapist will help the patient see and let go of defenses, which help her ignore her anxiety. Once she no longer ignores her anxiety, she will be able to regulate it and explore her feeling.

Th: Are you aware of feeling anxious?

Pt: Yes, but I'm better at getting rid of it now. [*She observes her anxiety for a moment and then ignores it.*]

Th: You are aware of your anxiety. How do you experience it?

Pt: All over, but I'm over it now. I'm okay. [*She observes her anxiety but cannot pay attention to it. Instead, she uses the defense of denial.*]

Th: But you look and sound quite anxious. [*Point out the patient's denial.*] Do you notice the anxiety in your body right now? [*Invite her attention to the anxiety.*]

Pt: That's true, but—

Th: [*Interrupts the defense.*] It's good that you notice. As we notice your anxiety, what do you notice in your neck? [*Mobilize attention to her anxiety.*]

Pt: Tension. [*Anxiety.*]

Th: That's a sign of anxiety. And in your shoulders?

Pt: Tension.

Th: That's another sign of anxiety. And your arms?

Pt: Tension.

Th: And in your legs?

Pt: Tension.

Th: And how is your stomach? [*Her anxiety goes into the striated muscles. The therapist assesses if the patient's anxiety is discharged in other channels.*]

Pt: I'm sick to my stomach. [*Smooth muscles. Anxiety is too high.*]

Th: Are you feeling nauseous?

Pt: Yes, but I do a lot of the time. [*Smooth muscles. Defense of ignoring her anxiety.*]

Th: That's another sign of anxiety. You are feeling anxiety in your shoulders, arms, legs, and stomach. [*Label her anxiety.*] How is your vision right now? [*Assess whether she is suffering from cognitive/perceptual disruption.*]

Pt: It's fine. Well, it's blurry, but it's like that a lot of the time. [*Cognitive/perceptual disruption.*]

Th: That's another sign of anxiety. How is your hearing?

Pt: It's fine.

Th: Are you experiencing any dizziness?

Pt: A little bit. [*Cognitive/perceptual disruption.*]

Th: And how is your thinking right now? [*Assess if she is experiencing cognitive/perceptual disruption in the form of dissociation, drifting thoughts, blanking out, or confusion.*]

Pt: It's a little cloudy. [*Cognitive/perceptual disruption.*]

Th: You are feeling anxiety in the form of tension in your shoulders, arms, and legs. You feel anxiety in the form of nausea in your stomach, and blurry vision, dizziness, and a little problem thinking. Do you see that now?

Pt: Yes.

Th: I'm going to invite you to join me here in paying close attention to the feelings in your body, the anxiety in your body, and any shifts in our connection [*defenses*] so we can see what's driving all this anxiety and these symptoms. [*Clarify the therapeutic task for the patient: to pay attention to her internal experience.*] Does that make sense to you?

Pt: Yes. But there's something else I would like to talk about. [*Defense of ignoring her anxiety.*]

Th: If we go to another topic, we would be ignoring your anxiety, and you would keep suffering from these symptoms. Would you like me to help you get rid of these symptoms?

Pt: Yes.

Th: Could we take a minute to pay close attention to these feelings and anxiety so we can see what's driving this anxiety? [*Mobilize the patient's will to engage in the therapeutic task.*]

Pt: Yes. [*Patient relaxes a bit in the chair.*]

Th: What do you notice feeling right now?

Pt: A little more calm. [*Mobilizing the patient's will deactivates the projection of her will onto the therapist, thereby reducing her projective anxiety.*]

Th: How do you notice that calm? [*Mobilize the patient's attention.*]

Pt: I'm less tense.

Th: How is your vision? [*Mobilize attention to her bodily experience.*]

Pt: It's fine now. [*Cognitive/perceptual disruption has disappeared.*]

Th: And how is your stomach?

Pt: It's fine now. [*Smooth muscle discharge of anxiety has stopped.*]

Th: Do you notice tension instead?

Pt: Yes, but it's not as bad as before. [*Anxiety goes into the striated muscles instead of smooth muscles or cognitive/perceptual disruption.*]

Th: Do you notice that when you ignore your anxiety it gets worse, but when we pay attention to your anxiety it goes down? [*Defenses dysregulate anxiety; attention regulates it.*]

Pt: I hadn't noticed that before.

Th: Do you see that connection now?

Pt: Yes.

Th: Would you like to see what the feeling is underneath that is driving this anxiety and creating these symptoms? [*Invite the patient to pay attention to the feelings triggering her anxiety.*]

Pt: Yes.

Th: What is the feeling here toward me that is making you so anxious? [*Since she began the session feeling anxious with the therapist, ask about feelings toward the therapist that are triggering this anxiety.*]

Therapists often ask, "Why do you assume it is a feeling toward the therapist?"

Imagine a dog that has been abused by a previous owner. When you approach the dog behind the fence, he barks at you. Since the previous owner abused him, the dog reacts with powerful feelings toward anyone who approaches him. Unable to hide his feelings, the dog needs a fence to keep from biting you. Patients who were hurt by others have these same powerful reactions and feelings. In contrast to a dog, they do not need a fence. They need defenses to keep them from expressing those ferocious feelings.

Vignette Three: Lack of Attention to Defense

Notice how the therapist assesses the patient's responses and sees that the patient is unable to pay attention to her defenses. Thus, the therapist helps the patient see and pay attention to her defenses. Otherwise, the patient would not let go of the defenses, and she would be unable to co-create a collaborative therapeutic alliance.

Th: What is your feeling toward him for slapping you?

Pt: I was surprised, but then I just ignored him. [*Defense. She does not describe her feeling, but how she ignored him and her feeling toward him for slapping her.*]

Th: But ignoring him is not your feeling. Ignoring is how you dealt with your feeling. You ignored it. Do you see that? [*Differentiate her feeling from her defense.*]

Pt: Yes, but I just don't see the point in looking at this. [*She observes her defense, but pays no attention to it, the symptoms it causes, or the price she pays for using it.*]

Th: You ignore your feelings.

Pt: Yes, I see no point in getting all caught up in feelings. [*She observes her defense but points out that it is syntonic for her.*]

Th: You see no point in paying attention to your feelings. You see no point in me paying attention to your feelings. You invite me to ignore your feelings too! What kind of therapist would I be if I said, "Oh, we should ignore your feelings"? [*Point out how her defense invites us to form a pathological relationship where neither of us pays attention to her inner life.*]

Pt: Not a very nice one.

Th: Why would you want to do that to yourself? [*Invite her to take a stand against ignoring her feelings.*]

Pt: It's not like I want that. [*She wants a healthy relationship but does not see how she invites an unhealthy one.*]

Th: That's why we have to look at this. You don't want a relationship where both of us agree to ignore your feelings, but when you ignore your feelings, you invite both of us to do just that: to dismiss and ignore your feelings [*Point out the effect of the defense on our relationship.*] Do you see what I mean?

Pt: Yes, I just hadn't thought about it before. [*She had not seen causality: her defenses create pathological relationships and presenting problems.*]

Th: As we think about this, what can we do about this destructive habit you've had of ignoring your feelings? [*Invite her to turn against her defense of ignoring.*] Because you see, as long as you ignore your feelings and invite me to ignore them, we'll have the same terrible relationship you had with your mother. [*Point out the price of her defense.*] Why do that to yourself? [*Invite her to take a stand against the defense.*]

Pt: I don't want to.

Th: What can we do about this habit of ignoring your feelings? [*Invite her to take a stand against the defense.*]

Pt: I don't want to ignore my feelings, and I don't want you to do that. [*She turns against the defense.*]

Th: If you don't ignore your feelings [*encourage her to let go of the defense*], what's the feeling toward me that led you to put up this wall between us? [*Encourage her to face the feeling the defense was covering.*]

Differentiating the Corners of the Triangle

Once the patient can pay attention to her feelings, anxiety, and defense in the present moment, can she differentiate the stimulus from her feelings, her feelings from anxiety, and her feelings from the defense she uses?

Differentiating the Stimulus from the Feeling

Sometimes the patient cannot differentiate what someone did to her from how she feels toward that person. In response, help her differentiate the stimulus from her reactive feeling so she can become aware of the feeling.

Th: What was the feeling toward him for slapping you?

Pt: I felt hurt. [*Patient confuses the stimulus with the feeling the stimulus triggered.*]

Th: He hurt you. [*Stimulus.*] And what is your feeling toward him for hurting you?

Pt: I felt betrayed. [*Patient confuses the stimulus with the feeling the stimulus triggered.*]

Th: He did betray you. [*Stimulus.*] What is your feeling toward him for doing that?

Pt: I felt abandoned. [*Patient confuses the stimulus with the feeling the stimulus triggered.*]

Th: He did abandon you! That's what *he* did. [*Stimulus.*] But the question for us is this: what is *your* feeling *toward* him for doing that?

Pt: I'm angry. [*Patient can now distinguish the stimulus (what he did to her) from her feeling toward him for doing that.*]

Suppose I walked up to you and rubbed some sandpaper harshly on your arm. You would not say you felt "sandpapered." You would say you felt angry toward me. Differentiate the stimulus from feeling so patients can become aware of their reactive feeling.

Differentiating the Feeling from Anxiety

If we ask, "What is the feeling toward her for throwing the engagement ring into the gutter?" the patient may reply, "I feel scared." "I feel afraid." "I feel anxious." "I feel frightened." He fails to distinguish the feeling toward his fiancé from the anxiety his feeling triggers. Patients who cannot differentiate their feeling from anxiety remain paralyzed by anxiety. Differentiate the patient's anxiety from his feeling and then invite him to face his feeling.

> Th: What is the feeling toward her for throwing the engagement ring into the gutter?
>
> Pt: I feel afraid.
>
> Th: That's your anxiety. If we don't cover your feeling with anxiety, can we take a look at the feeling toward her that is making you anxious?
>
> Pt: I feel afraid of her.
>
> Th: You probably were afraid of her, but right now, she's not here. So right now, what is the feeling toward her for throwing that ring into the gutter?
>
> Pt: I feel tense.
>
> Th: Tension is your anxiety. If we put this lid of tension off to the side, can we take a look at the feeling underneath that tension? What is the feeling toward her for throwing the ring away?
>
> Pt: I'm angry with her.

Anxiety signals that the rising feeling was dangerous in the past. In the example above, the patient covered his anger with anxiety. Help the patient push the anxiety to the side so he can face the feeling underneath and channel it into effective action.

Differentiating the Feeling from the Defense

When we ask the patient about her feeling, she may respond with a defense, unable to differentiate it from her feeling (Basch 1996). Notice how the therapist helps the patient differentiate her feeling from the defense. Otherwise, the patient's feeling will not be accessible.

> Th: What's the feeling toward him for throwing you out of the car?

Pt: I feel worried. [*Defense. Does not differentiate feeling from defense.*]

Th: Your mind goes off to worrying now, and there are a lot of thoughts now. If we put the thoughts to the side, can we take a look at the feeling underneath?

Pt: I feel he shouldn't have done that. [*Defense. She does not differentiate feeling from defense.*]

Th: That's your thought, but your thought is not a feeling. What's the feeling toward him for throwing you out of the car?

Pt: I feel stupid for being with him. [*Defense. She does not differentiate feeling from defense.*]

Th: Do you notice how there's some feeling toward your boyfriend, but then this critical part of your mind starts to turn the feeling toward him into criticism of you? Do you think that might be hurting you? If you don't turn the criticism onto you, what is the feeling toward him?

Pt: [*Sighs.*] I feel confused. [*Defense. She does not differentiate feeling from defense. Since anxiety is in the striated muscles her confusion is not a sign of cognitive/perceptual disruption.*]

Th: Confused is not a feeling. If you don't cover your feeling with confusion, can we have an uncensored look at this feeling toward him?

Pt: I feel empty. [*Defense. She does not differentiate feeling from defense.*]

Th: Empty is not a feeling. Emptying yourself is how you deal with your feelings. He threw you out of the car, and now you throw out your feelings. If you don't throw your feelings out and empty yourself, can we have an honest look at your feelings toward him?

Pt: I feel like running away. [*Defense. She does not differentiate feeling from defense.*]

Th: You can run away from your feelings, but no matter how far you run, your feelings are still in you. Running away is not working. If you don't run away from these feelings, are you willing to face them, so we can get to the bottom of what has been troubling you?

Pt: I feel irritated. [*Feeling plus defense.*]

Differentiating the Feeling from a Defensive Affect

Some patients use a defensive affect to cover up the underlying feeling.

Notice how the therapist assesses the patient's responses and sees that the patient cannot differentiate a reactive feeling from the defensive affect that covers her feeling. The therapist helps the patient make this distinction so she can feel her reactive feeling rather than suffer from her defensive affects.

> *Th:* How do you experience this anger toward him for insulting you in front of your friends?
>
> *Pt:* I want him back! I feel such a longing for him. [*She does not differentiate her anger from the defenses of longing, and reaction formation.*]
>
> *Th:* Longing is not your anger. [*Differentiate defense from feeling.*] You cover your anger with longing [*clarify the defensive function*], but when you cover your anger with longing, you remain stuck and confused. [*Price of the defense.*] If you don't hide your anger under this longing, can we see how you experience this anger?
>
> *Pt:* But I love him! [*She does not differentiate anger from her defense of reaction formation. She may love her boyfriend, but she uses her love to cover her anger toward him for insulting her.*]
>
> *Th:* I'm sure you do. But love is not anger. [*Differentiate her defensive affect from her anger.*] When you cover your anger with love, that hides the true complexity of what you really feel. [*Point out the defensive function.*] Do you see what I mean?
>
> *Pt:* You mean I cover my anger with positive feelings to make things "nicey" nice? [*She begins to see the defensive function of her love.*]
>
> *Th:* You put up this "nicey" nice façade, but that hides your other feelings. That façade gives false information to you and to him. Your façade says that you love him when he insults you. [*Point out the price of this defense.*] If you don't cover up your anger with this "nicey" nice façade [*invite her to turn against the defense*], how do you experience this anger toward him for insulting you?

One might ask, "Isn't her love real?" Of course, and so are her other feelings. After all, he insulted her! In this case, the patient used her love (a real fact) to cover her anger (another real fact). Another patient might cover her grief with the defensive affect of anger. Always differentiate the activating affect from a defensive affect.

To differentiate the feeling from a defensive affect, examine the process. Feeling triggers anxiety, then a defense. A defensive affect does not. Why not? The defensive affect already serves a defensive function. (See chapter 10.)

Causality

Feelings trigger anxiety, which triggers defenses, which cause the presenting symptoms. Once patients see this causality, their suffering begins to make sense. They see how defenses that helped in the past create suffering in the present. As a result, patients can turn against defenses more easily.

Defenses can prevent us from seeing causality. The father sexually abused the patient when she was a child. The therapist asks, "What is your feeling toward him for abusing you as a little girl?" The patient's awareness of her feeling will depend on how many elements of her experience she is aware of: the stimulus, the reactive feeling, anxiety, the defense, and the result of the defense. See figure 8.1 for the causal sequence of those elements.

1	2	3	4	5
Stimulus$\longrightarrow$	**Feeling** $\longrightarrow$	**Anxiety**$\longrightarrow$	**Defense** $\longrightarrow$	**Result of defense**
abuse	anger	striated	self-attack	experience of shame

Figure 8.1.   Sequence of the elements of causality

Every conflict has at least five components. When the patient cannot see the stimulus, feeling, anxiety, and defenses, she can see only her symptoms. As a result, she has a global, undifferentiated experience of displeasure. Help her recognize each of these elements and their relationships (Rangell 1985) as an understandable whole within herself.

At first, the patient may see only one element, equating it with the entirety of her being. Let us examine several examples of low self-observing capacity so we can show what the patient does and does not see. The patient above might say, "I am anxious." Yet she may not be aware of her anger or her defense of self-attack.

Or she might say, "I am an awful person." She is not aware of her anger, anxiety, or the function of her self-attack: to turn her anger back on herself. If you comment on how she attacks herself, she will deny it. "I'm just being honest about myself." Her awareness is limited to the result of her defense of self-attack: "I feel horrible about myself."

Or she might say, "I am shameful." Of the five elements listed above, she is aware of only the result of the self-attack: her internal experience of being "bad" and "shameful." At that moment, she is unaware of the memory of being abused, her rage, anxiety, or defense of self-attack. Thus, her shame *is not the entirety of her experience; it is the entirety of her present awareness—limited by her defenses.*

In each example, defenses prevent the patient from being aware of some part of the chain of causality. As a result, she has a mistaken sense of causality. For instance, she believes her defenses solve her problems rather than create them. Address the defenses that restrict the patient's awareness of causality. If we help her to feel her rage toward the abuser, notice the anxiety it triggers, and see her defense of self-attack, she can turn against the defense of self-attack. As a result, she will feel rage toward the abuser without attacking herself. She will feel rage toward him rather than identify with his shame. The shame will return to him where it always belonged.

Defenses interfere with the patient's awareness of her inner life: the stimulus, feelings, anxiety, defenses, and the results—presenting problems. The resulting incorrect causality keeps patients confused and unable to deal with their feelings effectively.

The following examples illustrate different problems of causality.

- *The patient is aware of the stimulus but not her feeling.* "He asked me to touch his genitals." When the therapist invites the feeling, the patient responds, "I don't feel anything."
- *The patient is aware of her feeling but not the stimulus.* "I'm so angry, but I don't know why. It just doesn't make sense."
- *The patient is unaware of the feeling triggering her anxiety.* "I don't know why I feel anxious now."
- *The patient is aware of her feeling but not her defense of self-attack.* "I'm angry with him, but, after all, I submitted to him."

- *The patient is aware of her defense and the result of it but not of the stimulus, her feeling, or anxiety.* "But I am shameful. I hate myself because I think I deserve it."
- *The patient is unaware of the stimulus, feeling, or anxiety triggering the defense.* "I don't know why I asked that guy to use me."
- *The patient is unaware of the stimulus, feeling, anxiety, or defenses causing her symptom.* "I don't know why I am so depressed."
- *The patient is aware of the result of her defense and her anxiety, but not of her defense, feeling, or the trigger to the feeling.* "I feel afraid and ashamed of myself."
- *The patient is unaware of how her defenses cause her presenting problems so she imagines other people create her problems.* "Other people have it in for me."
- *The patient is unaware of how her defenses make her feel worse.* "This therapy is making me worse!"
- *The patient is unaware of the stimulus, feeling, anxiety, or defenses causing her depression.* "Maybe my depression is genetic." We need to make meaning of our lives, but without an accurate understanding of causality, all we can do is create pseudoexplanations based on false causality.
- *The patient does not see how her defenses (things she does) create her suffering.* "No matter what I do, the same things keep happening." Since she does not see her defenses, she believes, "There's nothing I can do."

Vignette One: Causality Error

Notice how the patient does not see how a stimulus triggers her feeling. The therapist will help the patient differentiate the stimulus from the feeling and then help the patient see how the stimulus triggers the feeling.

Th: What are you feeling toward him?

Pt: I'm feeling left. [*The patient does not describe her feeling, but what someone did to her.*]

Th: "Left" is not a feeling, but it may be that someone has left you. Is that what you are describing?

Pt: Joe did leave me this weekend. He had promised to move in with me, and I had rented this apartment so we could live together. Then Sunday he broke up with me.

Th: What do you feel toward Joe for leaving you like that?

Pt: Like I said, I feel left. [*She does not distinguish the stimulus from the feeling.*]

Th: Of course, he left you. So what is your feeling toward him for doing that to you? [*Differentiate the stimulus from the feeling.*]

Pt: I feel angry.

Th: Of course, his leaving you [*stimulus*] triggers a lot of anger [*feeling*] in you toward him. [*Show causality: the stimulus triggers emotion in her.*]

Vignette Two: Causality Error

In this example, the patient does not see that feeling triggers anxiety, so she is aware only of her anxiety. The therapist will help the patient see how feeling triggers her anxiety. Then her anxiety makes sense and so does the therapeutic task: facing her feeling, so she does not have to be anxious instead.

Th: What do you notice feeling?

Pt: Tense. I've been anxious all day. I don't know why. It doesn't make any sense.

Th: Did something happen today that might have made you anxious?

Pt: I don't think so. I was calm until after class today.

Th: What happened at class?

Pt: Nothing much. The class was the usual. At the end of class I had to speak to the professor about whether I could get an extension on my paper. Since I lost a week in school due to the surgery, I'm a little behind. I told him that, but he said I couldn't get an extension.

Th: What is your feeling toward the professor for not giving you the extension?

Pt: No feeling really. [*Defense: denial.*] I mean that's his business, and he has a right not to give one if he doesn't want to. [*Defense: rationalization.*]

Th: That's your explanation for his behavior. If you don't cover this feeling with a reason, what's the feeling toward him? [*Identify the defense and invite feeling.*]

Pt: Angry, I guess. [*Feeling plus the defense of hypothetical speech.*]

Th: You guess? Either you are or you aren't. [*Block the defense.*]

Pt: No. I'm angry with him. It would have really helped if I had received the extension.

Th: Of course, so how do you experience this anger toward him? [*Invite the feeling.*]

Pt: [*Big sigh. She hunches her shoulders. Signs of anxiety in response to her anger.*] Tense.

Th: That's your anxiety, but if you don't turn your anger into anxiety, how do you experience this anger toward him?"

Pt: I'm furious. I know he gave one to this other student who didn't deserve it!

Th: Do you notice how this anger is triggering some tension and anxiety in your body now? [*Point out causality: feeling triggers anxiety in your body.*]

Pt: Yes, I hadn't noticed it before.

Th: Do you think this anger toward your professor may be what has been triggering your anxiety all day long? [*Make a causal link to the presenting problem.*]

Pt: That is when it started.

Th: This anger makes you anxious. It's like this anxiety attacks you just for feeling angry toward a professor. Would you like to face this feeling underneath the anxiety so we can help you get to the bottom of it?

Vignette Three: Causality Error

In this example, the patient does not see how feeling and anxiety trigger her defenses. The therapist will help her see this sequence. Then they can explore the patient's feeling so she does not hurt herself by using her defense.

Th: What is the feeling toward him for having this affair?

Pt: I think what a stupid person I was to see him. [*Defense: self-attack.*]

Th: Do you notice you talk about yourself instead of telling me about your feeling toward him? [*Point out the defense.*]

Pt: Oh.

Th: If you don't criticize yourself, can we see what your feeling is toward him?

Pt: I feel sad because it was painful. [*Defensive affect of sadness. She sees the stimulus (the affair) but not her reactive feeling.*]

Th: He had the affair and caused you pain. What is your feeling toward him for causing you such pain? [*Differentiate the stimulus and the feeling and then invite the feeling.*]

Pt: Anger.

Th: You feel angry with him for having the affair. So we see you felt angry with him, but then you criticized yourself instead, turning the anger back onto you. Do you see that? [*Show the causality of anger triggering the defense of self-attack.*]

Pt: I see it now. I didn't see it before.

Th: If you saw all this, you wouldn't need to be here. Then we saw that you feel angry toward him and then sadness comes in to cover your anger. Do you see that?

Pt: But I am sad. [*Does not see how sadness functions as a defense to cover her anger.*]

Th: Sure. You have many complex feelings: anger, guilt, grief, pain, and longing. The sadness is real, but the problem is how your sadness comes in to cover your anger. [*One part of reality can be enlisted to cover another part of reality.*] That keeps you in the dark. If you are sad, you feel it, but when you are angry, the sadness comes instead as a substitute, and then you get depressed. [*Point out the function and result of the defense: depression.*] Do you see what I mean now?

Vignette Four: Causality Error

In this example, the patient does not see that her defenses cause her presenting problem. As a result, she sees no reason to let go of her defenses or to engage in the therapeutic task. The therapist must help the patient see how her defenses create her problems so she can let go of them and engage in the therapeutic task.

Th: Do you notice how you distance yourself here from me as soon as we touch on your sadness?

Pt: I'm just trying to protect myself. [*The patient believes the defense protects her because she does not see how it hurts her.*]

Th: But is this distancing protecting you or is it keeping you lonely? [*Help the patient see how the defense hurts her.*]

Pt: [*Shifts in chair with rise of anxiety.*] Lonely, but then I feel safe. [*Failure to see how the defense endangers her.*]

Th: Are you feeling safe? You look anxious. It seems to me that distancing now deprives you of the support you came here to have. Distancing from your husband has created the distant relationship you have been complaining about. I can appreciate how distancing in the past helped you then, but would you agree that distancing creates the loneliness and isolation that you are suffering from right now. [*Correct her causality error: her defense does not create safety; it creates problems.*]

Pt: I see what you mean.

Empathize with her. Her defenses, adaptive in the past, are maladaptive today.

Causality Error Due to the Inability to See the Feeling

In the following example, the patient mistakenly believes the therapist causes her anxiety because she does not see the feeling that triggers it.

Pt: I'm afraid of you.

Psychodiagnosis: The patient is aware of her anxiety but not the feelings that trigger it. As a result, she mistakenly thinks that you, not her feelings, cause her anxiety.

False causality: You cause my anxiety.

True causality: My feelings toward you make me anxious.

Causality Error Due to Projection of the Superego

In the following example, the patient mistakenly believes the therapist is cornering her because she does not see how her defenses corner her.

Pt: I'm feeling cornered.

Psychodiagnosis: The patient's superego "corners" her, but the patient projects the superego onto the therapist, now believing he corners her.

Th: That's interesting because we have been talking about how this punitive mechanism has been cornering you by attacking you, putting you down, and telling you to give up. If you want, the two of us together could corner that punitive mechanism so it can no longer corner you.

Pt: [*Cries.*] I never thought of that.

Incorrect causality: "You are cornering me."

Correct causality: "I corner myself through self-attack."

Causality: Defenses Cause Presenting Problems and Symptoms

When formulating the triangle of conflict for a patient, note all the defenses she uses and the presenting problems they create. For instance, suppose a patient detaches, remains vague, does not declare a problem, and takes a passive stance. These defenses would create a failed marriage, poor relationships with office mates, and loneliness. These defenses would also sabotage a therapeutic alliance. Help the patient see how her defenses create her presenting problems so she can co-create a therapeutic alliance.

Syntonicity

The final element of self-observing capacity involves syntonicity: the inability to differentiate oneself from the defense. From the earliest days of life, we deal with our feelings through defenses. Learned implicitly and nonverbally, defenses become automatic habits. Therefore, we should not be surprised when a patient does not see defenses or assumes that "that's the way I am."

Syntonicity is often defined in terms of the patient not seeing his defenses or believing that they are helpful and adaptive. These beliefs indicate that the patient cannot observe or pay attention to his defense, or he fails to see causality. Syntonicity, narrowly defined here, refers to the patient's identification with the defense. If he does not disidentify with his defense, he continues to use it, making it impossible for him to gain deeper access to his inner life.

Syntonicity: Restructure the Patient's Identification with His Defenses

Although patients' defenses are *actions they do*, patients often mistakenly believe defenses are *who they are*. They identify with their defenses. As a result, no internal focus is possible. First, address the patient's tendency to ignore his defenses so he can observe and pay attention to them. Syntonic defenses repress anxiety and feeling; hence, the patient is not aware of them. Since he does not see his feelings, anxiety, or defense, he cannot differentiate the elements of conflict, nor can he see causality.

To help the patient disidentify from his defenses, help him see that he is not the same as his defense and that his defenses create his presenting problems. Defenses, which he thought were his friends, are his enemies. He has been satisfied with defenses, which create his dissatisfaction. He believes they are not the cause of his problems but the solution, a source of help rather than harm. The following examples illustrate the continuum from dystonicity to syntonicity of defenses.

The Spectrum from Dystonicity to Syntonicity

The following examples illustrate the spectrum of syntonicity, ranging from no defense to complete identification with the defense. The therapist who recognizes this spectrum can tailor her interventions accordingly.

1. "I want to be close to people." [*No defenses.*]
2. "I want to be close to people, but, for some reason, I pull back, and I don't like that I do that." [*The patient sees her defense and does not like it.*]
3. "I want to be close to people, but it doesn't happen. I don't know why." [*The patient does not see her defenses, the ways she avoids closeness. She feels conflict because she wants closeness.*]
4. "I'm not sure I want to be close to people. I could get hurt." [*The patient uses a defense (rationalization) but does not see it as a defense. She believes her rationalization is helpful and protects her, even though it prevents emotional closeness. She is identified with her defense of distancing, but since she says, "I'm not sure," she still feels a slight degree of conflict.*]
5. "I don't want to be close. You do!" [*She does not see her defense of projection onto the therapist, believing it to be a rational appraisal of him. She does not see any internal desire for closeness, nor does she see her lack of closeness or her defense as a problem.*]

She is identified with her defense and disidentified with her wish for closeness. She feels no internal emotional conflict.]

6. "I don't want to be close. I enjoy keeping people at a distance. I like seeing my boyfriend try to get close to me and thinking he is close to me when he really isn't." [*The patient does not see her defense of denial. Her enjoyment of pushing people away reveals that her defense is not a problem, but a source of pleasure! She is identified with her defense.*]

Differentiating the Patient from Her Defenses

Ego syntonic refers to behaviors, values, defenses, and feelings that are acceptable to patients or consistent with their self-image (S. Freud 1923/1961b). When these patients become aware of their defenses, they respond, "That's just the way I am." If you note how they detach, they reply, "I'm a detached person." Correct causality would be: "When faced with emotions, I detach from them. That choice is not me. I can make many choices, but, through habit, I choose to reveal only a tiny part of myself emotionally." These patients equate who they are with the act of defense ("I detach") or with the result of defense ("I'm an unemotional person"). They see their defenses as part of their very being.

As a result, if you confront their defenses, they experience you as criticizing them rather than describing the ways they handle their feelings. These patients see no reason to pay attention to, and turn against, defenses since "This is who I am." Therefore, we must help patients differentiate themselves from their defenses. First, help the patient observe and pay attention to his defenses, their function, and causality. Then address his identification with the defense.

Vignette One: Identification with the Defense

Notice how the therapist assesses the patient's responses and sees how the patient identifies with her defense. Thus, the therapist must help the patient see that the defense is not "who she is" but how she deals with her feelings.

Th: Do you notice how you detach from your feeling? [*Point out the defense.*]

Pt: That's the way I am. I'm detached. I'm not an emotional person. [*Identification with the defense.*]

Th: Detached is not the way you are. *Detaching* is how you handle your feelings. You detach from your feelings. [*Differentiate who she is from how she handles her feelings.*] Do you see what I mean?

Pt: Maybe I'm not an emotional person. [*Identification with the defense.*]

Th: That's not true. You have emotions, but you detach from them. [*Differentiate her feelings from her defense.*] Right now, you show me this façade of detachment instead of the feelings underneath. [*Differentiate the uninvolved, detached relationship from the therapeutic relationship.*] Are you willing to let me see who you really are under this façade of the unemotional woman?

The term *façade* differentiates the patient from her defense. Detachment, intellectualization, withdrawal, and lack of involvement function like masks, hiding the emotional person underneath. Help the patient differentiate who she is from the ways she hides herself.

Vignette Two: Identification with the Defense

Notice how the therapist assesses the patient's responses and sees that the patient does not differentiate who he is from the choice he makes about dealing with his feelings. The therapist uses a metaphor to help the patient see how defenses are choices, ways of turning off of "the road to feeling."

Th: Do you notice how you keep distancing yourself from your emotions? [*Point out the defense.*]

Pt: But that's the way I am. [*Identification with the defense.*]

Th: No, that's just a habit you have. When you have a feeling, you deal with that feeling habitually by detaching. It's a habit.

Pt: I thought that's all I am, a collection of habits. [*Identification with his defenses.*]

Th: Oh no. Imagine if you and I went for a drive. We come to an intersection, and you make a right-hand turn. Then we come to the next intersection, and you make another right-hand turn. And the same thing keeps happening until it becomes clear we're going around in circles, not getting anywhere. Now we wouldn't say that's "who you are," but we would say that you have a funny way of driving your car. [*Distinguish who he is from choices he makes.*]

Pt: [*Laughs.*] That's true.

Th: You know at an intersection you could go straight ahead, left, right, backwards, or even just leave the car in park, but we would notice that you have a habit of making only one choice. [*Point out how unconscious defenses limit the range of our conscious choices.*]

Pt: You mean there is a me here making these choices? [*Awareness of himself and his agency as separate from his choices.*]

Vignette Three: Identification with the Defense

In this example, the therapist uses another metaphor to help the patient differentiate a defense from his essence as a person. A defense has as little to do with a person's being as a leech has to do with the leg it is sucking on.

Th: Do you see how you turn this anger on yourself and start to criticize yourself?

Pt: I do that a lot.

Th: You notice that pattern here as a way to deal with your anger. [*Show causality: anger, anxiety, and the defense of self-attack.*]

Pt: I'm not sure it's that. That's just the way I am. [*Identification with the defense.*]

Th: That's not the way you are. It's sort of like, if you're in a jungle and you see a large tree, but it's all covered with vines. In fact, the vines are so large after so many years that you can barely even see the tree underneath. See, this healthy tree is you, but we have to pull off these vines of self-attack that have covered you up so we can see who you really are underneath all that. Do you see what I mean? [*Introduce a visual metaphor to help the patient distinguish himself from his defenses.*]

This example shows how patients can suffer from a problem in representation. We ask patients to see feelings, anxiety, and defenses that are invisible. Obviously, patients cannot see invisible things of which they are unaware. For that reason, provide visual metaphors to help patients form a picture of their inner life. For instance, if a patient has trouble understanding how one feeling can cover another, I will take two books from my bookshelf and show how one book (defensive affect) can make another book (the feeling) invisible when placed on top.

We do not ask if this patient can see a defense, strictly speaking. We ask if she can represent this sequence of events: feeling, anxiety, and defense. Usually, patients cannot. Provide visual metaphors so the patient can see how anxiety (like a policeman) comes in to punish her, or how self-attack (like a vine on a tree) strangles her. Visual metaphors help the patient picture invisible processes.

Sometimes therapists mistakenly refer to defensive behaviors as *parts of the self*. Defenses or identifications are no more "parts of the self" than a mask is a part of the face. Take the patient who covers her anger with sadness. We would not say her defense is a "part" of her. We would say *her defense is how she hides parts of herself*.

Failure to Differentiate the Patient from His Defenses Leads to Premature Challenge of Defenses

When the patient does not see his defense, does not see its price, or does not see that he is not the same as his defense, he is not differentiated from his defense. If you confront his defense, he will think you are attacking him as a person, rather than describing a way he handles his feelings. Therefore, never challenge or confront a defense until he can see his defense, its function, and the causality and can differentiate himself from the defense. Otherwise, your premature confrontation of the defense will cause a misalliance.

First, help the patient observe and pay attention to his defenses. Then help him differentiate his feelings from anxiety and from his defenses. Then help him see causality. Then help him disidentify with his defenses. These steps establish the therapeutic alliance. Now we can challenge or confront those defenses because the patient knows you are helping, not attacking him.

Differentiate the Depressed Patient from Her Defenses

Let's examine the phase of defense identification with depressed patients who identify with their defenses.

Vignette: Differentiating the Patient from Her Defenses

Notice how the therapist helps the depressed patient differentiate herself from her defense of cutting. Since the defense is so syntonic, we must take more time to help the patient see the defense and causality.

Th: What is the feeling toward him for throwing you out of the car?

Pt: I cut myself.

Psychodiagnosis: The patient equates her feeling of anger toward the boyfriend with her defense of cutting herself. If you explore her anger or confront her self-attack, she may punish and cut herself after the session. First, help her see and turn against this defense before exploring her anger deeply.

Th: Cutting yourself is not a feeling. Cutting is a way to deal with feelings. [*Differentiate the feeling from her defense of self-attack.*] There is some feeling toward him, but there's a critical system in your mind [*differentiate her from this automatic defense*] that takes this feeling and turns it on you [*describe the defense mechanism*]. Do you see that? Do you think that critical system might be hurting you? [*Differentiate her from the defense and help her turn against it.*] Could that critical system in your mind be making you depressed? [*Point out causality to turn the patient against the defense.*] Would you like to see what the feeling is toward him that's getting covered by this critical system in your mind? [*Invite her to face her feeling again.*]

Use abstract language like a "critical system in your mind" to help differentiate her from the defense, to observe self-criticism rather than engage in it. If we noted how she hurts herself, she would begin to hate herself again. "You're so right, doctor. This is just another sign that I am terrible. Look at the way I hurt myself!" Instead, refer to a "critical mechanism in her mind," a "habit," or a "thought pattern" to help her see these defenses while differentiating from them. Only when she sees and is fully differentiated from these defenses (no longer equating herself with self-attack), can we begin to talk about how she hurts herself.

Pt: That was so stupid of me.

Th: This is a critical mechanism in your mind. You have a feeling, and then this critical mechanism turns that feeling into criticism aimed back onto you. Do you think that critical mechanism is hurting you?

Differentiate the patient from an automatic habit. If we said she is criticizing herself, she might punish herself immediately for having done so. First, describe the defense as a mechanism that happens without her conscious will. Some wonder if this may be a useful way to talk to the patient but an inaccurate description. I would suggest it is accurate.

Procedural memory operates outside the patient's awareness, leading to habitual modes of behavior such as bicycle riding and self-attack. Differentiate unconscious habits from her conscious will. She can consciously choose not to use a defense only when she sees it.

Pt: I really messed that up.

- *Th:* So there's this critical part of your mind.
- *Th:* So there's this habit.
- *Th:* Is this a kind or a cruel way to treat yourself?

Pt: I just feel really anxious.

- *Th:* Do you notice how it's like a policeman comes in and Tasers you with anxiety? As if it's against the law for you to have this emotion of anger?
- *Th:* Do you see how this anxiety comes in to punish and attack you just for having a feeling? You must be upset with what this anxiety is doing to you, how it is trying to hold you back from what you want.
- *Th:* Do you see how it's like a perpetrator comes in the room and strangles you with anxiety just because you have this feeling?
- *Th:* Do you see how that mechanism comes in to attack and sabotage you right now?

Help the patient differentiate herself from the choices she makes, between the driver of the car and the roads she takes. By answering these questions, she experiences her agency. She sees the choices she could make and their consequences. Although these questions might seem rhetorical, in fact, they help the patient experience her agency. Her defenses are not her; they are choices made *by* her. Through awareness of choice, she becomes aware of herself as an agent, separate from her defenses.

Remind the Patient of Causality

Help patients see the effects their defenses have.

- What impact does this self-punishment have on you?
- Is this self-punishment your goal, or is it what you want us to overcome?

- Can you help me see how this self-punishment is benefiting you?
- Is this self-punishment giving you the results you want?
- Do you think this mechanism might be making you depressed?
- Do you think this way of treating yourself might be hurting you?
- When you say that, does it make you feel better or worse?
- Is this mechanism helping you get to the bottom of your difficulties, or is it getting in your way?
- When you say this to yourself, is that you or the internal punitive mechanism?
- Notice how you are tempted to give up on yourself? It sounds like you already tried that. What were the results?
- You see how you punish yourself now. Are we here to continue your father's dirty work, or are we here to make a different choice? [*Patient had an abusive father.*]

When the Patient Says, "I Don't Know"

This seemingly simple phrase, "I don't know," can mean many things, each of which requires a different response from the therapist. We will review an incomplete list of the meanings of this phrase to illustrate the psychodiagnosis of self-observing capacity.

- Example One

Th: What's the feeling toward him for throwing you out of the car?

Pt: I don't know. [*The patient is not aware of her anger because she uses so many defenses. When she says she doesn't know, she is stating a fact.*]

Th: It's hard for you to know what you feel. No wonder you feel stuck: without knowing what you feel, you don't know for sure what you want in this relationship.

- Example Two

Th: What's the feeling toward your lover for having stolen money from you?

Pt: I don't know. [*The patient does not want to admit her anger because she would have to face the need to leave him.*]

Th: I can appreciate that. When you do know what you feel, you will face some difficult choices.

Pt: That is true.

- Example Three

Th: What's the feeling toward me?

Pt: I don't know. I feel fine with you. [*The patient tries to avoid conflict with the therapist.*]

Th: I sense some reluctance here as if you are worried your feelings here could make things not fine.

- Example Four

Th: Notice how you detach here with me?

Pt: Yes.

Th: What can we do about that?

Pt: I don't know. [*Said with a smirk. The patient defies the therapist.*]

Th: Well, the good news is, you don't have to do anything about it. You can detach as much as you think would be helpful to you. [*Deactivate the defiance.*] It's just that as long as you detach, we won't be able to get to the bottom of your difficulties.

- Example Five

Th: Notice how you detach here with me?

Pt: Yes.

Th: What can we do about that?

Pt: I don't know. [*Said with a puzzled look. The patient does not know what the healthy alternative is to detaching.*]

Th: Well, if detaching is the unhealthy alternative, what would be the healthy alternative?

- Example Six

Th: What is the feeling toward him for betraying you?

Pt: [*Patient goes limp.*] I don't know. [*The patient experiences cognitive/perceptual disruption and goes blank.*]

Th: Did your mind just go blank there?

Pt: Yes.

Th: That's a sign of anxiety.

When the patient says she does not know the answer to your question, do not assume she does. Assess self-observing capacity carefully based on the total context. To avoid getting this response, avoid asking questions that will generate it (Mitchell 2007; H. S. Sullivan 1953a). If you ask questions far beyond her self-observing capacity, "I don't know" will be the result. Rather than ask for something she does not know, find out what defenses prevent her from knowing. Then help her see and let go of those defenses.

SUMMARY

We have outlined the basic self-observing capacities and common psychodiagnostic problems. The same principle for assessing and building capacity applies to anxiety, defenses, and transference resistance. Each time the patient presents with a defense, assess the patient's self-observing capacity. Then build the patient's self-observing capacity to reduce the syntonicity of the defense. Self-observing capacities must be mobilized in a certain order: observe feeling, anxiety, and defense; pay attention to feeling, anxiety, and defense; see causality; and differentiate the patient as a person from the defenses he uses.

RECOMMENDED READINGS

Ten Have de Labije, J. (2001). Red and green traffic lights on Davanloo's road to the unconscious. In *The Collected Writings of Josette ten Have de Labije* (pp. 97–110). Del Mar, CA: Unlocking Press.

CHAPTER NINE

Regressive Defenses

When working with patients in the fragile spectrum, we restructure the pathway of anxiety discharge, build self-observing capacity, and restructure regressive defenses. Regressive defenses make anxiety more dysregulated and reality testing more impaired, leading to severe regressions. Thus, it is essential to identify and restructure regressive defenses (Land 1991).

The term *regression* refers to regression from conscious to unconscious processes; temporal regression from mature to earlier forms of functioning; and formal regression to modes of expression that are less complex, structured, and differentiated (S. Freud 1914/1957b). Regressive defenses are examples of formal regression. Rather than experience their feelings internally, patients can use regressive defenses to get rid of their feelings through acting out, verbal discharge, splitting, and projection. They "relocate" parts of themselves in others and then lose the ability to differentiate reality from a fantasy (e.g., a projection).

Patient groups have specific defenses that require restructuring: fragile patients (splitting and projection); depressed patients (weepiness, turning rage on the self, and character defenses); somatizing patients (identifying with the object of one's rage); and impulsive patients (cursing, discharge, projection, and acting out).

Principle: *To restructure a regressive defense, (1) identify the regressive defense, (2) clarify its price and function, (3) invite the patient to let go of it, and (4) integrate the previously split-off feelings.*

ACTING OUT: PUNCHING WALLS OR THROWING OBJECTS

Patients who are unable to tolerate feelings internally, act out their feelings externally. Unable to bear a rise of feelings, they vent, yell, or hit things to get rid of the internal experience of feeling. Rather than feel rage toward a loved one, a man may punch the wall. He releases the rage while punishing himself with broken knuckles. Acting out *always* wards off the internal experience of feeling or provokes punishment for having it.

Vignette One: Making the Defense Dystonic

In the following example, the patient does not see the price of his defense of acting out. Thus, he is not yet motivated to let go of the defense.

Th: Rather than experience the rage toward Jane, you punched the wall instead. [*Identify the defense.*]

Pt: Right.

Th: But then who took the hit? Who got hurt? [*Point out the price.*]

Pt: Me.

Th: See how destructive this mechanism is? You felt the rage toward Jane, but then you were the one who got hurt! By turning the rage on the wall, you avoided facing your feelings toward her and punished yourself instead. Would you like to face this rage honestly in here so we can help you overcome this pattern of self-abuse?

Encourage the patient to feel his feelings internally as powerfully as possible so he can channel them into adaptive self-assertion rather than maladaptive self-destruction.

Vignette Two: Differentiating Feeling from the Defense of Acting Out

In the following example, the patient does not see the difference between experiencing a feeling internally within his body and acting it out externally. That is, he does not differentiate between his feeling and his defense, which helps him avoid the internal experience of his feeling.

Th: How do you experience this rage at Jane?

Pt: I slugged her.

Psychodiagnosis: The patient equates his feeling of anger with the defense of acting out.

Th: But slugging her is not your rage. Slugging is how you try to get rid of your rage, to keep from feeling it inside you [*differentiate the defense from feeling*], but this is very destructive. By hitting Jane, you kill off the love she could feel for you. [*The price of the defense.*] When you act out your rage, you push her away, and invite her to leave you. Why do that to yourself? [*Address the self-punishment to help him turn against it.*]

ACTING OUT IN RESPONSE TO A PROJECTION

A recovering drug addict abandoned his son when he was high on drugs. Rather than experience his guilt, however, he projected his superego onto everyone in his rehabilitation facility. "Who are you looking at?" he would ask. He projected his cruel superego onto others, imagining that they judged him. He became furious at these "judges," and then acted out toward them, trying to provoke them to punish him. Unfortunately, he failed to differentiate them from his projections.

Acting out is frequently accompanied by cognitive/perceptual disruption. The hippocampus, which integrates short-term memory, shuts down when anxiety is too high. That may be why impulsive patients often do not remember what happened when they act out.

CONTEMPT AND SARCASM

Contempt and sarcasm, regressive defenses against emotional closeness, prevent the establishment of a therapeutic alliance. Some patients mistake contempt and sarcasm for honesty. However, contempt and sarcasm devalue the other person rather than offer a complex, nuanced view. In fact, contempt is always a dishonest, partial picture of other people. And sarcasm offers a relationship based on disrespect, something that could never be the basis for a therapeutic alliance.

In the following example, the patient does not see the price of his defense, contempt. Notice the amount of time a therapist may need to take to help the patient see the price of his defense.

Pt: That was a stupid comment. I can't believe you therapists try to pull that kind of crap. Do you really expect me to take you seriously?

Th: Do you notice you referred to what I said as stupid?

Pt: Yes.

Th: Do you notice you also seem to regard it as normal not to take me seriously? [*Point out facts.*]

Pt: Of course.

Th: Do you notice this wall of contempt you are putting up here with me? [*Ask the patient if he sees this defense.*]

Pt: Do you have a problem with that? [*The patient implicitly reveals he sees it but asks a provocative question. Do not answer it or take the bait.*]

Th: There's this wall of contempt you are putting up here between you and me. You put up a wall by calling what I say *crap*. And you put up a wall by calling what I say *stupid*. This is very important for us to look at because as long as there is this wall of contempt here between you and me, there will be no way for this therapy to help you. So the first thing we need to ask is, "What do you want to do about this wall of contempt?" [*Point out the defense and its price. Mobilize his will to turn against the defense.*]

Pt: What? Do you have a problem with my honesty? [*Psychodiagnosis: the patient cannot differentiate honest communication of his feelings from the defense of contempt. He invites a battle of wills, something the therapist must avoid.*]

Th: We are not talking about honesty. We are talking about contempt. Right now, you are putting up this wall of contempt. And the question we have to ask is: what do you want to do about this wall? As long as there is this wall of contempt here, this relationship will be doomed to fail.

Pt: Maybe I don't care if this relationship fails.

Th: That may be. Perhaps you want this relationship to fail, and the good news is, if that's what you want, that's what you'll have. For as long as you maintain this wall of contempt, I will remain another useless person in your life, and you can make this into another useless, dead therapy in the graveyard of failed therapies. Your suffering can continue, but, as you say, that may be acceptable to you.

Pt: [*Tears in his eyes.*] It's not that bad. [*Partial recognition of his pain and suffering, accompanied by the defense of minimization.*]

Th: And you may not want it to be any better. Neither I nor anyone else can help you as long as you maintain this wall of contempt. This process will be doomed to failure like all your relationships. Then I can say, "I tried to help Jim, but he didn't want it." And we would have to say goodbye to each other. I can afford to fail. I can't help everyone, but then who remains the lonely man? Who continues to suffer? If you want only to maintain this wall of contempt, obviously there would be no reason for us to meet.

Pt: [*Cries.*]

Meet his hate with strength (Winnicott 1965). Tolerating contempt co-creates a sadomasochistic relationship, not a therapeutic one. You are his therapist, not his toilet (H. Eist, personal communication). Standing firm will give him the faith that you can help him turn against this destructive defense. To be effective, speak from a position of calm rather than anger. Otherwise, you will be caught up in the patient's defense, creating a battle of wills. Repeat the above interventions until the patient feels grief over the ways contempt destroys his relationships. Expressing contempt or sarcasm is not free association, but a sadistic attack. Block this defense, which sabotages therapy.

DEFIANCE

Unconscious defiance can take the form of a sarcastic tone of voice, a refusal to explore key issues and feelings, dismissive laughter, stubbornness, a passive, provocative stance, arrogance, or noninvolvement. The defiance may not be overt but enacted through behaviors. Why?

Most defiant patients were traumatized. Imagine a child being beaten. He gets an even worse beating if he defends himself. The experience of his will triggers anxiety, so inhibiting his will or using his counterwill (Rank 1936) becomes habitual and automatic over time. He develops character traits that allow him to express his rage through defiant behaviors while simultaneously triggering punishment from others.

Every patient begins therapy with the wish to share his feelings, and his fear of doing so. Some people bear this conflict internally, acknowledging both their wish and defense. Fragile patients sometimes cannot do this. They identify themselves with the defense: "I don't want to share." They project the wish to share onto the therapist: "You want me to share." Then they oppose the therapist's "will": "It is not my wish to reveal myself. I must defy your 'wish' that I reveal myself."

The patient is not defying you. *He defies the projections he places on you.* For instance, he wants to face his feelings. But he forgets his desires and projects them onto you. Now that you "personify" his desire, he defies or submits to "your" will. There appears to be a conflict between a pushy therapist and a resistant patient. In fact, the conflict is between his wish to reveal and his resistance to doing so.

Confronting defiance makes it stronger. If you mistakenly ask about his feeling toward you, he will become angry at the projection on you: "Trying to explore feelings shows that you want to explore and invade me. So I am angry at you." His anger toward this projection will only deepen the misalliance.

Defiance and submission are two sides of the same coin: "I project my will onto you. So I can defy or submit to 'your' will." Either way, he relates to a projection. To establish a therapeutic alliance, reduce defiance (Korff 1998) by deactivating the projection of will upon which defiance is based. Remind the patient of his desire. Once he experiences his will internally, he will not have to defy it "in" his therapist.

Mobilizing Will and Deactivating Defiance: Interventions

Since the patient defies the will he has projected upon the therapist, the therapist must deactivate the projection of will for the defiance to drop. To deactivate the projection of will, the therapist must mobilize the patient's awareness of his own will. The more the patient owns his will, the less he projects it upon the therapist.

Th: You seem withdrawn right now. Do you notice that? [*Identify the defense.*]

Pt: You seem to think this is a big problem [*defense: projection*], but I'm not so sure it's worth going into. [*Defense: defiance.*]

Th: Only you can know for sure whether this is a problem for you. [*Deactivate the projection: only the patient, not the therapist, can determine if something is a problem.*]

Pt: You seem to think I should do something about it. [*Implicit message: "I don't think so." Projection.*]

Th: But this is your life, your suffering, and it can be your happiness. Whether you do something about this is up to you. Perhaps you are satisfied with how things are. [*Deactivate the projection. He believed I was not satisfied. The question is whether he is satisfied with the results of his defenses.*]

Pt: I'm not sure I want to do anything about it at this time. [*Defense: defiance.*]

Th: Okay. [*Deactivate the projection that I will force him.*]

Pt: I feel you are trying to push me into doing this. [*Defense: projection.*]

Th: I can't. If you don't want to explore this issue, you don't have to. [*Deactivate the defiance.*] You have every right not to explore these issues. If this is not something you want to do, I have no right to insist that you do so. [*Deactivate projection.*] But if that's the case, why are you here? [*Point out the contradiction: you seek, yet refuse to do therapy. Why oppose yourself?*]

Pt: I'm telling you: I'm not so sure that this is really a problem.

Th: That may be. [*Avoid a battle of wills.*]

Pt: My wife thinks it is a problem. [*Defense: projection.*]

Th: Who's the one who came here? [*Deactivate projection.*]

Pt: I did.

Th: And did you come of your own free will?

Pt: My wife said I should. [*Defense: projection.*]

Th: But did you come of your own free will? [*Deactivate projection.*]

Pt: Yes, but that doesn't mean I want to get better. [*Defense: defiance.*]

Th: That's right. You may not want to get better. [*Side with the resistance.*]

Pt: You can't tell me I should. [*Defense: defiance.*]

Th: I'm glad we're in agreement. Only you can tell yourself whether you should get better. And let's face it, you have been living this life of a lonely, depressed man with a series of failed relationships for fifty-three years [*reflect reality*], and it has been working up until now. [*Mirror his denial.*] Why do anything different? If it's been working, why change? [*Reflect reality and his denial, and then side with the resistance. This deactivates his projection further.*]

Pt: [*Tears in his eyes.*] I tell you: it is working! [*Breakthrough of the feeling as the resistance breaks down. A last attempt at denial tries to prevent a breakthrough to the feeling.*]

Th: If this is not something you want to do, you don't have to. [*Deactivate defiance.*] Like you say, your life is working. [*Reflect his denial.*] If this is working for you, obviously, you should keep doing what works. [*Mirror the resistance.*] You know as well as I do that therapy is not necessary for you; it's completely optional. [*Deactivate defiance.*] Why do something you don't want to do?

[*Undo the projection so the conflict is between the patient and his defenses.*] Why should we pretend to do something, when you know you don't want to do it? If this is not something you want to do, you and I can shake hands and say our goodbyes, and you will go forth with my blessing. [*Deactivate the defiance.*]

Pt: [*He breaks down in tears and describes how devastated he was when his wife left him.*]

Deactivate Projection by Mirroring the Patient's Resistance

When the patient projects his will onto you, he is identified with his resistance, expecting you to argue with his position. When you mirror his resistance, he does not get the argument he expects (your resistance to him). Without that conflict between you and him, he cannot have the interpersonal conflict (the defense). As a result, he experiences an intrapsychic conflict instead, and his feelings will rise, and his defiance will decrease. The following examples show how to mirror the resistance to deactivate the projection of the patient's will upon the therapist.

- "I don't know if there is something you want to explore. Perhaps there isn't."
- "If you want to continue this way, you certainly can. After all, it is your life."
- "You have been carrying this depression for forty years. Why change now?"
- "If this is working for you, good for you."
- "You have every right not to look at this, but then we have to ask, 'Why are you here?'"
- "Your suffering is yours, and happiness can be yours. It's really up to you."
- "If this is not something you want to do, we won't. I have no right to explore any aspect of your inner life, but then I won't be able to help you."

Deactivate Projection by Mirroring the Patient's Denial

When the patient denies having a problem, he expects you to point out the reality he denies. Then your interpersonal conflict serves as a defense to ward off his feelings. Instead, mirror his denial. Then conflict is not between you and him, but between him and his defense. This leads to a rise of feelings and a drop in his denial. The following examples show how to mirror the patient's denial to deactivate the projection of his healthy awareness upon the therapist.

- "This may not be a problem for you."
- "You may be getting the results you want."
- "Your marriage, life, and work may be satisfying for you. Only you can know for sure."
- "There is no need to rush. You can wait as long as you think it would be helpful."
- "You may be comfortable with your symptoms as they are."

Principle: *Make sure the patient has a problem and he wants your help. Always emphasize his free will and his right to decide whether to do therapy. Once you deactivate his defiance, continue to mobilize his will. Remind him that our task is to work together to achieve his goals. Without his will, we cannot go forward.*

Use noninterpretive interventions to deactivate projections. Interpretation fails because it reinforces his projection: "Aha. You say this because you want to control me." Interpretation unwittingly strengthens his view of you as an invader whom he must defy.

We have focused on defiance resulting from the projection of the patient's will. Defiance can also result from projection of the superego. The patient imagines you secretly criticize him; then he either defies or submits to your imagined criticisms. In this case, deactivate the projection of the superego.

DISCHARGE: RAPID SPEECH

Rapid speech prevents the patient from paying attention to her anxiety and feelings. Her pressured speech also prevents genuine dialogue. Block this defense immediately and then help her observe, pay attention to, and regulate her anxiety. By listening to her rapid speech, you co-create a dismissive relationship wherein both of you ignore her feelings and anxiety.

Th: [*Speak very slowly to slow the patient down.*] Do you notice you are talking rapidly now? That's often a sign that you are talking over feelings and anxiety. I'm going to invite you to slow down right now so we can see what is going on underneath these words. Without saying anything for a moment, what do you notice feeling inside right now? [*Mobilize her attention to, and regulate, her anxiety.*]

As you speak slowly to block her defense of rapid speech, feeling and anxiety will rise.

Pt: I'm feeling really anxious, because I've got to tell you— [*Interrupt her defenses of rumination and rapid speech.*]

Th: Let's slow down and notice how you experience this anxiety inside. How do you experience this anxiety in your body right now? [*Slow the patient down, direct her attention to her feelings and anxiety, and block her defense of rapid speech. The longer she races, the more dysregulated she will become in the session.*]

Pt: Just really tense all over [*now the defense enters*], but see I've got all this stuff I need to get out.

Th: And I want to hear it all. I notice you are tense head to toe. Do you notice that? [*Draw attention back to her anxiety.*]

Continue to slow the patient down and draw her attention to her anxiety.

DISCHARGE: LOUD SPEECH AND YELLING

Patients talk loudly in the session (assuming they do not have a hearing impairment) to get rid of the internal experience of their feeling.

Psychodiagnosis: Inability to observe or pay attention to feelings, anxiety, or defenses. The patient may be projecting the superego onto you. Thus, he tries to yell over your imagined criticisms.

Vignette One: Blocking a Regressive Defense

In the following example, the patient does not see his regressive defense of loud speech. Notice how the therapist helps the patient see and let go of the defense so he can begin to face his underlying feelings.

Th: I don't know if you noticed, but you are talking quite loudly. That's usually a way to get rid of some feeling, but any feeling that you blow out of your mouth will be unavailable for our therapy. I'm going to ask you to talk quietly and slowly right now, so you can notice what you are feeling inside your body. What are you feeling inside, if you don't drown it out with all this loudness?

Monitor the patient closely when you block a regressive defense. In the next second the feeling rises, anxiety rises, and a regressive defense appears. After you block the defense, intervene as soon as anxiety rises *and before the next defense.* This may take only a second. Rapidly draw her attention to her feeling and anxiety so she can bear them without going to defense. The longer she bears this rise of the feeling, the more you build her capacity.

Vignette Two: Making Discharge Dystonic

A young man with a history of failed relationships has entered therapy following the loss of his most recent girlfriend. He repeatedly feels rage in relationships and sabotages them. He has just described an example where his girlfriend made him angry.

Th: She made you angry, you say.

Pt: Yes, we were at a concert, and I was talking to this other woman. My girlfriend was drunk and started yelling at me for talking to this other girl. So I started yelling at her. [*Defense of discharge.*]

Th: She yelled at you [*stimulus*]. Naturally, you felt angry toward her [*feeling*]. So how did you handle your anger?

Pt: I yelled back at her. She hit me, so when we got home I hit her back. [*Defense: discharge.*] Then she decided to leave.

Th: You felt angry with her, but rather than assert yourself and set a limit, you yelled at her instead. [*Differentiate the feeling of anger from the defense of discharge.*]

Pt: Are you saying I shouldn't have yelled at her? [*Defense: projection of his conscience.*]

Th: I'm not telling you to do anything. [*Block projection.*] I'm just saying that rather than feel your anger inside, you yelled at her instead. You blew the anger out of your mouth, rather than feel it inside and channel it adaptively by setting a clear limit with her. Do you see what I mean?

Pt: But the yelling is my anger! [*He cannot differentiate his feeling from his defense.*]

Th: Not at all! Rather than feel your anger and channel it in a healthy way with her, you yelled. By yelling at her, you killed off the love

she could feel toward you. By hitting her, you invited her to punish and reject you for being angry. I'm not saying you wanted her
to reject you. I'm just saying that's the effect. When you yell at and
hit a girlfriend, you invite her to punish and reject you. Do you
see what I mean?

Pt: But she deserved it. [*In the blindness of his rage and defense, he does
not see causality: his defense causes his presenting problem.*]

Th: But then who gets rejected? Who loses another relationship? Who
gets depressed again?

Pt: I do.

Th: When you handle your anger by yelling and hitting, you end up
lonely. Do you think these mechanisms of yelling and hitting
might be hurting you?

Pt: I see what you mean.

Th: Yelling at her and hitting her destroyed the relationship. This
may seem like a surprise, but I don't think you have an anger
problem. Anyone will feel anger if a girlfriend yells at them. The
problem is how you deal with your anger. Yelling and hitting invite her to punish you for being angry. Do you see what I mean?
[*Differentiate the feeling of anger from the defense by reminding
him of the price.*]

Pt: What am I supposed to do? Just stuff it inside? [*Defense: projection
onto the therapist.*]

Th: That's what you are already doing. You stuff the rage inside until it gets too high, and then you explode with your girlfriend,
but each time you explode, another relationship blows up, leaving this series of wrecked relationships behind you. Do you see
what I mean? [*Point out how denial of feelings leads to discharge,
destroying his relationships.*]

Pt: So what am I supposed to do? [*He invites the therapist to tell
him what to do so that he, the patient, can oppose and defy the
therapist.*]

Th: The good news is, you don't have to do anything. [*Deactivate defiance.*] If you want, we can face this rage as deeply as possible and
see if we can get to the bottom of what is driving this self-punishment so we can bring your suffering to an end. [*The therapeutic task.*] Or, if you want, you can stuff your anger, explode, and

continue this path of destroyed relationships [*the antitherapeutic task*], but the choice is yours.

Pt: Maybe I should stop this therapy and just avoid women for the rest of my life. [*The patient invites the therapist to argue for his healthy longings. This way he could avoid an inner conflict between his longings and his resistance.*]

Th: That's always an option. There is no law that says you have to be in therapy. [*Deactivate defiance.*] If avoiding women and relationships, remaining a lonely man to the end of your days, is the healthiest option for you, obviously that is what you should do. [*Mirror the resistance.*]

Pt: Are you making fun of me? [*He begins to realize how cruel his resistance is, but rather than tolerate his internal conflict, he projects onto the therapist.*]

Th: How can I be making fun of you when I am only repeating what you have said? You want to avoid women for the rest of your life and remain a lonely man. I assume you are not making fun of yourself. Right? [*Deactivate the projection.*]

Pt: Right.

Th: You have a right to avoid women and remain a lonely man. Would you agree? [*Mirror his resistance to deactivate the projection.*]

Pt: I know I have that right, but that's not really what I want to do. [*Turns against the resistance.*] I have to find some way to deal with these feelings so I don't keep being rejected.

DISCHARGE: CURSING

Patients who impulsively act out their rage frequently curse to get rid of rather than experience any rise in feeling. Block this defense to access the avoided feeling and build self-observing capacity. Cursing prevents the development of affect tolerance.

Intervention

The following intervention shows how to draw the patient's attention to his cursing. Notice how the therapist does not judge the patient. He simply draws the patient's attention to the defense's function: making feelings unavailable for the therapy.

Th: Do you notice you are using some curse words? It doesn't bother me personally. It's just that cursing makes some feelings unavailable for our work. Would you be willing to refrain from cursing here, so I can help you with all your feelings? Does that make sense to you?

DISCHARGE: TALKING OVER THE THERAPIST

Patients with low self-observing capacity impulsively talk over others as soon as they become anxious, preventing intimate relationships. They can talk over you as a way to talk over their feelings and anxiety. However, they may also talk over you because they fear what you might say (projection of the superego). If anxiety regulation does not work, assess whether the patient is projecting a judge onto you, and then deactivate that projection. (See projection section in this chapter, pp. 320–323, and chapter 11.)

Intervention

In the following example, the patient talked over the therapist as soon as he started to speak. Clearly, this would prevent the patient from hearing what the therapist said. But it also signals that the patient's anxiety is too high. Notice how the therapist brings the defense to the patient's attention without any sense of criticism.

Th: Do you notice you talked over me? It's good you see that. That's going to be a problem. Talking over me will prevent us from forming the healing relationship you need here to get better. Does that make sense? Would you be willing to listen until I finish speaking, so you can get the help you came here to receive?

If the patient says yes, her wish to open up will trigger a defense in the next second, unless you mobilize her attention to her feeling right away. Ask, "What do you notice feeling right now when you say that?" Once she sees her feeling or anxiety, show her causality: "Some anxiety comes up as soon as you say you want to collaborate with me. Do you see that?"

If this intervention does not work, the patient may be talking over you to prevent you from criticizing her. In other words, she is projecting the superego onto you. If so, explore how the patient is thinking about and perceiving you to deactivate this projection. (See the section on projection in this chapter, pp. 320–323, and chapter 11.)

DISSOCIATION

Dissociation is a regressive defense that creates the symptom of "multiple selves." Many therapies focus on the "integration of selves." This strategy merely "integrates" the products of a defense, not the person who uses it (Frederickson 2000, 2003). Integrate the warded-off feelings, not the results of defense.

Dissociation is a sign of cognitive/perceptual disruption, a brain malfunctioning due to excessive anxiety. As soon as dissociation occurs, stop exploring feeling and start regulating anxiety until the patient's cognitive/perceptual disruption and dissociation stop. If the patient has access to striated muscle tension, the so-called dissociation is a tactical defense of detaching. Anxiety in the striated muscles involves not only tension but also sighing respiration and clenching of the hands. However, a patient who is tense throughout his body, without sighing respiration, may have a freeze response associated with dissociation.

Vignette: Dissociation

Notice in the following example how the therapist begins to regulate the patient's anxiety as soon as he dissociates. The first concern of the therapist should be anxiety regulation before addressing the defense of dissociation itself.

Th: What's the feeling toward your father for beating you?

Pt: I just left.

Th: What do you mean?

Pt: It's like I went up on the ceiling. [*The patient's face is slack, his eyes are blank, and his body is limp—no striated tension.*]

Th: How is your thinking now?

Pt: It's a little fuzzy. I'm trying really hard to concentrate, but it's not working. [*Cognitive/perceptual disruption.*]

Th: Is there any ringing in your ears, or is your vision blurry? [*Assess the discharge pattern of his anxiety.*]

Pt: No ringing in my ears, but my vision is blurry. It's getting better now. [*Anxiety drops.*]

Th: As we step back to observe: your thinking was fuzzy, your vision got blurry, and you were having some trouble thinking. [*Encourage the patient to observe and label the symptoms to bring down his anxiety.*] How is your thinking now? [*Assess the anxiety.*]

Pt: It's fine now, and the vision is fine. [*Anxiety now goes into striated muscles, and cognitive/perceptual disruption is gone.*]

Th: There was some feeling toward your father. This feeling triggered anxiety. Then your mind conked out. [*Outline the triangle of conflict.*] Do you see that?

Pt: Yeah, I don't know why it did that.

Th: What was the feeling toward your father that made you so anxious? [*Inviting the feeling.*]

Pt: I must have been angry.

Anxiety may shift back into cognitive/perceptual disruption when you explore the feeling. If so, stop exploring the feeling, regulate the anxiety, and outline the triangle of conflict until the patient's anxiety returns to the striated muscles. Then encourage the patient to face his feelings at a higher level in a different example. As his affect tolerance rises, cognitive/perceptual disruption and dissociation will disappear.

EXTERNALIZATION

Externalization is a defense by which the patient blames others for the ways she hurts herself. The conflict begins with a stimulus that makes the patient angry. She wards off her anger by punishing herself. Unable to see how she punishes herself, she accuses others, blaming them for her suffering. Undo externalization to establish an intrapsychic focus. To do so, help the patient see that she does to herself what she blames others for doing to her. Once she can see that her defenses cause her suffering, she will have an internal focus that will lead to effective therapy.

Vignette One: Pointing Out Causality in Externalization

A depressed, masochistic patient reports that her husband asked if he could insert his fist into her anus as part of their lovemaking. She told him it was fine with her. A few minutes later in the session she continues.

Pt: He hurt me last night.

Th: How so?

Pt: He put his fist in my anus, and it hurt when he did it.

Th: He put his fist in your anus. Is that true?

Pt: Yes. I just told you he did.

Th: Do you mind if I offer you a different perspective?

Pt: Go ahead.

Th: He asked you whether he could put his fist in your anus. Right?

Pt: Yes.

Th: And at that point, you could have said yes or no, but you chose to say yes.

Pt: But he didn't want me to say no.

Th: So you said no to yourself instead. [*By saying yes to him, she said no to herself.*]

Pt: Oh.

Th: You told him yes. He could put his fist in your anus. In effect, you put his fist in your anus because you told him he could [*correct causality: she punished herself*], but then you blame him for your choice. You chose to say no to yourself, and you blame him for that choice. [*Externalization: rather than face how she punished herself, she blamed him.*] Do you see what I mean?

Pt: I didn't think of it that way.

Th: If we think of it that way, what did you feel toward him when he asked to put his fist in your anus?

Pt: I didn't like the idea. [*Defense: intellectualization.*]

Th: But what was your feeling toward him?

Pt: I was angry.

Th: You were angry with him. Then we see that the way you dealt with your anger was to turn the anger on yourself by inviting him to hurt you.

Pt: I had forgotten that I had been angry with him. [*Evidence of repression.*]

Th: Right. You felt angry with him, forgot your anger, and turned it on yourself by inviting him to hurt you. It was as if you were inviting him to punish you for being angry with him.

Pt: And then later I invited him to criticize the food I made for dinner. [*Increased insight into self-punishment as a defense.*]

She sees her conflict of anger, anxiety, and the defense of self-punishment, no longer blaming her husband for the ways she punishes herself. Now she has an intrapsychic focus. To better understand the process of unconscious causality in externalization, see table 9.1.

Table 9.1   **Unconscious causality in externalization**

Step one	*Stimulus*	Husband asked to insert his fist
Step two	*Feeling*	Anger
Step three	*Anxiety*	Striated muscles
Step four	*Defense*	Punish herself by saying yes and abusing herself
Step five	*Externalization*	Blaming him for her choice to punish herself

We cannot explore her anger at her husband at first because her anger is at a projection: her husband as an "abuser." First, undo the defense of externalization so she can see how she punished herself. Then help her face her rage at him for asking to insert his fist. Never explore rage before the defenses of blaming or complaining have been restructured.

Vignette Two: Deactivating Projection in Externalization

A patient enters the office quite agitated. For some weeks, he had accused his girlfriend of having an affair with another man. Now the patient was angry because she had broken up the relationship. She had tired of the accusations, distrust, and arguments, so she moved out. The patient wanted to talk about his anger toward her for breaking up the relationship.

Th: She broke up with you. Is that true?

Pt: What do you mean? Of course, it's true. I just told you that she broke up with me.

Th: Do you mind if I offer another point of view?

Pt: Okay.

Th: For weeks, you thought she was having an affair. Yet it's my sense that you have been having an affair with your projection. Rather than listen to her, you listened to your fantasy. You ignored her words; you paid attention to your fantasy. In effect, you had already broken up with her and were having an affair with your fantasy. You thought she was lying to you, but your story was lying to you and being unfaithful to your best interests. Now the story has you all to itself, because you chose it instead of her. Do you see what I mean?

Fearing the emotional closeness with his girlfriend, he used the defense of projection ("She is having an affair"). This allowed him to distance himself from her but at the price of damaging the relationship. Then he blamed her for the distress resulting from his own projection (externalization). His conflict was that he had a feeling (related to emotional closeness). This feeling triggered anxiety in his striated muscles. To ward off his feeling and anxiety, he used the defense of projection ("You are having an affair"). Since he did not see his projection and the ways it damaged his relationship, he assumed his girlfriend was damaging the relationship. So he used the defense of externalization ("She, not my projection, damages our relationship").

Therapists who do not see externalization make one of several mistakes. They empathize with the patient as a victim without examining how he creates his suffering. They explore the patient's rage toward his "victimizers," thereby reinforcing his victim stance. Therapists can also err by "problem solving," that is, helping the patient assert himself with "cruel" others. When the patient externalizes, he does not see how he punishes himself. He mistakenly thinks he needs to take a stand against his so-called abusers rather than take a stand against his self-abuse. Help him see his internal conflict (anger, anxiety, self-punishment followed by blaming someone else for the patient's choice to punish himself). Then he can let go of the defense, own his responsibility, face his feelings, and make new adaptive choices.

HELPLESSNESS AND PASSIVITY

Some patients lack abilities we have to develop. Others present as if they are less capable than they really are. The therapist asks, "Can we take a look at the feeling toward your father?" The patient who uses the defenses of helplessness and passivity responds:

- "I can't."
- "I'm not sure I have the energy."
- "I don't know what you mean by feelings. Do you have a list of feelings I could look at?"

- "I wish I could tell you."
- "What do you think I feel?"

Passivity and helplessness can be defenses or a transference resistance. ["*If I act incapable of giving something to this relationship, would you give to me what I withhold from you?*" *(will, engagement, attention, thought).*] This makes a therapeutic alliance impossible. Therefore, deactivate these defenses.

But, the reader may ask, "Isn't the patient merely depending on the therapist?" We must differentiate healthy from pathological dependency. Ideally, the therapist offers what the patient cannot give. Pathological dependency occurs when the patient asks the therapist to give what the patient withholds.

Vignette One: Pointing Out Reality

We can help some patients who use the defense of helplessness by pointing out the reality consequences of that defense. Helplessness does not help the patient.

Pt: I'm not sure I have the motivation for this. [*Defense: helplessness.*]

Th: That may be, but if you don't have the motivation, we can't help you get to the bottom of your difficulties. [*Point out reality.*]

Pt: Isn't there something you can do? [*Could you make up for what I refuse to give to this relationship?*]

Th: If you don't have the motivation, we will have to accept that you don't have what we need to get to the top of the mountain. We will have to part ways, while I take those with the motivation to the top of the mountain. [*Point out reality.*]

Vignette Two: Deactivating Projection

Some patients adopt a helpless stance by projecting their capacity onto the therapist. In these cases, the therapist must point out and deactivate the projection.

Th: What's the feeling you have toward her?

Pt: I wish I could tell you. [*Defense: helplessness.*]

Th: What can we do about that?

Pt: What?

Th: What can we do about that? If you can't tell us what you feel, we won't be able to help you. [*Price of his defense.*] So what can we do about that? [*Block helplessness by asking him what stance he wants to take regarding this defense.*]

Pt: Couldn't you tell me what I feel? [*Defense: helplessness to project responsibility onto the therapist.*]

Th: Neither I nor anyone else can tell you what you feel. Only you can do that. [*Block the projection.*]

Pt: But what if I can't tell what I feel? [*Defense: helpless position.*]

Th: Then you'll have a real problem on your hands. [*Block projection.*] You want me to help you with your feelings, but if you don't know what you are feeling right now, then obviously I won't be able to help you with it. [*Price of his stance.*]

Pt: Aren't you supposed to be able to help me figure out what I feel? [*Project responsibility.*]

Th: No. Only you can feel what you feel. [*Block the projection.*]

Pt: [*Fidgets and shifts in his chair. Sign of rise of feeling and anxiety. When the patient lets go of his defense, unconscious feeling, and anxiety rise. After this rise of anxiety, ask about the feeling.*]

Th: What do you notice feeling in your body right now?

Pt: Uncomfortable. [*Anxiety.*]

Th: Where do you notice that in your body?

Pt: Just tension in my back. [*Striated muscles.*]

Th: Tension in your back. That's anxiety. [*Label the anxiety.*] What's the feeling toward me that's triggering all this anxiety?

Some patients adopt a helpless position by denying their actual capacity, which they have demonstrated previously. In those cases, remind the patient of reality.

Pt: I can't do it.

Th: That's not true. You've already demonstrated that you can face these feelings [*list examples for the patient*]. Together we can do this, if you'll give yourself a chance. Are you worth the effort?

Separate the patient from his helplessness by pointing out his agency. He *tells* himself that he is helpless; he *makes* himself into an incapable man; he *takes* a crippled position. Contrast his healthy goals with the helplessness that could defeat them. To differentiate him further from his defense, ask, "Why perpetuate your suffering this way?" "Why do this to yourself?"

Deactivate projections by pointing out that the defenses hurt the patient, not the therapist. The patient—not the therapist—will have to take a stand against the defense or live with the consequences. The patient who waits for magic waits forever.

Vignette Three: Hopelessness When Denial Breaks Down

Sometimes hopelessness is a way to take a helpless stance. However, hopelessness can also be a sign of progress. For instance, a patient realizes it is hopeless to expect the world to be the same as her fantasy. The hopelessness of her fantasy emerges when her denial of reality breaks down.

Pt: I think it is hopeless for me to look for a job. I will just be rejected.

Th: I think it is progress; you can see that. You know as well as I do that since you are not fluent in English, it is impossible to get or hold a job as an executive secretary. [*Point out reality.*]

Pt: But then I will not be able to buy a house! [*Cries.*]

Th: That is true. You will not be able to buy a house if you apply for jobs you can't hold. [*Point out that behavior based on denial (looking for jobs she won't get) leads to defeat.*]

Pt: But I cannot get a job. [*Defense: denial. She can get a job in reality, but not the one she wanted in fantasy. Her tears signal that her denial in fantasy is breaking down.*]

Th: That is not true. You can get a job, but it is impossible to get the job you wanted, an executive secretary position. And how hard that is! This fantasy was so beautiful. And how hard it is to let go of that beautiful picture you had in your mind.

Pt: It was a very beautiful picture. [*She observes her fantasy without substituting it for reality.*]

Projection

Projection is a defense by which we attribute to someone else a feeling, impulse, quality, or wish belonging to ourselves. Our view of other people becomes distorted. Rather than face our anger, we imagine the other person is angry with us. Then we become afraid of or preoccupied with the imaginary anger we place on him.

This example illustrates a key distinction between repressive and regressive defenses. Repressive defenses effectively reduce our awareness of feeling, so anxiety drops. We associate these defenses with a functioning triangle of conflict: feeling evokes anxiety, which triggers defenses that make us less aware of feeling and anxiety.

Regressive defenses do not work this way. The patient who projects becomes more anxious, afraid of the person upon whom he has projected. His anger is not repressed out of awareness; he sees it in (projected onto) others. For instance, if angry with the therapist, he projects and believes the therapist is angry with him. Thus, he fears the supposedly angry therapist.

This fear, created by projection, we call *projective anxiety* (H. Davanloo, supervision 2002–2004). Regressive defenses like projection trigger continual free-floating anxiety. They create a feedback loop: feeling triggers anxiety, which triggers projection, adding projective anxiety—which leads to more projection and projective anxiety, and so on. We cannot regulate anxiety that is perpetuated by projection.

Restructure projection to undo the projective anxiety and establish an intrapsychic perspective. A patient who projects believes other people cause his anxiety and problems. To understand the difference between an intrapsychic and externalizing focus, see table 9.2.

Table 9.2   Externalizing versus an internal focus for therapy

Projection	Externalizing focus	Internal focus
Causality	"I am afraid of you." "My problem is outside me: it's you."	"I have feelings. They trigger anxiety. So I use the Defense of projection. Then I fear you." "My problem is how I deal with the feelings and anxiety inside me."
Goal of therapy	"I think the problem is you. You must prove to me that you are not the same as my projection. We are here to examine you, not my projection."	"I need to see the difference between you and my projection. Then I can face my feeling, so I won't have to get anxious and project instead."

Patients who project the image of an aggressor fear the therapist will traumatize them. But it is too late. The trauma they fear in the future already occurred in the past (Winnicott 1965). Their projections chronically distort reality inside and outside the therapy session.

Denial involves not seeing what *is* in myself. Projection involves seeing what *is not* there in someone else. We deny something exists within ourselves. We project that element onto others.

Denial of anger through negation: "I'm not angry."

Projection of anger: "You are angry at me."

Splitting: "Negative feelings like anger are 'not me.' Good feelings are 'me'" (H. S. Sullivan 1953b).

When the patient relates to her projection instead of you, her experience of you and the therapy becomes distorted and more negative. Viewing you through the filter of her projection, she becomes suspicious and hypervigilant. She can react to her projection upon you by hiding from, criticizing, or leaving you [*hoping she left the projection behind in the therapist's office*].

Projection distorts perceptions of reality to varying degrees. A patient who generalizes projects onto you but recognizes those same feelings and impulses within herself. In classical projection, the patient attributes her unacceptable unconscious tendencies to someone else who she believes possesses them (Knight 1940, 335).

Although often considered a primitive defense, projection occurs across the spectrum of psychoneurosis (Willick 1985). Thus, we need to assess the function of the projection; the content of the projection (Frosch 1983); the patient's self-observing capacity (Bateman and Fonagy 2004; A. Freud 1936; S. Freud 1923/1961c; Ten Have de Labije 2001) and symbolic thinking (Bateman and Fonagy 2004; Fonagy et al. 2002; Segal 1981); and the pathway of unconscious anxiety discharge (H. Davanloo, supervision 2002–2004).

Function of Projection

Assess the function of a projection before analyzing and interpreting its content. Projection functions as a distancing tactic when anxiety is discharged in the striated muscles.

Th: What is the problem you would like me to help you with?

Pt: [*Sighs.*] My wife says I am a control freak. [*Defense: projection.*]

Here, the projection allows the patient to remain uninvolved in treatment. In such a case, projection functions as a tactical, not a regressive, defense.

Th: Since your wife is not here, I can't help her. [*Block the tactical defense.*] So what is the problem you would like me to help you with?

In contrast, projection functions as a "relocation" strategy for frightening internal experiences when anxiety is discharged in cognitive/perceptual disruption.

Pt: I can see from your eyes that you hate me for not visiting my mother.

Here, the projection "relocates" the superego onto the therapist to avoid the conflict *within* the patient between his anger toward his mother and his inner judgment of it.

The Pathway of Unconscious Anxiety Discharge

The interventions used for projections vary according to the patient's pathway of unconscious anxiety discharge and self-observing capacity. When anxiety is channeled in the striated muscles, block the projection by inviting feeling. "There is that barrier again. If you don't put up that barrier, what is the feeling toward me?"

Projection can also result from cognitive/perceptual disruption. When projection causes a loss of reality testing, restructure the projection, differentiate the therapist from the projection, and then regulate anxiety (Cornelissen 2005). For instance, some patients who use projection present with tension from head to toe *but with no sighing or hand clenching,* and thoracic rather than abdominal breathing. This is a freeze reaction in which the patient equates the therapist with her projection. Deactivate the projection, regulate anxiety, and then explore the feeling. As long as the patient experiences cognitive/perceptual disruption, interpretation of projection can have little integrative effect.

The following vignette shows how to help the patient differentiate the therapist from the projection. No exploration of other issues will be useful until the projection is deactivated.

Pt: I'm afraid you want to hurt me. [*Defense: projection.*]

Th: Are you seeing me as an abuser again? [*Point out the projection causing the freeze reaction.*]

Pt: Yes, but maybe you will hurt me!

Th: If you think I am a potential abuser, you absolutely *must not* open up to me. [*Clarify the consequences of the patient's assumption (projection).*]

Pt: [*Rise of anxiety in the patient in response to drop in the projection.*]

Th: What do you notice feeling inside?

Pt: I don't think you are listening to me. [*Defense: intellectualization. This repressive defense reveals a rise of anger.*]

Th: It sounds like you had a reaction to what I said. What do you notice feeling toward me?

Pt: [*Sighs.*] Irritated.

Th: It sounds like you got irritated with me, and then your irritation traveled across the room where you thought I was irritated and wanted to hurt you. Do you see how your irritation toward me turned around on you? [*Point out the triangle of conflict: feelings, anxiety, and the defense of projection.*]

Pt: I didn't quite hear what you said there. [*Cognitive/perceptual disruption when the projection drops, feeling, and anxiety rises so the patient goes over the threshold of anxiety tolerance.*]

Th: Are you having a little trouble thinking right now?

Pt: I'm feeling a little dizzy.

Th: Let's take a moment to put this together. This dizziness is a sign of anxiety. So we are noticing you were a bit miffed with me. Then, when we noticed you had put that feeling onto me, your anxiety went up, and you got dizzy there. Do you see how that happened here? [*Offer repeated cognitive summaries of the process until the patient's anxiety is back in the striated muscles and the freeze reaction drops.*]

Self-Observing Capacity

Patients usually are unable to observe their projection or differentiate it from the person upon whom they project. ("No. That's not my opinion. That's how she is!") This inability is known as *symbolic equation* (Segal 1981). The patient equates reality with his fantasy (the projection). For instance, a patient reported something illegal he had done and then accused the therapist of judging him. *Step one*: He judged himself for his crime. *Step two*: he projected his inner judgment onto the therapist. Then he was unable to differentiate the therapist from his projection (Winnicott 1971).

Help him differentiate the therapist from his projection by mobilizing, in this order, the ability to (1) see and pay attention to the defense, (2) differentiate reality from fantasy, (3) see the price of the defense; and (4) bear the feelings and anxiety that arise when integrating what he had projected. Restructure the pathway of unconscious anxiety discharge, restructure projection, and build self-observing capacity so the patient can face his inner life rather than project it onto others.

Projection of the Superego: A Spectrum

One of the most common projections is projection of the superego. This projection occurs along a spectrum from good reality testing to loss of reality testing, and from the projection of a mature conscience to the projection of severe aggression onto others. The following examples show how projection of the superego can occur across the spectrum of psychoneurosis.

- *Psychotic level of character structure:* Projection of a pathological superego onto a figure in the outside world—loss of reality testing. A schizophrenic woman has a delusion: "I'm afraid the mayor wants to cut off my head." She feels murderous rage toward her boyfriend. Rather than feel the conflict between her rage and her judgment of it, she projects her superego onto the mayor. She cannot differentiate reality from her fantasy.

- *Borderline level of character structure:* Projection of the pathological superego onto voices. The patient is aware the voices are in his mind but disavows that he is punishing himself. He becomes angry with the therapist during the session. A moment later he says, "The voices in my head say I should kill myself." He turns the anger onto himself while attributing this self-attack to "the voices."

- *Neurotic level of character structure:* Projection of a healthy conscience. A patient reports something unethical she did. Then she says, "You probably don't think this is a good idea." The therapist replies, "I think that's your conscience talking."

This patient can differentiate the therapist from her attribution. In addition, notice the content of the projection. She does not project an unhealthy *part* of her superego but an integrated conscience.

Psychotic patients project an extremely severe superego onto others and fear it there, unable to differentiate their projection from reality. Patients at a borderline level of character pathology either project or identify with the pathological superego. Deactivating their projections can trigger some brief cognitive/perceptual disruption and grief and guilt. Neurotic patients integrate their projected conscience with less difficulty. See table 9.3.

Table 9.3 The spectrum of projection of the superego and reality testing

Level of character structure	Type of superego projection	Level of symbolic functioning
Psychotic	Experiences hallucinated voices, delusions of persecution	Loss of reality testing
Borderline	Alternately projects or identifies with the superego	Transient loss of distinction between the therapist and the projection
Neurotic	Demonstrates integrated superego	Ability to differentiate reality and fantasy

Content of the Projection—Parts of Oneself

Moderately resistant patients may project their conscience onto you ("You might not think that was a good idea"). Highly resistant patients may project their awareness of an internal problem ("My wife thinks there is a problem, but I don't"), or a desire for help onto others ("My doctor said I should come"), or onto the therapist ("What do *you* think I should work on?"). Fragile patients may project their will to do therapy upon you ("I'm afraid of the questions you want to ask me") and then become afraid of you. Patients with character disorders may project their superego ("I can see you think I'm a terrible person") and then fear or become angry at your imagined criticism.

- Example One—anger

Pt: [*Angry with the therapist.*] Are you angry with me? [*Defense: projection of anger.*]

Th: Do you notice you put your anger over onto me, as soon as you are feeling it yourself? If you don't relocate your anger, how do you experience your anger here toward me?

- Example Two—grief

Pt: [*Struggling with her grief.*] I'm sorry. I don't want to overwhelm you. [*The patient, overwhelmed with her loss, projects her grief onto the therapist.*]

Th: But who is feeling the loss? [*Block the projection.*]

- Example Three—awareness

Pt: My wife thinks this is a problem. [*Projection of his awareness.*]

Th: Since your wife is not here, I can't help her, but I'm wondering what the problem is with which you would like me to help you? [*Block the projection and invite him to declare an internal problem.*]

Pt: How should I handle this? [*Projection of his ability to solve his problems.*]

Th: Only you can know for sure. [*Block the projection.*]

- Example Four—superego

Pt: You probably think this is stupid. [*Psychodiagnosis: anxiety in the striated muscles.*]

Th: What's the evidence for that? [*Differentiate the projection from the therapist.*]

Pt: Well, you haven't said anything, but it could be true.

Th: But what's the evidence?

Pt: Well, there isn't any yet.

Th: There's a thought in your head that I think badly of you, but there is no evidence to support the thought in your head. Could this be your critical conscience inside you calling you names?

Pt: I'm always criticizing myself.

Th: Sometimes you criticize yourself, and sometimes you imagine your conscience is out here in me, when it's been in you all the time.

- Example Five—will

Pt: You want me to share my feelings. [*Projection of his will to share onto the therapist.*]

Th: But who is it who came here wanting to know what was driving his depression and anxiety? [*Deactivate the projection of will by reminding the patient of his will.*]

The patient will react in a specific way to the projection he has placed on the therapist. Table 9.4 shows these common reactions to projections.

Table 9.4 Projection and the resulting subjective state of the patient

Content of the projection	Result
Pathological Superego	Fears the therapist's judgment
Healthy desires	Passively waits for the therapist to take responsibility for the therapy. Or fears the therapist will make her reveal her inner life
Rageful impulses	Fears the therapist's rage
Loving desires	Fears the therapist will violate her boundaries

Whether projection is a tactical or regressive defense depends on the pathway of anxiety discharge, the self-observing capacities, the content that is projected, and the degree of symbolic equation. The highly resistant patient uses projection as a tactical defense to keep the therapist at a distance. His anxiety remains in the striated muscles. He uses repressive or tactical defenses and suffers no loss of reality testing. Block his projections, and return to the focus on feeling.

In contrast, the fragile patient uses projection as a regressive defense to relocate internal experience. Her anxiety is discharged into cognitive/perceptual disruption. She uses regressive defenses and suffers from a loss of reality testing. She becomes terrified. Unable to differentiate between reality and her projection, she suffers from projective anxiety. Now she has a misalliance with a projection rather than a therapeutic alliance with the therapist. Restructure her projection, regulate anxiety, and then explore feeling. Table 9.5 shows how to assess whether a projection is a tactical or regressive defense.

Table 9.5 Psychodiagnosis of projection as a tactical or regressive defense

Qualities	Projection as tactical defense	Projection as a regressive defense
Function	Keep the therapist at a distance	"Relocate" feelings or parts of the mind
Pathway of anxiety discharge	Striated	Cognitive/perceptual disruption
Reality testing	Intact	Impaired or lost

Table 9.5   (continued)

Other defenses	Tactical, repressive, and character defenses	Regressive and character defenses
Projective anxiety?	No	Yes
Intervention	Block the projection, and then return to the focus.	Restructure the projection until reality testing and striated muscle tension returns, and then explore the feeling triggering the projection

See figure 9.1, which shows the sequence of interventions to use when assessing whether projection is a tactical or regressive defense.

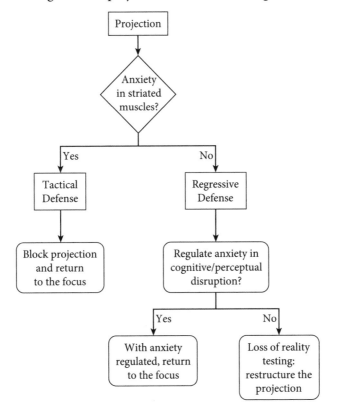

Figure 9.1   Psychodiagnosis of projection

If the projection is a regressive defense, the patient will experience a loss of reality testing, unable to differentiate the therapist from the projection. If the patient relates to a projection rather than the therapist, she will be in a misalliance with the projection rather than a therapeutic alliance with the therapist. Figure 9.2 shows the steps of assessment and intervention when addressing three common types of projection.

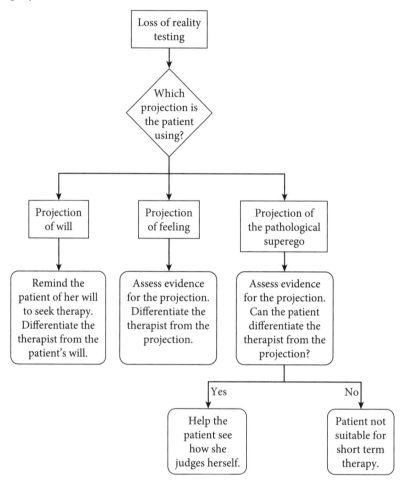

Figure 9.2   Restructuring the loss of reality testing in patients who project

PROVOCATION

Some patients have trouble tolerating their guilt. To avoid their guilt and the need to repair the damage they have inflicted on a relationship, they either punish themselves or provoke others to punish them. Help the patient see his guilt and how he provokes others to punish him. This will help establish an intrapsychic focus for the therapy.

Pt: I knew I shouldn't be doing this. It didn't feel right, but after I had sex with that bimbo at the bar, I came home. My wife asked me how my day was, and I snapped at her. I don't know what it was, but I was so pissed off at her. I was getting a glass of water at the sink. I don't even know what she said. All I know is I blew up, turned around, and threw a glass of water in her face. She got all pissed off and told me to get the hell out of the house if I was going to treat her like that. I left the house for a while to cool down.

Th: It sounds like you were not feeling too good about having sex with the woman at the bar. What was that feeling?

Pt: I felt guilty. My friends have talked about stepping out on their wives and how great it was, but it didn't feel so great to me.

Th: You felt guilty for having sex with this other woman, but the way you dealt with the guilt was to go home and provoke your wife to punish you, even though she didn't know the real reason. [*Point out the defense of provoking punishment from others to avoid his guilt.*]

Pt: I hadn't thought of that. I was just angry with her for being hard on me. [*Accuses his wife of being hard on him, yet his defense of self-punishment was hard on him.*]

Th: You thought she was being hard on you. Yet by throwing the water on her for no reason, you were hard on her, and you invited her to punish you. You felt guilty, but rather than face your guilt, you goaded her into punishing you. [*Point out how he projects his inner judgment onto his wife rather than feel his guilt.*]

Pt: That's true. I didn't feel right about it afterward.

Impulsive patients provoke others to punish them rather than feel guilty for their own misdeeds. Then they resent the "punishing" person rather than their defense of provoking punishment.

SOMATIZATION

Patients somatize in session in response to a rise of feelings. They do not usually see the link between a rise of feelings and the defense of somatization. Help the patient see the following sequence: rise of feelings, anxiety, and the defense of somatization. (See chapter 7 for examples.)

WEEPINESS

Tears come in to cover up anger. As soon as weepiness begins, intervene to avoid a depressive regression in therapy. Help the patient see how tears come in to wash away her anger. Then show her how this defense makes her depressed, unable to take effective action. (See chapter 10 for more information on weepiness.)

SUMMARY

Address regressive defenses systematically to develop an intrapsychic perspective. Remind the patient of reality: "You hoped you could leave your rage in my office when you left last time, but now we can see that no matter how far you run, your feelings are still inside you. No matter where you go, there you are." "You thought the hospital was persecuting you, but now we can see how you have been persecuting yourself. The hospital is not making you feel worse. Your self-persecution and self-attack is making you feel worse. The bad news is this: you are hurting yourself. The good news is that, since you are the one doing it, it could be entirely under your control."

Regressive defenses perpetuate the patient's anxiety, making it worse. Restructure them to regulate anxiety, mobilize self-observation, and then explore feelings.

To restructure regressive defenses, help the patient sequentially

1. Observe and pay attention to regressive defenses and the warded-off feelings
2. See causality
3. Differentiate reality from projections
4. Let go of regressive defenses

Build these capacities so the patient will be strong enough to bear the unlocking of unconscious feelings. By doing so, you will avoid misalliances, regression, and patient drop out.

RECOMMENDED READINGS

Coughlin Della Selva, P. (1996). Restructuring regressive defenses. In *Intensive short-term dynamic psychotherapy: Theory and technique* (pp. 79–103). New York: Wiley.

Davanloo, H. (1990). ISTDP with highly resistant depressed patients. In *Unlocking the unconscious* (pp. 1–27). Chichester, UK: Wiley.

Davanloo, H. (1990). The technique of unlocking the unconscious in patients suffering from functional disorders. part 1: Restructuring the ego's defenses. In *Unlocking the unconscious* (pp. 283–306). Chichester, UK: Wiley.

Korff, P. von (1998). Early management of unconscious defiance in Davanloo's intensive short-term dynamic psychotherapy, part 1. *International Journal of Short-Term Dynamic Psychotherapy, 12,* 183–208.

RECOMMENDED MATERIALS

You may want to visit http://www.istdpinstitute.com/DVDs/ and get the DVD series on restructuring projection in a borderline patient. It will help you see projection, what causes it, and how to intervene in different ways to help restore the patient's reality testing.

If you would like to view the video on projection presented by Jon Frederickson, visit the URL below. The video offers several examples of projection along with specific interventions for them.

Projection (December 20, 2012). http://www.youtube.com/watch?v =pPY2wKhiSWA.

CHAPTER TEN

Defensive Affects

D efensive affects are feelings that result from or function as defenses. Patients in the fragile spectrum suffer from overwhelming feelings, which result from regressive defenses. Projection floods them with projective anxiety. Defensive weepiness overwhelms them with depression. Externalization fills impulsive or paranoid people with endless rage.

Suppose a man projects, imagining others are angry or critical of him. In response, he will remain chronically angry, fearful, or depressed about this imaginary rejection. Unable to differentiate others from his projection, his feelings can escalate and become catastrophic. In a few patients, dysregulated emotions result from neurocognitive deficits or brain injury. For most people, however, dysregulated feelings function as or result from regressive defenses. Thus, the therapist must help the patient see and turn against defenses generating those defensive affects.

For instance, a patient projects her self-judgment onto her boyfriend, believing he will judge her. She feels sad and depressed as a result. If we encourage her to feel her sadness as deeply as possible, she will feel more depressed, unable to see her projection. Never explore defensive affects. Deactivate the defenses that create them or help the patient differentiate feelings from defensive affects.

This point is important for all expressive therapies. According to psychotherapy research, up to 10 percent of patients can become worse with an experiential therapy (Lilienfeld 2007). Why? Exploring and deepening defensive affects strengthens patients' regressive defenses, leading to increased depression, anxiety, and somatic symptoms. Experiencing defensive sadness increases depression and hopelessness. Expressing defensive rage increases acting out, projection, and destruction of relationships. Thus, differentiating feelings from defensive affects is essential to avoid harming patients in an emotion-focused therapy.

DIFFERENTIATING EXPRESSIVE CRYING FROM DEFENSIVE CRYING

Expressive crying and grief, though painful, remind us of our loss and our capacity to love. We feel relieved and lighter after expressive crying. Before the start of genuine grief, sympathetic nervous system activation rises as the patient wards off the grief. But as defenses drop and the patient cries, this sympathetic activation decreases and parasympathetic activation increases. The breathing and pulse rate slow, the patient cries, and her mouth produces more saliva (Fogel 2009; Gross, Fredrickson, and Levenson 1994; Hendriks, Rottenberg, and Vingerhoets 2007; Rottenberg, Gross, and Gotlib 2003). Expressive crying flushes out toxic stress hormones from the body and calms the patient (Fogel 2009, 110–112; D. Sullivan, Block, and Pena 1996; Walter 2006).

In contrast, defensive affects of sadness and weepiness ward off other feelings. Table 10.1 presents common types of genuine grief and defensive crying (see Fogel 2009, 112–113).

Table 10.1   Types of crying

Type of cry	Features	Therapist countertransference
"Good" crying	Awareness of one's bodily experience of feeling. Calming, brief, easily soothed, most likely to have tears.	Patient feels nurturing and affection.
Protest crying	Intense, loud, angry sobbing, helpless and unsoothable. Exhausted rather than relieved.	Pateint feels apathy, irritation, pushed away, or guilty.
Infantile crying	Lip quivering, trembling, may be tearless, repeated stereotypical movements. May be related to infantile attachment trauma.	Patient feels unreachable, lost inside of herself.
Unprovoked or prolonged crying	Unprovoked by any obvious thought or stimulus, based on imaginary stimulus or unacknowledged grief.	Therapist feels confused, unable to find an explanation for the crying.

Table 10.1 (continued)

Dramatic crying	Not clearly connected to an emotion. Socially inappropriate, dead feeling inside. Possibly linked to childhood rejection and acting out to get attention.	Therapist feels manipulated by attention seeking. Tries to avoid the patient's entreaties.

Sources: T. Alexander 2003; Mills and Wooster 1987; J. Nelson 2000.

Protest crying can occur when the patient projects the superego onto the therapist: "You withhold from me, so I can hope for nothing from you." The patient becomes lost in sad hopelessness in front of the seemingly withholding therapist. Do not explore her feelings of rage and hopelessness, the result of projection. Instead, address the projection.

Infantile crying can occur when a patient who punishes herself, fears that the therapist will punish her. Fearing the "punitive" therapist, she cries with fearful trembling. Or a patient may feel anger while covering it with anxiety (which looks like infantile crying).

Unprovoked crying does not occur except in neurological conditions. Otherwise, a stimulus (either real or imaginary) always triggers crying. Prolonged crying, which brings no relief, is a defense (warding-off feeling) or the result of a defense. For instance, if a patient with a severe superego calls herself ugly, she may project her superego onto her boyfriend: "He thinks I'm ugly." In response, she cries without stopping and finds no relief. She is not grieving a genuine loss in reality. Instead, she suffers from an imaginary loss created by her projection (a constantly "rejecting" boyfriend). The crying can't stop until her projection stops. These patients do not suffer from dysregulated affects but from dysregulating defenses.

For instance, rather than express her rage for not getting the attention she wants, she may hide it under dramatic crying. Dramatic crying can also be a form of discharge to get rid of the internal experience of her guilt and prove how badly she feels.

Sometimes therapists confuse these defensive affects with genuine sadness. The following criteria differentiate genuine grief from defensive weepiness.

Process: Sadness and grief trigger anxiety and defenses. Since weepiness either functions as a defense or results from one, it does not trigger anxiety and defenses. Weepiness emerges after defenses, for example, projection or externalization. Or it arises after anger to ward it off.

Real versus an imaginary stimulus: Grieving involves a genuine loss, for example, "My husband died of cancer." Defensive sadness involves imaginary loss, for instance, a patient with a history of choosing abusive men claims that all men are bad and that she will never find a good one. In response to her projection that all men will be bad to her, she cries over imaginary losses in the future.

Physiological activation: Genuine grieving involves parasympathetic activation during which the body relaxes, the patient sighs, and cries with a loose belly, and tears flow freely. She feels more deeply connected to herself and the therapist. Defensive "sadness" involves continuous sympathetic activation during which the body remains tense, the heart rate and breathing remain elevated, the throat is tight, and the patient does not experience a deeper connection to herself or the therapist.

Unconscious signaling: Rising grief triggers anxiety in the form of tension in the striated muscles. Once the patient feels the grief, anxiety drops. The belly and throat relax and parasympathetic activation dominates. In contrast, during weepiness, tension continues with heightened sympathetic activation.

Defense activation: Grief triggers defenses and emerges more fully when the patient lets go of her defenses. In contrast, weepiness functions as or results from regressive defenses; it does not evoke them.

Architecture of the experience: Grief rises and falls in the shape of a wave. In contrast, weepiness fluctuates according to the amount of anger it must ward off or the projection the patient is using.

Result of experiencing the feeling: Genuine grieving brings relief and clarity. Defensive sadness brings no relief or clarity, just exhaustion and increased pain. For instance, the woman who projects that her boyfriend will reject her feels no relief after crying because she believes she is still with an imaginary rejecter in whom she has no hope.

Weepiness: Intervention

Weepiness arises as soon as the depressed patient begins to experience her rage. If the weepiness is not rapidly addressed, she becomes more depressed in session. In this example, notice how the therapist identifies the patient's weepiness immediately and mobilizes her attention to stop the regression. Once the regressive defense stops, explore the feeling again. Emotion differentiation is essential to emotion regulation (Barrett et al. 2001).

Th: What is the feeling toward your boyfriend for dumping you on Valentine's Day?

Pt: I'm upset. [*Defense: cover word.*]

Th: Clearly he upset you. That's what he did. What's the feeling toward him for doing that?

Pt: I'm angry. [*Becomes tearful. Defense: weepiness.*]

Th: Do you notice how these tears come in right now? [*Mobilize patient's attention to the defense.*]

Pt: [*Nods.*]

Th: Notice how these tears come in to wash away your anger as soon as you feel it? [*Label the defense.*]

Pt: I feel sad now. [*Psychodiagnosis: she does not differentiate her defensive sadness from her anger nor does she see its function: to cover up her anger.*]

Th: Do you see how this sadness and tears come in to cover up and wash away your anger? [*Point out the function of the defense.*]

Pt: I think so.

Th: Do you think that these tears are washing away your anger? Do you think these tears might be making you depressed? [*Link the defense to her presenting problem.*]

Pt: Absolutely.

Th: Would you like to take an honest look at this anger so it won't have to get covered with tears and so we could help you overcome this depression? [*Mobilize the patient's will to engage in the therapeutic task.*]

Initially, she cannot feel her anger nor differentiate it from defensive affects such as anxiety and sadness. Once weepiness begins, help her observe its defensive function. Once the weepiness stops, invite the feeling again.

Defensive Weepiness in Response to Self-Attack

Notice how the therapist identifies and draws the patient's attention to the defense of self-attack immediately. In this way, the therapist interrupts the regression into depression. Then the therapist helps the patient face the feeling covered up by the self-attack.

Th: How do you experience this rage toward your boss for putting you down?

Pt: I should have finished college. If I had, I wouldn't be in this situation. I'm such an idiot. [*Cries. Defense*: *self-attack.*]

Th: You are describing yourself now, but do you notice you were freer to describe your boss a minute ago? [*Point out the defense.*]

Pt: Yes, but—

Th: [*Interrupt the defense of self-attack.*] But if we don't describe you, can we take a look at your boss? It sounds like you have a feeling toward your boss. Could we take a look at the feeling toward your boss?

Pt: Okay. [*Weepiness stops.*]

Th: What is the feeling toward him?

Pt: Anger.

If the therapist does not block self-attack, weepiness and depression will deepen in the session. Exploring weepiness will make the patient feel even more depressed, and her self-attack will resume the next time she feels angry. Always block the self-attack that causes weepiness and help the patient see its defensive function. Then you will have blocked the self-attack, which causes a regression into depression.

Weepiness in Response to Projection of the Superego

In this example, the patient hates herself and projects that men will think she is fat and ugly. The therapist explores to find out if the patient is projecting the superego onto him. Then the therapist helps the patient see the difference between him and her projection. Then he helps her see how she judges herself internally. Once this is clear, the therapist can explore the feeling toward him. As long as she projects her superego onto the therapist, she will feel a weepy despair of ever being accepted by the superego/therapist.

> *Th:* Since we are also forming a relationship here, I wonder how that fear is in operation here with me? [*Explore to see if she is project-ing onto the therapist.*]
>
> *Pt:* I'm afraid you are judging my weight. [*Cries. Defensive affect re-sulting from her projection.*]
>
> *Th:* What's the evidence that I'm judging your weight? [*Block the projection.*]
>
> *Pt:* No evidence really. But you can see I'm overweight.
>
> *Th:* But who just called you overweight? [*Block the projection.*]
>
> *Pt:* I did.
>
> *Th:* You just called yourself overweight. So who has that thought?
>
> *Pt:* Me.
>
> *Th:* You are judging your weight, but then you put that judgment onto me. Do you see how that just happened? [*Point out the projection.*]
>
> *Pt:* I do now. [*Teariness has stopped.*]
>
> *Th:* If we put that judgment off to the side, if you don't judge yourself, can we take a look at the feeling toward me right now?

The patient was angry with me, judged her anger, and then pro-jected that I judged her. This triggered her weepiness. Angry with men, she punished herself through self-judging, and then imagined they would judge and reject her. Once we cleared up her projection, her weepiness stopped. Deactivate the projection that creates the weepi-ness, and the weepiness will stop.

Grief is a response to real loss: a spouse dies. *Defensive weepiness* can be a response to an imaginary loss: the patient fantasizes that a man will reject her. In the first example, grief is in response to an exter-nal stimulus in reality. In the second example, weepiness is in response to an internal stimulus in her imagination. She projects onto her date, imagines him rejecting her, and becomes sad. She is not aware of how she rejects herself. She is aware that she believes men will reject her. Then she can fear, be angry at, or feel sad over these "rejecting" men. But these feelings are in response to her projection. Do not explore any feelings resulting from projections. Instead, identify and clarify the defense of projection.

If we explore the patient's rage toward a projection she puts onto others, she will become more enraged, keep equating others with her projections, and become more entrenched in the victim stance. *Help her differentiate other people from her projections to establish an intrapsychic focus.* Then explore the feelings triggering the defense.

DEFENSIVE RAGE

Defensive rage is based on the defenses of projection and externalization or it wards off grief. Sometimes therapists confuse defensive rage with genuine rage. The following criteria differentiate genuine from defensive forms of rage.

Process: The feeling of anger occurs before anxiety and defense. Defensive rage comes up after feeling and anxiety. For instance, defensive rage occurs after the feeling of grief to ward it off.

Real versus an imaginary stimulus: Genuine anger results from a stimulus in reality. For example, "My husband hit me." Defensive anger involves imaginary stimuli based on defenses such as projection. For instance, a patient who criticizes himself projects that other people do not respect him. He is continually furious with them for their supposed disrespect. Genuine anger goes toward a real enemy; defensive rage goes toward an imaginary one. Suppose a patient yells at and insults her husband until he finally stomps out of the house. Then she is angry with him for "abandoning" her. Yet through her provocation, she artificially created her enemy (Bergler 1961).

Physiological activation: When the impulse of genuine rage passes, the patient relaxes and feels relief. In contrast, the experience of the impulse in defensive rage, expressing rage toward a projection, gives no relief. The patient is still relating to a terrible, unchanging person: the projection. Since projection continues, so does the defensive rage.

Unconscious signaling: Genuine anger triggers anxiety in the body. Once the patient feels the anger, anxiety drops. Defensive anger, the result of a defense (usually projection), does not trigger anxiety or defenses. Thus, raging at length without defenses arising is defensive anger.

Defense activation: Genuine rage triggers defenses and emerges more fully when defenses drop. Defensive rage functions as a defense, so it doesn't trigger repressive defenses. Instead, projection or externalization create and sustain the defensive rage.

Architecture of the experience: Genuine rage rises and falls in the shape of a wave. Defensive rage rises rapidly due to projection and remains high as long as the patient projects. Defensive anger remains chronically elevated because of chronic projection.

Result of experiencing the feeling: The experience of genuine anger brings relief and clarity. Defensive rage leads to no relief, only exhaustion and despair. The patient who chronically projects onto his wife feels perpetual rage or despair. The pseudoclarity that results is merely the result of a deepened belief in the projection: "I always knew she was a completely horrible person." The experience of defensive rage encourages the patient to project more, develop a more distorted sense of others, and become increasingly hopeless.

Differentiating Normal Rage from Defensive Rage

Normal rage occurs in response to a stimulus in external reality: you hit me. Defensive rage (based on projection) occurs in response to a wrong done in fantasy: I imagine you are judging me, and then become enraged with you. If someone harmed the patient in reality, explore the reactive rage as deeply as possible. Do not explore rage resulting from projection. Instead, address the projection to establish an intrapsychic focus. Let us look at some additional factors that differentiate genuine from defensive rage (Bergler 1959, 69–70).

Use: Normal rage is used *exclusively* for self-defense. Defensive rage is used indiscriminately.

Object: Normal rage is toward a real enemy who hurt you. "He called my work a piece of trash in front the entire class." Defensive rage is toward an imaginary enemy, created by distorted fantasies or projections. "I just knew she would say I should visit her on Sunday, so I let her have it before she could say a word." Normal rage is provoked by others. Defensive rage *provokes* a fight.

Guilt: Normal rage does not provoke guilt because it is proportional, directed toward the person who attacked. "The normal person doesn't pick a fight; he . . . defends himself when attacked" (Bergler 1948, 29). Neurotic rage always triggers guilt because it goes out on the wrong person to a disproportionate extent. The patient's projections trigger his rage, not the other person's actions.

Dose: The amount of normal rage corresponds to the provocation. Defensive rage corresponds to the fantasy or projection. A small slight plus projection triggers an excessive response.

Purpose: Normal rage has the purpose of stopping an enemy. Defensive rage has the purpose of triggering retaliation and punishment from an imaginary enemy.

Normal rage: I consciously intend to harm the other.

Defensive rage: I unconsciously arrange to harm myself.

Timing: The healthy person waits to express his rage when it is adaptive and his enemy is vulnerable. He can wait. Defensive rage occurs immediately without an ability to wait.

Stimulus: Normal rage is a reaction to a real stimulus in the external world. Defensive rage is often a reaction to an imaginary stimulus in the internal world.

Provocation: Normal rage cannot be easily provoked. Defensive rage can.

Pleasure: Normal rage does not bring pleasure. It is done as a necessary but disagreeable job. We experience defensive rage as exciting and pleasurable in advance, even though it provokes punishment in the end.

Does the patient seek success or defeat?: The normal person fights to succeed. The neurotic person provokes fights to lose, even though he claims he wants to win. His pattern of defeats, however, reveals *the underlying result and aim: suffering.*

Defensive Rage to Cover Grief

Sometimes patients use defensive rage to cover up their grief. In this example, notice how the therapist assesses the patient's response and sees the defense of devaluation. If the patient devalues her husband, she can claim she lost nothing. But to ward off the grief, she must be enraged forever at a devalued husband. Thus, the therapist must help the patient see and let go of her devaluation so she can face what she did value in him and has lost forever.

Th: I'm sorry to hear of your husband's death. I know how hard this has been for you during this ordeal with his cancer. How are you feeling now?

Pt: [*Tears.*] I'm glad the SOB is dead. What a relief! When I look back, I wonder what good he ever was to me. [*Defensive rage based on devaluation.*]

Th: It's as if you want to cover your tears with the rage instead. If only he had been worthless, then you wouldn't have to bear this loss of what was good in him. [*Point out the defense.*]

Pt: A lot of good it does me now. [*Defense: devaluation.*]

Th: He did a lot of good for you then. But death does you no good right now. Death took him away.

Pt: [*Cries.*]

Defensive Rage in Response to a Projection

The following example concerns a fragile patient who constantly fears that other people want to hurt her.

Pt: I gave a presentation at work yesterday and the evaluator came in to sit next to my boss. After my presentation the evaluator was really critical. He said he didn't know what I was talking about. He said my presentation was unclear, and that I had not even spoken on the right topic. I was afraid he was going to get me fired. Fortunately, my boss spoke up and said she thought my presentation was clear, and that the topic was one she had suggested to me. I didn't really have to fear my boss, but now I'm afraid the evaluator is going to retaliate and get me fired. [*Having been angry at the evaluator for criticizing her, she projects her anger onto him, fears he will hurt her, and is then angry at him as a imaginary retaliator.*]

Defensive Anger Due to Projection of the Superego

Notice how the therapist assesses the patient's response and sees that the patient projects her superego onto the therapist and does not differentiate him from her projection. Thus, the therapist must deactivate the projection so the patient will have a therapeutic alliance with him instead of a misalliance with her projection. As long as she projects a superego onto him, she will be enraged with him.

Pt: I'm angry with you because I can see you are judging and criticizing me. [*Projection of superego.*]

Th: What is the evidence I am judging you? [*Point out reality.*]

Pt: I just feel that way.

Th: I understand you feel that way, but my question was different. What is the evidence to support your feeling? What is the evidence I am judging and criticizing you?

Pt: Well, there isn't any evidence yet. But there could be!

Th: There is no evidence that I am criticizing you. So where is that thought of criticism coming from? Who is having that thought?

Pt: I am.

Th: You are having a critical thought but then you attributed it to me. But now we can see that the critical thought is in you. Is there a tendency for you to be too hard on yourself?

Pt: Yes. I criticize myself all the time.

Th: Can we take a look at what is underneath that self-criticism right now?

Help the patient see the difference between the therapist and the patient's projection of the superego so she can observe her defense of self-criticism and the anger she is criticizing. Then explore any angry feelings coming up toward the therapist.

Defensive Anger Based on Externalization

In this example, notice how the therapist helps the patient see the choices she made that caused her suffering. The therapist will focus on elements of reality upon which they agree. Then he will use those elements of reality to help the patient see how she caused her suffering.

Pt: [*Arrives to the session twenty minutes late.*] I'm so angry with Sadie. She wanted to catch a ride with me downtown when I came to my session. But then she was late. I told her we had to leave at two o'clock. But she wasn't ready. I told her I had to leave because our session is at three o'clock. But then she was so slow getting out of the shower and then getting dressed. I kept telling her we had to go but she didn't listen. She kept making me wait. So she made me late today. I'm so angry that she doesn't respect my time or listen to me.

Th: Who made the decision to wait? [*Point out to the patient her role.*]

Pt: She did, because she was late. [*Externalization.*]

Th: Who made the decision to wait for her?

Pt: I did, but she wasn't ready yet.

Th: You waited for her. So you made yourself late. But you blame her for your decision to wait for her. And you blame her for your decision to make yourself late. Do you see what I mean? [*Point out the externalization.*]

Pt: But she made me late! [*Externalization. Psychodiagnosis: the patient cannot differentiate the stimulus (daughter's lateness) from her defense (self-punishment through choosing to be late).*]

Th: That's not true. [*Differentiate reality from fantasy, her actions from her daughter's actions, and her responsibility from her daughter's.*] She chose to be late. Then you had two options: you could choose to leave on time by yourself or choose to be late with her. You chose to be late with her. That was your choice. But then you blame her for your choice.

Pt: But she wasn't listening to me! [*Externalization: the patient didn't listen to herself. She does not differentiate the stimulus (daughter not listening to her) from her defense (not listening to herself).*]

Th: Of course not, but that wasn't the problem. The problem was that you weren't listening to yourself! If she doesn't listen to you and you don't listen to you, then you have a problem. If she doesn't listen to you, but you listen to yourself anyway, you don't have a problem. It's as if you were waiting for her to listen to you before you were going to listen to yourself and leave. Do you see what I mean? [*Point out what she did (not listen to herself) and how she projects that onto her daughter ("She doesn't listen to me").*]

Pt: If I had just come on time, I would not have been stewing there for twenty minutes. [*Patient begins to realize the price of her defense.*]

Th: Can we take a look at what happened? What did you feel when she was delaying?

Pt: Anger.

Th: You felt angry. That makes you anxious. Then rather than just feel the anger and go on your way, you punished yourself for being angry by making yourself late and you punished yourself for being angry by cheating yourself out of twenty minutes of your therapy time. [*Point out the triangle of conflict.*] And then you blamed your daughter for your choice to punish yourself. [*Point out the externalization.*]

Pt: That certainly fits my pattern, doesn't it? I hadn't seen how I blamed her for what I was doing to myself. [*Patient now sees the defense.*]

Externalization leads her to take a victim stance: she complains about and blames others for what she did to herself. She raged at her daughter, unable to see how she hurt herself. As long as she blames her daughter, her rage will escalate. Whenever you see a victim stance, start looking for the externalization that sustains it.

Defensive Anger Due to Denial of Responsibility

In this example, notice how the therapist helps the patient see how he blames his partner for his choices. The therapist helps the patient see elements of reality. Then the therapist helps the patient see the choices he made that caused his suffering. As long as he does not see the choices he made that caused his suffering, he will believe his partner caused his suffering and be eternally angry with her for his choices.

Pt: I'm so furious with my girlfriend. She decided to take this teaching job here, which will last another year, and I came along. But I hate this city. I hate the people here. My job sucks, and there is no way to find something better in my specialty here. I was yelling at her last night about how much I hate this place. She just says that her contract lasts another year, and then we can move. But I just resent her so much for taking this job.

Th: Who decided to move with her? [*Point out reality.*]

Pt: I did.

Th: It was your choice, but you yell at her for what you chose.

Pt: But she was the one who wanted to move.

Th: And at that time you could have said you wouldn't move. But you chose to move here with her. That was your choice. And she is not responsible for your choice. You are. But you try to have it both ways. You chose to stay with her and you punish her for your choice. You decided she was more important to you than where you live. But now that you are here, you resent her for your choice.

As the patient recognizes how he projects the responsibility for his choice onto his girlfriend, his rage drops rapidly. Once he admits his destructive self-abandonment, we have an intrapsychic focus. We can focus on his defense, not her move.

GUILT

Misunderstandings occur when we confuse *healthy guilt* with *neurotic guilt*. (See Bergler 1959, 71–73.) Healthy guilt and neurotic guilt differ in the following ways.

Subject matter: Healthy guilt is for what you did—you hurt someone. Neurotic guilt is often displaced. A patient feels neurotic guilt over forgetting someone's name. In fact, she hates the guy. So she punishes herself for the lesser crime.

Quantitative factor: The amount of healthy guilt corresponds to the wrong deed you committed. Neurotic guilt corresponds to the need for self-punishment.

Expiation: Normal guilt can be expiated by repairing the damage you inflicted on the relationship. Neurotic guilt cannot be expiated because it is how we punish ourselves.

Time limit: Normal guilt disappears because you repaired the damage you caused. Neurotic guilt never disappears. The self-punishment continues.

Self-limitation versus self-aggravation: Normal guilt is self-limiting through reparation and compassion for self and others. Neurotic guilt grows in intensity as the patient misuses more elements of reality to torment herself with new "crimes."

Exhaustibility: Normal guilt is a realistic response to a real deed and, therefore, exhaustible. Neurotic guilt is an unrealistic form of self-punishment, which is inexhaustible.

Battlefronts: Genuine guilt is for a real deed. Neurotic guilt is connected to a substitute. A man feels guilt for criticizing a colleague in a meeting, which is a substitute for the real deed over which he feels guilt: convincing the boss to fire the colleague.

Type of guilt: Normal guilt is realistic. Neurotic guilt is an unrealistic form of self-punishment.

Outcome: Normal guilt rises and then ends with reparation. Neurotic guilt is forever.

THE STRUCTURE OF FEELING EXPERIENCE

Greenspan and Shanker (2006) proposed a hierarchy of feeling capacities: (1) to attend to and regulate feelings; (2) to express, understand, and signal with a wide range of feelings; and (3) to construct representations and be able to differentiate them from reality. A patient who cannot pay attention to her feelings and identify the needs they signal cannot regulate or express them adaptively. If a patient cannot pay attention to her anger when a boyfriend criticizes her, she will not be able to identify her need to set a self-protective limit, nor express it. Unable to pay attention to or identify her anger, she may unconsciously turn it onto herself, become depressed, and suffer from "affect dysregulation." Or she may project her anger onto her boyfriend and then remain paralyzed by fear of him. Unable to pay attention to the bodily experience of her feelings, her ability to represent them is impaired. She cannot use her feelings as a source of conscious information.

Feelings represent a continuum from nonawareness (the emotion is simply acted out) to complete awareness (the feeling is experienced and verbally labeled). Table 10.2 illustrates how patients represent their feelings.

Table 10.2   Hierarchy of feeling states

Representational states	Examples
Abstracted feeling states: Words have a combined affective/cognitive meaning and refer to specific differentiated feeling states.	Joy, anger, anxiety, sadness, disgust, shame, guilt
Expressions of global feelings	"I feel awful."
Verbalization of organized somatic feelings	"My heart aches."
Verbalization of disorganized somatic feelings	"When she stares at me, it's as if my body explodes into a thousand pieces."
Verbalization of intention in behavioral terms	"I want to push you."
Verbalization of behavior	"I grabbed her."
Organized somatic description	"My heart hurts.
Disorganized, fragmented, primitive somatic pattern	"My blood vessels were going to explode."
Complex gestural communication	Angry or loving facial expressions
Direct discharge of behavior	Hitting, biting, hugging, holding
Simple gestural communication	Smiles, nods, frowns

Source: Greenspan 1997, 230.

Feeling states can be categorized as prebehavioral, behavioral, and verbal representations. Verbal representations of feeling can be behavioral intentions, fragmented somatic states, organized somatic states, and abstract, differentiated feeling states. The patient who represents his feelings in disorganized somatic terms or in behavioral or gestural terms is more likely to be impulsive. For instance, he may tell you he wants to hit someone but not know the feeling he has: anger. Or he says he is angry but cannot tolerate the experience of it in his body so he acts out instead. A patient who represents his anger as a disorganized somatic state might say, "I feel like I could explode into a thousand pieces." But he won't be able to label his feeling as anger.

ASSESSMENT OF IMPULSIVITY

This *hierarchy of affect symbolization* (how we put feelings into words) allows us to assess impulsivity in fragile patients. To assess, first ask if the patient has impulsively acted out in the past. Second, assess the patient's affect tolerance, maturity of defenses, anxiety tolerance, and affect symbolization.

Affect tolerance: Patients who have good impulse control can label and tolerate the rise of the feeling without acting out. Patients with poor impulse control cannot tolerate the experience of anger. Instead, they try to get rid of it by moving their bodies, getting up out of the chair, and raising their voices. They act out impulses to avoid the internal experience of the feeling. Encourage them to tolerate the feeling without resorting to discharge. Blocking discharge helps the patient develop a higher tolerance of the rage, thereby reducing impulsivity. When he wants to talk about and act out his impulse, ask about the experience of anger in the body. The longer he can tolerate his anger without acting it out, the greater his affect tolerance. The lower the affect tolerance, the sooner he acts out.

Maturity of defenses: Patients with good impulse control use repressive defenses that keep anger out of awareness. Patients with poor impulse control use regressive defenses: acting out, discharge, racing speech, and projection. They project their impulses or superego onto others whom they imagine to be hostile. Then they act out with the people on whom they project.

Anxiety tolerance: Patients who discharge their anxiety into the striated muscles usually have good impulse control. However, patients whose anxiety is discharged into cognitive/perceptual disruption use projection more frequently.

Affect symbolization: Patients with good impulse control can label their feeling of anger and describe how they experience the feeling and impulse in their body. Patients with poor impulse control describe their feeling as disorganized somatic states ("I feel like I want to explode") or as a behavioral intention ("I want to hit him"), after which the patient, unable to tolerate the experience of the anger, begins to punch the air with his fist. He does not just describe a feeling; he enacts it. Some impulsive patients suffer from "trigger language." The word *anger* may trigger action in the patient rather than reflection (Ekstein 1966). The therapist might say, "You seem angry." A reflective patient would respond, "You're right. I do feel angry." An impulsive patient for whom language has a trigger function will pound his fist and yell, "You're goddamn right I'm angry!"

FEELINGS AND SYMBOLIC FUNCTIONING

For feelings to become part of our symbolic world, we must separate perception from action, which are not separated in young children and impulsive adults. An impulsive adult feels an impulse and punches the wall without delay. He cannot observe or pay attention to his feeling or think about how best to channel it. Impulse becomes action without any intervening awareness or attention to the feeling. Such patients are not conscious of what they feel when they act. Unable to express verbally or to think abstractly about their feelings, these patients remain in an action mode (Greenspan and Shanker 2006, 467).

For instance, a patient who threatened people with knives in his group home suddenly ran out of my office. Another person could say, "My legs feel like I want to run out of the office." Someone else with more awareness could say, "I'm afraid of you." And a patient with much higher capacity could reflect, "I'm aware I'm angry with you for saying that. In the past I felt like running away from you as if *you* were angry with *me.*"

Some might call the patient who ran out of my office impulsive. This describes the quality of the symptom but not its cause. The patient cannot observe or pay attention to his feeling (anger), anxiety, or defense (projection). Unable to observe or pay attention to his feelings, he is not conscious of them. Unable to differentiate me from his projection, he must run away from me. His so-called impulse is not a feeling but a reaction to the projection he placed on me. He did not run away from a therapist but from a projection.

The second patient can observe his legs (the defensive action) but not his feeling, anxiety, or the defense of projection. The third patient, who says he is afraid of his therapist, can observe the result of his projection, but not his act of projecting. Unaware of his anger and his projection of it, he assumes he is afraid of the therapist. Since the last patient can see his feeling (anger) and the defense of projection, he no longer feels the urge to run away from a projection.

Each patient wanted to run away from a projection. The feeling seems catastrophic in the first case because the patient cannot see his projection, differentiate his therapist from his projection, or differentiate past experience from the present. The loss of reality testing causes catastrophic feelings.

To regulate emotions, *activate the missing self-observing capacities.* In the first patient, we would separate the projection from the therapist, differentiate past and present, mobilize the patient's ability to observe and pay attention to anxiety in his body, mobilize his ability to observe and pay attention to the feeling triggering his anxiety, and mobilize his ability to see causality—when he feels angry, he gets anxious and then projects his anger and acts out toward his projections. Then his impulsivity drops because he can differentiate the therapist from his projection.

When impulses result from projection, help the patient see the projection and regain his reality testing before exploring the feeling. Help impulsive patients who experience a fast rise of feeling to observe and pay attention to the physical experience of the feeling in the body without enacting it. These skills build the capacities for feeling tolerance, impulse control, "the construction of internal representations, and higher levels of consciousness" (Greenspan and Shanker 2006, 467).

When the patient can pay attention to and put those feelings into words, the feelings no longer trigger unreflective action. He can represent them as words, images, and fantasies that acquire many meanings. Rather than suffer from "impulses" resulting from projections, he experiences feelings triggered by real stimuli, which he can channel into effective action.

SUMMARY

So-called *dysregulated affects are the result of dysregulating defenses.* The issue is not regulation of the dysregulated affect but helping the patient see the defenses that create it, especially projection. Krystal (1974, 1975, 1988, 1998), in his studies of alexythemia, proposed that these patients suffer from hyposymbolization, dedifferentiation, and affect regression. Patients who ignore the physical experience of their feelings cannot label them. If patients cannot differentiate the therapist from a projection, we will have dedifferentiation and regression.

The term *affect regression* is a misnomer. Affects do not regress. The patient's regression in reality testing leads her to confuse the therapist with her projection. Fearing her projection as if it were real, she is in a genuine catastrophe. Patients suffering a flashback cannot differentiate the present from the past, the therapist from an abuser. They relive rather than remember the past. This regression in reality testing leads to catastrophic affects.

Any feeling can be too much to bear if the patient has to bear it alone without the support of another caring human being. Patients become overwhelmed by defensive affects for that reason and others. Defensive affects become overwhelming when there is a loss of reality testing—an inability to differentiate a past trauma from current reality, a loss of reality testing due to projection, a loss of reality testing due to loss of differentiation between the observing ego and experiencing self, increasing defensive affects to cover other feelings (e.g., weepiness to cover rage or rage to cover grief), and increasing defensive affects to punish the patient for an expression of rage (e.g., a rise in shame and self-attack). If the patient is experiencing a feeling while in the presence of a projection, she will be bearing her feeling alone and will become overwhelmed.

For the traumatized patient "every emotional experience resonates as if it were the recurrence of the trauma" (Wurmser 2003, 226). We can tolerate a feeling experienced as a memory in the past. "I remember feeling this way when I was with my uncle Ed in Iowa." The feeling rises and subsides because the patient differentiates the past and present. When reliving a trauma, feelings do not subside because the patient equates the present feeling with the past trauma (Segal 1981). In his mind, he *is* with Uncle Ed.

All patients within the spectrum of fragility suffer from defensive affects. Identify, clarify, and restructure the regressive defenses causing the defensive affects. When the patient *tolerates her genuine feelings without using regressive defenses*, she can bear an unlocking of the unconscious.

PART THREE

Helping the Highly Resistant Patient

CHAPTER ELEVEN

Superego Pathology

In part 1, we learned the basic principles of assessment applicable to all patients. In part 2, we learned additional principles of assessment and intervention for patients in the fragile spectrum. Now we will address the principles and interventions for highly resistant patients.

These patients use a special group of defenses based on the enactment of identifications within the superego. Since these defenses have a different structure from the defenses discussed previously, they require a special set of interventions designed to address the identifications on which these defenses are based. Since these defenses occur on a spectrum of syntonicity, they require a spectrum of interventions designed to help patients see them. But before we look at those defenses, we will first examine the concept of the superego.

A woman living with an abusive husband says she does not deserve anything better in life. An adolescent girl claims she is proud of her ability to cut her arms and starve herself. A young man fails a test in medical school, feels enormous shame, and then commits suicide. An out-of-control internal judge punishes these patients continuously. Why?

We have a conscience, a capacity for guilt, a moral sense of what is right and wrong that gives meaning to our lives, an ideal image toward which we strive, or an inner voice saying we should not do something. We live according to internalized standards that guide our actions. They lead us to approve of deeds consistent with our values, or disapprove if they are not (S. Freud 1923/1961). When we have hurt someone, we feel guilt and reach out to repair the damage we caused (Klein 1975a, 1975b). As a result, we may feel self-love as a reward for living up to our internal ideals (Brenner 1955). These aspects of our inner life comprise the system "superego" (Barnett 2007).

Superego originally referred to the conscience (S. Freud 1923/1961c; Roth 2001), the ego ideal (S. Freud 1923/1961c), the pursuit of suffering (Bergler 1948, 1952, 1961; S. Freud 1923/1961c), and a "grade" within the ego (S. Freud 1923/1961c; 1940/1963). Later thinkers defined *superego* as stored up-aggression—*daimonium* (Bergler 1952) and a collection of identifications (Britton 2003; Kernberg 1975). Others have linked the concept of the superego to our capacity for guilt (Klein 1975a, 1975b) and to our drive to know the truth (Grotstein 2004, 2010; Reiner 2010). For the sake of clinical clarity, we will define the *pathological superego* as a collection of identifications that patients can enact as defenses. All later references to the superego will be to the *pathological superego*.

HOW IDENTIFICATIONS ARE FORMED

Children learn by imitating others and form these memories in implicit memory (Schore 1991). These memories serve an adaptive purpose. Each time the child encounters a given person, nonconscious memory tells her what to anticipate and how to respond adaptively (Hartmann 1964). These memories, enacted frequently enough as defenses, become habits that form our character structure (S. Freud 1917/1961a; Grigsby and Stevens 2000). As implicit memories, they continue to guide behavior nonconsciously during adulthood (Hassin et al. 2006).

We imitate others unconsciously, but we may enlist identifications for the purpose of defense. We may identify with others to avoid complex feelings related to loss (Davanloo 1990, 2000; S. Freud 1917/1961a; 1940/1963). A man wears his father's clothes after his father's death. We may identify with a dangerous person to become the source of danger so that the dangerous caretaker is still someone we can have hope in (Fairbairn 1954; Guntrip 1968). For instance, a little boy with a violent father claims that he, the boy, is dangerous. Meanwhile, he views his father as kind and not so dangerous. We may identify with others to ward off feelings of guilt over destructive wishes toward the caretaker (Klein 1975a, 1975b). These are not conscious thoughts. These are just conscious descriptions of tacit behaviors. But the main reason we develop these identifications? To avoid sharing feelings or impulses that could jeopardize a relationship we need for survival. We hide the feeling we have and identify with the person we are with.

WHY IDENTIFICATIONS ARE FORMED

When a parent damages the bond with his or her child, the child feels reactive rage (Benjamin 1993; Bowlby 1969, 1973, 1980). However, expressing this rage could further damage the bond or provoke additional retaliation. Unfortunately, the caretakers may provoke the child's rage many times, arousing guilt over his impulses (A. Freud 1936; Klein 1975b; Schore 1994). For the small child, a fantasy can trigger as much guilt as a deed (Klein 1975a, 1975b).

The child protects his mother by turning rage onto himself. "I don't feel guilty over the rage toward my mother. I become her and punish myself for having been enraged." Through this "gift of love" he rejects his inner life to keep his bond with her (Benjamin 1993).

Patients who turn rage on themselves usually suffered from a traumatized bond in early life. This triggered powerful unconscious, primitive murderous rage toward the loved one who damaged the bond, as well as guilt over that rage. In response to these mixed feelings, the child's guilt often triggers a pattern of unconscious self-punishment and self-sabotage (Davanloo 1990; Klein 1975a, 1975b). These patients punish themselves eternally for their rageful impulses toward early caretakers.

It may seem bizarre to attribute murderous impulses to small children, yet their play constantly reveals themes of adults being killed, eaten, or jailed and then brought back to life. Children are helpless with little autonomy under the power of others. What is worse, the child usually needs help from the person causing the rage. Unable to rely on his parent for help with his feelings, he relies on his defenses instead, especially the defense of identifying with the parent.

When enacting these identifications becomes automatic and habitual, adult patients deprive, hurt, and punish themselves or others. What was an occasional defense becomes a habitual pattern of defense use that chronically creates symptoms. We must help these patients see and turn against defenses based on identifications with aggressors.

HOW IDENTIFICATIONS ARE EXPRESSED AS DEFENSES

The child can enact an identification in one of three ways. For instance, a child with a critical mother may identify with her mother and criticize herself when she is angry. She may identify with her mother and criticize her little sister's anger. Or she may project and believe other people will criticize her for being angry. Thus, she can ward off her anger by enacting the identification with her mother in three different ways. She can do to herself what her mother did to her. She can do to others what her mother did to her. Or she can fear that others will do to her what her mother did to her.

When the adult patient does to herself what her mother did to her, we call this a *character defense*. When she does to the therapist what was done to her, we call it a *transference resistance*. When she imagines that the therapist will do to her what her mother did to her, we call it *projection of the superego* or a *transference of defense* (A. Freud 1936).

IDENTIFICATION AS A PROBLEM OF SELF-OBSERVING CAPACITY

The child wards off feelings toward aggressors by identifying with the aggressors. This preserves a jeopardized attachment. These defenses occur when the child is immature and cannot reliably distinguish between reality and fantasy. These identifications also occur when the child's mind cannot differentiate reality from projections she receives. The child who criticizes herself like her mother did, does not see that she attacks herself. She believes mother's criticism is simply true.

When adult patients attack themselves, they also show a transient loss in symbolic thinking. They think they are innately unlovable, bad, or evil. Symbolic equation (Segal 1981) occurs when patients cannot distinguish reality (the therapist) from fantasy (the projection). In the group of defenses we examine here, the patient cannot distinguish reality (herself) from fantasy (the self-attack). Naturally, if the little girl equates reality and fantasy ("I am bad"), mother remains good, and the girl has successfully warded off her rage (Klein 1975a, 1975b; Segal 1981; Winnicott 1965). Self-attack begins early in life when the child believes if something bad happens, she must be bad (Ferenczi 1950; Piaget 1970). She understands herself and others through concrete operational thought (Piaget 1970). Adults using self-attack often regress to concrete operational thought (Leahy 2001).

The patient who believes she is bad needs help to see (Gray 2005) and differentiate herself from self-attacking defenses. S. Freud (1940/1963, 180) called this the "slow demolition of the hostile superego."

Identifications: Why the Superego Becomes So Harsh

Since the *superego* is a concept, it cannot act. Hence, we define the superego as a collection of pathological identifications (Britton 2003; Kernberg 1975) that patients enact as defenses (A. Freud 1936).

Harsh identifications are not always accurate photographs of parents. Their harshness stems from two sources:

- *Reality:* The parents were harsh.
- *Misperceptions:* the child views the parents through neurocognitive deficits, an immature brain, or projections.

The child who has harsh parents judges himself harshly. In contrast, a child with neurocognitive deficits, such as sensory integration problems, may experience his mother's attempt to dress him as a painful attack. Because he misperceives her, he may identify with a harsh, attacking mother. A normal child, frustrated by his mother, will feel rage, but he may project his rage onto her and say, "Mom is angry and mean." Then he identifies with this distorted image of a "depriving" mother. For instance, an angry four-year-old boy may think his mother rejects him while she cares for his younger siblings. She is not rejecting him. She is, however, less available. But he views her through the lens of his anger. Thus, identifications with an aggressor (A. Freud in Sandler and A. Freud 1985, 404) can be based on reality or misperceptions or both.

How Identifications Are Structured

Patients' identifications with aggressors (S. Freud 1940/1963) manifest as unconscious, primitive defenses (Gill 1963, 144). Suppose a patient had a critical mother. She will form a memory not just of her mother but of the *relationship* with her mother. This memory is understood as an object relation (Kernberg 1975): a memory of herself (self-presentation), her critical mother (object-representation), and the affect between them (e.g., anger). Thus, any time a feeling rises in therapy, that feeling is connected to a memory of a past relationship (a criticizing mother and a criticized child). When anger arises, the highly resistant patient enacts that memory in the form of a defense: self-criticism, criticizing someone else, or projecting that someone wants to criticize her.

Let's suppose the patient had a judgmental father. In therapy, the patient can enact an identification with the father who judged her in three ways:

- She judges herself (character defense) as her father judged her.
- She judges you (transference resistance).
- She imagines that you judge her (projection of the superego).

When she treats herself as her father did in the past, this is a character defense (Kernberg 1984; Reich 1933): "I'm such an idiot." In the transference resistance, she treats others as her father treated her (Kernberg 1984; Reich 1933): "You are such an idiot!" In the paranoid solution, she imagines others will judge her as her father did in the past: "Everyone thinks I'm an idiot." Identified with the child, she regards you as identical with her father: "You, the therapist, treat me like an idiot." This is projection of the superego, or a transference of defense (A. Freud 1936).

To summarize, patients can enact identifications with aggressors in three ways: character defense, transference resistance, and projection of the superego. Table 11.1 illustrates these patterns within the spectrum of superego pathology (Kernberg 1975).

Table 11.1 Superego pathology

Early relationship: "Dad judges me."

Type of defense	Character defense			Transference resistance			Projection		
Structure of the defense	I judge myself.			I judge others			I project and believe that you judge me.		
Severity of syntonicity	I am some-times critical of myself.	I am an idiot.	I deserve to die.	I am some-times critical of others.	You are an idiot.	You deserve to die.	I think you are critical of me.	You think I'm an idiot.	You want to destroy me.

These defenses occur on a spectrum of reality testing ranging from a patient who wonders if you are critical to a patient who believes you want to kill him. Another patient may view his self-attack (symbol) as if it is correct (reality). "I am evil." This is symbolic equation (Segal 1957). He may also view his projection (symbol) as if it is true (reality). "You are evil and don't care about me." To establish reality testing and an internal focus, differentiate reality (the patient or other people) from judgments.

The capacity to tolerate internal conflict also exists on a spectrum. A relatively healthy patient tolerates internal conflict: "I have angry feelings and criticize myself for having them." The less healthy patient admits he is angry, but projects his internal judgment onto others. "They don't like me." A less healthy patient denies his anger, projecting it onto others whom he judges. The borderline patient alternates: at one moment, he believes you judge him; the next moment he judges you. Meanwhile, he constantly judges himself.

INTERNAL STANDARDS

Defenses based on pathological identifications create symptoms known as *superego pathology*. Ideally, we pursue our desires while living in accord with values that give meaning to our lives. Unfortunately, however, some patients misuse values in the service of self-punishment. The patient who fails to live up to standards may

- Judge herself for failing to live up to her standards, thereby suffering from chronic self-punishment.
- Project her inner judge onto others, believing they criticize her. She may even provoke them to punish her.
- Judge others rather than herself.
- Escape judgment by claiming to be the same as her ideal or by having immoral standards.

The Ego Ideal: Who We Are versus Who We Wish We Were

None of us is the same as we wish we were (the ego ideal) (Chasseguet-Smirgel 2003). Being human, we will never incarnate our ideals. They are like the North Star, providing a framework of meaning: what we value and aim for.

A patient who cannot bear not being the same as his ideal, handles this conflict in one of four ways:

- *He hates himself.* "I'm not the same as my ideal, but I can be loyal to it by hating myself."

- *He hates and devalues ideals (or respected people) rather than hate himself for having failed to live up to them.* "Since I've learned about some of her character flaws, now I know that Mother Teresa was just a hypocrite." Depression results because his life lacks meaning without ideals.

- *He claims to be his ideal, denying reality.* Living this lie, he fears others will expose him as a fraud. To ward off his fear, he demands that his followers admire him as if he were the ideal or face expulsion from the group. Reality threatens his denial. At the same time, he devalues others for failing to be ideal. So cults become paranoid to keep reality from threatening the leader's denial.

- *He idealizes someone who claims to be ideal.* He follows the idealized person's instructions with the hope of one day becoming the ideal himself. He shifts his attention away from who he is to who he wishes he were. By doing so, he loses sight of the reality of his being. In these forms we recognize how narcissism can be a defense against harsh self-judgment.

When we violate our standards, we can face our guilt and engage in reparation. We can forgive ourselves as inevitably flawed humans who will never be perfect. A patient with superego pathology believes she deserves everlasting suffering, punishment, and perhaps even a death penalty, suicide.

Healthy or Unhealthy?

A healthy patient sees reality. An unhealthy patient views herself through the filter of harsh judgment, which substitutes for realistic appraisal. She sees only those parts of herself consistent with her self-attack, ignoring her strengths and abilities. She insists that she (a flawed human being) should become ideal. She cannot distinguish fantasy (ideals) from reality. The patient's ideal may enact her identification with an aggressor. Suppose a parent criticized her for not being perfect. Now she attacks herself through perfectionism, directing rage toward herself rather than toward her critical father.

A healthy patient considers herself to be worthy of constant acceptance and guidance. She regards her value as unconditional given her innate worth as a human being. The patient who identified with an aggressor does not accept herself. She believes she *has* no intrinsic worth. She believes she must be perfect to *become* worthy of love.

The healthy patient pays attention to her inner life, trusting it to guide her. The unhealthy patient, identified with an aggressor, ignores her inner life, trusting her self-doubt for direction.

In summary, in response to experienced aggression by others, the child identifies with aggressive caretakers. These identifications, enacted as character defenses and transferences, create her presenting problems, perpetuating her suffering. Thus, we must help the patient see and turn against those character defenses and transferences to reach the buried mixed feelings (Davanloo 1990, 2000; S. Freud 1940/1963; Gray 2005).

LEVELS OF SUPEREGO PATHOLOGY

Since superego pathology exists on a continuum we must assess a variety of patient capacities. Can the patient bear her guilt or does she project that others judge her? Does her internal judgment help guide her to better action or has it become a means to torment or even kill her? When she projects her internal judgment onto others, can she see that or has she lost her reality testing? The following section will show criteria for four levels of superego pathology.

Healthy: The patient feels guilt, remorse, and concern for others. Conflict is intrapsychic. She loves herself and her ideals. She accepts herself while living a life based on her values.

Neurotic: The patient feels guilt, remorse, and concern for others, but her defenses of self-punishment, self-shaming, and self-attack lead to depression and anxiety. She misuses ideals to attack herself. Rather than tolerate her internal experience of guilt, sometimes she believes it is due to criticism by others.

Borderline: The patient has trouble bearing her guilt, remorse, or self-concern due to severe self-attack. She projects her superego onto others and becomes afraid of their judgment ("Other people are trying to make me feel guilty.") Alternatively, she projects her forbidden impulses onto others and judges them. She no longer experiences her conflicts intrapsychically, but interpersonally. Projection leads her to become paranoid, fearing punishment from others, or she denies feeling guilty to avoid severe self-punishment.

To avoid the severe self-attack, she uses denial and splitting. She may hold high values but act against them without being troubled by the contradiction between her values and her actions. When she falls short of her ideal, her self-devaluation creates severe mood swings. In response, she may abandon the pursuit of ideals and devalue them and anyone who has them, living a life without meaning.

The patient enacts pathological identifications as character traits and tolerates them. For instance, a borderline patient slapped himself during the session when he said something he regarded as stupid. Since his father called him names and slapped him, the patient regarded hitting himself in session as normal.

The borderline patient transiently loses sight of the difference between the reality of the therapist and the projections she places on him.

Psychotic: This patient projects primitive, aggressive images onto others. She lives in constant fear because she loses sight of the difference between other people and her projections. She suffers from a severe loss of reality testing (Meissner 1984; Kernberg 1975).

Psychodiagnosis of Superego Pathology

Defenses that enact identifications sabotage therapy. They function as resistances to the experience of feelings and the emotional closeness that results from sharing them. They create symptoms of depression, anxiety, self-destructiveness, self-reproach, impoverishment of the personality, and sterile relationships.

Below we examine these defenses and offer interventions for them.

Type One: Judging Oneself

The patient can judge herself as she was judged. She may experience this as a critical voice in her mind or a critical thought she has about herself or it can take the form of conscious self-hatred. The following vignettes show this spectrum of self-judgment from someone with a relatively healthy conscience to someone who suffers from severe self-hatred.

Experiencing one's superego as critical

Some patients are aware of their self-criticism, as if it is an internal irrational voice.

Pt: I told Bill I didn't want him to take that job because we would have to move. I would have to give up my job. The kids would have to lose all their friends here. But I've been feeling like I shouldn't have done that, like it was selfish of me to say that.

Th: It's as if a policeman [*superego*] comes into the room to attack you as soon as you stand up for what you want. It's as if it's against the law to do that. [*Differentiate the patient from her internal critical voice by showing her how she condemns herself after asserting herself.*]

Identification with a pathological introject

Self-attack occurs when the patient attacks herself as someone attacked her in the past.

- *Self-attack as a defense against the experience of rage:* Self-attack is always a defense. For instance, a woman reported that a teenage daughter criticized her unfairly.

Pt: I'm a terrible mother. I don't know why you keep working with me. I'm not getting any better. Don't you think the clinic will finally decide I shouldn't be in therapy because it's taking too long? [*Defense: self-attack.*]

Th: What is the feeling you have toward your daughter for criticizing you like that?

Pt: I think I'm a terrible mother. [*Defense: self-attack.*]

Th: That describes you, not your feeling toward your daughter. Do you notice how this mechanism in your mind is criticizing you right now? [*Point out the defense.*]

Pt: But I am a terrible mother. [*Defense: self-attack.*]

Th: Do you notice how this mechanism in your mind is criticizing you right now?

Pt: Yes, but I think it is right. [*Now she sees the defense, but it is syntonic.*]

Th: This mechanism that is criticizing you right now—do you think it might be hurting you? Do you think it might be getting you down? [*Point out causality: the defense hurts her.*]

Pt: Yes.

Th: You think this critical mechanism might be getting you down. Do you think it might be making you depressed?

Pt: Oh, definitely. [*Her anxiety drops as she steps back and observes the defense.*]

Th: If we put that critical mechanism off to the side, could we shift perspectives for a moment and see what the feeling is toward your daughter instead?

Pt: Okay.

Th: You mentioned that you have been trying hard, and your daughter criticized you in a way that was unfair. Let's see what the feeling is toward your daughter for being unfair to you.

Pt: I didn't like it. [*Defense: intellectualization.*]

Th: What's the feeling toward her for doing that?

Pt: Anger?

Th: You felt angry toward her for doing that.

The patient turns the rage on herself through self-attack, becoming depressed. Her self-esteem plummets because condemnation from her internal world replaces realistic appraisal from the external world (Jacobson 1971, 90). Whenever patients report low self-esteem, look for the defenses creating it.

Help the patient pay attention to the function, not the content, of the judgment. Point out how a critical voice in her mind attacks her. Once she can see the defense of self-attack, focus on the underlying feelings. The following are common forms of self-attack:

- "I am bad, stupid, a failure, ugly, fat, and no good."
- "I am not good enough."
- "I will never be able to . . ."
- "I don't deserve . . ."
- "I shouldn't feel . . ."

Each of these statements guarantees the patient's suffering will continue, defends against feeling, and rejects the patient and her feelings. Self-attack creates depression and low self-esteem. Self-esteem is like a tree that she can nurture or chop down with little cuts of self-attack.

In the following example, the patient suffered from a psychotic depression, delusions of persecution, and auditory hallucinations. She had suffered from physical and sexual abuse as a child. Because her ability to observe and think are so impaired at this stage, I address her self-attack in a different way.

Pt: I'm terrible. God does not love me. I know he could not love me. Otherwise, I would not have had all these traumas. I had these traumas because I am bad. [*Her self-attack is syntonic. She cannot see how she treats herself. She does not see this defense against her rage toward the people who hurt her. For her, her badness is a fact, not a description. She equates herself with this symbol of badness.*]

Th: Since I haven't cured you yet, I must be bad too. How should I punish myself, do you think? [*Present a mirror to her. Enact her pattern of self-attack so she can see it.*]

Pt: [*Surprise and a smile.*] What? Oh, Dr. Jon, you should not punish yourself. [*She does not yet see her self-attack.*]

Th: I should have cured you by now, and the fact that I haven't cured you yet means I am bad. And since I am bad, I deserve to be punished. How do you think I should punish myself? [*Mirror the pathological logic her punitive mother used on the patient, which the patient just used on herself.*]

Pt: [*Laughs.*] Oh, you are funny. You can't help it that you haven't cured me yet. I am much better now.

Th: But you still aren't cured. And that means I am bad. And since I'm bad, I deserve to punish myself. How should I punish myself, do you think? [*Mirror the punitive logic of her superego.*]

Pt: [*Laughs.*] Now I see. You are doing to yourself what I have been doing to me. [*Now she sees how she has punished herself.*]

Th: You could punish yourself, and I could punish myself, and then we could suffer together. [*Mirror the relationship she had with her mother.*]

Pt: [*Laughs.*] Oh, that would be horrible. Do you think I am not bad?

Th: No, I don't think you are bad. I think you are mad! I think you are really angry at the people who caused those traumas. [*Point out the rage she warded off through self-attack.*]

Pt: Oh, you think I turn the anger on me rather than feel it toward my mother? [*Now her awareness is much higher.*]

Th: Do you think so?

Pt: Yes.

Th: Shall we take a look at that anger toward your mother, so you don't have to turn it on yourself instead? [*Mobilize her to the therapeutic task.*]

- *Self-attack as a defense against the experience of guilt*: Self-attack is a defense that wards off feelings. Sometimes the patient can use this defense to direct rage against himself rather than toward someone else. Here we see how the patient can use self-attack to ward off his genuine guilt over hurting someone else.

Pt: I feel so terrible about the way I talked to Jane last night. I'm such a terrible person.

Th: What happened?

Pt: I told her I don't want to make love to her so often because I find her too fat. I told her I think she is ugly. She cried and cried. Don't you think that was just terrible of me? [*He invites the therapist to be his superego so he can feel judged by me rather than by his own conscience.*]

Th: Do you? [*Block the projection.*]

Pt: I do. I think I was perfectly awful to her.

Th: How did you make it up to her?

Pt: What?

Th: You said you think you were awful to her. So I'm wondering how you made it up to her?

Pt: I didn't.

Th: [*Silence.*]

Pt: Are you thinking I should have? [*Projection onto the therapist.*]

Th: Given that you think you were perfectly awful to her, only you can know whether you want to make it up to her or not. [*Block his projection.*] That may not be something you need to repair.

Pt: I hadn't thought about that. I just figured if I told her I felt terrible, that would be enough. [*He attacks himself rather than reach out to her.*]

Th: You thought if you attacked yourself, that would be enough.

Pt: It's true. I didn't actually tell her I was sorry.

Th: It's as if your self-attack was a substitute for apologizing to her.

Pt: I didn't come back to her afterward about it.

Th: In a way, attacking yourself became a substitute for reaching out to her. Was this self-attack a way to avoid facing your guilt, reaching out to her, and repairing the damage? [*Point out the function of the defense.*]

Pt: I think that's the same thing I did with Paula.

This patient uses self-attack to avoid facing his guilt. Always differentiate self-punishment (narcissistic self-absorption) from healthy guilt (relational reparation). When patients fail to apologize and engage in reparation, their so-called guilty feelings have a defensive function.

- *Self-attack as a defense against the experience of pride*: A patient reports that she won a baking contest at her church but puts herself down to avoid the envy of her friends and her pleasure in defeating them.

- *Self-attack in response to tensions between the ego and the ego ideal:* Patients may attack themselves to ward off grief when they fail to live up to their ideals.

Pt: I should have been able to get that job. I must have done something wrong. [*Here the patient is saying to herself: "I should be the same as my ideal. Since I am not, I must torment myself by searching for the answer so next time I can incarnate that ideal."*]

A patient may suffer mood swings, feeling excited when she momentarily appears to be ideal. Then she becomes severely depressed when she fails. Another patient punishes herself for failing to be like someone she knows. She loves an ideal image, the person whom she idealizes, but detests the reality of her essence. She condemns herself for not being ideal. By comparing herself with a fantasy image, she becomes blind to the truth of her own experience. She relates to a belief ("I should be like someone else") rather than reality.

Character defense—identification with a pathological introject enacted habitually (see chapter 12 for more examples)

The patient wards off anger toward earlier aggressive figures by treating herself aggressively the ways those figures did. She does to herself what others did to her.

Pt: [*Talks rapidly.*]

Th: Do you notice how you talk rapidly right now? [*Defense identification.*]

Pt: Yes, I always do that.

Th: That's often a way of talking over your anxiety and feelings. If we slow down for a moment, are you aware of feeling anxious right now here with me? [*Address the character defense: she ignores herself, enacting an identification with someone who ignored her feelings.*]

Pt: I hadn't thought of that before.

Th: You hadn't thought about how you might be talking quickly over your feelings and anxiety. Are you aware of feeling anxious right now?

Pt: It's no big deal. [*Patient talks quickly again. Character defense of self-dismissal.*]

Th: You say it's no big deal that you are anxious. Do you notice how you dismiss your anxiety right now as if it is no big deal? [*Implicit description of the identification: an object relation of an ignoring mother and ignored child.*]

Pt: Yes.

Th: When you dismiss your anxiety as no big deal, is that a caring way to treat yourself or might it be a dismissive way to treat yourself? [*Help the patient see the cruelty of ignoring her feelings.*]

Pt: I guess it's dismissive. I just hadn't thought about it before.

Th: That's why it's important for us to think about it now. So you see that it is dismissive to call your anxiety no big deal. Has it been a habit to ignore your feelings and anxiety by talking over them?

Pt: I do talk fast all the time. That's true, and I don't usually stop to notice if I'm anxious or not.

Th: You talk over your anxiety rather than pay attention to it. If you ignore your anxiety, it just—

Pt: Escalates.

Th: Would it make sense to pay attention to this anxiety so you could get a handle on it? Otherwise, if you keep ignoring it, it could get worse. [*Invite the patient to turn against the defense and pay attention to her feelings instead.*]

Pt: That makes sense. [*The patient now observes the price of the defenses.*]

Th: As we begin to pay attention to your feelings and anxiety, are you worth this attention in your opinion? [*Mobilize the unconscious therapeutic alliance.*]

Pt: [*Begins to tear up. Rise of guilt and grief over past self-neglect as she turns against the defense.*]

Th: Some painful feeling comes up.

Pt: I'm feeling some pain in my chest.

Th: Some painful feeling comes up as you make this choice to pay attention to your anxiety instead of ignore it.

Each time we help the patient see a character defense and turn against that identification, we have deactivated part of the pathological superego. She must see and turn against these identifications before we explore rage toward her parents. Otherwise, she will identify with them in session and turn the rage back onto herself. This is especially true for depressed patients.

Complete identification with the pathological superego

This type of patient consciously pursues self-defeat, delighting in self-destructiveness as an ideal (Kernberg 1975, 121). She destroys herself to triumph over a therapist she envies (Klein 1975b). A chronically depressed woman presented for a consultation because she was stalemated in a twenty-year-long therapy. She had responded minimally to treatment and not at all to medications. In the session, she quickly became defiant, projecting her healthy desires onto the consultant, whom she could oppose. The following vignette occurred two hours into the interview.

Th: Do you notice how you deaden your emotions?

Pt: I want to be dead. [*Said defiantly.*]

Th: Obviously, if that's what you want, it can be easily arranged. As you know, neither I nor your therapist can stop you from killing yourself if that's what you want. [*Deactivate the omnipotent transference: she believes I can keep her alive if she wants to kill herself.*]

Pt: That's true.

Th: If you want to deaden your emotions and go through life as an emotionally dead woman, you can do that too. Obviously, if going through life as an emotionally dead woman is helpful to you, you have an obligation to deaden yourself. [*Mirror the pathological superego, which says, "Deadening yourself will help you." Help the patient see rather than identify with the pathological superego by mirroring it.*] But then, as long as you deaden your emotions, you'll have a dead therapy. And you can continue to have a dead therapy for another twenty years if you think that would be helpful to you. [*Mirror the pathological superego.*] But then, neither I, your therapist, nor anyone else would be able to help you. [*Point out the destructive impact result of identifying with her pathological superego.*] Why do that to yourself?

Pt: [*Begins to cry.*] I guess I've f—ed up major big time. [*She begins to feel grief and guilt over how she has hurt and deprived herself.*]

In this example, I deactivated the patient's identification (Ten Have de Labije 2001, 2005, 2006, 2009a). Her defiance (the character trait) enacted a pathological identification. She invited me to speak for her healthy strivings while she opposed them. She gained "a pathological freedom from the superego by identifying with it" (Kernberg 1975, 123). By refusing to join me in the therapeutic task, she hoped to ensure its defeat. By deactivating her identification, I helped her change.

At mild levels of superego pathology, the patient suffers from internal conflict, criticizing herself for forbidden wishes and feelings. At severe levels of superego pathology, the patient avoids internal conflict by projecting healthy wishes or her pathological superego. She can project her healthy strivings onto the therapist, so the therapist becomes responsible for the therapy's progress. She can project her rageful impulses onto others, fearing their attacks. Or she can project her loving impulses onto others, fearing they will violate her boundaries.

Type Two: Judging Others

The patient can enact the identification by judging others as he was judged. This is a manic defense against guilt: "I don't suffer from a superego! I *am* a superego to others." Like the boss who said, "I don't have ulcers. I give them!"

Being a superego to others

This type of patient comes across as bossy, officious, and superior. He projects his impulses onto others whom he punishes. He judges others quietly to avoid judging himself. At severe levels of superego pathology, the patient no longer complains privately; he judges people in person. When you point out his impulses, he (to avoid his guilt) may claim that you are judging him. Then he becomes angry at, or fearful of, the supposedly judging therapist.

In the following example, the patient, unfaithful to his wife, believes his girlfriend is unfaithful to him. Rather than experience guilt over betraying his wife, he punishes his girlfriend for his deed.

Pt: I called her (the girlfriend) five times in an hour, and she didn't pick up. I really got frantic that she was going out with someone else. I got so enraged I couldn't stand it.

Th: You were afraid she was betraying you.

Pt: Yes.

Th: Isn't it interesting that you accuse her of what you are doing to your wife? [*Point out the projection.*]

Pt: What?

Th: Isn't it interesting that you accuse your girlfriend of doing to you what you are doing to your wife?

Pt: I hadn't thought of that.

Th: That you condemn her for what you have done. [*Point out how he judges her.*]

Pt: [*Becomes anxious.*] Are you saying I should condemn myself? [*He tries to make the therapist into a judge, whom he can oppose and argue with.*]

Th: Only you can know whether you should condemn what you did or not. [*Block the projection.*]

Pt: I see what you're saying. I accuse her of doing what I did to my wife. [*He can see the projection. Next, help him face his guilt rather than ask his girlfriend to bear it for him.*]

Sometimes, when patients enact the pathological superego ("You are not helpful"), therapists assume they have done something wrong.

They feel bad and apologize to the patient. Remember: the patient accuses the therapist, *just as his superego accuses him*. If you find yourself worrying about his criticism, pause and reflect. Notice your fear of his criticism and its content. Now you know how he criticizes himself.

In the next example, a patient suffering from borderline personality disorder alternately punishes himself or the therapist. Notice how the therapist addresses this particular defense in a noninterpretive fashion.

> Pt: [*His voice is on the verge of yelling.*] That is the most stupid thing I have ever heard. Where did you get that, from a book? Don't you have anything useful to say? Every time I'm hearing this worthless stuff from you, and it doesn't help. I'm not getting any better. I keep coming and nothing changes. All I hear is this worthless, stupid crap that doesn't help. What do you have to say for yourself? [*The patient attacks me, letting me know how he attacks himself. An interpretation would trigger another attack. So I speak from within the role of the attacked person.*]
>
> Th: Well, much of what you say is true. A lot of what I say is off target. Sometimes it's stupid. Sometimes what I say is useless and doesn't help. I can't argue with that. All I can hope is that what I say is *good enough, enough of the time*, that, in the end, we can have a good result. [*The therapist's steadiness shows that he survived a devaluing attack by the patient without attacking in turn and without collapsing into depression as the patient usually does.*]
>
> Pt: [*Relaxes into his chair.*] Gosh. I wish I could say that.

Transference resistance: enactment of a past relationship

Moderately resistant patients use defenses to resist feelings. In contrast, highly resistant patients enact a past relationship (the *transference*) to *resist* feelings, hence, the term *transference resistance*. (See chapter 13, on transference resistance.) In the transference resistance, the patient often treats the therapist as his parents treated him.

Type Three: Projection of the Judge

To avoid his internal judgment, the patient may project and imagine that the therapist judges him. This projection can range from a mild thought the patient has about the therapist to a complete conviction that the therapist judges him. The following examples will exhibit this spectrum of reality testing.

Projection onto others of an integrated conscience

When patients have excellent reality testing, they are aware of their projection. And what they project is usually a healthy integrated conscience—that is, a conscience they can acknowledge as their own which has reasonable judgments.

Pt: You probably don't think this is a good idea.

Th: I think that's your conscience talking (Blackman 2004).

In the next example, the patient needs more help to see how she projects her inner judge onto others.

Pt: I don't think my staff will like it if I give myself a raise but not them. [*Defense: projection.*]

Th: Who is having that thought? [*Draw attention to the location of the patient's thought, so she can more easily see her projection.*]

Pt: I am.

Th: In fact, you won't like yourself if you give yourself a raise, but not them. [*Point out her internal judgment.*]

Pt: That's true.

Th: And maybe if you could accuse them of being your conscience [*point out how she projects her conscience*], you could resent them instead of what your own conscience is demanding of you.

Pt: That's true because I am already judging myself, and they don't know about any of this yet.

Projection of a punitive superego

In the following example, the patient projects her inner judgment onto her colleagues, believing they judge her. She must see her projection before she can see her inner judgment. The patient believes her colleagues will judge her for seeking medical leave to avoid an overseas assignment in a dangerous area. Having lost many physical functions following an accident, she lacks the strength necessary for the assignment.

Pt: I'm afraid, if the rest of my office finds out I am requesting medical leave, they'll really get angry with me. [*Defense: projection of her superego onto the office staff.*]

Th: Are you having some doubts yourself?

Pt: Well, I'm not sure my medical issues are really severe enough. [*Defense: denial.*]

Th: What are they?

Pt: I've got fifty percent lung function, according to the doctors, and I can't carry more than twenty pounds, or else it will cause problems with the surgery I had on my neck.

Th: You have fifty percent lung function, and you can't carry more than twenty pounds when you are required to carry how much?

Pt: Eighty pounds.

Th: You can carry twenty but are required to carry eighty. And you have doubts about your ability to do this? [*Point out the denial.*]

Pt: I see what you mean. If I can carry only twenty, I can't carry eighty.

Th: It sounds like you are criticizing yourself for taking medical leave when, in fact, you qualify for it.

Pt: I feel I should be able to. [*Defense: denial.*]

Th: Even when you can't. You criticize yourself for taking medical leave and even try to ignore reality by asking yourself to do what you cannot do. [*Point out the denial.*]

Pt: [*Smiles a smile of recognition.*] That's true.

Th: It sounds like you are relieved not to have to go, but you punish yourself for not going. You imagine they would be angry with you and punish you, but it is you who is critical and punitive to yourself. Do you see what I mean? [*Point out her conflict: her wish to take a leave, and the defenses of self-punishment and projecting her superego onto others.*]

Pt: But I think they would be angry. [*Defense: projection of her superego.*]

Th: Some of them might be in the future, but right now we see that you are criticizing yourself. You are punishing yourself. They aren't doing that. [*Point out her self-punishment to deactivate her projection that others want to punish her.*]

Pt: That explains why I have been doing favors for other people.

Th: As if to ask for their forgiveness.

Pt: Yes—for not going on the assignment.

In the next example, a patient suffering from social anxiety fears women will not find him attractive. This case illustrates how to help a patient see his projection onto others through Socratic questioning. Notice how the therapist then points out causality, showing the patient he is afraid of projections he places on women. He is not afraid of the women themselves.

> *Pt:* I'm going out tonight, but I don't think they will find me attractive. [*Defense: projection.*]
>
> *Th:* Who has that thought? [*The patient, although neurotic, fails to distinguish his fantasy from reality. First distinguish his internal judgment from his projection of it onto others.*]

Pt: Me.

Th: Who had the thought yesterday that you were not attractive?

Pt: Me.

Th: And who had the thought the day before that you were overweight?

Pt: Me.

Th: So who has those self-critical thoughts?

Pt: Me.

Th: And who is accused of having those thoughts?

Pt: These women.

Th: Do you see how these are your self-critical thoughts and that you put those thoughts onto women? [*Determine if he can differentiate his self-criticism from his projections.*]

Pt: Yes.

Th: It is understandable you feel anxious when you date. You aren't afraid of the women. You are afraid of the critical mechanism that you place on those women. [*He does not fear women but the projections he places on them. Differentiate these women from his projections.*]

Pt: I have those thoughts all the time. [*But he does not distinguish his thoughts (projections) from reality.*]

Th: And when you put them on the women, it is no wonder you get anxious. You have an internal judge. Then, when you put that judge onto these women, you are afraid and uncomfortable. You're not afraid of the women. You're afraid of that judgmental image you place on those women. [*Point out the conflict: closeness, anxiety, project a judge on women, then fear the projections he places on them. Differentiate women from his projections.*]

Pt: That explains why I get so anxious before the date.

Th: You haven't met the woman yet, but you are busy meeting these images of a judge [*projections*] before the date. That would make anyone anxious!

Pt: [*Laughs.*]

Externalization: projection of the superego—blaming and complaining

In externalization, the patient has a feeling, becomes anxious, and punishes herself. Unable to see her defense of self-punishment, she blames others or complains about how they punish her. Blaming them, she remains blind to the ways she punishes herself. *Blaming and complaining are results of externalization.* "I don't punish myself, other people do. I can be angry at them rather than face how I hurt myself." Restructure externalization to establish an internal perspective. (See chapter 9 on restructuring regressive defenses.)

Projection of the pathological superego to avoid the experience of guilt

These patients avoid guilt by projecting the superego onto others. Then they anticipate judgment from these supposed "judges," whom they regard as "unfair" or "critical." Or they provoke others to judge them. "I knew you wanted to punish me, and now I have the proof!"

A woman projects her superego onto her husband. Since she believes he is an unfair judge, she believes he deserves all of her retaliatory rage. She becomes blind to the fact she is hurting someone she loves and is killing off the love he feels toward her. By projecting her superego, she avoids her guilt, but at the price of damaging her marriage. She no longer sees causality. Attacking her supposed judge, her rage (based on the projection) blinds her to the fact that she is destroying her marriage.

In the following example, notice how the therapist blocks projections, showing the patient how her defensive affects result from her projections, not from her husband's actions.

Husband: We had an argument the other night. And, since we were ratcheting up, I said, "Let's hold off until we see Jon on Monday. Let's talk about this then, and see if he can help us."

Th to wife: What do you notice feeling?

Wife: I feel angry. I feel like he is telling you how he did so well, and how I was out of control. I feel like he is misrepresenting me, as if I'm "all bad," and he's "all good." [*She judges herself as "all good" or "all bad," but projects, claiming he judges her.*]

Th: That may be what you heard, but that is not what he said. He said you two had an argument, and he said he thought it would be good if the two of you talked to me about it today. He did not portray himself as "all good," nor did he portray you as "all bad." [*Block the projection. Point out reality.*]

Wife: It feels that way. [*Projection. She ignores what he says and pays attention only to the feeling her projection creates.*]

Th: Of course it feels that way. If you assume he is calling you "all bad," you will feel the feelings that go with that assumption. [*Her projection, not her husband, creates the feeling.*] That's why we have to clarify that what you assumed is not the same as what he actually said. [*Distinguish the projection from her husband.*]

Wife: I just feel you are not getting a realistic picture of what happens between us. He is much worse to me than he acts in here. [*Now she judges her husband and invites me to judge him too.*]

Th: I'm sure that both of you are able to sink to lower levels, but that is not you. We know that at your top functioning, you both are incredibly competent. But we see that under stress, your ability to function drops precipitously. That's why we have to look at the feelings underneath that make you so anxious. [*Mobilize the patient to the therapeutic task: to face the feelings that lead her to punish herself by projecting her punitive superego onto her husband. Differentiate her as a person from the way she functions when suffering from projection.*]

Oscillating projections onto the therapist

Patients at a neurotic level of character pathology enact their identifications by doing to themselves what others did to them, doing to the therapist what was done to them, or thinking the therapist is going to do to them what was done in the past.

Patients at a borderline level of character pathology do something different. This type of patient may criticize himself, and then shift and accuse you of criticizing him, then shift again and criticize himself.

When he enacts an identification, at one moment he acts out the role of the criticized child, at the next moment the role of the criticizing parent (Kernberg 1975, 1976). The therapist must quickly address these shifts in order to make sense of the session.

At one moment, the patient experiences the therapist like the superego. The next moment, he behaves like a superego to the therapist. When these roles oscillate, the patient has a borderline level of character pathology (Kernberg 1975).

Sometimes a patient shifts rapidly from the position of a primitive superego to a mature conscience and back (Wurmser 1978, 156–157). She denies moral standards and rules only to recommend them in the next moment. She feels intense rage and punishes herself. Suddenly, she blames her husband for punishing her and attacks him instead. Momentarily, she has no compassion for her husband. Why? Her rage is not toward him, but toward a projection she placed on him. She does not distinguish him from her projection. She dehumanizes him as the "cause" of all her suffering. She does not see how she inflicts suffering on herself.

Patients with a borderline level of character pathology identify with the pathological superego or project it onto the therapist. Their reality testing and capacity for symbolic thinking collapse. Thus, no exploration of feeling is useful until the therapist restructures the defenses of splitting and projection.

SPECTRUM OF IDENTIFICATION: SYNTONICITY

The following statements illustrate the spectrum of syntonicity:

Parent to child in the past:	"You are bad."
Patient to self today:	"I'm sometimes too critical of myself." "Maybe I should criticize myself." "I should criticize myself." *[Some differentiation since the patient recognizes her agency: one who "should" criticize herself. The "tyranny of the shoulds" (Horney 1950) is a sign of superego pathology.]* "I hate myself." *[Less differentiation. "I hate myself" indicates an implicit awareness of agency since she realizes she does this to herself.]* "I'm bad." *[The patient, now identified with the critical parent, does not see how she criticizes herself.]* "I'm evil." *[No differentiation of herself from her identification.]*

When a patient says she is evil, she equates the image (evil) with reality (who she is). She believes the self-attack is a fact, not a way she abuses herself. Self-reproach and self-deprecation become substitutes for realistic self-appraisal (Britton 2003). She views herself through devaluing rather than loving eyes (J. Ten Have de Labije, personal communication).

A healthier patient says, "It is a fact that I am fat. That's not my problem. The problem is that I misuse that fact to punish myself. When I am angry with people I love, I turn the anger onto myself and call myself names, like *fat*. I protect others from my anger by hating myself instead. I used to say, 'I am fat' rather than 'I am angry with my boyfriend, who treated me badly.'" She knows the criticism does not fit the reality of who she is. Her self-criticism is consciousness dystonic (Sandler and A. Freud 1985). She does not accept self-devaluation as accurate.

At severe levels of superego pathology, the patient will not see her self-attack as a cruel way to treat herself, but as an accurate description of who she is. She cannot differentiate herself from her defense. If she sees her self-attack, she may not see that it hurts her. If she sees how it hurts her, she may say she deserves it.

For instance, a patient, having shared deep grief with me, suddenly apologized to me then said, "I am a piece of shit."

Th: Could this be a form of self-criticism?

Pt: It's a feeling. I feel like shit.

Th: That's not a feeling. That's how you treat yourself. After all, if I spent all day telling you that you are a piece of shit, by the end of the day you would be feeling "shitty," right?

Pt: That's true.

Th: If you tell yourself that all day, you'll feel shitty too. Do you think this self-berating might be hurting you?

Pt: Yes.

The patient can't differentiate herself from an identification, which she enacts. If she were in a play, acting the role of a punitive parent, she could separate herself from her role in the play. But in therapy, she does not see she is acting like her father. She does not see that she is attacking herself. When acting like her father, she thinks that self-devaluation helps her and is satisfying. Like her devaluing father, she says, in effect: "I'm just doing this for your own good."

Syntonicity and Self-Observing Capacity

The patient enacts identifications with ignoring, neglecting, and denying parents. If he ignores, neglects, and denies his feelings, his character defenses will undermine his ability to perceive reality (Kernberg 1975).

Defenses reject reality and our feelings. The defenses do not observe the truth. They reject it, distorting the patient's awareness. The patient, enacting an identification, looks at himself through dismissive eyes. This identification does not protect him or give him a realistic appraisal. That is why we say: "This mechanism probably saved your life in the past, and we should thank it for how it protected you then. But what protected you in the past is destroying your life today."

The superego "has to sanction [our] perceptions, thoughts, and sensations . . . *if they are to be felt as real*" (my italics) (Nunberg 1955, 148). Thus, the patient who identifies with a dismissive parent dismisses his experience as not real. He dismisses the therapist's words as not real. Any failure in the nonpsychotic patient to see reality is the result of superego pathology. "Oh, that feeling isn't real." "That problem doesn't exist." "You don't need to pay attention to that." Paying attention to and remaining in harmony with reality protects the patient from suffering (Sandler in Sandler and A. Freud 1985, 303). A patient who ignores reality cannot live in harmony with it. As a result, he suffers.

Syntonicity and Observing Causality

Patients who do not see causality believe their defenses are helpful and satisfying. The failure to see causality results in several thinking errors: (1) victim stance ("Why do bad things keep happening to me?"), (2) circumstantial thinking ("Things just happen to me" "It's just one thing leading to another"), or (3) a paranoid stance ("People have it in for me" "Things will never work out for me"). Let us examine a series of statements involving incorrect causality in patients with syntonic character pathology.

- "You hurt me."

True causality: "When you point out something I do to myself that hurts me, I feel guilty over how I have treated myself. Rather than feel my guilt and sadness, and face how I hurt myself, I accuse you of hurting me."

- "This therapy is making me worse."

True causality: "When feelings are aroused in therapy, I punish myself. Since I don't see how I punish myself, I see only the resulting suffering. So I assume the therapy makes me worse rather than my defenses of self-attack and self-criticism." [*Of course, we assume the therapist is not causing the regression.*]

- "Things keep happening to me, and I don't know why."

True causality: "When angry, I lash out at boyfriends and provoke them to punish me by leaving. I don't notice how my defenses sabotage my relationships. So I don't see how I make these things happen."

- "I keep getting blindsided by my wife. She yelled at me again before I got out of bed."

True causality: "When my wife verbally abuses me, I ignore it. Then I have a wishful fantasy that she will be different tomorrow. When she verbally abuses me tomorrow, I am 'blindsided' because she bumps into my fantasy. She didn't blindside me. I blind myself to reality each time she verbally abuses me by paying attention to a wishful fantasy."

Blindness to defenses means blindness to causality. When we do not see how we create our suffering, we assume others cause it. As a result, we pay attention to other people instead of the defenses creating our suffering.

Ignoring inner experience opposes the therapeutic task: attention to and acceptance of one's internal life. A successful defense "is always something dangerous." It either restricts our awareness of reality or falsifies it (A. Freud in Sandler and A. Freud 1985, 195). Help patients turn against defenses so they can see reality.

UNCONSCIOUS GUILT VERSUS SELF-PUNISHMENT

We can differentiate three types of guilt: healthy guilt over misdeeds, conscious neurotic guilty feelings that have a defensive function, and unconscious guilt due to unconscious murderous rage toward loved ones. Unconscious guilt due to unconscious murderous rage is a primary engine of psychopathology (Davanloo 1990, 2000). Patients who are unable to bear or face this unconscious guilt ward it off through self-punishment. Help patients face their murderous rage and unconscious guilt so they can overcome the self-punishment, which has perpetuated their suffering.

A patient with healthy guilt faces the wrong he has done to someone and engages in reparation (Klein 1975a, 1975b). He feels empathy for their suffering.

But the patient may avoid healthy guilt through

- Denying his deed.
- Acknowledging his deed, but denying any reason to feel guilt for it.
- Punishing himself to avoid guilt and reparation.
- Projecting onto others, believing they judge him and want him to feel guilty. In this paranoid/schizoid solution, he does not bear his guilt (Klein 1975a, 1975b).

When the therapist points out how the patient hurts herself, the patient may avoid feelings of guilt and grief by

- Punishing herself: "I know. I'm terrible."
- Punishing the therapist: "What you are doing is not helpful enough. I can't believe you get paid for doing this." Now the patient criticizes the therapist, doing to him what she was doing to herself.
- Accusing the therapist of punishing her: "Why are you always putting me down? I feel like all you do is criticize me!" Since she does not see how she criticizes herself, she assumes the therapist criticizes her. She becomes angry at the "critical" therapist rather than at the defense of self-criticism.

Therapists often reassure patients of their good intentions to dispel projections. This reduces the patient's fear temporarily but not permanently. If she does not learn to see how she projects and punishes herself, her suffering will continue.

Some patients invite others to punish them. A man with a long criminal history provoked other people verbally to beat him up. He felt rage toward a neglectful, alcoholic mother and absent father. The guilt over his rage led him repeatedly to provoke people to attack him. Now his guilt could feel rational. After all, he had done something wrong (being verbally abusive). He could feel some relief when someone else punished him. A beating was less severe than the several decades of prison he had inflicted on himself.

The patient may punish himself or provoke punishment rather than suffer the pangs of his own guilt. He withdraws narcissistically into self-punishment rather than reach out to the person he hurt. Self-punishment becomes a substitute for genuine guilt and reparation.

Chronic self-punishment creates symptoms of emptiness, frag-mentation, boredom, and irritability. Patients do not experience these symptoms as deficits but as tormenting forms of self-punishment, which are substitutes for healthy guilt (D. Carveth 2001). "Those of us who consider the admission of sin and wrongdoing an intolerable in-sult to our narcissism and find conscious guilt unbearable, are forced to resort to symptom formation. The suffering entailed in our symp-toms gratifies the superego need for punishment and, at the same time, evades unbearable conscious guilt" (D. Carveth and J. Carveth 2003, 2).

We can also avoid our guilt through helplessness and the victim stance, denying our agency, responsibility, and choices. "I couldn't help it," rather than "I made this choice." "It wasn't my fault," rather than "I was at fault because I chose to have the affair." "It just happened" rather than "I made it happen." "There was some distance in our rela-tionship," rather than "I distanced myself from my wife." Demoralizing language denies the patient's agency and responsibility (D. Carveth and J. Carveth 2003, 3). Self-punishment wards off *conscious* guilt (D. Carveth 2001) for deeds and *unconscious* guilt due to fantasies linked to early traumas (Davanloo 1990, 2000).

Therapists often conflate guilt and self-punishment. Healthy guilt derives from our love for others (D. Carveth 2002; S. Freud 1923/1961c; Klein 1975a, 1975b). Self-punishment is a defense against guilt (Carveth 2002, 182–183; S. Freud 1923/1961c; Safa-Gerard 1998). Instead of reaching out to the one she hurt, the person may reveal her self-punishment. She says how "awful" she feels and reproaches her-self. Rather than repair the relationship, she asks the other person to repair her! "I hurt you, so comfort me."

Shame can also ward off guilt. Healthy shame signals that we have failed to live up to our own standards and mobilizes us to act according to them. When we do not repair the external relationship, unhealthy shame wards off the experience of healthy guilt and reparation. We shame ourselves rather than reveal our shameful deed to others and repair the damage we caused.

"Guilty" feelings also have a defensive function. Patients who say, "I feel so guilty," are often taking an irresponsible position. "As long as I feel 'guilty,' I don't have to repair the damage I caused. I don't have to *respond* to her pain." "I feel so guilty" can be a substitute for genuine reparation. The patient can sit around having "guilty feelings" and avoid her genuine guilt and responsibility, or she can face her guilt, apologize, and repair the relationship. Feeling bad simply because someone found out you did some wrong is a prestage of morality. "Guilty" feelings are not the critical element in developing a healthy superego (A. Freud in Sandler and A. Freud 1985, 412).

Sometimes therapists try to "analyze away" these painful feelings rather than help patients bear them. Protecting patients from the truth is not compassion, but abandonment. Our task is to face the truth *together*, no matter how painful. The therapist may need to ask the patient, "Your guilt is so painful that you would rather escape it and punish yourself instead?" "The point of compassion is not to eliminate suffering, but to lead a person to the truth so he will be able to lead a life of truth" (Almaas 1987, 92).

Compassion merely on the side of feeling good is pseudocompassion. We must feel compassion not only for the patient's pain, guilt, and shame, but also for her wish to face the truth and live closer to her ideals. The therapist's attention to this complexity helps the patient tolerate the pain of seeing the truth. Help the patient face her guilt to address the defense of self-punishment. We must replace self-punishment "with the capacity for guilt, repentance, and reparation" (D. Carveth 2002, 186).

Treat neurotic "guilty feelings" as a defense. Do not explore them. Help patients face genuine guilt over what they have done, and their unconscious guilt over fantasies of murderous rage toward loved ones. Once the patient can face the deep experience of unconscious murderous rage, guilt, grief, longing, love, and pain over the broken bond, self-punishment is no longer necessary as a defense.

MIRRORING SUPEREGO PATHOLOGY

Patients with superego pathology vary in their ability to differentiate themselves from the identification they enact. As a result, they require a spectrum of interventions to help them see their defenses. These interventions range from cognitive to enactive interventions. The type of intervention needs to be matched with the degree of self-observing capacity the patient has. Now we will show a spectrum of self-observing capacity and the range of interventions necessary to help patients with superego pathology.

Low Superego Pathology

A patient with low superego pathology will criticize herself very gently and can be helped readily to see and turn against the defense.

Pt: I don't think I can do it.

Th: Do you notice how you underestimate yourself? [*Point out the character defense.*]

Pt: I hadn't seen that, but I see it now.

Low to Moderate Superego Pathology

In this example, the therapist needs only to point out the conflict between the patient's defense and his goal for the patient to turn against the defense.

Pt: I don't think I can do it.

Th: Do you notice how you underestimate yourself?

Pt: But what if I can't do it? [*The patient is identified with his defense.*]

Th: You have come here to overcome this problem you have at work where you hold yourself back and let others surpass you, right? [*Clarify his goal.*]

Pt: Yes.

Th: And you have asked me to help you get to the bottom of what leads you to hold yourself back as soon as you declare a goal at work, right? [*Clarify the therapeutic task.*]

Pt: Yes.

Th: You give up on yourself and tell yourself you won't be able to do it. That's how you hold yourself back from your goal right now. Do you see what I mean? [*Clarify how his defense defeats his goal in this moment. Create an intrapsychic focus.*]

Pt: I'm holding myself back here? [*Begins to see his defense.*]

Th: When you doubt your capacity here, you hold yourself back. On the one hand, you want to go full speed ahead. On the other hand, this punitive mechanism in your mind doubts you and tries to get you to put on the brakes. Do you see what I mean? [*Point out the conflict.*]

Pt: I do now. [*Sees the conflict.*]

Th: Do you want to doubt yourself a little bit more now, or shall we take a look at the feelings underneath that have been driving this self-sabotage? [*Point out the choice: avoid his feelings or face them. Use a destructive defense or turn against it.*]

Pt: I've got to stop doubting myself. [*Patient turns against the defense.*]

Moderate Superego Pathology

In this example, the patient is more identified with the defense. The therapist first describes and then mirrors the defense so the patient can see and turn against it.

Pt: I don't think I can do it.

Th: Do you notice how you underestimate yourself?

Pt: But maybe I'm really not able to. [*She is identified with her superego and does not see it.*]

Th: Do you notice how you portray yourself as if you are incapable? [*Point out how she treats herself.*]

Pt: It's not that I want to portray myself that way, it's just I think I am incapable. [*Identification with her superego.*]

Th: [*Silence. Since she portrays herself as incapable, she expects the therapist to offer the capacity that she "cannot." If the therapist does not become active in response to her passivity, her defense will fail, and feeling and anxiety will rise.*]

Pt: [*Becomes anxious.*] Isn't there something you can do? [*Projection of her healthy desires onto me while she remains identified with her pathological superego.*]

Th: If you really are as incapable as you say, we won't have what we need to succeed. If I give one hundred percent and you can give only ten percent, you'll just have a ten percent result. [*Deactivate the projection of her healthy desires onto me. Deactivate the omnipotent transference. I can give only one hundred percent. I cannot give, in addition, the ninety percent she claims she cannot give to the therapy.*]

Pt: That's all I've had in therapy. [*Rise in the alliance. She admits that she has had only ten percent results.*] I just think therapy can't help me. [*She thinks therapy can't help her. I have to help her see that her passivity can't help her.*]

Th: Actually, you just said that you think you can't help yourself. And the good news is, you don't have to if you don't want to. [*Mirror her pathological superego.*] After all, since therapy hasn't succeeded before, you may not want to invest in yourself again. [*Mirror her pathological superego.*]

Pt: Funny you say that, since I had that thought before I came here today. [*She begins to see her pathological superego.*]

Th: Sure, and let's face it: you don't have to invest in yourself if you don't want to. [*Mirror her pathological superego.*]

Pt: I want to! I just don't know how. [*Defense: helplessness.*]

Th: You don't have to invest yourself until you know how. There's no rush. [*Mirror her pathological superego.*]

Pt: But there is. I'm thirty-eight, and I'm still not married. I can't keep delaying, or else I'll never get married or have a family. [*The patient acknowledges her healthy strivings and sees her conflict more clearly.*]

Do not interpret the patient's defenses when she identifies with them. If the therapist gives voice to the patient's defense, the patient can more easily see it within herself. So-called paradoxical techniques (M. C. Nelson 1962, 1968; Farrelly 1974; Spotnitz 1985; Weeks and L'Abate 1982; Weeks 1985) build her self-observing capacity. Mirror the pathological identification so she can see it and differentiate from it.

Never mirror the patient's self-destructive wishes and thoughts if she is feeling angry toward you, or if you want to argue with her. You will create a misalliance. Mirroring the pathological superego is effective only when the therapist feels no wish to control, argue with, or oppose the patient.

Severe Superego Pathology

The therapist is working with an impulsive patient in her twenties who picks abusive boyfriends. Notice how the therapist works very carefully only with the concrete facts the patient presents and then shows the patient causality. In response to the patient identifying with her defense, the therapist mirrors the defense several times to help the patient see and let go of it.

> *Pt:* I was really furious with my boyfriend for dumping me. So I went to the bar, got drunk, and then got in a fight and got beat up. I think it was because I had vodka. [*Patient blames the vodka for her problems rather than her self-punishment, a defense against her rage. No intrapsychic perspective.*]
>
> *Th:* You were angry. And, rather than feel the anger toward your boyfriend, you got drunk, got in a fight, and invited people to beat you up. [*Point out the conflict.*]
>
> *Pt:* I didn't invite them to beat me up. [*She does not see how she arranged her punishment.*]
>
> *Th:* You got drunk, got in a fight, and, by getting into a fight, invited people to fight you and see if they could beat you up. [*Point out causality: getting into a fight invited others to fight and hurt her.*]
>
> *Pt:* Oh, yeah. [*Said offhandedly. Syntonicity.*]
>
> *Th:* And that may be acceptable to you. [*Mirror the syntonicity.*]
>
> *Pt:* No, that's bad. I don't want to get beat up. [*She sees that getting beaten up is bad, but she does not see how she invited this punishment to avoid feelings of rage toward her boyfriend.*]
>
> *Th:* Although you don't want to get beat up, you find yourself drinking alcohol and getting into fights where you get beat up. [*Mirror back what she can see so far.*]
>
> *Pt:* Are you saying I shouldn't drink? [*She projects her healthy awareness onto the therapist.*]
>
> *Th:* I have no right to tell you what to do. If drinking leads to fights, and fights lead to getting beat up, and getting beat up is okay with you, obviously there's no reason to change your drinking. [*Mirror*

her pathological superego. This allows her to see it and blocks the projection of her healthy capacities onto the therapist.]

Pt: Except the getting beat up part is not okay with me. [*The defense of self-punishment becomes less syntonic.*]

Th: I see. [*Therapist waits as the patient struggles with this conflict: drinking creates results she does not like.*]

Pt: I know I shouldn't drink. [*Projection of her healthy awareness. "Should" implies that this is not her opinion.*]

Th: It's not a matter of "should." [*Block the projection of her healthy awareness.*] It's really a matter of what choice works for you. You can drink and get beat up or not drink and not get beat up [*mirror her conflict*], but, in the end, it's about how you want to treat yourself. [*Keep the focus intrapsychic: her feelings, her defenses, and her results.*]

Pt: But this getting beat up is bad. [*Higher anxiety and feeling indicate her destructive behavior is becoming more dystonic.*]

Initially, the patient failed to see causality. She thought other people hurt her. In fact, she hurt herself by getting into a fight. Mirroring her defense helped her see and turn against it.

When the patient sees her defense and how it hurts her, she will experience guilt and grief over the suffering she has inflicted on herself. This step will trigger defenses against the guilt and grief. In response, mirror the patient's degree of conflict. She says, "That's a problem," in an offhand manner. Her words suggest she wants to change. Her offhand manner suggests she does not want to. Mirror the conflict between *what* she says and *how* she says it. "So although that's a problem (dystonicity), it may be one you can live with" (syntonicity). Mirror the conflict between what she says (dystonicity) and does (syntonicity).

Often, therapists mistakenly mirror the patient's healthy words, but not the unhealthy behavior. Suppose the patient says, "That's a problem," with an offhand manner. If the therapist eagerly responds, "You can see how that is a problem now," the patient will respond halfheartedly "Yeah." The therapist listened to the patient's words but not her passive behavior. Mirror the degree of conflict shown between her words *and* behavior (Reich 1933). This can range from no conflict at all (complete identification with the defense) to extreme conflict (guilt over how she has hurt herself).

Mirroring the toxic identification enhances the patient's reality testing (Wexler 1975). She can see the self-destructive defense and repudiate it. Rather than resist the therapist (who personified her healthy strivings), she can resist her pathological identifications (M. C. Nelson 1962, 121). When the patient identifies with her defense, mirror it. This ego-strengthening technique allows partial breakthroughs of grief and guilt until she tolerates her internal conflict rather than using projection to avoid it.

Mirror the precise degree of the patient's conflict.

Moderate superego pathology: mirror conflict. "Part of you wants to overcome these difficulties but another part of you wants them to continue."

Severe superego pathology: mirror the *absence* of conflict. "That may not be a problem for you."

Patients who use words to act out a pathological relationship are less accessible to rational communication. When the patient enacts an identification, the therapist should shift to enactive interventions. Rather than interpret the unconscious identification, the therapist enacts it. Do not explain; demonstrate. An enactive style of communication undercuts the patient's resistances and communicates with the patient on his level (M. C. Nelson 1968). This is different from role-playing a conscious role (Sherman 1968). Here, the therapist enacts the identification the patient acts out unconsciously so she can observe and question it.

The therapist mirrors the incongruity between the content and the emotional implications of the patient's expressions (Sherman 1968, 115). The patient might say, "What I'm going to say is so stupid." This is verbal self-abuse. Yet her tone of voice implies that she is not being unkind to herself, just honest. So the therapist mirrors her self-abuse, "You took the words out of my mouth," bringing these incongruities to the patient's attention.

When the therapist sides with the resistance, he appears as if he is the mirror image of the patient. "[T]he patient recognizes himself unconsciously . . . in the therapist's resistance-joining remarks." This is because the identification the therapist enacts "is a function of the unconscious part of the patient" (Brandt 1968, 124).

Vignette: Mirroring a Character Defense

Notice how the therapist points out the patient's character defense (not committing to himself) and then mirrors the defense until the patient lets go of it.

Pt: I'm not totally committed to the therapy.

Th: Although this is your goal, you are letting me know you are not that committed to you. [*Point out how the patient treats himself. This establishes an intrapsychic perspective.*]

Pt: I was thinking it was about the therapy.

Th: It's really about you. It's your goal, and you are not committed to it or to you. And the good news is, you can be as committed or as uncommitted as you want to be to yourself. [*Point out reality and mirror his pathological superego.*]

Pt: [*He shifts in his chair and laughs nervously. Rise of anxiety due to addressing his defense.*] I'm just concerned about how long the therapy could take.

Th: That makes sense. If you don't commit to your goal and to yourself, how long will therapy take? [*Causality: defenses create the problem—a prolonged therapy.*]

Pt: I get your point.

Th: What level of noncommitment do you think would be in your best interest? [*Mirror his pathological superego.*]

Pt: [*Laughs. Smiles. Rise of anxiety.*] I want to say, "Of course I want to commit to myself!" [*Rise of alliance.*]

I mirror the patient's pathological stance. By seeing it in me, he sees how he hurts himself. With his final statement, he begins to take a stand against his self-neglect (Brandt 1968, 126). Sometimes therapists ask, "Isn't this a departure from reality when you act as if you agree with a pathological identification?" No. You reveal the toxic identifications in the patient's mind so he can now see and turn against them.

REFLECT THE DEGREE OF SYNTONICITY OF CONFLICT

When addressing conflict, we must also attune empathically to the presence or absence of awareness of conflict. The degree of conflict takes place on a spectrum from no awareness of conflict to complete awareness. The following examples illustrate the spectrum of conflict and some interventions appropriate for them.

- *No conflict regarding a desire for closeness*

Pt: I want to be close to people. [*No anxiety or defense.*]

- *Awareness of conflict that is dystonic*

Pt: I want to be close to people, but I pull back from them, and I don't like that I do that. [*Conflict: I want to be close, but I pull back. Dystonic.*]

Th: You don't want to pull back because that interferes with your goal. [*Reflect her conflict of wanting closeness, avoiding it, and not wanting to avoid.*]

Pt: Yes, it gets in my way.

Th: If you don't pull back now, what are you feeling right now here with me?

- *Conflict without awareness*

Pt: I want to be close to people, but it doesn't happen. I don't know why. [*Said with a dismissive shrug. The patient wants closeness but is unaware of her defenses, unlike the previous patient.*]

Th: You want to be close to people, but you don't know how you manage not to be close. [*Mirror her conflict.*] But that may not be a problem for you. [*Mirror the syntonicity indicated in her tone of voice.*]

Pt: It is a problem because I can't get married if I don't get close to people. [*Not knowing is becoming dystonic.*]

Th: If you don't recognize how you keep people at a distance, you won't get married. And you say that would be a problem. [*Mirror the dystonicity: not knowing means her problem will continue.*]

Pt: Do you think I keep people at a distance? [*Projection.*]

Th: Only you can know for sure. [*Block the projection.*]

Pt: I must because my last boyfriend said I did. [*Projection.*]

Th: But in your opinion? [*Block the projection.*]

Pt: I did yell at him a lot, and I threw the engagement ring into the gutter. [*Alliance is improving.*]

Th: You think that yelling at him a lot and throwing the engagement ring into the gutter could have kept him at a distance. [*Link her defenses of discharge and acting out to the problem.*]

Pt: Yes. I didn't see it at the time though.

- *Disavowal of conflict*

Pt: I'm not sure I want to be close to people. [*The patient denies a wish for closeness.*]

Th: That may not be something you want. [*Mirror her disavowal of conflict; do not attribute to her a wish for closeness she has not expressed.*]

- *Projection of conflict*

Pt: I know you think I should want closeness, but I don't want it. [*Patient denies she wants closeness. She projects onto the therapist. She tries to have a conflict with the therapist rather than bear it within herself.*]

Th: If you don't want closeness, you have every right to avoid it. I have no right to ask you to want something you don't want. [*Reflect her denial and block her projection of the desire onto the therapist.*]

- *Denial of conflict*

Pt: I don't want to be close with my wife. And I don't see that as a problem. [*Defense: denial.*]

Th: That may not be something you want to change. [*Mirror the patient's denial and stated absence of conflict.*]

Pt: My wife thinks it's a problem. [*Defense: projection.*]

Th: Since she's not here, I can't help her with her problem. [*Block the projection.*]

Pt: I don't know why I should be here. [*Inviting the therapist to state a reason so he can oppose the therapist.*]

Th: Neither do I. I mean, if this is not a problem for you, why would you come here for a nonproblem? [*State incompatible realities.*]

- *Pleasure in the identification with the resistance*

Pt: I don't want to be close. I enjoy it when he thinks we are really close, and meanwhile I'm a million miles away, and he doesn't know it. [*Manic identification with the rejecting role. Pleasure in rejecting her boyfriend secretly without his knowledge.*]

Th: You don't want to be close, and that's a source of pleasure to be able to be distant without him knowing it. Perhaps that is your goal. [*Mirror her identification, her pleasure, and her absence of conflict.*]

Pt: I don't know if I would say it's my goal. [*Begins to move away from the syntonic identification with the rejecting role.*] It's just what happens when I distance myself.

Th: If you remain distant with men, you should have distant relationships with men. [*Mirror her pathological superego.*]

Pt: That sounds sick. [*Beginning to turn against the defense.*]

Th: What makes you say that? [*Mirror her pathological superego.*]

Pt: Choosing to have distant relationships doesn't sound right.

Th: It doesn't have to sound right to feel right. If being distant feels right, why not? [*Mirror her pathological superego.*]

Pt: I have actually thought that, but when I hear you say it, it sounds crazy. [*Greater capacity for tolerating internal conflict.*]

Mirror the exact degree of, or lack of, conflict the patient experiences. Mirroring a lack of conflict might seem counterintuitive. Some therapists reflect the conflict they want to see rather than the degree of conflict the patient experiences. Instead, we must relate to the level of conflict the patient has in order to be as attuned as possible to the patient.

When the patient fully identifies with the defense, do not mirror conflict the patient does not experience. Mirror the defense. When the patient partially identifies with the defense, mirror conflict ("Part of you is here for a positive purpose, but at the same time, you sabotage yourself. You seem to be at war with yourself."). When the patient is differentiated from the defense, encourage her to turn against it: "Underestimating yourself like this will only perpetuate your self-defeat. Why do that to yourself?"

COUNTERTRANSFERENCE AND SUPEREGO PATHOLOGY

The patient can project onto the therapist her wishes and impulses or her superego (Racker 1968). This leads to two issues of countertransference for therapists. The therapist identifies with the patient's wishes. As the sole advocate, the therapist begins to overwork in therapy and starts to feel depressed, suffering from the patient's resistance. Or the therapist identifies with the patient's superego. Now the therapist feels critical of the patient and pathologizes her. Once the therapist understands with what aspect of the patient he is identifying, he can better empathize with the patient's inner conflict. As a result, the therapist can then help the patient integrate her wishes, feelings, impulses, and superego rather than project onto others.

The patient's attacks can also trigger the therapist's unresolved superego issues (Racker 1968, 174–180). We can become depressed under the force of the patient's criticisms or disappointment. Or we may become angry at or feel persecuted by the patient. Masochism makes us not only seek failure but fear it (Racker 1968). As a result, the therapist's masochism blinds him to the patient's good and healthy aspects. Masochism acts like a filter, enabling the therapist to see only the patient's healthy wishes or only the aggression, resistance, and defenses. The therapist who sees only the patient's healthy wishes, masochistically submits to the patient's defenses and resistance, calling that stance *empathic listening*. The therapist who sees only the patient's pathology, becomes a superego to the patient (A. Freud 1936). "The truth is that the neurotic is the prisoner of his resistances and needs constant and intense help from the analyst if he is to liberate himself from his chains" (Racker 1968, 178).

The masochistic therapist can fall into two traps. He can remain passive in the face of resistances, failing to fight for the patient. Or he can become overactive, fighting for the patient who does not fight for himself. Collaborating with the patient's defenses and resistance reveals the therapist's wish to be frustrated by him rather than to frustrate his defenses and resistance. To recognize the good and bad in the patient we must recognize the good and bad in ourselves. To remember the good in the patient while addressing his superego means remembering the good in ourselves as well as our own superego difficulties. "[E]xperiencing the patient as one's self [is] the basis for understanding" (Racker 1968, 179). If we see only the good or only the bad, we fail to identify with the entire patient. To see only pathology in the patient requires no genius on the part of the therapist, only projection.

SUMMARY

The superego is best viewed as a system (Barnett 2007). It encompasses the conscious and unconscious parts of the mind that criticize and judge our actions, provide our internal ideals, serve as our "inner voice" or conscience, constitute our capacity for guilt and remorse, insist on the need for self-punishment, and provide our inner sense of morality.

These elements of our humanity are shaped by culture and religion, but they are formed in the crucible of early relationships. Ideally, through childhood and adolescent development, the young adult emerges with the capacity to lead his life in accord with his inner standards, ideals, and values. Some, given their insecure attachments in early life, trauma, and other factors, develop superego pathology based on defenses, which enact pathological identifications.

The superego is a concept. Thus, it cannot act (Ryle 1984). To be clear clinically, focus on the defenses the patient uses that enact identifications within the superego.

Superego pathology takes three basic forms. The patient judges himself, judges others, or projects that others judge him. These forms occur on a spectrum of reality testing. As a result, interventions must be tailored to the patient's capacities.

Often the major obstacle to effective work is the therapist's own problems. If we doubt ourselves, we will not recognize the defense of self-doubt. What we condemn in ourselves, we will judge in others. If we blame others for how we hurt ourselves, we will not see the patient's externalizations. Anything we ignore in ourselves, we will ignore in our patients. The therapist needs supervision and personal psychotherapy to help the patient on this mutual journey.

Defenses are our conditioning, not our essence. In a sense, there is no such "thing" as a superego. There are only our defenses, which can put us in a trance. We have these defenses, but we can forget the person who has them. Acceptance of who you are undermines the habit of self-rejection. Trying to reject, push away, or fix oneself are forms of self-hatred. Who you are is what is here. You are here to discover who is always here: the person hidden under the habits of self-hatred.

RECOMMENDED READINGS

Barnett, B. (2007). *"You ought to!" A psychoanalytic study of the superego and conscience.* London: Karnac Books.

Carveth, D. (2001). The unconscious need for punishment: Expression or evasion of the sense of guilt? *Psychoanalytic Studies*, *3*(1), 9–21. http://www.yorku.ca/dcarveth/guilt.html.

Carveth, D. (2002). Self-punishment as guilt evasion: Theoretical issues. *Canadian Journal of Psychoanalysis*, *14*(2), 177–198.

Davanloo, H. (1990). Clinical manifestations of superego pathology. In *Unlocking the unconscious* (pp. 163–192). New York: Wiley.

Davanloo, H. (1990). Clinical manifestations of superego pathology, part II: The resistance of the superego and the liberation of the paralyzed ego. In *Unlocking the unconscious* (pp. 193–216). New York: Wiley.

Frederickson, J. (2010) Separating ego and superego in a recovering drug addict. http://www.istdpinstitute.com/resources/.

RECOMMENDED MATERIALS

If you would like more information on working with projection in a borderline patient, visit http://www.istdpinstitute.com/DVD/. There you can purchase a DVD series that focuses on restructuring projection.

CHAPTER TWELVE

Superego Pathology: Addressing Character Defenses

T he patient who uses a character defense does to himself what someone did to him in the past (Fenichel 1945, 1954, 114; S. Freud 1917/1961a; Kernberg 1975, 1984). If a parent ignored his feelings or devalued him, he ignores his feelings or devalues himself. By enacting a past relationship he wards off feelings and desires rising in therapy (Greenson 1967; Kernberg 1980, 156–157).

Some patients use repressive defenses and then shift to enacting a past relationship to avoid experiencing feelings. This enactment can take the form of the transference resistance, doing to the therapist what was done to the patient in the past. Or the patient may use character defenses and treat himself as he was treated. Character defenses are often demonstrated in the patient's character traits and nonverbal behavior rather than in his associations (Kernberg 1984, 211). The more severe the patient's character pathology, the more pathological traits function simultaneously as character defenses and transference resistance (Kernberg 1984, 210–211).

Thus, every character defense reveals the history of the patient's suffering (Kernberg 1976, 79; Reich 1933, 158). For example, a patient spoke of problems in his relationship with his girlfriend. I noted that, although he said this issue was important, he described it in a nonchalant manner. As I focused on his detached stance, he realized that he expected me to tolerate his distance and noninvolvement without complaint, just as his mother expected of him. He began to sob. This illustrates how character defenses enact an identification with the aggressor (A. Freud 1936). In this enactment, the patient simultaneously dismissed his feelings (character defense) and his therapist (transference resistance). His character defense functioned simultaneously as a transference resistance.

A character defense is revealed in *how the patient is with you*: how he acts, behaves, and relates. We are less interested in *what* he says than *how* he says it. For instance, character defenses can take the forms of a manner of talking, gait, facial expressions, typical attitudes such as smiling, derision, haughtiness, overcorrectness, or the *manner* of politeness (Reich 1933, 47). The constant use of a defensive "attitude" indicates that repressed feeling is continually present. The patient's rudeness, excessive politeness, indifference, or criticalness (Fenichel 1954, 114) becomes a resistance in therapy.

The character-disordered patient says he will do something, but he doesn't. He collaborates verbally, but not nonverbally. He says he wants to look at a feeling, but avoids eye gaze, looks uninvolved, sits in a detached posture, and speaks with a dismissive tone of voice. The words are right but not the music. He *says* he wants to be involved but *acts* uninvolved. He *says* he is angry, but *sounds* detached. When his words don't match his behavior, trust his behavior, not his words. Comment on what he does, not on what he says.

An exclusive focus on the patient's words underestimates the importance of his behavior. If you interpret, the patient responds with more enactment. For instance, if you interpret to a patient that he detaches to avoid emotional closeness, he will enact his character defense of detaching: "I suppose you may have a point." To address a character defense, point out the enactment (Reich 1933, 27). "You detach from your feelings and from yourself right now here with me." Character defenses must be our first priority when they occur because they prevent any genuine emotional connection.

Therapists often mistakenly believe the character-disordered patient sees his defenses and how they create his presenting problems. When the patient *enacts* a character defense, he does not observe it. Thus, no interpretation or confrontation is possible.

Principle: *First block the enactment of the character defense, point out the patient's behaviors, and then invite him to see how he relates to himself.*

In the following example the therapist points out the patient's behaviors and then invites the patient to see the pattern of those behaviors: a pathological way of relating to herself, the character defenses.

Th: What is the feeling toward him for hitting you?

Pt: I just forget about it. [*Character defense: she enacts her identification with a forgetful, dismissive parent by doing to herself what her parent did to her—ignores herself.*]

Th: You forget about the hit. You forget about the bruised lip. You forget about the pain. [*Point out the behaviors.*] Do you notice how you forget and ignore yourself and your feelings? [*Invite the patient to see the pattern of these behaviors: how she relates to herself.*]

Sometimes therapists ask prematurely, "Do you see how you dismiss yourself?" But the patient does not yet see her behavior, much less that she ignores herself. Always point out the patient's behaviors first. Then she will more easily see the *pattern of the behaviors,* which is the character defense itself: how she treats herself.

Pt: It's no big deal.

Th: You say the hit is no big deal. You say the bruise is no big deal. You say the pain is no big deal. Do you notice how you dismiss and ignore your feelings? [*Describe the facts and then the pattern of how she relates to herself.*]

Once the patient can see how she relates to herself (the character defense), help her see the price of those defenses.

- "When you turn this criticism back onto yourself, does this mobilize you or paralyze you?"
- "When you turn this criticism back onto yourself, does it make you feel good or does it make you feel depressed?"
- "When you say his hit is 'no big deal,' does that help you create the kind of relationship you want with your boyfriend?"

Once the patient begins to see that her character defense is causing her presenting problems and symptoms, we can help her disidentify with the defense.

- "Is turning anger onto yourself your friend, or could it be your enemy?"
- "Is dismissing yourself what you want to do, or is this what you want to change?"

Then we can mobilize her will to the therapeutic task.

- Would it make sense to you that we take a stand against this self-dismissal that has been hurting you?"
- "Is this self-attack something you would like to overcome?"
- "Do I have your permission to interrupt anytime I sense you might be dismissing yourself or disrespecting yourself?"

STEPS IN ADDRESSING CHARACTER DEFENSES

Since character defenses are based on the enactment of an identification and since they are usually syntonic, they require several steps of defense work before they become dystonic.

1. Point out the patient's concrete behaviors.
2. Point out how she relates to herself (the enactment of the character defense).
3. Help her see the price (how the defense creates her presenting problems and symptoms).
4. Mobilize her to turn against the defense and engage in the task.

As soon as she turns against a character defense, feelings will rise within a split second, then anxiety and a new character defense. Intervene before the next defense so she can see when it occurs.

- "What do you notice feeling when you say you want to take a stand against that mechanism?" "What do you notice feeling when you say you want the two of us to join forces against that mechanism?"
- "Notice how that anxiety comes in to attack you right now just for saying you want to take a stand against that punitive mechanism? As if it's against the law to take your side instead of the side of self-attack?"

Intervening immediately before the defense helps her recognize and differentiate herself from it. She learns that self-attack does not happen randomly but predictably: anytime she expresses her feelings and desires.

Every time we reject our emotional experience in the present moment we identify with someone who said, "You should be different from how you are now." Through the character defense we try to be what we are not, to feel what we do not feel, and to want what we do not want. A dismissive parent's judgment becomes a substitute for the patient's self-awareness, direct perception, and knowledge. Help the patient create a space between herself and her defenses. Focus on her feelings, her essence, which has always existed underneath these defenses. Help the patient *consciously defend herself against these attacking defenses.* The experience of her emerging feelings and will differentiates her from the defenses so she can more easily let go of them.

Mobilizing the will helps the patient differentiate herself from her identifications. Ask her what she wants. Remind her of her desire that conflicts with the enacted desire of others seen in character defenses ("Would you please ignore your feelings right now?"). Love of the emotional truth of this moment replaces habitual ignoring. Awareness of emotional reality replaces judgment. Questions such as "Is this your will?" are not rhetorical. They invite her to pay attention to the desire at the center of her life. They help differentiate her being from the character defenses, which have hidden it.

Once the patient has differentiated herself from these identifications and can defend herself successfully against them, she can face her rage. She must disidentify with those character defenses. Otherwise, when she faces her rage toward others, she will identify with them and turn the rage onto herself again.

STRUCTURALLY PRIMITIVE THINKING

Character defenses are formed when children think with a preoperational level of intelligence (Piaget 1970). When using character defenses, a patient is often stuck in preoperational thinking, unable to observe these defenses or cognitions based upon them (Leahy 2001; McCullough 2000). "I am evil." Piaget (1970) described the structural process of this kind of thinking as centration. "It's all my fault." The patient focuses on one dimension and cannot consider other perspectives. Thus, he forms a global conclusion about himself or others based on this limited perspective. "I'm a shit." For instance, if he notices a fault in himself now, he ignores his qualities in the past. "I always mess up relationships." The adult using preoperational thought will see himself as the sole cause of an event, rather than consider the roles of other people. "My wife wouldn't have had the affair if I had been more understanding of her." Due to centration, he cannot "decenter" to stand outside and observe his thinking or enactment. Thus, when we point out his character defense ("Do you notice how you call yourself names?"), he may process your intervention from within preoperational thought. "But I really am an idiot!"

POINT OUT HOW A CHARACTER DEFENSE IS AN ENACTED IDENTIFICATION

When the patient attacks herself, her attention is focused on the *content* of her self-attack: "I'm ugly." Shift her awareness from the content to the process of her judgment. Do not argue with her about her attractiveness. Point out the identification: how she relates to herself. "Do you notice how you put yourself down right now?" Block and label each character defense immediately. Help her become aware of and disidentify with her self-attack.

Clarification of Character Defenses: Identify the Defense as a Pathological Way of Relating to Herself

Draw the patient's attention to each character defense until she experiences it as a painful symptom, "a foreign body which [she] wants to get rid of" (Reich 1933, 50).

- "How do you feel when you talk to yourself that way?"
- "Do you see how you minimize your feeling? Is that fair to you?"
- "It's a shame to talk over your important feelings. Don't they deserve our attention?" (Warshow 2008)
- "Do you notice how you undermine yourself?"
- "Do you see how you devalue yourself?"
- "Do you notice how you reject your feelings and yourself right now?"

Clarification of the Price of the Defense

Help the patient see how the defense causes the patient's presenting problems. If the patient can see how the defense is no longer her friend but her enemy, she can more easily let go of the defense.

- "Do you notice how you want to deny and avoid the reality of my compassion? Wouldn't that be sad if you deprived yourself that way here with me?"

- "Do you notice how you condemn yourself now rather than just feel your guilt?"
- "Do you hear how you condemn yourself now? Is this self-condemnation helping you or is it deadening you, killing you off piece by piece?"
- "Is this self-condemnation an expression of love for him, or an expression of hatred for yourself? Does hating you help him?"
- "Is it true you are worthless? Or is this self-condemnation worthless? Do you want to give to your son your love or your self-hatred? What will be helpful to him?"
- "Does this contempt for yourself help you to reach out and be a better mother? Or does this contempt for yourself lead you to withdraw from him even more?"
- "You've told me you desperately want to defeat this depression. Unfortunately, your passive detached state will perpetuate it. It's your choice if you want us to take a look at how you are feeling in this moment here with me" (Warshow 2008).
- "Is this self-hatred the best in you? Or is it hiding the best in you?"
- "You just called yourself an idiot. Is that something you need to hear more often?"
- "Is this judgment helping you, or it is just making you feel bad?"
- "What does that judgment keep you from seeing in yourself?"
- "What does your judgment want to make sure you don't see?"

Clarification: Differentiate the Patient from the Defense

Patients have used character defenses so long that they assume the defense is who they are. Hence, the therapist must differentiate the patient from the defense.

- "You are not the problem. This punitive judgment is the problem."
- "That punitive part of your mind is not protecting you. It is attacking you."
- "You can hide yourself in this cloak of shame and embarrassment. But, if you do, how will we be able to know and support you? Why should you be ashamed or embarrassed by this

natural feeling? It's sad to see you shaming yourself. Would you agree?" (Warshow 2008)

Vignette One: Differentiating the Therapist from the Projection

In this example, the therapist has to differentiate the patient from his defense and then help the patient differentiate the therapist from the projection.

Pt: When I shared that fantasy with you I began to think how sick it was for me to think that about you and your wife. [*Character defense: self-contempt.*]

Th: We see two things: you had a fantasy toward me. That is not the problem. The problem is that there's this punitive part of your mind that punishes you for even having a fantasy about me. [*Point out the character defense.*]

Pt: I am worried about your reaction. [*Defense: projection.*]

Th: But even before you came here today you called yourself *sick*. Even before you came here you judged your fantasy. [*Point out her internal judgment.*]

Pt: Yes.

Th: Then we see how you put that judge onto me. But this was your own internal judgment—condemning yourself for having a fantasy. [*Point out her internal self-attack and undo the projection of her superego.*]

Pt: [*Tears.*] I was afraid.

Th: You are afraid of how harshly you will judge yourself if you share your feelings with me. But you forgot that you were afraid of how harshly you would judge yourself. You put the judge on me and then thought you were afraid of me. But you are also trying to defend yourself from this internal judge that condemns you. [*Point out how she is defending herself, not from her parents or me but from her internal judgment.*]

The patient becomes anxious not only because of an urge she is tempted to share. She is afraid of how severely she may punish herself. She doesn't have to fear her parents anymore. They are not in the therapy office. If she can see how her self-attack is the danger, she need no longer fear the therapist. Then we can face the rage her defense is covering.

Vignette Two: Clarifying the Price of a Character Defense

Notice how the therapist helps the patient see the character defense of self-attack and then clarifies the price of the defense. Only when the patient sees the price does she begin to let go of the defense.

Th: You see this self-attack. Are you willing to defend yourself from it? Are you willing to take a stand for you instead of taking a stand for self-attack?

Pt: I don't know. [*Character defense: I abandon myself and refuse to protect myself from my own self-attack.*]

Th: You don't know whether you will take your side instead of the side of self-attack. [*She takes the side of her identification with an abandoning parent rather than take her own side.*]

Pt: I'm more afraid others will attack me. [*Defense: projection of the superego.*]

Th: That makes perfect sense to me. If you are unwilling to defend yourself against your own self-attack, you will be unable to defend yourself against the attacks of others.

Pt: Maybe I don't love myself. [*Character defense: self-hatred.*]

Th: If you don't accept your love, you won't be willing to accept the love of others. As long as you reject yourself, you will continue to choose men who reject you. Why do that to yourself? [*Identify the price of the defense.*]

Pt: [*Rise of feeling. Tears in her eyes.*] Maybe that is how I love.

Th: But whenever your love goes against your freedom, you are doing something else in the name of love (Osho 1977). What you call *love* I call *self-hatred*. [*From the perspective of an abandoning parent, the child shows her love for her mother by abandoning herself. But from the perspective of the patient, this is self-hatred.*]

Pt: [*Sigh. Tears streaming down her face.*]

Vignette Three: Clarifying the Price of a Character Defense

This vignette illustrates how to persist so the patient can recognize a defense. When patients have attacked themselves for so many years, self-attack appears to be an obvious truth rather than a form of cruelty to oneself.

Pt: I know that was stupid of me to say. [*Character defense: self-denigration.*]

Th: Wow! Do you see what you just did?

Pt: What?

Th: Do you see how you just verbally abused yourself? [*Point out the character defense.*]

Pt: Well, it was stupid. [*Character defense: self-devaluation.*]

Th: Is that a kind or a cruel thing to say yourself?

Pt: It was stupid.

Th: Keep repeating that to yourself, and let me know how you feel. [*Draw her attention to the defense and the impact it has on her.*]

Pt: It was stupid. It was stupid.

Th: How does that make you feel when you say that to yourself?

Pt: Bad.

Th: When you verbally abuse yourself, you make yourself feel bad. Why do that to yourself?

Pt: [*Tears.*] I always do that to myself.

Th: You refuse to defend yourself against this verbal abuse.

Pt: I hadn't even thought of that. [*Character defense: ignore yourself and your pain.*]

Th: You didn't think of defending yourself against this verbal abuse.

Pt: But shouldn't I think about my mistakes?

Th: How many times did you make that mistake?

Pt: Once.

Th: And how many times did you remind yourself of it and call yourself stupid?

Pt: Probably hundreds of times.

Th: So is that thinking about a mistake or is it self-torture?

Pt: I see your point.

Th: You can torture yourself, or you could defend yourself against this torturous habit. What shall we do?

Notice the stepwise manner in which the therapist helps the patient:

Step One: Help the patient observe her defenses (how she treats herself).

Step Two: Help the patient pay attention to her defenses.

Step Three: Help the patient differentiate her defenses from feeling and anxiety.

Step Four: Help the patient see causality.

Step Five: Help the patient turn against her defenses.

Step Six: Help the patient bear the feelings that emerge when she turns against her defenses.

As soon as the patient neglects, ignores, or dismisses herself, interrupt her. Label her behavior, using her concrete words. Once she can see her behaviors, she can see her defense. In this case we had an interesting question, "Shouldn't I think about my mistakes?" Thinking about a mistake once so you can correct it is thinking. Ruminating about one's mistakes thousands of times is self-torture. And it should be labeled that way. Patients with character defenses often cannot differentiate thinking from the misuse of their thinking for the purpose of self-torture. This differentiation is essential.

If the patient faces her rage toward an aggressor before she has let go of her character defenses, she will immediately turn the rage back onto herself, becoming more depressed and symptomatic. The patient must turn against these character defenses before it will be safe to explore high levels of rage. To turn her against the defense, show her how she relates to herself.

- "Do you notice how you dismiss yourself?"
- "Do you notice how you laugh at your pain?"
- "Do you notice how you give up on yourself and abandon yourself?"

Only when the patient can see how she relates to herself, can we begin to help her see how she relates to the therapist. "Do you notice how, when you dismiss your feelings and laugh them off that you invite me to do the same?" "If we ignore your feelings and anxiety together, what kind of relationship will we have? Will that be a healing relationship or a dismissive relationship?"

Use the patient's words to show the patient the precise way she dismisses herself. Always repeat the patient's words (e.g., "No big deal") so she can see the pattern of self-dismissal. Also, her use of the word *it* is the rug under which she sweeps her feelings and her boyfriend's deeds. "*It*'s no big deal." "I don't make much of *it*." "I forget about *it*." The word *it* hides the stimulus: her boyfriend slapped her in the face and gave her a bruise. Do not use the word *it*. Always describe the facts her *it* hides: the hit, the bruise, and her pain.

Also notice the sequence: show the ways she says these things are no big deal. After three examples she can look at them and recognize the pattern of self-dismissal. She can't see the pattern right away because she doesn't see the facts. If you ask immediately if she sees her self-dismissal, she won't know what you are talking about. Help her see the facts so she can recognize the pattern.

Do not point out the price of the defense until the patient can see the defense. Always point out the behaviors, and then ask if she can see the defense, "Do you notice how you dismiss and ignore your feelings?" Do not say, "We see this is how you ward off your feelings." You may see this, but the patient may not.

In the following example, the patient does not see the defense because she does not see the pattern of her behaviors. Notice how the therapist points out the patient's behaviors until she can see them and then asks if she can see the pattern: the defense.

Pt: I don't see how I'm ignoring my feelings.

Th: When you say his hit is no big deal, is that a way to pay attention to his hit or ignore it?

Pt: Ignore it. But I don't see why I should pay attention to it.

Th: You can see, when you say his hit is no big deal, that is a way to not pay attention to his hit. When you say the bruise is no big deal, is that a way to pay attention to the bruise or to look away?

Pt: To look away.

Th: When you don't pay attention to the hit and you look away from the bruise, do you see how you ignore the hit and your bruise?

Pt: Yes.

Repeat the patient's words to show everything she does not think about. Establish a concrete chain of facts, illustrating how she ignores herself and her feelings. This careful, step-by-step defense identification helps her shift from enacting to observing her defense. If she does not see how she forgets the slapping, the bruise, her feelings, and herself, she won't see the evidence that she ignores herself. Always help her see the defense before pointing out its function and price. Otherwise, what you say will make no sense to her. If she does not see the defense, do not argue with her. Point out the evidence so she can see her defense.

After identifying the character defense to the patient, clarify its price and function and then help her differentiate herself from and turn against it. Always point out how the defense creates the patient's presenting problems and symptoms.

Th: When you ignore his hit and the hits of other boyfriends, you show them that hitting you is no big deal, and it's acceptable to you. No wonder you stay with abusive boyfriends. You say their abuse is no big deal. When you say getting hit is no big deal, could this be a reason you have trouble leaving bad relationships?

The patient has indicated that she gets into bad relationships and has trouble leaving them. If we can show how her defense hurts and traps her, she will be more motivated to let go of it. Here is another example of clarifying the character defense.

Th: Notice how you laugh over your pain? [*Identify the character defense.*]

Pt: Yes.

Th: Is your pain funny? [*Make the defense dystonic.*]

Pt: No.

Th: What kind of relationship would we have if we sat here and agreed your pain is funny and laughed at it? [*Draw the patient's attention to the relational price of her defense.*]

Pt: Not a good one.

Th: This laughter and covering of your feelings, does this protect you or your father who molested you? [*Draw the patient's attention to the function of the defense.*]

Pt: It protects him.

Th: Who shall we protect here: him or you? [*Invite the patient to turn against her defense of self-dismissal.*]

Pt: Me.

Every time the patient lets go of a character defense, she lets go of an identification within the pathological superego. Within a split second, the patient may experience a new self-attack, self-hatred, self-criticism, self-dismissal, or projection of the superego. This pattern explains why these patients often suffer severe regressions. As soon as she lets go of her character defense, ask what she feels before the next defense occurs. This helps build her capacity to tolerate her feelings without attacking herself. Let's continue with our example.

Th: What do you notice feeling as you take this stand for you instead of your father?

Pt: [*Sadness rises in her face.*] I'm afraid. [*Anxiety attacks her for taking her side.*]

Th: It's wonderful you notice. See how this punitive mechanism comes in now to attack you just for taking your side instead of your father's? [*Show causality: turning against the identification triggers anxiety. Help her differentiate herself from her defense.*]

Pt: I didn't see it before.

Th: But notice now how this punitive mechanism comes in here to punish you? It's as if a policeman comes in to Taser you with anxiety, as if you broke the law by taking your side. Do you notice that? [*Again pointing out causality and separating her from her defense.*]

Pt: Yes.

Th: Shall we break the law and take your side? [*Invite the patient to engage in the therapeutic task: let go of the defense and face her feelings instead.*]

Pt: Sure.

These interventions differentiate the patient from the character defense. Now she can feel the rage toward her molesting father without turning it onto herself.

SUMMARY

A character defense not only wards off feeling, it is a way of relating to oneself. Point out how the patient treats herself and help her pay attention to her self-abuse. This focus will help the patient see, pay attention to, and let go of these forms of self-maltreatment. Once she has let go of the identification with an earlier aggressor, we can begin to explore her rage toward that figure.

The playwright Henrik Ibsen once said that we must be careful not to take away the lie that holds a person's life together. But lies do not hold a life together; they tear it apart. "You aren't good enough." "You deserve to die." "You don't deserve anything good." When we believe our lies or the lies told to us, we suffer. By helping the patient moment by moment see the lies she has been whispering to herself, we free her from the identifications of her past and from her self-torture.

CHAPTER THIRTEEN

Superego Pathology: Transference Resistance

Therapy invites an emotionally close relationship. Based on earlier life experience, the patient has mixed feelings, which she avoids through defenses and the transference, the two main strategies for resistance (S. Freud 1926/1961d).

The highly resistant patient is torn: she wants to rely on *and* to distance from the therapist. We can resist therapy for several reasons: to avoid feelings (repression), to enjoy gratifications such as punishing others or avoiding responsibility for our lives (secondary gain), to pursue a longing for an external good object (primary gain), or to punish ourselves due to guilt over unconscious rage (superego resistance) (S. Freud 1926/1961d). In each case, defenses and transference resist the rise of any "material derived from the unconscious" (Fenichel 1945, 27).

WHAT IS TRANSFERENCE RESISTANCE?

We should differentiate feelings, transference resistance, and projection. Unconscious feelings rise when the therapist tries to form a relationship. As we described earlier, using the abused dog analogy, any time we become closer to people, feelings rise in the body as part of our nonconscious perception of threat or safety (Andersen et al. 2005; Hassin et al. 2006; Panksepp and Biven 2012).

Some patients cannot tolerate the experience of these feelings. Instead, they resort to projection: "I'm not angry at you. You are angry at me."

Rather than feel his feelings, the fragile patient projects them onto others. His projection ("The therapist is angry") is not transference, but a defense against experiencing feelings *toward* the therapist.

In contrast, the highly resistant patient avoids his feelings toward the therapist by using repressive, tactical, and character defenses. As the therapist addresses the defenses against feeling, however, they begin to work as a system. The patient begins to enact a relationship from the past, the transference, to resist the rise of feelings toward the therapist (Davanloo 1990; S. Freud 1912/1957a, 1926/1961d; Strachey 1934). Hence, the term *transference resistance*.

Now the defenses work together to form a pathological relationship. For instance, as a therapist worked with a patient, the patient became vague. After a few minutes, the patient became withholding. Rather than use defenses to avoid feelings toward the therapist, the patient began to act like his withholding mother (transference resistance). As the therapist addressed this withholding behavior, the patient began to feel rage at the therapist. Then his mother came to mind, whereupon he experienced complex mixed feelings toward her. The sequence was (1) a rise of feelings toward the therapist based on earlier experience with a withholding mother, (2) resistance of those feelings by enacting the relationship he had with his mother (withholding from the therapist), (3) dissolving of the resistance with the therapist, (4) emergence of feelings of rage toward the therapist, and (5) experiencing of a link to feelings toward his mother in the past. Now he could experience feelings toward her without enacting the past relationship with others.

To summarize, the patient experiences mixed feelings based on earlier relationships. Rather than experience those feelings (based on an earlier relationship), the highly resistant patient resists them by enacting a past relationship. The fragile patient resists them through the defense of projection.

Earlier in the book we showed how to address repressive defenses, which help us avoid feelings. Then we showed how to work with regressive defenses, which cause a regression in reality testing and functioning. In this section of the book we are addressing character defenses and the transference resistance, two ways of enacting past relationships. Since these forms of resistance are based on the enactment of a past relationship, we have to address their relational implications.

We handle character defenses by pointing out how the patient relates to himself (his enactment of a past relationship). We handle the transference resistance by pointing out how the patient relates to the therapist. Although we have addressed these in separate chapters, highly resistant patients use both character defenses and the transference resistance to avoid feelings and the therapist. So you will need to address both of them to help the patient become free of superego pathology.

The transference resistance creates a past pathological relationship rather than a healing therapeutic alliance, prevents emotional closeness in relationships, prevents the patient from experiencing the feelings triggering his defenses and anxiety, encourages him to fail at the pursuit of unrealistic wishes rather than to succeed at the pursuit of realistic healthy desires, enables him to identify with his character defenses, and perpetuates his suffering.

The Spectrum of Resistance

Patients can resist the rise of feelings in many ways, but we can see patterns of resistance across the spectrum of psychoneurosis. The following list shows the spectrum of resistance from moderately to highly resistant patients.

- Moderately resistant patients use tactical and repressive defenses to repress feelings.
- Fragile patients resort to regressive defenses to "relocate" their feelings, internal judgment, or defenses.
- Some highly resistant patients use repressive defenses and then shift to using character defenses and a transference to resist the experience of feelings.
- More highly resistant patients begin therapy using character defenses, enacting a relational pattern they use throughout their lives. They exhibit these character traits more in nonverbal behavior than in their associations (Kernberg 1984, 211). As the therapist addresses those character defenses, the patient begins

to enact that past relationship directly with the therapist (the transference resistance) (Fenichel 1945; Kernberg 1984, 218–221; Reich 1933).

The transference resistance is dissolved through (1) identifying, clarifying, and confronting it in the here and now between the therapist and patient; and (2) the resulting breakthrough of feelings, which reveals its origin and purpose.

The Evolution of the Transference Resistance

The highly resistant patient starts out using defenses against offering a presenting problem.

- "I'm not sure I have an internal problem." [*Defense: denial.*]
- "You should ask my wife. She's the one who had the idea I should come to therapy." [*Defense: projection.*]

Address each defense until the patient declares a presenting problem for which he seeks help. Then find out if he wants to engage in therapy. If so, then address his defenses against offering a specific example where his problem occurs. Then explore that example, addressing his defenses against feeling.

During these interventions, a shift occurs. The patient begins to distance himself from the therapist. He looks away, avoiding the therapist's eyes. His posture changes: he crosses his arms and legs or slouches in the chair. He speaks in a dismissive and detached tone of voice. He uses verbal tactical defenses such as hypothetical speech, vagueness, generalization, and diversification. These defenses not only ward off feeling, they ward off the therapist. These interpersonal defenses signal a rise of feelings toward the therapist.

When a patient uses defenses to prevent contact with the therapist, do not try to explore feelings. You would not try to walk into someone's house when the door is locked. Instead, address these defenses against human contact first. When the patient lets go of those defenses, feelings will become more accessible.

Since these defenses work together to create a pathological relationship, point out that relationship. Each defense becomes a brick in the wall the patient erects between himself and others. Shift your focus from individual defenses to the pathological relationship they create (Benoit 1990, 1991).

> *Th:* Do you notice how you are looking at the floor? [*Defense identification.*]
>
> *Pt:* Yeah. What? Am I supposed to look at you?
>
> *Th:* I just wondered if you noticed how you avoid my gaze. [*Transference resistance identification.*]
>
> *Pt:* I find it easier to think when I look away.
>
> *Th:* You find it easier to think when you avoid my eyes. [*Identify the transference resistance.*]
>
> *Pt:* [*Sighs, shifts in his chair.*] Yes. [*Looks out the window.*]
>
> *Th:* Do you notice how you look out the window when you talk to me? [*Identify the transference resistance.*]
>
> *Pt:* [*Looks back at the therapist and then slouches in his chair.*] I like the view.
>
> *Th:* How involved would you say you are here today? [*Identify the transference resistance.*]
>
> *Pt:* I think I'm very involved.
>
> *Th:* You said you're a lawyer. If a prospective intern were sitting like this in your office for an interview, how involved would you say she was? [*Identify the transference resistance.*]
>
> *Pt:* Not too involved, I guess. [*Patient begins to see his transference resistance.*]
>
> *Th:* How involved? One hundred percent, fifty percent, twenty percent?
>
> *Pt:* I'd say about twenty percent.
>
> *Th:* What can we do about this eighty percent that's missing here? After all, if you're only twenty percent here, you'll just have a twenty percent result. [*Clarify the transference resistance: its price.*]

He has trouble tolerating the conflict between sharing feelings and using defenses. So he tries to transform his internal conflict into an interpersonal one with the therapist. Do *not* confront his defenses yet. Help him see them and their price first. If you respond to his provocations, the conflict will be between the two of you instead of within him.

Shift from Defense to Transference Resistance Identification

Previous sections of the book have shown how to address defenses. Now we will show how to address defenses when they function as a transference resistance.

Th: Do you notice how you are going up in your head now, getting a little distant? Do you notice how you are pulling away and avoiding looking at me? [*Identify signs of the transference resistance.*]

Pt: Yes.

Th: What will be the impact on our work here if you withdraw and become distant? [*Point out the price.*]

Pt: I probably won't get anywhere.

Th: What do you think we can do about this tendency to withdraw so we can have a better result? [*Encourage the patient to let go of the transference resistance.*]

Pt: I guess I need not to withdraw and go up in my head.

Th: If you don't withdraw and go up in your head, what do you notice feeling here toward me? [*The emergence of the transference resistance suggests that feelings are rising toward the therapist. When the patient lets go of the resistance, ask about those feelings.*]

Let us look at two examples to illustrate the difference between working on defenses versus working on the transference resistance.

Address defense: "Do you notice you detach from your feelings?"

Address transference resistance: "Do you notice this wall of detachment you put up now between you and me?"

Within the transference resistance, always emphasize the relational implications of the defense. Emphasize how the defenses create a treatment-destructive relationship.

Steps in Addressing the Transference Resistance

Sometimes the patient enacts a transference resistance at the beginning of a therapy. Usually, it evolves. First, the therapist invites the patient to form a therapeutic alliance. Then the patient starts to have feelings toward the therapist. Then the patient starts to distance himself from the therapist and those feelings through enacting a past relationship: the transference. Whenever the transference resistance arises, the sequence for handling it always remains the same (Worchel 1986a, 1986b):

1. The therapist invites a close relationship.
2. The patient experiences feelings toward the therapist based on past relationships.
3. The patient enacts a past relationship (character defense or transference) to avoid experiencing those feelings.
4. The therapist addresses the character defenses and transference resistance until they collapse.
5. The patient experiences feelings toward the therapist.
6. The patient experiences links between feelings toward the therapist and feelings toward someone in the patient's past.

Structure of the Transference Resistance

In the transference resistance, the patient does to you what his parent did to him or he acts as if you are doing what his parent did to him. This enactment takes nonverbal and verbal forms. For instance, he may act like his passive, withdrawn father, inviting you to be active and forthcoming. Or he may act like his cold, withholding mother, inviting you to be warm and giving. The therapist often feels angry, experiencing what the child felt when treated in these ways (T. Ogden 1982; Racker 1968).

The transference resistance has the structure (Troendle 2005) of an internalized object relation (Kernberg 1975). Table 13.1 shows the structure of the internalized object relationship as it is enacted in therapy.

Table 13.1   Structure of the transference resistance

Patient's enactment	Therapist's expected role
I am passive.	You must be active.
I ignore my inner life.	You must pay attention to it.
I oppose therapy.	Convince me to do it.
I don't have hope.	You must have hope.
I don't have the energy.	You must have it.
I am not an emotional person.	You must be emotional

Key insight: the patient avoids feelings by enacting one role in a past relationship and inviting the therapist to enact the other.

The patient avoids an intrapsychic conflict by creating an interpersonal conflict

The patient simultaneously wants to face and avoid his feelings. To avoid his intrapsychic conflict, he creates an interpersonal one. "I don't depend on anyone who could withhold from me like my mother did. Instead, I act like my withholding mother, and you depend on me!" This explains why patients say

- "You think I should look at this." [*Projection:* "*I don't want to look inside. I withhold from you like my mother did with me.*"]
- "You seem to think this is important, but I don't see why." [*Projection.* "*You want to look at my inner life. I withhold any desire to relate, just like mother did to me.*"]
- "What do you think is my problem, doctor?" [*Projection:* "*I don't know; you must know. I withhold from you like my mother withheld from me.*"]

When the patient projects his healthy desires, the therapist can unwittingly speak up for them. Then conflict occurs between the therapist and the patient rather than within the patient. The patient enacts one role in a past relationship, unconsciously inviting the therapist to enact the other role. If she does, the therapy becomes stuck. If she doesn't, the patient's resistance fails, and change occurs.

The patient cannot access deep feelings in other relationships as long as she wards off the therapist. If there is a problem in the therapeutic relationship, explore it first before exploring feelings in other relationships. You might think of the relationship with the therapist as the front door of a house. If it is locked, there is no way to view other rooms in the house. So work on the front door, the relationship to the therapist. Once the transference resistance is dissolved and you gain genuine contact with the patient, exploring feelings in other relationships will be fruitful.

PSYCHODIAGNOSIS OF THE TRANSFERENCE RESISTANCE

To intervene, the therapist must assess the type of transference resistance and the element of it that is in the forefront. The sequence of psychodiagnosis occurs as follows:

1. The patient enacts the transference resistance.

2. Psychodiagnosis of the element in the forefront occurs.

3. The therapist intervenes to deactivate the resistance.

4. Decreased resistance leads to rise of unconscious feeling and anxiety.

5. The next patient enactment of transference resistance occurs. The sequence continues as before.

In the transference resistance, each patient response expresses one of four elements:

- An identification with a parent
- A projection of healthy desires onto the therapist
- An invitation for the therapist to take an omnipotent stance
- A regressive wish

Each intervention deactivates one of those elements, as the following interventions will illustrate.

Psychodiagnosis of Response and Therapist Intervention

When assessing the transference resistance, note which element of the transference resistance is in the forefront: identification with a parent, projection of healthy desires, regressive wish, omnipotent transference. Once you understand which element is in the forefront, you will know which intervention will be most helpful in the moment.

Patient Response: Identification with a Parent

In the transference resistance, the patient can enact an identification with a parent's defense. In the following example, the patient enacts the role of an avoidant parent who leaves all the responsibility for the relationship to the child. Notice how the therapist deactivates the patient's identification with the parent.

Pt: But this makes me anxious. I don't want to be anxious.

Th: If avoiding what makes you anxious is keeping you calm and giving you the results you want, then obviously that is what you should do. But as long as you avoid what makes you anxious, we cannot help you with it. We have two choices. We can avoid what makes you anxious, and then the anxiety will be in charge. Or we can face what makes you anxious so you can be in charge. But as long as you avoid what makes you anxious, this therapy cannot help you.

Principle: *Deactivate the patient's identification by mirroring his stance and pointing out reality—therapy will fail. The conflict is between reality and his resistance to it.*

Patient Response: Projection of the Patient's Healthy Desires onto the Therapist

In this element of the transference resistance the patient projects the child's desires onto the therapist. Meanwhile, the patient remains identified with the parent. Notice how the therapist deactivates the patient's projection. By doing so, the therapist avoids an interpersonal conflict with the patient, so the patient begins to experience an intrapsychic conflict instead.

Pt: I know you think I should take a look at this.

Th: Only you can know whether it would be in your interest to look at it.

Principle: *Block the projection of the patient's healthy wishes. Do not advocate for his wish to look inside; leave that task in his hands.*

Patient Response: Expression of the Regressive Wish

The transference resistance always involves regressive wishes, which cannot be satisfied in reality. The therapist must point out and deactivate those regressive wishes. If the therapist tries to satisfy those regressive wishes, he will fail, and the therapy will remain stuck.

Detached or uninvolved transference resistance: "Heal me emotionally while I remain emotionally uninvolved." "Help me while I hide from you."

Oppositional or defiant transference resistance: "Heal me while I oppose you. I expect my behavior to have no impact on our success."

Passive or helpless transference resistance: "I will be passive. You must give the activity I refuse to offer."

Do not gratify regressive wishes. Instead, remind the patient of reality: regressive wishes are impossible to satisfy, and they lead to a failed therapy.

Pt: I was hoping I could just let this therapy happen to me.

Th: And how long will that take?

Principle: *Point out reality: the regressive wish is not possible.*

The conflict is not between you and the patient. The conflict is between reality and the patient's resistance to it. Resistance leads to self-defeat. Healthy relationships operate according to certain laws, which we violate at our peril. Passivity, detachment, defiance, and helplessness do not work. No therapy can succeed under those conditions.

Patient Response: Inviting the Therapist to Take an Omnipotent Stance

To succeed in any relationship, both partners must put 100 percent of their effort toward a shared goal. In the transference resistance, the patient proposes an impossible, omnipotent role for the therapist.

> *Detached or uninvolved transference resistance:* "I will give twenty percent of my involvement. Then I want you to offer one hundred percent of your involvement plus the eighty percent I withhold." The therapist cannot give what the patient withholds.

> *Oppositional or defiant transference resistance:* "I want you to put one hundred percent of your effort to the therapy while I work one hundred percent against it. You will need to give your one hundred percent, the one hundred percent I am not giving, plus one hundred percent to counter my opposition." Yet no therapist can give 300 percent!

> *Helpless or passive transference resistance:* "I cannot do this. You must do whatever I say I can't do. Carry me on your back so I don't have to take the steps in my journey." Or, "Change me magically by your omnipotent interpretation so I don't have to change how I deal with my feelings." "You must give your one hundred percent and my hundred percent."

Principle: *Deactivate the omnipotent transference by reminding the patient of reality.*

In summary,

1. Help the patient disidentify with the parent.
2. Deactivate the projection of his healthy desires onto the therapist.

3. Deactivate the omnipotent transference.

4. Clarify the regressive wish and its realistic consequences.

5. Help the patient let go of the resistance.

These interventions put together facilitate a "head-on collision" (Davanloo 2000; Kalpin 1994) between the patient and his resistance. His resistance defeats him as someone defeated him in the past. This experience of internal conflict between the patient and his resistance leads to a breakthrough of feeling. To facilitate that intrapsychic crisis, the therapist will assess which element of the transference resistance is in the forefront (see figure 13.1).

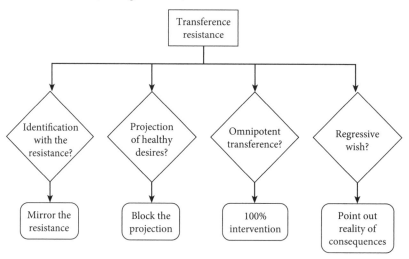

Figure 13.1 Decision tree for psychodiagnosis of the transference resistance

The Process of Change

We must first help the patient see and differentiate himself from this habitual pattern of behavior so he can make a different choice in his relationships. Changing the transference resistance takes place in three stages:

1. Differentiate the patient from the resistance (Coughlin Della Selva 1996; Davanloo 2000, 2001; Ten Have de Labije 2001).

2. Mobilize and strengthen the patient's awareness of his healthy desires (Coughlin Della Selva 1996; Davanloo 1990, 2000, 2001; Lebeaux 2000; Ten Have de Labije 2001).

3. Help the patient make a healthy choice (Coughlin Della Selva 1996; Davanloo 1990, 2000, 2001; Ten Have de Labije 2001).

To differentiate the patient from the resistance, help him see his defenses and then help him see the ways he relates to you. Then help him see the price of his noncollaboration. Since he is enacting a past relationship automatically and habitually, he does not see his resistance. Therefore, you must persistently point out his defenses and relational behavior so he can see the difference between who he is as a person and how he wards you off.

The patient's resistance is not a "part" of him. It is merely an automatic, habitual pattern of behavior. We must differentiate the person from his choices, his essence from his conditioning. Once he can see his resistance, he can make different conscious choices, rather than be the hostage of automaticity.

To strengthen the patient's awareness of his healthy desires, remind him of his goals and the ways the resistance defeats them. By strengthening his capacity to observe his feelings, anxiety, and defense, we help him become aware of himself as someone differentiated from his behaviors. Now he can observe automatic reactions rather than identify with them. He learns to see the difference between his essence as a person and his resistance.

Once these three stages have been accomplished, the transference resistance drops, and feelings break through. Although we must also mobilize self-observing capacity and work with character defenses, here we will focus only on deactivating the transference resistance.

Deactivating the Passive/Helpless Transference Resistance

The examples below illustrate common forms of the passive/helpless transference resistance and ways you can deactivate it. Notice how pointing out reality is key to addressing this resistance.

- Example One

Th: What's the problem with which you would like me to help you?

Pt: I was hoping you could tell me what my problem is. [*Invitation to form a passive transference resistance.*]

Th: That's not something I can do. Only you can know if you have an internal emotional problem. [*Confront his regressive wish with reality.*]

Pt: But you have all this training. Surely you can tell me if I have a problem or not.

Th: Not really. Since I haven't heard anything from you, I have no idea whether you have an internal emotional problem or not. Only you can know for sure. [*Deactivate the projection onto the therapist.*]

Pt: Let me tell you about what's going on in my marriage. [*The patient lets go of the passive transference resistance momentarily and talks more collaboratively.*]

- Example Two

Pt: Why do I do this? [*The patient, having faced a destructive defense, intellectualizes to avoid the painful feelings that would rise if he faced his self-destructiveness. He invites the therapist to share insights while the patient passively is "healed."*]

Th: The question isn't why you do this, but what do you want to do about this destructive habit of devaluing yourself because this would be a disaster for our relationship. [*Block the passive transference resistance.*]

- Example Three

Th: What's the feeling toward him for kicking you out of the house?

Pt: I don't know how to feel. [*Metacommunication: "Work hard for me while I take a helpless stance. Offer to this therapy what I am 'unable' to give."*]

Th: Do you notice how you underestimate yourself right now? [*Point out the defense.*]

Pt: What?

Th: Do you notice how you underestimate yourself right now? You say you don't know how to feel; yet every baby in the world feels. You have felt. Do you see now how you underestimate yourself and put yourself down? [*Point out the defense.*]

Pt: I do put myself down a lot. I know that. [*She sees her defense.*]

Th: That's important here because if you underestimate yourself and put yourself down here, we won't have your full capacities to achieve your goal. [*The price of the defense.*]

Pt: But what if I'm not able to feel? [*Metacommunication: "Heal me emotionally while I have no feelings."*]

Th: Then we won't be able to succeed. [*Contrast her regressive wish with reality.*]

Pt: [*Anxiety indicates a rise of complex transference feelings.*] Can you give me a list of feelings? [*Another form of helplessness.*]

Th: The issue isn't a list. The issue is that you say you cannot feel. If that is true, then therapy cannot help you. [*Contrast her regressive wish with reality.*]

Pt: Isn't there something you could do? [*Metacommunication: "Please take on the omnipotent transference."*]

Th: No. I can do what I can do, but I can't feel your feelings for you. If you cannot feel, then we have to accept that you don't have the capacities necessary to do therapy. [*Mirror her resistance to deactivate the projection onto the therapist. Then point out the reality consequences.*]

Pt: [*Sigh.*] Now I'm angry with you. [*Weakening of the transference resistance allows feelings to rise.*]

Th: How do you experience that anger toward me physically in your body?

Therapists often wonder, "Wasn't the patient's anger a result of your stance with her?" No. Every time she became angry with people, she covered it up with a helpless stance. Focusing on the transference resistance allows the covered-up feelings to rise.

- Example Four

Pt: I'm not sure I have the energy to do this. [*Metacommunication: "You will need to provide the energy I can't offer."*]

Th: That will be a problem. [*Block the transference resistance.*]

Pt: Isn't there something you can do? [*Invites the therapist to take on the omnipotent transference.*]

Th: No. If I give one hundred percent here and you give one hundred percent, we can have a very good result. [*The therapeutic alliance and its result.*] But if I give one hundred percent and you can give only twenty percent, we'll just have a twenty percent result. [*The transference resistance and its result.*] If twenty percent is all you can give [*mirror the pathological superego*], then a twenty percent result is all we can hope for. [*The price of the resistance.*]

Pt: But what if I can't do it? [*Invite the transference resistance.*]

Th: If you can't do it, I can't carry you on my shoulders the rest of the way. [*Deactivate the omnipotent transference and regressive wish.*] We'll have to accept that you won't be able to achieve your goal. [*The price.*]

Pt: [*Begins to cry.*] But I can't go on this way! [*Turning against the resistance.*]

Th: I hear you, but, as long as you give up on yourself, this is the result you'll have. [*The transference resistance creates this terrible result.*] What can we do about this destructive habit of giving up on yourself? [*Encourage him to turn against the resistance.*]

Pt: I guess I have to stop giving up on myself. But I was hoping you could do something. [*Metacommunication: "I hoped you could heal me while I give up on myself."*]

Th: I'm glad to help you. But I have to accept I can't help you while you give up on yourself. If you don't have the energy to do this, I can't do it by myself. [*Deactivate the omnipotent transference.*]

Pt: [*Cries.*] That's what my fiancée said. I gave up on our relationship and I lost the best woman I ever had. [*Now faces the price of his resistance.*]

In the passive or helpless transference resistance, patients present as if they are less capable than they are. When working with the passive or helpless transference resistance, the therapist asks a question and the passive patient will reply: "I don't know." [*Metacommunication: "Figure that out for me while I remain passive."*]

The therapist can respond in one of these ways:

- If you don't, who will? [*Deactivate projection of the omnipotent role onto the therapist.*]

- Do you notice you are going a little passive now? [*Identify the resistance.*] What impact will that have on our work? [*Invite the patient to notice the price of his resistance.*] When the patient answers, ask him: "So what can we do about this passivity because this is going to get in your way?" [*Deactivate the projection. The patient will have to end his passivity for therapy to succeed.*]

In the passive/helpless transference resistance, the patient invites the therapist to give what the patient withholds. Some wonder, "What if he cannot answer these questions in therapy?" We ask questions children can answer: "What is the feeling toward him?" "Does putting yourself down make you feel good or does it hurt you?" Questions for the heart do not require great abilities of the head.

People demonstrate skills and intelligence every day. The patient may be an emergency room nurse or a skilled carpenter. But in therapy, "helpless" patients hide their real abilities under a façade of pseudoincapacity. They enact the same pathological relationship in marriage, friendships, and at work. There are exceptions, of course, such as people suffering from Asperger's syndrome or other neurocognitive deficits. For most patients, however, helplessness is a transference resistance.

Yet sometimes it can be hard to differentiate the projection of will in the fragile patient from the passive transference resistance of the highly resistant patient. Table 13.2 shows the differences in psychodiagnosis that allow you to differentiate these two forms of resistance.

Table 13.2   Differentiating projection of will from the passive transference resistance

Elements for psychodiagnosis	Projection of will	Passive transference resistance
Anxiety	Cognitive/perceptual disruption	Striated muscles
Defense structure	Regressive defenses	Repressive and tactical defenses
Reality testing	Impaired	Good
Reaction to therapist's "will"	Fear of the therapist's "will"	Comfortable with the therapist being active while the patient remains passive
Extent of the resistance	Single defense	The entire relationship
Response to deactivating projection of will	Drop in projective anxiety and patient engages in the task	Patient remains passive

When the therapist deactivates projection of will, the fragile patient's projective anxiety drops and she readily engages in the therapeutic task. Her projection of will was the only defense preventing her from engaging in the therapeutic task. In contrast, the patient with a passive transference resistance uses many defenses that operate together to form a pathological relationship. Thus, addressing only one defense leaves the rest of the defenses functioning so they can form the passive transference resistance.

Deactivating the Oppositional or Defiant Transference Resistance

These examples illustrate common forms of the oppositional/defiant transference resistance and ways you can deactivate it. Notice how deactivating the projection of will onto the therapist is the key intervention.

- Example One

Th: What's the problem you would like me to help you with?

Pt: I don't want to f__ing depend on you!

Th: Thank you for being so collaborative. [*This is not said sarcastically but honestly. The patient's response was very helpful to the therapist. His response has just let the therapist know exactly what help is necessary.*] Although your feet have brought you here, you are also letting me know you don't want to depend on me. [*Avoid the battle of wills. Point out the contradiction between what he did (come to the session) and said ("I don't want to f__ing depend on you!")*]

Pt: You can't make me depend upon you. [*Patient invites a battle of wills.*]

Th: That's true. I'm glad you realize that. [*Deactivate his projection.*] You can depend upon me if you want, or you can decide not to. Only you can make that decision. [*Point out reality.*] If not depending on me is helpful to you, you have an obligation not to. [*Deactivate the projection that I want him to depend on me.*]

Pt: [*Tears in his eyes. With this deactivation of the projections, the patient experiences conflict between his wish to depend, and his resistance to doing so. He begins to talk more openly.*]

- Example Two

Pt: I'm not sure I want to get better. [*Invites the transference resistance. Metacommunication: "I don't want to get better. Make me better against my will."*]

Th: There's no law that says you have to get better if you don't want to. [*Mirror the denial to deactivate the projection of his desire to get well onto the therapist.*]

Pt: I don't want to get better. [*Invites the transference resistance.*]

Th: Okay. [*Pause. Avoiding a battle of wills deactivates the patient's defense.*]

Pt: [*Shifts in his chair and becomes anxious.*] Well? [*Invitation to a battle of wills.*]

Th: Well what?

Pt: Aren't you going to say something about my not wanting to get better? [*Invites the therapist to get into a battle of wills.*]

Th: Why should I? If you don't want to get better, you have every right to make that choice. [*Point out reality.*] I have no right to tell you what to do. [*Deactivate the defiant transference.*]

Pt: But don't you think that's unhealthy? [*Projection onto the therapist.*]

Th: Only you can know if it's unhealthy for you to not want to get better. [*Point out his choice.*] Neither I nor anyone else can stop you from making your choices. They're yours. [*Deactivate the omnipotent transference.*] If you don't want to get better, that's the result you'll have. [*Point out the price of the resistance.*]

Pt: [*Shifts in his chair with a rise of anxiety.*] Aren't you going to fight for me? [*Invitation to the transference resistance.*]

Th: Why should I fight for you when you have decided you are not worth fighting for? [*Outline the transference resistance.*]

Pt: [*Rise of anxiety.*] That's a sad thought.

Th: You are aware that it is sad that you treat yourself as if you are not worth fighting for. [*Mirror the healthy desire of the patient.*]

Pt: Yes.

Some patients invite you to be the spokesperson for their healthy desire so they can oppose you and ignore their internal conflict. Deactivate the projection by mirroring his defenses and reminding him of the price. Avoid a battle of wills between you and him. The conflict is between him and the resistance that is creating his suffering. He will try to make the conflict interpersonal. Keep it intrapsychic.

Defiant patients may respond to the therapist's question, "What is the feeling toward her?" by saying, "I just don't share feelings." [*Metacommunication: "Heal me while I refuse to reveal what I want you to heal." Omnipotent transference.*]

The following examples show how to address this same patient response from four different perspectives within the transference resistance.

1. *Block the omnipotent transference.*

Th: Then we won't be able to get to the bottom of your difficulties.

2. *Block the projection of the patient's healthy will onto the therapist.*

Th: The good news is you don't have to. There is no rule that says you have to share your feelings with me. [*Reality: he can choose to share or not to share.*] It's just that as long as you don't share your feelings with me, I'll just be another useless therapist. Why do that to yourself? [*Reality: "I can't help you with something you don't share with me." Show the price of the transference resistance: it perpetuates his suffering.*]

Pt: I know you think I should share my feelings. [*Projection: "Tell me so the conflict is between us, instead of within me."*]

Th: Only you can know if it is in your best interests here to share your feelings. [*Block projection.*]

Pt: But you're a therapist. You must have an idea about this. [*He invites the therapist to say he should share so they could have a battle of wills.*]

Th: I have no right to tell you what you should do. This is your life, your feelings, and your issues. Only you can know for sure what you should do for yourself. [*Block the projection of his healthy desire onto the therapist.*]

Pt: [*Shifts in chair. Rise of anxiety.*] I was angry with her for dumping me. [*He begins to share his feelings.*]

After the patient has described a conflict with his wife, a rise of the feeling and anxiety may lead to a defiant transference resistance. He may ask, "Do you think I have a problem?" Or, "What do you think I feel?" Or, "What feeling should I have?"

Avoid the battle of wills. Instead,

1. *Deactivate the projection of his awareness.*

Th: Only you can know for sure. [*Deactivate his attempt to be passive while you are the "omniscient" being. If you "know," he will argue with you rather than attend to his inner experience.*]

2. *Deactivate the projection of his suffering.*

Th: Is it your misery or not? [*The patient fails to see how self-destructive defenses cause his suffering. Block the projection by returning the question to him. If he admits his misery, he can be in conflict with his transference resistance.*]

3. *Deactivate the projection of his healthy desires.*

Th: If our work fails, it is your misery and your suffering. If our work succeeds, it will be your happiness and your freedom. *[Identified with his defenses, the patient imagines he is defeating you instead of himself. Remind him how his defenses defeat his goals.]*

4. *Mirror the patient's defense to deactivate his identification with the resistance.*

Th: You may not have a problem. It is for you to decide.

Th: If this is working for you, obviously it's what you should do. *[Deactivate the projection. He must declare whether or not this is a problem.]*

Pt: Why should I change? *[Metacommunication: "Tell me why I should change, so I can argue with you."]*

Th: Perhaps you shouldn't. *[Deactivate the projection. Now the battle is between him and his resistance.]* You love your resistance. You have lived with this crutch your whole life. Why change now?

Principle: *Mirror the resistance to block the projection.*

The patient habitually frustrates his loved ones, making them suffer as he did in the past with a frustrating parent. He replicates a past relationship rather than allow a new one to flourish.

Deactivating the Uninvolved or Detached Transference Resistance

These examples illustrate common forms of the uninvolved/detached transference resistance and how to deactivate it. Notice how within each form of the transference resistance (passive, uninvolved, defiant, etc.) the patient can act out the identification with the parent, project his healthy desires, engage in the omnipotent transference, or enact a regressive wish.

- Example One

Th: She dumped you. What are you doing with your feelings?

Pt: I'm dead to my feelings. *[Transference resistance. Metacommunication: "Heal me while I pretend to be dead."]*

Th: But this cannot be psychotherapy of the dead. If you are emotionally dead, then this can be only a dead therapy. *[Confront his regressive wish with reality.]*

- Example Two

Th: What is the feeling toward this woman who dumped you?

Pt: There's nothing there. [*Invitation to detached transference resistance. Metacommunication: "Heal me emotionally while I present nothing to heal."*]

Th: That's going to be a problem.

Pt: Why?

Th: Because if you have no emotions, we can't help you with any emotional problems. [*Contrast his regressive wish with reality.*]

- Example Three

Th: You mention a problem regarding intimacy with your wife.

Pt: There's a reluctance. [*Invitation to a detached transference resistance. Metacommunication: "Relate to me while I remain uninvolved."*]

Th: You mean *you* are reluctant?

Pt: I guess you could say that. [*By not declaring yes or no, the patient enacts the transference resistance.*]

Th: You guess? Either you are reluctant or you aren't. It doesn't make a difference to me. Which is it, in your opinion? [*Block his detached/uninvolved transference resistance.*]

Pt: I'm reluctant.

Th: You are reluctant to be intimate with your wife.

This patient tried to distance himself rather than co-create a healing therapeutic alliance.

When the therapist asks a question about a feeling, the uninvolved patient will reply:

Pt: I don't have any feelings. [*Metacommunication: "Heal me emotionally when I have no feelings."*]

The following examples show how to address this same patient response from four different perspectives within the transference resistance.

1. Deactivate the omnipotent transference.

Th: That's going to be a problem because if you don't have any feelings, then obviously I won't be able to help you with your emotional difficulties. [*Mirror his resistance (he has no feelings) and reflect the price.*]

Pt: But like I told you, I'm an unemotional person.

Th: And if that's true, then we won't be able to get to the root of your emotional difficulties.

Pt: I can see that. But I thought that was your job. [*Projection.*]

Th: No. I can't get to the bottom of your emotional problems if that isn't something you want. And if you don't have emotions, as you say, then obviously there would be nothing for me to get to the bottom of.

Pt: So what do we do? [*Projection. Metacommunication: "You, the therapist, do something."*]

Th: Good question. As long as you take this position of the unemotional man, the therapy will be useless to you. What can we do about this unemotional position you are taking? [*Invite him to turn against his resistance. Point out its price and function: to destroy another relationship and perpetuate his loneliness.*]

Pt: I'm not sure I want to do anything about it. [*Inviting the therapist to take on the omnipotent role. Metacommunication: "Heal me while I refuse to collaborate."*]

Th: Okay. [*Pause. Mirror the resistance.*] You have every right to keep this façade of the unemotional man. It's just that if you continue this way, this therapy will end in defeat. [*Patient begins to cry, turning against the transference resistance.*]

2. *Point out denial of agency.*

Pt: I feel detached and distant.

Th: You are detaching from your feelings and distancing yourself from me right now.

3. *Deactivate the projection of the patient's healthy desire onto the therapist.*

Pt: How long will this therapy take? [*Projection of responsibility onto the therapist.*]

Th: That depends on your motivation. [*Point out the patient's responsibility.*]

Pt: I don't know if I should commit myself to this or not. [*Metacommunication: "Commit to me while I refuse to commit to myself."*]

Th: You can be as committed or as uncommitted to your therapy as you want. [*Deactivate the projection onto the therapist.*] How uncommitted would you like to be to your own goal? [*Mirror the resistance.*]

Pt: [*Laughs.*] I want to say, "Of course, I want to be committed to my goal," but I feel like holding back. [*The patient begins to turn against the transference resistance.*]

4. Deactivate the projection of the patient's awareness onto the therapist.

Pt: I hear what you are saying, but I don't think these defenses are hurting me. I think they are holding me together. [*The patient invites the therapist to be the spokesperson for his healthy awareness.*]

Th: You know better than I if this is damaging your life. [*Deactivate the projection by returning the responsibility of knowing to the patient.*] Perhaps your detachment is creating the emotional closeness you want in your marriage. If it is, you should keep detaching. [*Mirror the resistance by encouraging him to do what he is doing and also mirror his denial that detaching hurts him.*]

Mirroring the resistance helps the patient see the discrepancy between his behavior and the results he wants. This keeps the conflict between him and his resistance, thereby undermining it.

Deactivating the Patient's Transference Resistance

A patient who enacts the transference resistance cannot see it or how it causes his presenting problems. Help him see and turn against it.

1. *Point out reality and mobilize the conscious therapeutic alliance.*

Pt: I have a hard time relating to people. [*Defense: vagueness.*]

Th: Actually, you just said you have an easy time rejecting people and pushing them away. [*Confront the denial.*] Is that the optimal level of functioning you are looking for? [*Mobilize the conscious therapeutic alliance.*] (Coughlin 2009)

Pt: [*Tears in her eyes.*] I feel like there's a little girl in a cave afraid of the light outside the cave. [*Unconscious therapeutic alliance: imagery depicts how her resistance traps her in a cave of defenses.*]

Th: How sad that you have imprisoned yourself in that cave of rejection. How long must you suffer in the darkness? [*Mobilize the unconscious therapeutic alliance.*]

Pt: [*Burst of grief.*]

Vague language reinforces the resistance. Speak to the unconscious (H. Davanloo, supervision 2002–2004). Use terms and phrases that highlight the price of the resistance: *great pain, suffering, loneliness, failure, doomed, in prison, die without your children knowing you, perpetuating your suffering, this is the cancer of your life.* Remind the patient of her suffering so she will turn against her resistance.

2. *Mobilize the unconscious therapeutic alliance against the resistance.*

Th: This is self-destructive, isn't it? You [*the patient*] come here under your own will to get to the core of your problems and at the same time you [*the transference resistance*] defeat the goal you have set. Why perpetuate your misery this way? [*Ask the patient why she punishes herself to turn her against the resistance.*]

3. *Mobilize the unconscious therapeutic alliance by reminding the patient how his resistance defeats his goals.*

Th: You have come here of your own free will to overcome this depression, anxiety, work problems, and problems in your marriage. You said you no longer want to feel depressed. You want to live a life no longer crippled by anxiety. You want to succeed in your work finally so you can advance rather than continue to be bypassed by others. And you said you want to have a loving relationship with your wife rather than the distant estrangement you now have. Is this still true? [*Point out his goals.*]

Pt: Yes.

Th: Although you want to overcome these difficulties and have a better life, at the same time we see how this self-destructive detachment is sabotaging your therapy. You detach with your wife and end up with a detached marriage. You detach at work and end up unconnected to your goals. You detach here with me, and then you sabotage your own goals here. [*Transference resistance.*] Why would an intelligent man like you want to do that to yourself?

Pt: I don't.

Th: You don't want to sabotage yourself. That is not your intent [*validate the patient*], but it is what you are doing. [*Point out his splitting: the difference between what he says and does. The patient pays attention to what he says (healthy) but ignores what he does (unhealthy). What he does is his character pathology.*] So what can we do about this detachment here because, as long as you detach, we will have the same disastrous result you have everywhere else?

Deactivating the Projection of the Patient's Awareness onto the Therapist

To avoid experiencing the conflict between his resistance and the problems it causes, the patient projects his awareness onto the therapist. That way he can be in conflict with the therapist rather than with his resistance. To avoid this interpersonal conflict, the therapist must deactivate the projection of awareness.

1. *Deactivate the Projection of Healthy Awareness:* A patient described her self-neglect as something furthering her "spiritual path." Then she projected this awareness onto her therapist.

Pt: You probably think this is a problem. [*Defense: projection.*]

Th: Did you ever think that maybe if you neglect yourself enough, you might end up in better shape in the next reincarnation? [*Mirror her resistance to block the projection onto the therapist.*]

Pt: I actually did have that thought.

Th: What's a little suffering now if it leads to realization in the next lifetime? [*Mirror the resistance to block the projection of her healthy awareness onto the therapist.*]

Pt: Except I can't afford to neglect myself now because it's affecting my daughter. [*She acknowledges her healthy awareness. Feeling and anxiety rise as she tolerates the conflict between her wish to have a better life and her defense of self-neglect.*]

A patient, married to a verbally abusive husband, projects her awareness onto the therapist. Notice how the therapist mirrors her defenses to avoid an interpersonal conflict. As a result, the patient experiences conflict within herself.

Pt: I know you think that this is self-neglect, but I think you're wrong. There's a virtue to being patient. [*Inviting the therapist to talk about the price of her defense so they could have a battle of wills.*]

Th: How wonderful that you have found a solution to your difficulties. How long would you like to wait? [*Mirror her resistance to block the projection of her healthy awareness onto the therapist.*]

Pt: [*Rise of anxiety.*] It's not how long I would *like* to wait. It's just that I have to right now. [*Defense: helplessness, denying her agency.*]

Th: It's not that you would like to wait. [*Mirror her move toward health.*] It's just that waiting is what you are doing. You are doing

what you don't like. [*Point out her internal conflict.*] You can wait
as little as you want, or you can wait as long as you want. [*Point
out her agency.*] And it may be that a long wait is in your best
interest. [*Mirror the resistance.*]

Pt: But I can't keep going this way! [*She moves toward health.*]

Th: Is it possible you are underestimating yourself? If you've waited
thirty years, surely you could wait a few more. [*Mirror the resistance to block her projection.*]

Pt: Okay. I get it. I realize I keep myself stuck in the marriage by telling
myself this stuff, but I still don't see how I'll get out of this mess.
[*The patient lets go of the defense of denial and the transference
resistance.*]

2. *Deactivate the omnipotent transference:* Highly resistant patients invite the therapist to assume omnipotent responsibility
for the therapy. "I, the patient, am identified with my resistance.
You must identify with my wish to get well. Try to defeat me
[*as the resistance*] while I try to defeat you. The responsibility
for success lies with you." But no therapist can be omnipotent.

A patient who identifies with his resistance sees causality
incorrectly.

Incorrect causality: "My problems are created by other people or cir-
cumstances—sometimes even by my therapist. My defenses are
good and protect me."

Correct causality: "I use defenses that create my problems and hurt
me."

Incorrect causality: "If I identify with my resistance, I will defeat the
therapist, causing him to suffer."

Correct causality: "If I identify with my resistance, I will defeat my
positive goals, causing myself to suffer."

A patient, identified with his resistance, can defeat any therapist.
He may respond: "I hear what you are saying, but I still think that shutting down protects me." [*Metacommunication: "Take an omnipotent
position and try to convince me to do otherwise."*]

Mirror the resistance and then remind the patient of reality: You
know better than I if shutting down is damaging your life. If you shut
down, then obviously there is no way for me to help you with this. And
in the end, let's face it: the end result here can be failure and suffering,

or your success and freedom. It's really up to you. [*Do not take the omnipotent role and argue with the patient.*]

Therapists who assume omnipotent responsibility for change become burned out, frustrated, and feel guilty for "failing to help the patient." Yet no therapist can succeed if the patient wants to oppose, detach, or remain uninvolved.

- The therapist enacting the omnipotent role
  - Becomes active to compensate for the patient's passivity or "incapacity"
  - Argues with the patient
  - Ignores signs of resistance from the patient and tries harder instead by asking the patient to offer what the patient withholds or by offering to the patient what the patient withholds
  - Provides all the will to engage in the therapeutic task, activity, emotional involvement, motivation, desire, or curiosity

Frustration in the therapist is often a sign of resistance in the patient. The therapist may harbor a secret belief that therapy is not succeeding because she is not good enough. She should ask herself, "What am I giving that the patient is withholding?" "How am I taking on the omnipotent transference?"

3. *Mobilize the unconscious therapeutic alliance:* When the patient does not let go of his transference resistance, point out how it defeats his goals. This knowledge mobilizes the patient's healthy wish to achieve his goals, a wish that previously was unconscious. Hence, the term *unconscious therapeutic alliance.*

- *Point out causality (the transference resistance will create failure) to mobilize the patient to turn against the resistance.*

Th: As long as you remain helpless, vague, and incapable of saying what you feel
  - we will be unable to get a clear idea of your internal difficulties and I won't be able to help you.
  - I cannot understand you or be helpful to you.
  - our work will remain in limbo.
  - this process will end in defeat.
  - you will not reach the goal you set for yourself.
- *Invite the patient to assess the price of his resistance.*

Th: If you avoid these feelings, what impact will that have on your goal to have more emotionally intimate relationships?

- *Mobilize the unconscious therapeutic alliance by noting the conflict between the patient's goals and his transference resistance.*

Th: As long as you have this *need to control*, we cannot arrive at the core of your problems. *You decided to come here to understand your problems.* But you censor yourself. *You sabotage your own goal and defeat yourself.* If you have this need to defeat yourself, why should we meet here and have this interview? (Troendle 2005, my translation)

Th: And now you say you believe that you deserve to be punished by your wife for thirty-one years. Yet we see that it is not only your wife, but you have punished yourself for thirty-one years. You chose her. You stayed with her. And you have continuously invited her to punish you. This is a profoundly destructive element in your personality. Now by punishing yourself and even trying to convince me why you should do so, we see the destructive part of your personality.

Pt: I can see I am hard on myself.

Th: Hard on yourself? This is the cancer of your life. This is how you have been making yourself depressed for decades. And you can continue to punish yourself the rest of your life if you want and remain a depressed, lonely man. But there is no way therapy can succeed if this is the choice you make.

Pt: I don't want to depend on you.

Th: That's okay. You don't have to. You have every right not to depend on me and not to let me get close to your intimate feelings. That may not be something you want to do. [*Deactivate the defiant transference resistance.*] Obviously, you have been able to keep men at a distance for many years and, if it is in your best interests to do that with me, that's what you should do. It's just that as long as you maintain this wall between you and me, then I will be just another useless man in your life, this will be a useless therapy, and your loneliness and isolation will continue.

The transference resistance sabotages a healing relationship, perpetuating the patient's suffering. Point out how it dooms the therapy to fail, perpetuates his misery, frustrates his own goal, guarantees he will remain a lonely man, sets him up for self-defeat, and ensures that this therapy will end up in the graveyard of failed relationships (H. Davanloo, supervision 2002–2004).

Problems When Addressing the Transference Resistance: Premature Confrontation

Do not confront the transference resistance until the patient can observe and pay attention to his transference resistance, and see causality—the resistance creates his presenting problems. Premature confrontation will create a misalliance. Identified with the resistance, he will believe you are attacking him as a person. He no longer experiences you as his ally against attacking defenses. First, identify, clarify, and separate him from the transference resistance. Then confront it.

Premature confrontation of the transference resistance results in iatrogenic rage toward the therapist. This creates several kinds of misalliance: (1) depressed patients "flatten out" or become depressed; (2) fragile patients become defiant or project; (3) patients with functional disorders suffer increased somatization; and (4) highly resistant patients become defiant. Exploring iatrogenic rage deepens the misalliance. [*Metacommunication: "I did not hear you confronting my behaviors. I heard you attacking my very person."*] This rage is based on a misunderstanding, not on unconscious transference feelings.

If a misalliance occurs due to premature confrontation, apologize for the misunderstanding to repair the alliance. Then clarify the therapeutic task, his goals, and the defenses that are preventing him from reaching his goals, and differentiate him from the transference resistance. Once he realizes that you are confronting his resistance, not his person, he will recognize you are trying to free him from self-sabotaging behaviors. Then, confronting the transference resistance deepens the alliance. The greater the differentiation and the higher rise of complex feelings toward the therapist, the more you can confront the transference resistance.

Compassionately addressing the transference resistance flies in the face of our socialization. We are socialized not to interrupt defenses but to reinforce them! Think of the family gathering where Uncle Peter brings up a taboo subject. Suddenly Mother stands up and provides the defense: "Okay everyone. Let's go into the dining room for dinner."

This is valuable in the living room. But colluding with defenses is destructive in the therapy office. Interrupt the transference resistance so you can co-create a therapeutic alliance. The *therapist and patient* must be willing to experience anxiety for the sake of their mutual growth. We can avoid anxiety or face it together to deal with feelings. "To treat the patient with true compassion involves overcoming our own internal resistance to fostering adaptive discomfort" (N. Kuhn 2011, personal communication).

NonInterpretive Focus on the Transference Resistance

Interpretation often supports the defense of intellectualization. This does not lead to change (H. Davanloo, supervision 2002–2004; Reich 1933). In fact, it can strengthen the transference resistance. The passive patient waits to be cured by the therapist's interpretations. The defiant patient experiences an interpretation as the therapist's attempt to control him. The uninvolved patient can listen to interpretations while remaining uninvolved.

Interpretation *enacts* the omnipotent transference. "If I listen to his words, I'll be healed magically by his efforts, not my own." In the transference resistance, the patient uses words to enact a pathological relationship. For instance, he might say, "Yeah, that's my goal here, but I'm not totally committed to it." By his detached tone of voice and posture, he enacts the transference (Havens 1986, 1993)! Since he uses words for the purpose of enactment, interventions must be enactive. Use enactive, noninterpretive interventions to deactivate the transference resistance.

SUMMARY

When we explore feelings, the highly resistant patient enacts a past relationship to keep the therapist at a distance—the transference resistance. Shift from defense work to transference resistance work. Remind the patient of his goals and desires. Emphasize your role as his ally to help him achieve his goals. This establishes a positive working alliance, the most potent factor in therapy outcome. Remind the patient that his healthy goals conflict with his resistance, which will defeat him. Instead, you and he can join forces so he can achieve what he longs for.

Help the patient see the destructive impact on his life when he avoids closeness with you. As you do, let his experience of complex feelings continue to rise. Mobilize him to let go of the transference resistance. Remind him of his positive goals. Ask questions of the unconscious such as, "What is the crime that makes you punish yourself this way?" Respond to cues from the unconscious therapeutic alliance. Focus on his longings for freedom while confronting his self-destructive defenses to maximize the tension between him and his resistance. Eventually, an unlocking of unconscious feelings begins.

RECOMMENDED READINGS

Benoit, C. (1990). Management of transference resistance in Davanloo's intensive short-term dynamic psychotherapy. *International Journal of Short-Term Psychotherapy, 5*, 277–296.

Benoit, C. (1991). Management of transference resistance in Davanloo's intensive short-term dynamic psychotherapy, part II. *International Journal of Short-Term Psychotherapy, 6*, 145–161.

Davanloo, H. (2000). Head-on collision with the resistance. In *Intensive short-term dynamic psychotherapy* (pp. 235–253). New York: Wiley.

Kalpin, A. (1994). Effective use of Davanloo's "head-on collision." *International Journal of Short-Term Dynamic Psychotherapy, 9*, 19–36.

CHAPTER FOURTEEN

Breakthrough to the Unconscious

Through the restructuring of anxiety and defense, the therapist helps the patient develop the capacity to bear her feelings to the greatest degree possible with regulated anxiety. When the therapist has helped the patient turn against enough defenses and resistances, feelings rise in the body until the patient experiences an impulse in the body, signaling that access to unconscious feelings is possible. The therapist helps the patient face these feelings as deeply as possible toward the figure with whom she is in conflict. When the patient experiences this rage without defenses, unconscious rage emerges: a fantasy of killing this figure. The therapist encourages the patient to picture this fantasy in her imagination while feeling her rage. When the patient does so in fantasy, the patient's body relaxes with the passage of the rage.

At this moment, the patient often begins to feel a wave of guilt and painful feelings. During this passage of feelings, the image of one of the patient's early caretakers comes to mind. This transfer of images tells us that the conscious rage toward a current figure is connected to unconscious rage toward a past figure. This transfer of images is the beginning of what we call the *unlocking of the unconscious.*

We encourage the patient to face these feelings toward the earlier figure. As the patient feels those powerful feelings where they really belong, memories emerge, allowing us to see into the patient's repressed unconscious life. When the patient can feel these feelings deeply toward the people toward whom they belonged in the past, these feelings do not have to be directed toward others in the patient's current life. Once the patient can feel her unconscious guilt over her unconscious rage, this guilt no longer drives the patient's self-punishment. The more deeply the patient can experience her powerful mixed feelings toward her caretakers, the more she can embrace all of her inner life. Thereby, she becomes a more integrated person and acquires a more integrated and realistic view of other people. She no longer needs to use anxiety or defenses to cover her feelings. Although earlier phases of the work can cause significant symptom change, significant character change results from the unlocking of repressed, unconscious feelings.

STAGES IN THE PHASE OF PORTRAYAL

When the patient's unconscious therapeutic alliance becomes stronger than her resistance, feelings break through, signaling the beginning of an unlocking of the unconscious. At this point, the patient experiences the impulse in her body. Perhaps her hand forms a fist or we see a choking impulse in her hands.

Stage One: Invite the Patient to Portray the Impulse

Once the patient experiences the impulse in her hands, her defenses have dropped, and the unconscious is accessible. At that point, invite the patient to portray the impulse in her imagination.

Th: If that impulse went out on him, if you were out of control like a wild animal, how do you picture that impulse going out onto his body?

Pt: You mean if I really did it? I never would.

Th: Of course, but in thoughts, words, and fantasy, in your mind how do you picture that rage going out onto him?

The patient pictures in fantasy how her rage would go out onto the person who hurt her. The therapist gently encourages the patient to picture the image in her mind. When the impulse of her murderous rage has passed, her body will relax, and tension will go out of her body.

Stage Two: Invite the Patient to Face the Complex Feelings

With the passage of the murderous impulse, a wave of painful feelings may spontaneously arise toward the murdered figure. Encourage the patient to face those feelings as deeply as possible. As she experiences those painful feelings, the unconscious will unlock: the image of an earlier figure in her life spontaneously appears in her mind.

With some patients the complex, mixed feelings will flow readily immediately. If not, encourage the patient to picture what she does with the murdered body, how she prepares it for burial in a loving way, what kind of service she holds, and how she says her final goodbye to the murdered figure. This kind of picturing helps the patient access the painful, mixed feelings and put them into words.

Stage Three: Unlocking of the Unconscious

The patient experiences how the feelings toward the current figure are transferred from feelings toward an earlier figure in her life. As she experiences those complex feelings toward the original figure, memories come to mind that help her see how unconscious feelings from the past have driven her recent behavior and symptoms. Since her defenses are out of the way, the therapist only needs to encourage the patient to face her feelings as deeply as possible and to elaborate on the memories that arise.

Once the unlocking of the unconscious occurs, the process unfolds naturally with little assistance from the therapist. However, therapist mistakes can prevent the unlocking. We will address below the primary problems that occur.

PROBLEMS BEFORE THE STAGE OF PORTRAYAL

Problems often occur during the state of portrayal because the therapist has failed to properly assess the patient's responses while inviting feeling. The following examples show common errors in assessment while inviting feelings that will prevent an unlocking of unconscious feelings.

Mistakes in Focusing on Feeling

Patients do not get to a breakthrough to unconscious feelings if those feelings have not risen enough or defenses and anxiety have not been sufficiently restructured. To get a sufficient rise of the feeling, maintain a focus on the feeling, the experience of the feeling, and the experience of impulse—in that order. When the patient reveals the experience of impulse through a movement in her body, the rise of the feeling and drop in defense and resistance is enough for a breakthrough to occur.

Skipping the Step of Labeling the Feeling

Before exploring the patient's impulse, first help the patient let go of defenses so she can label her feeling and experience it.

Th: What is the feeling toward him for throwing you out of the car?

Pt: I think it was really terrible of him to do that. [*Defense: intellectualization. The patient has not yet labeled her feeling: anger.*]

Th: What is it you want to do to him? [*The therapist mistakenly jumps to portrayal when the patient cannot label her feeling, experience it, or experience her impulse.*]

Solution:

Th: I agree it was terrible, but that still doesn't say what you feel toward him for doing that. If you don't cover your feeling with a thought, what is the feeling toward him? [*Address the defense, and then invite the feeling to maintain the focus. The patient must be able to experience her feeling and impulse before the unconscious can unlock.*]

Skipping the Step of Experiencing the Feeling

Before inviting the patient to portray her impulse, she must first be able to label her feeling and let go of enough defenses that she can experience her feeling physically in her body. In the following example, the therapist mistakenly invites the patient to portray her impulse before the patient is able to experience the anger physically.

Th: What is the feeling toward him for throwing you out of the car?

Pt: I'm angry with him.

Th: How do you experience that feeling physically in your body?

Pt: [*Sitting still with flat affect.*] I want to run that car right over him. [*The patient does not describe how she experiences her anger: defense. Her lack of affect reveals that she is either detaching from her emotion or distancing herself from the therapist, either of which would prevent her from getting access to her deeper feelings.*]

Th: How do you picture that in your mind? [*The therapist jumps to portrayal when the patient cannot describe how she experiences the anger or impulse physically in her body. This is an insufficient rise in feeling for a portrayal.*]

Solution:

Th: You say that in such a detached way. Do you notice how you detach from your rage right now? [*Address the defense so she can begin to experience her feeling and impulse.*]

Skipping the Step of Experiencing the Impulse

For the patient to have access to unconscious feelings, she must have turned against enough defenses that she can label her feeling, experience it physically, and experience her impulse. In the following example, the patient does not experience her impulse.

Th: How do you experience that anger physically in your body?

Pt: I feel a heat coming up from my body going out to my arms.

Th: What's the impulse that comes with that feeling?

Pt: They want to grab. [*Her arms lay in her lap limp. Defense against the experience of her impulse.*]

Th: How do you experience that impulse?

Pt: I don't. [*Defense against the experience of her impulse. No breakthrough to the unconscious is possible with that defense.*]

Th: If those arms grabbed him, how do you picture that in your mind? [*The therapist jumps to portrayal and ignores the defense against experiencing the impulse.*]

Solution:

Th: You say you want to grab him, but then you go limp. Do you notice that? What will happen if you keep going limp in the face of your rage? [*Address the defense and help her see the price so she will turn against it and experience the impulse.*]

In each of these cases, the patient may comply and visualize her rage but without feeling it. This is not a breakthrough to rage, but intellectualizing about it. The patient remains detached from the physical experience of her feelings. By doing so, she merely repeats her habitual defenses. This is not helpful. In these examples, the therapist skips one or two of the steps of feeling activation: (1) address defenses and invite the feeling until the patient can label it; (2) address defenses and invite the feeling until the patient can describe how she experiences the feeling in her body; and (3) address defenses and invite feeling until the patient experiences the impulse physically in her body. If you bypass any of these steps, you will not mobilize enough of the feeling to get a breakthrough to the unconscious. The patient must be able to label her feeling, experience it physically in her body, and experience the impulse associated with the feeling for a breakthrough to occur.

Skipping the Step of Experiencing the Feeling in the Body

Impulsive patients often skip the experience of their feeling to act it out instead. The therapist must block the use of acting out, and then build the patient's affect tolerance to make the unconscious available. In the following example, the therapist mistakenly explores the patient's impulse, when the patient avoids the physical experience of his feeling.

Th: What is the feeling toward him for taking your girlfriend?

Pt: I feel like I could explode! [*Yells. Defense: discharge. Primitive somatic representation of emotion. Unable to label his feeling as an abstract state: anger.*]

Th: And what is that feeling?

Pt: Rage.

Th: How do you experience that rage in your body?

Pt: [*Begins punching with his fists and stomping the floor with his feet. The patient goes to impulse immediately, bypassing the experience of his rage. Impulsive patients often act out an impulse to avoid the internal experience of their rage. Bypassing this phase prevents the patient from building his capacity to bear feelings at higher levels without acting out.*]

Th: And if that went out on him, how do you picture it? [*The therapist mistakenly encourages the defense of acting out.*]

Solution:

Th: I see that's what you want to do. You want to get this rage out of you by moving rather than to let yourself feel it inside. If you don't shake this feeling out of your body, could you let your feet stay still on the floor, and leave your arms on the armrest? [*Block the defense of discharge.*] How do you experience this rage in your body now? [*Build his capacity to pay attention to and experience his rage without acting out or discharging.*]

An impulsive patient in this situation will vent most of his rage externally rather than experience it internally. This will prevent an unlocking of the unconscious. The visualization allows him to engage in the same acting out and discharge that gets him into trouble in his outside life. It is not helpful. Any defenses you do not address earlier will prevent an unlocking later. They can stop the patient from feeling the impulse, portraying the rage, or experiencing the mixed feelings toward the damaged figure and having the unlocking.

Mistakes in Focusing on Defense

In moderately resistant and fragile patients, mistakes can occur due to problems in the phase of inviting the feeling and defense identification. In highly resistant patients, problems usually occur because the therapist has trouble addressing character defenses and the transference resistance. If character defenses and the transference resistance are still operating, no breakthrough to the unconscious is possible. If the patient is enacting his identification with a past figure, he cannot face his rage toward that figure.

A patient who was angry with her detached father experienced an impulse toward him.

Th: How does that rage go out onto him?

Pt: I just feel indifferent. [*Character defense.*]

Th: If you don't cover it with indifference, how does the rage go out on him? [*The therapist explores feeling but ignores the patient's identification with her indifferent father, a defense that will prevent a breakthrough of rage toward the father.*]

Solution:

Th: Now you become the emotionally dead daughter, indifferent to yourself just as your father was indifferent to you. But are we here to cover yourself with his façade, or are we here to find out who you really are under this façade of indifference?

Deactivating a character defense can be the pathway to breakthroughs with the highly resistant patient. If feelings do not break through, shift from defense identification to transference resistance identification. What role is the patient playing and what role is the patient inviting you to play to avoid an intrapsychic conflict? (See chapter 13.)

Defenses against Experiencing the Impulse

As soon as the patient begins to experience the impulse, defenses may come in. The following examples illustrate how different defenses can prevent the patient from experiencing his impulse. This patient just expressed the impulse to choke her ex-boyfriend.

Instant Repression

In the following vignette, the therapist helps the patient see and let go of the defense of instant repression.

Th: How do you experience that impulse in your hands?

Pt: [*Having just described her wish to strangle an ex-boyfriend who tried to rape her, the patient's hands form a circle as if they are around his neck.*] I don't. [*Her hands drop.*]

Th: Do you notice how you dropped your hands? Do you notice how you just dropped your power? [*Point out the defense.*]

Pt: I didn't, but I do now.

Th: If you let those hands power up, could we take a look at that impulse? [*Encourage the patient to turn against the defense and experience her impulse instead.*]

Negation

In the following vignette, the therapist blocks the patient's defense of negation so that feelings can rise.

Th: What do you want to do with that fist?

Pt: I don't want to do anything with it. [*Defense: denial. The patient's fist drops.*]

Th: And yet there was a fist there. If you form the fist again, what do you notice feeling when you let yourself feel your power?

Pt: I feel some heat rising up in me. [*Return of feeling.*]

Th: If those fists did what you would never do, how do you picture those fists going out on him, in your imagination? [*I offer the patient the defense of displacement during this first portrayal. During later portrayals, she will be able to acknowledge her impulse as her own without this graded approach.*]

Minimization

In the following example, the therapist helps the patient see the defense and also the price: it creates her symptoms. This is essential in this phase of the work, so the patient will completely let go of the defense, allowing the feelings to rise.

Th: How do you experience that impulse in your hands?

Pt: It's not an impulse to choke him, just to push him. [*The patient uses the defense of minimization. If not addressed, this defense would prevent a breakthrough to the unconscious.*]

Th: Now you water down your impulse. Do you notice how you hold yourself back now? Isn't this the same pattern that has been getting you in trouble? You held yourself back just before you would have won first prize in the karate contest. You held yourself back so you wouldn't surpass your twin sister at graduation. And now you hold yourself back again. But if you hold back your rage now, it will just come back on you again, and we won't overcome this tendency to inhibit yourself. Are we here to hold you back? Or are we here to overcome that self-destructive habit? [*Label the defense, then confront the patient with the self-destructive impact of the defense, and then invite her to make a choice: continue with a self-destructive defense or turn against it now.*]

Pt: I'm here to stop doing that. [*The patient turns against the defense.*]

Th: If you don't hold back this rage and those fists, how do they come out on him in your imagination?

Somatization

In the following vignette, the therapist helps the patient see the defense of somatization so he can let go of the defense, allowing the rage to be felt toward the other person.

Th: How do you experience that impulse in your hands?

Pt: [*Hands drop.*] I'm having trouble breathing. I feel like my throat is closing up. I need to get my inhaler. I think I'm having an allergic reaction. [*The patient somatizes.*]

Th: Do you notice how you start to choke just after your hands looked like they were going to choke him? Do you notice how the impulse goes on your throat instead of going onto his? [*Point out the link between the rageful impulse and the somatization. If not addressed, the defense of somatization prevents a breakthrough of murderous rage toward someone else since it keeps going back on the patient instead.*]

Depression

In the following vignette, the therapist identifies and blocks the defense of self-attack, which makes the patient depressed. If not addressed, that defense and the resulting depression would prevent an unlocking of the unconscious.

Th: How do you experience that impulse in your hands?

Pt: [*Slumps in chair. Tension leaves the body.*] I'm such a terrible person to feel this toward you. After everything you did for me, here I am wanting to hit you. I am an ungrateful piece of crap. [*Turning of rage onto the self makes him depressed.*]

Th: Wow! Do you see how the rage is going back onto you now? See how that old mechanism is coming in here to hurt you? If you don't protect me and hurt yourself instead, can we turn the rage toward me and see how you experience that impulse toward me?

Defenses against Picturing the Impulse

Sometimes patients experience the impulse and declare what they want to do, but then ward off portraying their murderous wish. In each case, address the defense. Otherwise, the patient will not portray the murderous wish, and no unlocking of the unconscious will occur. The following examples illustrate different defenses patients can use to avoid portraying their impulses.

Using Reality as a Defense: "But I would never do that."

A patient often will bring in reality to ward off his feelings. In response, the therapist must validate the patient's perception of reality and then encourage the patient to explore another aspect of reality: his feelings and impulses. When the therapist invites the patient to face an impulse, the patient may respond by denying that he would ever engage in that impulse in reality.

Th: Of course, in reality you never would, but we are not talking about reality. In fantasy, in your mind, how do you picture this if in your imagination you lost complete control of yourself?

Projection of Will (Compliance): "Do I have to?"

If the projection of will has not been completely restructured earlier, it may emerge again when the therapist invites the patient to face his impulse. At this point in the work, the therapist will confront the patient's use of projection and its price. Then the therapist will invite the patient to face his impulse. When the patient asks if she has to look at her inner life, the therapist will intervene as follows.

> *Th:* Of course not. You can avoid facing this murderous rage toward your ex-husband. [*Deactivate the projection of will.*] But as long as you keep avoiding this murderous rage toward your ex-husband, what will happen? [*Point out the price of the defense.*]
>
> *Pt:* I'll just stay depressed.
>
> *Th:* Right. And you can stay depressed another five years if you want. I can't stop that, but then I have to ask you, "Why perpetuate your suffering this way?" You can face this rage toward him in fantasy, or turn it on yourself in reality. But then, who suffers? [*Point out the price of the defense.*]
>
> *Pt:* Me.
>
> *Th:* Are we here to help you perpetuate your suffering or bring it to an end? [*Invite her to let go of the defense.*]
>
> *Pt:* Bring it to an end.
>
> *Th:* If we bring it to an end, how do you picture this rage going out onto him, if you lost total control like a wild animal?

Denial: "I just don't feel that way."

When the therapist invites the patient to face his impulse, the patient may suddenly deny the impulse the therapist can see in the patient's body. The therapist can point out the evidence that flies in the face of the patient's denial and then point out the price. In the following vignette, the therapist challenges the patient's denial and reveals its price so the patient can let go of his denial and face the impulse he denied.

> *Th:* Now you try to erase your feelings you have described over the past twenty minutes. You said you feel angry with her for harassing you through the courts. You said you feel heat in your body. Your hands formed fists. Then you said you wanted to hit her and silence her. Then who do you silence here? [*Challenge the defense.*]

Pt: I guess you'd say me. [*Projection.*]

Th: Who would you say? [*Block the projection.*]

Pt: Me.

Th: Exactly. Yet who is it you want to silence?

Pt: Carol.

Th: So if you don't silence yourself, how does this rage go out onto her in your imagination?

If denial comes in at this point, after the phase of defense identification, challenge the defense directly.

Defenses against the Experience of Complex Mixed Feelings

After the patient has pictured her murderous fantasy, defenses can ward off the experience of complex mixed feelings. Handling these defenses is essential. Otherwise, a breakthrough only to rage will encourage the patient to engage in splitting (Klein 1975a, 1975b). She will view others only in terms of her rage, denying what was good and loveable in them. This helps her avoid the unconscious guilt and grief, which have driven her self-punishment. It also perpetuates splitting within herself and splitting of her images of others (Grotstein 1985). Thus, resolving the defenses against bearing the guilt over unconscious rage is essential if we are to get character change.

Vignette: Continued Rage as a Defense

The patient has killed her father off in her imagination but continues to beat the body after he is clearly dead. This continued rage is a defense against facing the complex feelings over the murder she has just portrayed. Notice how the therapist blocks the defense and invites the patient to face her warded-off complex feelings.

Pt: And then I take a baseball bat to his head again.

Th: But you already flattened it. You cut his head off. You cut out his heart and mutilated the genitals of this father who molested you. He is dead. What does he look like now that you have finally killed him in this picture? [*Block the defense of attacking a dead body as if it is not dead. Invite her to look at her crime to access her complex, mixed feelings.*]

Pt: It's pretty ugly. [*Vague.*]

Th: What do you see?

Pt: [*Tears form in her eyes as she describes his body and the guilt emerges.*]

Vignette: Detaching

After having portrayed the impulse toward a loved one, the patient may envision walking away from the body and, thus, from her feelings. Notice how the therapist points out the defense and its price. In this example, the patient has killed off her father in her imagination and described his body.

Pt: And then I just walk away. To hell with him!

Th: You walk away from your feelings, but isn't that obeying him? He said, "Let me molest you while you walk away from your feelings." And now you obey him, but are we here to walk away from your feelings or face them? Who is going to win this time, you or he? [*Point out her defense (identification), its price, and encourage her to turn against it.*]

Pt: Me.

Th: If you don't walk away from your feelings, because you loved him too at one time, what do you do with his body if you honor all of your feelings?

Pt: I would wash it and prepare it for burial.

Th: How do you imagine washing his body in a loving way? [*Encourage the patient to face her complex mixed emotions toward a father who betrayed her.*]

Pt: [*Cries.*]

Vignette: Devaluation

Sometimes patients avoid their complex mixed feelings by devaluing the murdered figure. Notice how the therapist identifies the defense and points out its price.

In this example, the patient has imagined murdering her much-older brother who molested her for six years. He was her closest relationship during those years due to the neglect in her family. She has just described what his body looks like after she had killed him, gutted him, cut out his penis, and put it in his mouth.

Th: What is the feeling in you as you look at his body?

Pt: I just want to put it in a trash bag and put him out in the trash.

Th: Just like you did with your feelings for so many years. Even when you told your mother about his molestation, she said, in effect, put your feelings in the trash and you did. But if we don't trash your feelings, if we treat all of them with respect and care, what do you do with his body to prepare it for burial? [*Point out the defense, it price, and help her turn against it.*]

Pt: I felt really abandoned when he got married. [*Unconscious therapeutic alliance.*]

Th: Of course, because you felt he had been married to you as a little girl. You had been his secret wife.

Pt: [*Sobs.*]

Vignette: Defenses of Splitting and Devaluation to Avoid the Experience of Guilt

Sometimes the patient avoids her guilt over murderous rage by judging the person she killed in her imagination. Rather than feel guilt over her murderous rage, she judges and devalues him, saying he deserved the rage and not other mixed feelings. This defense against facing her mixed feelings means that she will continue to punish herself. In this example, the patient has just described her murderous rage toward an ex-husband who had an affair.

Th: What's the feeling now as you look at his dead body?

Pt: He deserved it. [*Defense. She does not describe her feelings.*]

Th: This man you loved, with whom you raised children, with whom you had been happy, deserved to be killed? Deserved to have his belly slit open? Deserved to have his genitals cut off? Deserved to be run over by a car? Is that true? Or is that a way you avoid the complex feelings you have toward this man you loved with all your heart?

Pt: [*Tears.*] It just hurts so much to remember that.

Th: But we mustn't forget any part of you or your feelings. Otherwise, you leave this room a heartless, unfeeling criminal, and we know that's not the whole truth of you.

Pt: That's true.

Th: So what's the feeling as you look at his dead eyes looking up at you?

Pt: I want to say, "I'm sorry."

Th: How do you tell him?

Pt: [*Cries.*]

Vignette: Avoiding the Eyes to Avoid the Experience of Guilt

After having pictured the impulse, the patient may avoid looking at the murdered figure or his eyes. This is a defense against experiencing his guilt and mixed feelings. Notice how the therapist identifies the defense and encourages the patient to face his mixed feelings. In this example, the patient has just pictured the murder of his father who physically abused him.

Th: What is the feeling as you look at his eyes?

Pt: He's face down. [*Defense.*]

Th: If you turn him over?

Pt: His eyes are closed. [*Defense.*]

Th: If they are open?

Pt: I don't look at them. [*Defense.*]

Th: If you don't avoid his eyes, what is the feeling in you as you look at his dead eyes looking up at you lifelessly?

Pt: Well, now I feel guilty.

Th: Let yourself feel that guilt as deeply as possible.

Patients avoid looking at the eyes to avoid the experience of guilt. Sometimes patients gouge out the eyes of the figure to avoid being seen and to avoid experiencing their guilt.

Vignette: Identification with the Object of Her Rage

The patient can avoid facing mixed feelings by identifying with the murdered figure. The therapist must take care to identify this defense, or else the patient will suffer severe symptoms. In this example, the patient has just pictured killing her ex-lover in her imagination. She is looking in his face while experiencing powerful painful feelings.

Th: Whose face comes to mind right now?

Pt: Mine. [*Identification with the murdered body.*]

Th: So it is your body you have murdered. What is it you do with your body?

Pt: I burn it.

Th: Isn't this what you've done in your life—burn it up? [*Point out how she turns the rage onto herself and the price of doing so.*]

Pt: [*Cries.*]

Th: If you don't turn this murderous impulse back onto you, whose face comes to mind?

Pt: My mother's. [*Massive wave of grief and guilt unfolds.*]

The patient turned the rage toward her mother onto herself to avoid facing the complex, mixed feelings she felt toward her mother.

INVITING FEELINGS AND BREAKTHROUGH TO FEELING WITH A MODERATELY RESISTANT PATIENT

The following transcript continues the case we read in chapter 1, where the patient had turned against his defenses and experienced a rageful impulse toward his doctor.

Vignette Four (minutes 38–42)

Now we will continue during the phase of the breakthrough to unconscious feelings.

Th: How do you tear her to pieces? If you're totally honest, how do you tear her to pieces? [*I invite him to picture this impulse in his mind while feeling the rage in his body.*]

Pt: Just like, you know, disassembly. It's just a disassembly issue, you know [*makes a tear-apart gesture*]. And, again, it's like, you know, I would never do this.

Th: But this is the fantasy. [*Remind the patient to imagine this impulse in his mind, in fantasy, thoughts, and ideas.*]

Pt: This is fantasy.

Th: If you go totally berserk—

Pt: This is fantasy.

Th: You disassemble her. How do you disassemble her? How do you tear her apart?

Pt: I just grab the arms and aaaaarrgh! [*A tear-apart gesture.*]

Th: Tear her arms.

Pt: Tear her arms off, yeah.

Th: What else?

Pt: [*Sighs.*] Tear her head off. Yeah that was just—Tear! Tear! Tear! Tear! If that was just totally in fantasy, I would never, ever do this to anybody. [*Remember how he had no feeling earlier below the head: an unconscious identification with the body whose head is torn off.*]

Th: Obviously, but in fantasy you tear her arms off, you tear her head off, you— [*Encourage him to visualize the sadistic impulse as vividly as possible so all his rage goes out onto the doctor in fantasy rather than onto his body in reality.*]

Pt: Yeah, I just really rage beyond belief.

Th: And just picture that. You tear her arms off. You tear her head off. What else? What else do you tear?

Pt: Legs.

Th: Mmm-hmmm. Tear her legs off?

Pt: I just grab them and just snap! I mean, I just snap! Snap! Snap! Snap! Snap! Yeah, it's just, you know.

Th: Tear her legs off.

Pt: Just brute force, snap! You know, no knives, no guns, nothing of that nature, it's just snap!

Th: It's just tearing.

Pt: Just tear! Tear the body apart because that's what's been happening to me. My body's been torn apart. [*The patient links the sadistic impulse to his symptoms.*]

During the next several minutes (minutes 47–56), he gazes at the head and eventually makes the connection to his mother, an emotionally disturbed woman who ignored the patient's feelings. I note that he was enraged with his mother and unconsciously wanted to tear her to pieces too, which led to a pattern of tearing himself to pieces. All of which reveals his love for her, his guilt, and his rage. After a brief passage of guilt, the impulse of rage emerges toward his mother. We resume the session.

Th: But if we're completely honest, because you've been tearing yourself to pieces for years.

Pt: Yes.

Th: And now we know who it's really been that you wanted to tear up. [*His mother.*]

Pt: Yeah.

Th: If we face this totally honestly.

Pt: Yeah.

Th: Because we need to make sure that the right person—that the rage really goes where it belongs—

Pt: Yeah.

Th: And not on your body.

Pt: Yeah.

Th: Because if it keeps going on your body, you could get killed.

Pt: That's true, that's true.

Th: If you totally unleash—I know it's very uncomfortable to face this honestly, but if we really, for the first time, face it totally honestly and all the rage went on her body, how do you picture that, physically, if we're just totally honest. If it's all going on her body now, not yours. How do you picture it?

Second Breakthrough of the Murderous Rage

At this point we see the unlocking of unconscious repressed feelings. Now we understand that the patient's rage toward the physician was connected to unconscious rage toward his mother. With this shift from the physician to his mother, the unlocking begins. We invite the patient to experience these feelings as deeply as possible so we can identify the repressed feelings that have been driving his anxiety and defenses.

Pt: Arrrrrgh-arrrrrgh-arrrrgh! Same thing again. Want to grab, just want to shake, just want to say, "Why don't you listen! Tell you I'm not feeling good. I don't feel right. Why don't you listen? Why do you just tell me there's nothing wrong, everything's okay. You're fine, you know, I'm the person who's sick. There's nothing wrong with you, you know. You're perfectly okay." Yeah. And look at the hands, look at the hands.

Th: And what do the hands want to do?

Pt: The hands just want to grab. They just want to grab. They want to bang. It's just like, you know— "Why are you trying to control? Why are you trying to lie and tell me that you have to do this, people are watching you. Why are you making up stuff, you know, to say that you have to behave better, you have to do this, you have to that, you know. Why are you trying to control me so damn much?"

Th: If all that rage in your head goes out to your hands onto her, how do you picture that? If there are no words, but just let your hands do all the talking, what do your hands do to her body? If you let yourself feel this completely—

Pt: Arrrrrrrrgh! Arrrrgh, boy. Again, I just grab. I just grab. I just grab so hard. I just grab so damn hard and say, "Why don't you let me go! You have to let me go!"

Th: So, if you don't hold onto your rage anymore, but let it go right into her, how do you picture your hands letting go of all that rage onto her?

Pt: Just grabbing, just shaking, just saying, you know, "Let me go! Let me go! Let me GO!"

While experiencing his murderous rage toward his mother, he spontaneously remembers his mother's death. Just before she died, she yelled at him, accusing him of abandoning her when he had spent an afternoon seeing some friends. He sobs while remembering his pain and hers, and his inability to heal her pain.

Vignette Five (minutes 62–73)

We return to experiencing the full extent of his murderous rage.

Th: If you let all this pain in you go out through your arms onto her, how do you finally finish her off?

Pt: Arrrrgh! Ah-haaaah! Ahhhh! Tear her apart. Just tear her apart. I don't even see any blood. It's just yank! Tear! "Just get out of my life! Get it over with! Get rid of it!"

Th: How do you tear her apart?

Pt: Just grab the arms, grab hard, and just yank! Just yank! Just yank! Just pull hard! Pull hard! Pull hard! Pull really hard.

Th: What have you yanked off?

Pt: Arms. Yanked the arms off. Yanked the head off. Yeah, got the head off. Arrrrgh.

Th: Anything else?

Pt: Maybe grab the breasts, just yank!

Th: Yank the breasts off.

Pt: Yank the breasts off. Just yank! Yank! Yank!

Th: Uhm-hmmm. And what else? If you're totally berserk—

Pt: Totally berserk.

Th: No restraints.

Pt: No restraints, no restraints.

Th: The restraints are over.

Pt: The restraints are over. Sexual attack, I don't know, not attack, I don't—

Th: No restraints.

Pt: No restraints, no restraints, I—

Th: Sexually, how do you attack? [*Emergence of fusion of his sexual and murderous impulses.*]

Pt: I just go in, I just f__ing. I just go, go, go, go, go! And just release! Arrrrgh! I just release! Release! "Held me back so long! You can't date! You can't do this," you know. You're just constrained. You know, "you can't have relationships. You know, you just, you're not allowed to do that, you know. No, you can't do that! No, you can't do that, you know. You can't have girls. You can't date girls. You can't do anything with girls, you know, that's just not—you know, you have to—you know. You just—you know. Grandmother doesn't like this, you know. You have to conform, you know. You have to not do this. You have to not do that, you know. You have to restrain yourself."

He recounts an incident illustrating this problem during high school.

Th: Once you've gone, and gone, and gone, and gone, and released,

Pt: Yeah.

Th: Anything else you do, if we're totally honest with your anger, on her body? Anything else?

Pt: I think there would be—I would stab, knife, and just— [*Makes several stabbing motions.*]

Th: Where would you stab her?

Pt: Chest/upper body. Just throw it in, just go, go, go, go, go, go, go! [*A symbolic rape.*]

Th: Anything else?

Pt: Beat her rear end.

Th: How do you beat her rear end?

Pt: Belt. It's, you know. "You've been in control, in control over me. I'm going to control you now. I'm the one calling the shots. I'm not, you know—"

Th: What else? How do you beat her?

Pt: Make her bend over, strap her rear end hard. Just really let her have it good and hard and go for it—Ahhhh, there's just sexual tension release, really real damned release here. Ugh! Really release. Reeeeally release. It's like, you know, "you've been a bad girl, and you really deserve this, ugh! Arrrgh!" Whew.

Th: So, beating her and beating her, and then there's a huge sexual release.

Pt: Yeah, yes, yes, yes, yes, yes! Whew! Thank you. This has been really wild, but I had to talk about it. [*The tension and impulse go out of his body as he relaxes back into the chair. The rageful impulse has finally passed. Now I will inquire about other feelings to see if he can access the previously unconscious mixed feelings toward his mother.*]

Th: Sure.

Pt: Had to talk about it.

Th: And so as we look at her body now on the floor, her legs are torn off. Her breasts are torn off. Her arms are torn off. Her head is torn off. What does her face look like, after all this? [*I invite the patient to look at her face to mobilize unconscious guilt feelings related to his murderous rage.*]

Pt: Shock. Like, "how could you do this? How could *you* do this? How could *you* do this?"

Th: And what's the feeling inside you, as you look at her eyes?

Pt: "Why did you do this to me?" I'm going someplace here and stay with me.

Th: Um-hmmm.

De-repression of the Oedipal Conflict

In the following material, the patient reveals important parts of his history. The patient's father suffered a severe, incapacitating illness during the patient's childhood. In response, his mother put him in the father's role, asking him to take on responsibilities no child could bear.

Pt: I think something was going down here and why the frustration. With my father not there, because of his illness, I think she was expecting me to be the husband. She was expecting me to be the husband. I wasn't her husband. I was her son! "You are not my wife. You are my mother! I'm your son, not your husband! You take your problems to your husband! You trust your husband. So he didn't go when the doctor told him you were dying the first time. So, he didn't tell you, and you didn't find out until later. You just don't cut him off and say, you know, I don't go to you anymore. Now Jim (the patient's pseudonym) becomes the substitute husband. Jim gets to deal with me. Jim gets to deal with all my issues. I have to end up talking to Jim. No, I'm the child here! I'm not the adult! I'm not the husband! It's not my responsibility to have to deal with you!" [*This de-repression of memories, his sudden awareness and analysis of his Oedipal conflict, and related feelings constitute the beginning of the "unlocking of the unconscious."*]

Th: Just let it out. There's a lot of painful feeling here. Just let it out.

Pt: Yes. Yes, yes, yes! I'm still—My childhood is not there. It disappeared. It was—God! [*Begins to cry.*]

Breakthrough of Grief

The remainder of the session is a series of breakthroughs of grief over numerous losses (father, mother, sister, and his own childhood).

Th: Just let it out.

Pt: I never—gone—I was supposed to have a childhood.

Th: Just let it out. There's a lot of grief, just let it out.

Pt: I was just an adult from too damn young! I had to be there! I had to watch my father have that seizure when I was eight years old. I had to be the one who had to stand up. "You were there, but I had to be the damn adult! I had to start taking over! I had to do so damn much! So damn much! Nobody here to do anything for me."

Th: For you. Just let it out. You were all alone. Just let the grief out. There's tremendous pain.

Pt: Nobody there to do anything for me, damn it. I just have to take care of myself. Always have to take care of myself.

Th: By yourself.

Pt: By myself! Always by myself, damn it!

Th: Just let it out.

Pt: Always by myself!

Th: Just let it out. You don't have to talk over the pain.

Pt: Always by myself! No damn help! You go and try and get help and you get told, "Well, you know, take some drugs, go away." No damn help! [*He spontaneously links his frustration with the female doctor and murderous rage toward his mother: two women who were of no help.*]

Th: Just like your mom.

Pt: Yep, no help! No help. Can't get any help here, you know. Got to go elsewhere.

In the midst of deep grief he reveals that after the death of his parents at age nineteen, no family members offered any help. Indeed, several ran off with family assets! He recounts how his doctor underestimated his toughness.

Given what he describes, he clearly has a great deal of unresolved grief over his mother's death. So I return him to the scene of his mother's dead body and how he pictures burying her. He says he never really had a chance to say goodbye because the last time he saw his mother in the minutes before she died, she was yelling at him. He pictures being able to finally tell her of his love. His grief and guilt pour out as he recounts his regrets over not being able to undo her suffering.

Vignette Six (minutes 81–105)

We return at minute 81 during another wave of grief.

Pt: I just wanted to help you so damn much. I didn't want you to go through what you went through! I didn't want that to happen to you! I didn't want that to happen to you. I didn't want my father to be sick. I didn't want you to have to go through so much damn pain! But I couldn't do anything to help! I couldn't do a damn thing to help! I couldn't stop it. [*He had been enraged with his mother. One way he dealt with the rage was to turn it on himself by identifying with his mother's accusations: "You could have done more." By accusing himself this way, he could punish himself unconsciously for his murderous rage. Now with the passage of the rage and guilt, we learn of his mother's accusations and his identification with her punitive voice.*]

Th: You couldn't stop her pain.

Pt: I couldn't stop her pain. I couldn't help. I could not help!

Th: Just let it out. You couldn't stop her pain.

Pt: I couldn't stop her pain. I could not help. I could not help.

Th: What else would you say to her, as your final goodbye?

Pt: Only believe in me. Believe that I will succeed.

Th: Believe that I will succeed.

Pt: Believe that I will succeed.

Th: Please believe me.

Pt: Believe.

Th: Please believe in me.

Pt: Yes, yes, yes.

Th: Anything else you want to say to her as a final goodbye?

Pt: Don't be afraid. Don't be afraid. God is with you. Don't be afraid.

Th: God is with you. What would you say to her that you would want her to carry with her for eternity that she could never forget?

Pt: I am always with you.

During minutes 84–104 he continues to grieve as he shares the details of her death and funeral and how his extended family abandoned him. He pictures giving her the kind of funeral she would have wanted, not the drab one she actually received. And he sobs as he imagines singing at her funeral, something he was not allowed to do by his family. He then recounts how, after his mother's death, his younger sister never got a chance to live up to her potential. He mourns the life she never had and the one he lost too.

SUMMARY

This transcript illustrates how systematic invitation of the feeling and defense work clears the way for the patient's unconscious feelings to rise. During the portrayal, keep addressing defenses so an unlocking can occur. Encourage the patient to feel his grief, guilt, and love as deeply as possible. By facing his complex feelings as deeply as possible, he regains a complex feeling for and understanding of his loved ones. And by experiencing his complex feelings, he becomes reunited with his own humanity. For, as Martin Buber said, "The world is not comprehensible, but it is embraceable: through the embracing of one of its beings."

RECOMMENDED READINGS

Davanloo, H. (1990). The technique of unlocking the unconscious, part I: In *Unlocking the unconscious* (pp. 101–124). New York: Wiley.

Davanloo, H. (1990). The technique of unlocking the unconscious, Part II: Partial unlocking of the unconscious. In *Unlocking the unconscious* (pp. 125–162). New York: Wiley.

CHAPTER FIFTEEN

Consolidation

A ll interventions help increase the patient's capacity to experience a breakthrough to unconscious feeling. Once the patient has experienced a breakthrough of unconscious feeling and memories, the therapist interprets the de-repressed material.

Summarize the session for the patient. Begin by outlining the initial conflict, the feeling the patient had, the anxiety in the body that was aroused, the defenses the patient used, and the symptoms they caused. Then link the patient's feelings in the beginning of the session to unconscious feelings that arose during the breakthrough. Link the conscious feelings in the present to unconscious feelings from the past so the patient sees those connections. Then link the unconscious guilt to the self-punishment the patient has suffered. Link physical symptoms in his body to the damage he inflicted on the other person's body during the breakthrough. Show how he attacks himself in the ways he attacked the person in the portrayal. Then point out his mixed feelings toward that person so the patient develops a more complex, integrated view of the other person and himself. Then invite the patient to the therapeutic task. If he wants, the two of you can face these previously buried emotions so he can overcome his symptoms and suffering. If he agrees, you will have co-created a conscious and unconscious therapeutic alliance.

Include the following ingredients in a consolidation at the end of the session:

1. Outline the initial conflict.
2. Point out the anxiety the patient experienced and the feelings that triggered it.
3. Point out the defenses the patient used in session and the symptoms they cause.

4. Point out the mixed feelings that arose and then link those feelings to unconscious feelings toward figures in the patient's past.

5. Point out the guilt and how it has driven the patient's self-punishment.

6. Help the patient bear her mixed feelings to reach a more complex experience of herself and others.

7. Then point out the therapeutic task and the reasons for undertaking it: to overcome the patient's problems and presenting symptoms to achieve her goals in life.

The consolidation helps the patient understand the relationships between her inner life and her outer problems. Help the patient see how the buried feelings triggered her anxiety and defenses, creating her symptoms. These insights lead to a better treatment outcome.

What follows is the phase of consolidation at the end of the first session of the patient we looked at in chapters 1 and 14.

Th: You were obviously feeling enraged with the misdiagnosis, failure to diagnose, failure to be really aggressive on the parts of the doctors—

Pt: Right.

Th: And obviously you're feeling very enraged, which is not your problem, interestingly.

Pt: Right.

Th: Your problem is not that you were enraged. Your problem was that, when you felt this enraged, it aroused tremendous anxiety.

Pt: Yes.

Th: And now we see that the situation with the doctors was echoing the situation with your mother, with your sisters, with family members that again it was a situation of someone who was not there for you. [*Link past and present.*]

Pt: Right.

Th: You know, someone who has abandoned you, who's supposed to be responsible, caring for you, abandoning you, not taking care of you, being neglectful—like your mother.

Pt: Yep.

Th: And what we saw was this tremendous, murderous rage really wanting to tear this doctor apart, which aroused tremendous anxiety. But we also saw that this rage you felt actually had to do with your mother and that you loved your mother greatly, but that there's this tremendous rage over her demand, her control, her denying your feelings, not wanting to know your feelings, wanting to control and suppress and hold down any of your feelings, any of your initiative— [*Link his rage toward the doctor to the unconscious rage toward his mother.*]

Pt: Yeah.

Th: To be doing what she wanted.

Pt: Right.

Th: But we see that underneath that, you felt this tremendous rage, murderous rage, wanting to tear her to pieces.

Pt: Sure.

Th: And it sounds like you felt such guilt about this because it's clear from the scene of the funeral that you loved your mother dearly. [*Link his rage toward his mother to his guilt and love, the experience of complex mixed emotions.*]

Pt: Yeah.

Th: You had a powerful love for your mother—

Pt: Absolutely.

Th: And that you felt such tremendous guilt about wanting to tear your mother to pieces, that you were tempted to tear yourself to pieces. [*Link the unconscious rage toward his mother to his guilt, which led him to turn the rage upon himself and identify with her.*]

Pt: Sure.

Th: With very harsh self-criticism, and with very harsh self-judgment.

Pt: Yes.

Th: And then we're understanding too, that in this murderous rage really wanting to tear her to pieces the way you would verbally tear yourself to pieces for years. [*Link the unconscious rage to his unconscious self-punishment.*]

Pt: Yeah.

Th: That there was in this rage, there was also this wish to sexually assault her, which helps us understand some of your difficulties over the years about sexuality and the difficulty of being able to ejaculate. [*Link his sexual/rage impulse to his sexual symptom.*]

Pt: Yep, yep, yep.

Th: We see that that got tangled up in there too.

Pt: Sure did.

Th: And we see also that, with all this rage toward your mother and the guilt and the self-punishment, and the getting tangled up with love and so on with women, that we see also another element. You'd always actually really loved your mother.

Pt: Yes.

Th: And you had this terrible situation with your mother that even in the death scene you're imagining wanting to tell her that you loved her and wanting her to believe that you loved her.

Pt: Yes.

Th: That her inability to believe in your love has been a source of tremendous pain.

Pt: I think so.

Th: And you were left with the sense that any emotion, whether it was your rage, whether it was your grief, whether it was your success, whether it was your joy, all of these, you got the impression, would hurt your mother. She said don't bring me a feeling; quit doing that. And we see how this has influenced your relationship with your current wife. [*Link his defenses against closeness with his mother to the relationship with his wife.*]

Pt: Yes.

Th: I'm not convinced that her diagnosis really requires you to hold back emotions so much. I think this is the template you brought to that relationship. [*Point out how the transference of his mother onto his wife does not fit the reality of his wife.*]

Pt: Yeah.

Th: You were brought up with a sense that your emotions have to be held back from a woman, because you learned with your mother that that was the way you were supposed to love her; that if you really loved your mother, you would hide your emotions. [*Point out the origin of the defenses.*]

Pt: Yeah.

Th: Whereas, in fact, in most relationships, we achieve closeness by sharing emotions.

Pt: Yes.

Th: Sharing emotions is how we get close. And yet you got the impression that sharing emotions would hurt someone, rather than give them an opportunity to feel closer and know you more intimately.

Pt: Yeah.

Th: And we see that even here today part of what we were struggling with is sharing these emotions with me. Because that template was there: How close am I wanting to really be with Jon? And do I really have permission to actually reveal all these emotions and have the relief and comfort of having someone truly be with me, wanting to know my emotions. [*Link defenses against closeness with his mother, his wife, and the therapist.*]

Pt: Sure.

Th: Because remember also, when you were killing your mother, there was a sense of, you don't want to know what my feelings are.

Pt: Right.

Th: And you've always had the sense that no one really does want to know my emotions. It's okay for me to know other people's emotions, and so on and so forth, but it's not okay for me to know mine. [*Link his mother's rejection of his feelings to his rejection of his feelings.*]

Pt: Right.

Th: It suggests that one thing to really look at is to explore in a sense, with your wife, how much of your emotions she would like to know. It will allow her a certain kind of closeness.

Pt: Yeah.

Th: It's probably scary for her not knowing what you feel and wanting a closeness of knowing what you feel.

Pt: Yes, yes.

Th: This all comes together in a very powerful way. Although we don't know what's causing the sleep difficulties and the sudden energy losses that are happening at work, we're certainly seeing how the suppression of emotion through the pseudorelaxation and through the tension, holding that down, has been very exhausting. [*Link defenses to his symptoms.*]

Pt: I should note that the energy loss was not starting at work. It happened outside of work. It's been random.

Th: But we can also see how suppression of the emotion and the tensing up that you've been doing would be very exhausting. [*Point out the effect of his defenses.*]

Pt: No question. No question!

Th: And we're also able to see that you're able to feel and experience a lot more emotion than you ever gave yourself credit for before.

Pt: Right.

Th: And by experiencing those emotions as deeply as you did, you're feeling much less tense. [*Link his drop in anxiety to having faced his feelings.*]

Pt: Yeah, no question. No question.

Th: Have any other connections been occurring to you as a result of what we just said?

Pt: [*Sighs.*] You're right, that I've got to talk to [his wife] more and, you know, I know that she's going through some health problems of her own. I know that one of the reasons I've held back is that we've been investigating some thyroid issues and I felt guilty during this—part—I knew things were wrong. I shoved off my stuff, saying, "Let me get you fixed first and as soon as you're fixed, then"— Well, it didn't quite work out that way, but you know that certainly ticked on—

Th: That helps us understand that you were abandoned as a child in so many ways, and yet, with [your wife] by not revealing your emotions, you leave yourself in an abandoned position because you don't give yourself a chance to see how much of your emotion [she] could stay with, and how much emotional closeness the two of you could have to let your relation develop into a much more emotionally intimate way. You don't have to repeat the past of simply being a caretaker with [her], but you could actually have emotional closeness with her. That wasn't possible back then. [*Link the defense of emotional distancing with the price: he leaves himself in an abandoned position, lonely and isolated.*]

Pt: Right, I've got to get out of the caretaker thing. I mean, she's doing the best that she can. She does drive some. She does do things. It's not like she's not housebound, but there's probably some resentment on my part that I am picking up some stuff, but I'm probably overblowing it at this point in time.

Th: It's probably quite strong, and that's something we could come back to, because it would make sense that there are probably mixed feelings, and the more we face them here, the more we can help your tension level go down. [*Point out the therapeutic task.*]

After the patient describes his work situation briefly, the therapist continues:

Th: It sounds like the more we help you deal with all the stuff that's been backed up underneath, that when you're dealing with these tensions, you won't be feeling such a pressure from underneath.

Pt: We're going after the big stuff, which is what we've got to do.

OUTCOME AND COURSE OF TREATMENT

Following this session, the patient's somatic complaints ended. His sleep disorder of thirteen years ended. His sleep returned to normal, his shaking stopped, his physical collapses stopped, his headaches lessened dramatically, and there were no further reports of bowel complaints. His wife had to drive him to this first session. He drove by himself to the next session two days later—the first time he had driven for a long distance in months. And he did this after having returned to work that morning. He never lost another day of work to physical collapse. His headaches ended completely after session seven.

The treatment continued for ten sessions. Many breakthroughs of murderous rage, guilt, and grief toward the mother occurred. However, the major work later in treatment involved transforming pathological mourning over multiple losses into normal grief, and, through the grieving, overcoming his resistances to emotional closeness.

At the beginning of treatment, he was so crippled by his collapses that he was working from home in bed. At the end of treatment, he was promoted to the highest professional position he ever had. His doctor exclaimed, "This is the best you've ever looked in years." His blood pressure had dropped thirty-one points. He stopped all medications and his neurological treatment. His headaches stopped after the seventh session. He reported that he had formerly thought of himself as "introverted," but now he says, "that's out the window." Cognitively, he said, "It's like the lights are back on." His relationships with his wife and family were closer. He described himself as more open and friendly than ever before. "I've got my life back. More than back. I've got something different." "I'm a happy man. I never had this level of happiness. This is a new peak level. Not there in fifty-two years. I'm going to have a lot more happiness and pleasure in my life. I got the tools. Life is going to be different from this point forward."

SUMMARY

Rather than speculate about what is underneath the defenses, help the patient turn against them. Eventually, repressed feelings rise to the surface. Then trust the patient's unconscious to bring forth the relevant feelings and memories to the surface. Whereas some therapists interpret to bring material to the surface, here we interpret only after unconscious material has risen. We do not speculate about what is underneath. We interpret and put together only what has been de-repressed. By doing so, we help the patient develop an integrated understanding of his inner life that links his unconscious feelings with his conscious suffering, his past with his present, and his inner life with its outer expressions.

CHAPTER SIXTEEN

Conclusion

I n intensive short-term dynamic psychotherapy we help the patient see the triangle of conflict (feelings, anxiety, and defenses), which creates her presenting problems and symptoms. Once we have consensus on the problem for which she wants our help and consensus on what causes her problem, we can get consensus on the therapeutic task.

The patient's task is to see and let go of defenses that have hurt her, to face rather than avoid what makes her anxious, and to experience her warded-off feelings as deeply as possible. This therapeutic task requires emotional courage on the part of the patient. Likewise, the therapist must point out rather than avoid the patient's defenses. The therapist must also help the patient face what she fears. And the therapist must help the patient face her feelings as deeply as possible rather than avoid them. This takes emotional courage on the part of the therapist.

Persisting in the face of the patient's defenses is a form of love. Willingness to face the patient's rage when you address her defenses is also a form of love and a way of being present to the patient. Developing this courage as a therapist and a patient is a lifelong task in the service of our own growth and development.

In therapy, choosing to go against conditioning (defenses) is our continual act of self-transcendence and self-creation (Berdyaev 1944). No matter how conditioned we are by our past and genetics, we always have a choice we can make in response to conditions, even if, at worst, our only choice available is the attitude we take (Frankl 1959). Each choice, moment by moment, creates the meaning of our lives. And, fortunately, at each moment we have the chance to make a different choice, rather than remain imprisoned by our habitual defenses.

At each moment in therapy, the patient faces a question: What will I choose? Will I accept or reject my inner life? The therapist, too, faces a choice: Will I help the patient let go of his defenses or collaborate with them? Will I reach out or pull back?

We began this book with the question of why we suffer. Then we showed various ways to end suffering. And now we conclude by talking about the person we find under the defenses. Defenses are impersonal habits. Our task is always to reach out to the person hidden underneath the conditioning.

Sadly, the patient often cannot differentiate himself as a living reality from the ideas he has about himself. He understands himself as a static object, not as a dynamic person. Yet he is always something greater and other than his concepts, which can only point to the living reality of him as a person. The patient is not his defenses, his habits, or his resistances. These impersonal automaticities only point to his slavery and determinism, not to his innate capacity for love and freedom.

Likewise, therapists can also forget to differentiate the living person of the patient from the defenses he has. We propose impersonal entities like "ego" and "superego" and forget this crucial question: "Who is the person who observes and criticizes himself?" When we forget, the patient becomes an impersonal object directed by impersonal forces. We lose sight of the patient as a person, an existential center who creates himself. The person is not merely some contents but a creative act, a triumph over the determinism of defenses and genetics.

This determination of himself from within, arising out of freedom, is personality (Berdyaev 1944, 26–27). Everything done to him in the past is impersonal. That is why the present moment is so important. The creative act in this moment reveals who the patient is becoming.

This is why, when asked to define a person, Martin Buber answered, "A mystery." We are always coming to know a person, whose potentials and future choices will reveal ever-new dimensions of his being. A person is always unknowable (Frank 1983), not only because living reality always surpasses our static concepts, but also because we cannot know what potentials may yet be realized in the coming to be of this person. That is why, as Bakhtin (1981) said, "The final word has not been written" about any person. Any comment the patient makes about herself can only point to the larger reality of who she is and could become. Likewise, any interpretation the therapist makes cannot define the patient, but merely point to the potential person who has been hidden under her defenses.

As Frieda Fromm-Reichmann said, "The patient does not need an interpretation, but a new experience," (Hornstein 2000), but an experience of what? Bion (1970) proposed that we become transformed by becoming at one with the emotional Truth of this moment. With the collapse of the impersonal defenses, the person emerges in the form of feeling. Through feeling, the patient comes face to face with the mystery of her being, something larger than any thoughts or ideas she had before. This direct experience of her being transforms who she thought she was, but, more important, it transforms *who she is becoming*.

That is why we do this work.

References

Abbass, A. (2004). Treatment of fragility. Presentation at the Washington School of Psychiatry, Washington, DC.

Abbass, A. (2005). Somatization: Diagnosing it sooner through emotion-focused interviewing. *Journal of Family Practice, 54*(3), 215–224.

Abbass, A. (2007). Bringing character changes with Davanloo's intensive short-term dynamic psychotherapy. *Ad Hoc Bulletin of Short-Term Dynamic Psychotherapy, 11*(2), 26–40.

Abbass, A., Kisely, S., and Kroenke, K. (2009). Short-term psychodynamic psychotherapy for somatic disorders. *Psychotherapy and Psychosomatics, 78*, 265–274.

Abbass, A., Lovas, D., and Purdy, A. (2008). Direct diagnosis and management of emotional factors in chronic headache patients. *Cephalagia, 28*(12), 1305–1314.

Abbass, A., Town, J., and Driessen, E. (2012). Intensive short-term dynamic psychotherapy: A systematic review and meta-analysis of outcome research. *Harvard Review of Psychiatry, 20* (2), 97–108.

Ainslie, G. (2001). *Breakdown of will*. Cambridge: Cambridge University Press.

Alexander, F. (1950). *Psychosomatic medicine*. New York: W. W. Norton.

Alexander, T. (2003). Narcissism and the experience of crying. *British Journal of Psychotherapy, 20*(1), 27–37.

Almaas, H. (1987). *Work on the superego*. Berkeley, CA: Diamond Books.

Andersen, S., Reznik, I., and Glassman, N. (2005). The unconscious relational self. In R. Hassin, J. Uleman, and J. Bargh (Eds.), *The new unconscious* (pp. 421–484). New York: Oxford University Press.

Arnsten, A. (1997). Catecholamine regulation of the prefrontal cortex. *Journal of Psychopharmacology, 11*(2), 151–162.

Arnsten, A. (1998a). The biology of being frazzled. *Science, 280,* 1711–1712.

Arnsten, A. (1998b). Development of the cerebral cortex: XIV. Stress impairs prefrontal cortical function. *Journal of the American Academy of Child and Adolescent Psychiatry, 37*(2), 1337–1339.

Austin, J. (2006). *Zen-brain reflections: Reviewing recent developments in mediation and states of consciousness.* Cambridge, MA: MIT Press.

Bakhtin, M. (1981). *The dialogical imagination.* (M. Holmquist, Ed.; C. Emerson and M. Holmquist, Trans.) Austin: University of Texas Press.

Bargh, J., and Chartrand, T. (1999). The unbearable automaticity of being. *American Psychologist, 54,* 462–479.

Barnett, B. (2007). *"You ought to!" A psychoanalytic study of the super-ego and conscience.* London: Karnac Books.

Barrett, L., Gross, J., Conner, T., and Benvenuto, M. (2001). Emotion differentiation and regulation. *Cognition and Emotion, 15,* 181–211.

Basch, M. (1996). Affect and defense. In D. Nathanson (Ed.), *Knowing feeling: Affect, script, and psychotherapy* (pp. 257–270). New York: W. W. Norton.

Bateman, A., and Fonagy, P. (2004). *Psychotherapy for borderline personality disorder.* Oxford: Oxford University Press.

Beauchaine, T. (2001). Vagal tone, development, and Gray's motivational theory: Toward an integrated model of autonomic nervous system functioning in psychopathology. *Development and Psychopathology, 13,* 183–214.

Beck, A., and Emery, G. (1985). *Anxiety disorders and phobias: A cognitive perspective.* New York: Basic Books.

Beck, A., Rush, A., Shaw, B., and Emery, G. (1979). *Cognitive therapy of depression.* New York: Guilford Press.

Benjamin, L. (1993). *Interpersonal diagnosis and treatment of personality disorders*. New York: Guilford Press.

Benjamin, L. (1995). Good defenses make good neighbors. In H. Conte and R. Plutchik (Eds.), *Ego defenses: Theory and measurement* (pp. 53–78). New York: Wiley.

Benoit, C. (1990). Management of transference resistance in Davanloo's intensive short-term dynamic psychotherapy. *International Journal of Short-Term Psychotherapy, 5,* 277–296.

Benoit, C. (1991). Management of transference resistance in Davanloo's intensive short-term dynamic psychotherapy part II. *International Journal of Short-Term Psychotherapy, 6,* 145–161.

Berdyaev, N. (1944). *Slavery and freedom*. New York: Scribners.

Bergler, E. (1948). *The battle of the conscience*. Washington, DC: Washington Institute of Medicine.

Bergler, E. (1952). *The superego: Unconscious conscience—the key to the theory and therapy of neurosis*. New York: Grune and Stratton.

Bergler, E. (1959). *Principles of self-damage*. New York: Philosophical Library.

Bergler, E. (1961). *Curable and incurable neurotics*. Madison, CT: International Universities Press.

Berntson, G., Cacioppo, J., and Quigley, K. (1991). Autonomic determinism: The modes of autonomic control, the doctrine of autonomic space, and the laws of autonomic constraint. *Psychological Review 98,* 459–487.

Berntson, G., Cacioppo, J., and Quigley, K. (1994). Autonomic cardiac control: I. Estimation and validation from pharmacological blockades. *Psychophysiology, 31,* 572–585.

Bion, W. (1970). *Seven servants*. New York: Jason Aronson.

Birnbaum, S., Gobesske, K., Auerbach, J., Taylor, J., and Arnsten, A. (1999). A role for norepinephrine in stress-induced cognitive deficits: Alpha-I adrenoceptor mediation in the prefrontal cortex. *Biological Psychiatry, 46,* 1266–1274.

Blackman, J. (2004). *101 defenses: How the mind shields itself*. New York: Taylor and Francis.

Blair, C., Granger, D., and Razza, R. (2005). Cortisol reactivity is positively related to executive function in preschool children attending Head Start. *Child Development, 76*(3), 554–567.

Blum, H. (1985). *Defense and resistance: Historical perspectives and current concepts.* New York: International Universities Press.

Bowlby, J. (1969). *Attachment and Loss, vol. 1: Attachment.* New York: Basic Books.

Bowlby, J. (1973). *Attachment and Loss, vol. 2: Separation: Anxiety and anger.* New York: Basic Books.

Bowlby, J. (1980). *Attachment and Loss, vol. 3: Loss—sadness and depression.* New York: Basic Books.

Bradley, S. (2000). *Affect regulation and the development of psychopathology.* New York: Guilford Press.

Brandt, L. (1968). The unobserving participant. In M. Nelson, B. Nelson, B. Sherman, and H. Strean (Eds.), *Roles and paradigms in psychotherapy* (pp. 120–149). New York: Grune and Stratton.

Bremner, J., Randall, P., Scott, T., Bronen, R., Seibyl, J., Southwick, S., et al. (1995). MRI based measurement of hippocampal volume in patients with combat related post-traumatic stress disorder. *American Journal of Psychiatry, 152,* 973.

Bremner, J., Narayan, M., Anderson, E., Staib, L., Miller, H., and Charney, D. (2000). Hippocampal volume reduction in major depression. *American Journal of Psychiatry, 157,* 115–127.

Brenner, C. (1955). *An elementary textbook of psychoanalysis.* New York: International Universities Press.

Britton, R. (2003). *Sex, death, and the superego: Experiences in psychoanalysis.* London: Karnac.

Carveth, D. (2001). The unconscious need for punishment: Expression or evasion of the sense of guilt? *Psychoanalytic Studies, 3*(1), 9–21. Retrieved from http://www.yorku.ca /dcarveth/guilt.html.

Carveth, D. (2002). Self-punishment as guilt evasion: Theoretical issues. *Canadian Journal of Psychoanalysis, 14*(2), 177–198.

Carveth, D., and Carveth, J. (2003). Fugitives from guilt: Postmodern de-moralization of the new hysterias. *American Imago, 60*(4), 445–479.

Cassidy, J. (1994). Emotion regulation: influences of attachment relationships. In N. Fox (Ed.), The development of emotional regulation: Biological and behavioral considerations. *Monographs of the Society for Research in Child Development, 59*(2–3), 228–249.

Chasseguet-Smirgel, J. (2003). *The ego ideal: A psychoanalytic essay on the malady of the ideal.* New York: Free Association.

Clyman, R. (1992). The procedural organization of emotions: A contribution from cognitive science to the psychoanalytic theory of therapeutic action. In T. Shapiro and R. Emde (Eds.), *Affect: Psychoanalytic perspectives* (pp. 349–382). Madison, CT: International Universities Press.

Cooper, S. (1998). Changing notions of defense within psychoanalytic theory. *Journal of Personality, 66,* 947–964.

Cornelissen, K. (2005). Understanding and undoing projection: The alien. *Ad Hoc Bulletin of Short-Term Dynamic Psychotherapy 9*(3), 24–50.

Coryell, W., and Norton, S. (1981). Briquet's syndrome (somatization disorder) and primary depression: Comparison of background and outcome. *Comprehensive Psychiatry, 22,* 249–256.

Coughlin, P. (2009). Developing the therapeutic alliance in ISTDP. Presentation at the Washington School of Psychiatry, Washington, DC.

Coughlin Della Selva, P. (1996). *Intensive short-term dynamic psychotherapy: Theory and technique.* New York: Wiley.

Coughlin Della Selva, P. (2001). Dynamic assessment of ego functioning in Davanloo's ISTDP. In J. Ten Have de Labije (Ed.), *The working alliance: Whose intrapsychic crisis?* (pp. 117–147). Amsterdam: VKDP.

Cramer, P. (1991). *The development of defense mechanisms: Theory, research, and assessment.* New York: Springer-Verlag.

Cramer, P. (1997). Evidence for change in children's use of defense mechanisms. *Journal of Personality, 66,* 335–357.

Cramer, P. (1998). Coping and defense mechanisms: What's the difference? *Journal of Personality, 66*, 919–946.

Cramer, P. (2003). Defense mechanisms and physiological reactivity to stress. *Journal of Personality, 71*, 221–244.

Cramer, P. (2006). *Protecting the self: Defense mechanisms in action.* New York: Guilford Press.

Cramer, P. (2008). Seven pillars of defense mechanism theory. *Social and Personality Psychology Compass, 2*, 1963–1981.

Damasio, A. (1994). *Descartes' error: Emotion, reason, and the human brain.* New York: Putnam.

Damasio, A. (1999). *The feeling of what happens: Body and emotion in the making of consciousness.* New York: Harcourt Press.

Darwin, C. (1998). *The expression of the emotions in man and animals* (3rd ed.). London: Harper Collins. (Original work published 1872.)

Davanloo, H. (1987). The unconscious therapeutic alliance. In P. Buirski (Ed.), *Frontiers of dynamic psychotherapy* (pp. 64–88). New York: Brunner and Mazel.

Davanloo, H. (1990). *Unlocking the unconscious.* New York: Wiley.

Davanloo, H. (2000). *Intensive short-term dynamic psychotherapy.* New York: Wiley.

Davanloo, H. (2001). Intensive short-term dynamic psychotherapy. Extended major direct access to the unconscious. *European Journal of Psychotherapy, 2*, 25–70.

Davidson, R. (2004). Well-being and affective style: Neural substrates and biobehavioral correlates. *Philosophical Transactions of the Royal Society of London B, 359*, 1395–1411.

De Rijk, R., Kitraki, E., and De Kloet, E. (2010). Corticosteroid hormones in stress and anxiety: Role of receptor variants and environmental inputs. In H. Soreq, A. Friedman, and D. Kauger (Eds.) *Stress—from molecules to behavior* (pp. 119–150). Weinheim, Germany: Wiley-VCH.

Deschields, T., Tait, R., Geller, J., and Chibnall, J. (1995). Relationship between social desirability and self-report in chronic pain patients. *Clinical Journal of Pain, 11*, 189–193.

Dozier, M., Stovall, K., and Albus, K. (1999). Attachment and psychopathology in adulthood. In J. Cassidy and P. Shaver (Eds.), *Handbook of attachment: Theory, research, and clinical applications* (pp. 497–519). New York: Guilford Press.

Duffy, C. (1997). Implicit memory: Knowledge without awareness. *Neurology, 49,* 1200–1202.

Eigen, M. (1998). *The psychoanalytic mystic.* New York: Free Association.

Ekman, P. (1992). Facial expression of emotion: New findings, new questions. *Psychological Science, 3,* 34–38.

Ekman, P. (2003). *Emotions revealed: Recognizing faces and feelings to improve communication and emotional life.* New York: Henry Holt.

Ekman, P., and Davidson, R. (Eds.) (1994). *The nature of emotions.* New York: Oxford University Press.

Ekstein, R. (1966). *Children of time and space, of action and impulse: Clinical studies on the psychoanalytic treatment of severely disturbed children.* New York: Appleton-Century-Crofts.

Elster, J. (1999). *Strong feelings.* Cambridge: MIT Press.

Elster, J. (2000). *Ulysses unbound.* Cambridge: Cambridge University Press.

Erickson, S., Feldman, S., and Steiner, H. (1997). Defense reactions and coping strategies in normal adolescents. *Child Psychiatry and Human Development, 28,* 45–56.

Evans, F. (1996). *Harry Stack Sullivan: Interpersonal theory and psychotherapy.* New York: Routledge.

Fairbairn, W. (1954). *An object relations theory of the personality.* New York: Basic Books.

Fanselow, M., and Dale, G. (2003). The amygdala, fear, and memory. *Annals of the New York Academy of Science, 985,* 125–134.

Farrelly, F. (1974). *Provocative therapy.* Fort Collins, CO: Shields Publishing.

Fenichel, O. (1945). *The psychoanalytic theory of neurosis.* New York: W. W. Norton.

Fenichel, O. (1954). *The collected papers of Otto Fenichel, second ser.* (H. Fenichel and D. Rapaport, Eds.). New York: W. W. Norton.

Ferenczi, S. (1950). Stages in the development of the sense of reality. In *The selected papers of Sandor Ferenczi: Vol. 1. Sex in psychoanalysis.* New York: Basic Books.

Fogel, A. (2009). *The psycho-physiology of self-awareness: Rediscovering the lost art of body sense.* New York: W. W. Norton.

Folkow, B. (2000). Perspectives on the integrative function of the sympatho-adrenomedullary system. *Autonomic Neuroscience, 83,* 101–115.

Fonagy, P., Gergely, G., Jurist, E., and Target, M. (2002). *Affect regulation, mentalization, and the development of the self.* New York: Other Press.

Fosha, D. (2000). *The transformative power of affect.* New York: W. W. Norton.

Franchini, K., and Cowley, A. (2004). Autonomic control of cardiac function. In D. Robertson et al. (Eds.), *Primer on the autonomic nervous system* (pp. 134–138). Amsterdam: Elsevier Academic Press.

Frank, S. (1983). *The unknowable.* Athens, OH: Ohio University Press.

Frankl, V. (1959). *Man's search for meaning.* Boston: Beacon Press.

Franklin Institute. (2004). The human brain. Retrieved from http://www.fi.edu/learn/brain/stress.html.

Frederickson, J. (2000). There's something "youey" about you. *Contemporary Psychoanalysis, 36*(4), 587–617.

Frederickson, J. (2003). The eclipse of the person in psychoanalysis. In R. Frie (Ed.), *Understanding experience: Psychotherapy and postmodernism* (pp. 204–224). London: Routledge.

Frederickson, J. (2005). ISTDP with a patient suffering from long-standing somatic complaints. *Ad Hoc Bulletin of Short-Term Dynamic Psychotherapy, 9*(1), 15–35.

Freud, A. (1936). *The ego and the mechanisms of defense.* Madison, CT: International Universities Press.

Freud, S. (1957a). The dynamics of transference. In J. Strachey (Ed. and Trans.), *The standard edition of the complete psychological works of Sigmund Freud* (Vol. 12, pp. 97–108). London: Hogarth Press. (Original work published 1912.)

Freud, S. (1957b). On narcissism: An introduction. In J. Strachey (Ed. and Trans.), *The standard edition of the complete psychological works of Sigmund Freud* (Vol. 14, 99. 69–102). London: Hogarth Press. (Original work published 1914.)

Freud, S. (1958). The neuro-psychoses of defence. In J. Strachey (Ed. and Trans.), *The standard edition of the complete psychological works of Sigmund Freud* (Vol. 3, pp. 43–68). London: Hogarth Press. (Original work published 1894.)

Freud, S. (1961a). Mourning and melancholia. In J. Strachey (Ed. and Trans.), *The standard edition of the complete psychological works of Sigmund Freud* (Vol. 14, pp. 239–258). New York: W. W. Norton. (Original work published 1917.)

Freud, S. (1961b). Two encyclopaedia articles. In J. Strachey (Ed. and Trans.), *The standard edition of the complete psychological works of Sigmund Freud* (Vol. 18, pp. 235–259). New York: W. W. Norton. (Original work published 1923.)

Freud, S. (1961c). The ego and the id. In J. Strachey (Ed. and Trans.), *The standard edition of the complete psychological works of Sigmund Freud* (Vol. 19, pp. 3–66). New York: W. W. Norton. (Original work published 1923.)

Freud, S. (1961d). Inhibitions, symptoms, and anxiety. In J. Strachey (Ed. and Trans.), *The standard edition of the complete psychological works of Sigmund Freud* (Vol. 20, pp. 75–175. New York: W. W. Norton. (Original work published 1926.)

Freud, S. (1963). An outline of psychoanalysis. In J. Strachey (Ed. and Trans.), *The standard edition of the complete psychological works of Sigmund Freud* (Vol. 23, pp. 144–207). London: Hogarth Press. (Original work published 1940.)

Freud, S., and Breuer, J. (1883–1895). *Studies on hysteria.* Harmondsworth, UK: Penguin Press, 1974.

Freud, S., and Jung, C. (1994). Letter to Jung, 1906. *Freud/Jung letters* (W. McGuire, Ed.). Princeton, NJ: Princeton University Press.

Frijda, N. (1986). *The emotions.* Cambridge: Cambridge University Press.

Frosch, J. (1983). *The psychotic process.* New York: International Universities Press.

Gaylin, W. (1990). *On being and becoming human.* New York: Penguin Books.

Gaynor, D., and Egan, J. (2011). Vaso-vagal syncope: The common faint (What clinicians need to know). *Irish Psychologist, 7*(37), 176. Retrieved from http://hdl.handle.net/10147/135366.

Gellhorn, E. (1967). *Principles of autonomic-somatic integrations: Physiological basis and psychological and clinical implications.* Minneapolis: University of Minnesota Press.

Gill, M. (1963). *Topography and systems in psychoanalytic theory.* New York: International Universities Press.

Goldstein, D. (2004). Merging of the homeostate theory with the concept of allostatic load. In J. Schulkin (Ed.), *Allostasis, homeostasis, and the costs of physiological adaptation* (pp. 99–112). Cambridge: Cambridge University Press.

Goldstein, D. (2006). *Adrenaline and the inner world: An introduction to scientific integrative medicine.* Baltimore: Johns Hopkins University Press.

Gottwik, G., Orbes, I., Tressel, F., and Wagner, G. (1998a). Application of Davanloo's intensive short-term dynamic psychotherapy in the treatment of patients with agoraphobia, fainting attacks, panic, somatization, and functional disorders. Part 1: Technical and metapsychological roots of the technique. Initial phase of the trial therapy. *International Journal of Intensive Short-Term Dynamic Psychotherapy, 12,* 77–103.

Gottwik, G., Orbes, I., Tressel, F., and Wagner, G. (1998b). Application of Davanloo's intensive short-term dynamic psychotherapy in the treatment of patients with agoraphobia, fainting attacks, panic, somatization, and functional disorders. Part 2: The first breakthrough. Initial phase of the trial therapy. *International Journal of Intensive Short-Term Dynamic Psychotherapy, 12,* 105–123.

Gottwik, G., Orbes, I., Tressel, F., and Wagner, G. (1998c). Application of Davanloo's intensive short-term dynamic psychotherapy in the treatment of patients with agoraphobia, fainting attacks, panic, somatization, and functional disorders. Part 3: Partial unlocking of the unconscious. *International Journal of Intensive Short-Term Dynamic Psychotherapy, 12,* 125–149.

Grawe, K. (2007). *Neuropsychotherapy: How the neurosciences inform effective psychotherapy.* Mahwah, NJ: Lawrence Erlbaum.

Gray, P. (2005). *The ego and the analysis of defense,* (2nd ed.). New York: Jason Aronson.

Greenson, R. (1967). *The technique and practice of psychoanalysis, Vol. 1.* New York: International Universities Press.

Greenspan, S. (1997). *Developmentally based psychotherapy.* Madison, CT: International Universities Press.

Greenspan, S., and Shanker, S. (2006). A developmental framework for depth psychology and a definition of healthy emotional functioning. In *Psychodynamic diagnostic manual* (pp. 431–482). Silver Spring, MD: Alliance of Psychoanalytic Organizations.

Grigsby, J., and Stevens, D. (2000). *The dynamics of personality.* New York: Guilford Press.

Gross, J., Fredrickson, B., and Levenson, R. (1994). The psychophysiology of crying. *Psychophysiology, 31*(5), 460–468.

Gross, J., and Levenson, R. (1997). Hiding feelings: The acute effects of inhibiting negative and positive emotions. *Journal of Abnormal Psychology, 106,* 95–103.

Grotstein, J. (1985). *Splitting and projective identification.* New York: Jason Aronson.

Grotstein, J. (2004). The seventh servant: The implications of a truth drive in Bion's theory of "O." *International Journal of Psychoanalysis, 85,* 1081–1101.

Grotstein, J. (2010). Foreword in Reiner, A. *The quest for conscience and the birth of the mind* (pp. 1–11). London: Karnac.

Guntrip, H. (1968). *Schizoid phenomena, object relations, and the self.* New York: International Universities Press.

Haan, N. (1977). *Coping and defending: processes of self-environment organization*. New York: Academic Press.

Hamill, R., and Shapiro, R. (2004). Peripheral autonomic nervous system. In D. Robertson et al. (Eds.), *Primer on the autonomic nervous system* (pp. 20–28). Amsterdam: Elsevier Academic Press.

Hartmann, H. (1964). *Ego psychology and the problem of adaptation*. New York: International Universities Press.

Hassin, R., Uleman, J., and Bargh, J. (Eds.) (2006). *The new unconscious*. New York: Oxford University Press.

Havens, L. (1986). *Making contact*. Cambridge, MA: Harvard University Press.

Havens, L. (1993). *Participant observation*. Northvale, NJ: Jason Aronson.

Hendriks, M., Rottenberg, J., and Vingerhoets, A. (2007). Can the distress-signal and arousal-reduction views of crying be reconciled? Evidence from the cardiovascular system. *Emotion, 7*(2), 458–463.

Horney, K. (1950). *Neurosis and human growth: The struggle toward self-realization*. New York: W. W. Norton.

Hornstein, G. (2000). *To redeem one person is to redeem the world: The life of Frieda Fromm-Reichmann*. New York: Free Press.

Izard, C. (1994). Innate and universal facial expressions: Evidence from developmental and cross-cultural research. *Psychological Bulletin, 115*, 288–299.

Jacobson, E. (1971). *Depression: Comparative studies of normal, neurotic, and psychotic conditions*. New York: International Universities Press.

Jamner, L, Schwartz, G., and Leigh, H. (1988). The relationship between repressive and defensive coping styles and monocyte, eosinophile, and serum glucose levels: Support for the opioid peptide hypothesis of repression. *Psychosomatic Medicine, 50*, 567–575.

Janig, W. (2003). The autonomic nervous system and its coordination by the brain. In R. Davidson, K. Scherer, and H. Goldsmith

(Eds.), *Handbook of Affective Sciences* (pp. 135–186). New York: Oxford University Press.

Janig, W. (2007). *The integrative action of the autonomic nervous system: Neurobiology of homeostasis.* Cambridge: Cambridge University Press.

Joels, M., and Karst, H. (2010). Effects of stress on the function of hippocampal cells. In H. Soreq, A. Freidman, and D. Kaufer (Eds.) *Stress—from molecules to behavior* (pp. 55–70). Weinheim, Germany: Wiley-VCH.

Kalpin, A. (1994) Effective use of Davanloo's "head-on collision." *International Journal of Short-Term Dynamic Psychotherapy, 9,* 19–36.

Katon, W., Lin, E., Von Korff, M., Russo, J., Lipscomb, P., and Bush, T. (1991). Somatization: A spectrum of severity. *American Journal of Psychiatry, 148,* 34–40.

Kaufmann, H. (2004). Evaluation of the patient with syncope. In D. Robertson et al. (Eds.), *Primer on the autonomic nervous system* (pp. 217–220). Amsterdam: Elsevier Academic Press.

Kelly, V. (1996). Affect and the redefinition of intimacy. In D. Nathanson (Ed.), *Knowing feeling: Affect, script, and psychotherapy* (pp. 55–104). New York: W. W. Norton.

Keltner, D., Ekman, P., Gonzaga, G., and Beer, J. (2003). Facial expression of emotion. In R. Davidson, K. Scherer, and H. Goldsmith (Eds.), *Handbook of affective sciences* (pp. 415–432). New York: Oxford University Press.

Kennard, M. (1947). Autonomic interrelations with the somatic nervous system. *Psychosomatic Medicine, 9*(1), 29–36.

Kenny, A. (1998). *Action, emotion, and will.* London: Routledge.

Kernberg, O. (1975). *Borderline conditions and pathological narcissism.* New York: Jason Aronson.

Kernberg, O. (1976). *Object relations theory and clinical psychoanalysis.* New York: Jason Aronson.

Kernberg, O. (1980). *Internal world, external reality.* New York: Jason Aronson.

Kernberg, O. (1984). *Severe personality disorders: Psychotherapeutic strategies*. New Haven, CT: Yale University Press.

King, A., Taylor, C., Albright, C., and Haskell, H. (1990). The relationship between repressive and defensive coping styles and blood pressure responses in healthy, middle-aged men and women. *Journal of Psychosomatic Research, 34,* 461–471.

Klein, M. (1975a). *Love, guilt, and reparation and other works, 1921–1945*. New York: Delacorte Press.

Klein, M. (1975b). *Envy and gratitude and other works, 1946–1963*. New York: Delacorte Press.

Knight, R. (1940). Introjection, projection, and identification. *Psychoanalytic Quarterly, 9,* 334–441.

Kohut, H. (1977). *The restoration of the self*. New York: International Universities Press.

Kohut, H. (1984). *How does analysis cure?* Chicago: University of Chicago Press.

Korff, P. von (1998). Early management of unconscious defiance in Davanloo's intensive short-term dynamic psychotherapy, part 1. *International Journal of Short-Term Dynamic Psychotherapy, 12,* 183–208.

Krystal, H. (1974). The genetic development of affects and affect regression. *The Annual of Psychoanalysis, 2,* 98–126.

Krystal, H. (1975). Affect tolerance. *The Annual of Psychoanalysis, 3,* 179–219.

Krystal, H. (1988). *Integration and self-healing: Affect, trauma, alexithymia*. Hillsdale, NJ: Analytic Press.

Krystal, H. (1998). Desomatization and the consequences of infantile trauma. *Psychoanalytic Inquiry, 17,* 126–150.

Kuhn, T. (1962/1970). *The structure of scientific revolutions*. (2nd ed.) Chicago: University of Chicago Press.

Land, J. (1991). Regressive defense in psychoanalysis and intensive short-term dynamic psychotherapy: Technical and theoretical considerations. *International Journal of Short-Term Dynamic Psychotherapy, 6,* 243–258.

Leahy, R. (2001). *Overcoming resistance in cognitive therapy*. New York: Guilford Press.

Lebeaux, D. (2000). The role of the conscious therapeutic alliance in Davanloo's intensive short-term dynamic psychotherapy. *International Journal of Intensive Short-Term Dynamic Psychotherapy, 14*(1), 39–48.

LeDoux, J. (1998). *The emotional brain*. London: Weidenfeld and Nicolson.

LeDoux, J. (2000). Cognitive-emotional interactions: Listen to the brain. In R. Lane and L. Nadel (Eds.), *Cognitive neuroscience of emotion* (pp. 129–155). Oxford: Oxford University Press.

LeDoux, J. (2002). *The synaptic self: How our brains become who we are*. New York: Viking Penguin.

Levenson, R. (2003). Autonomic specificity and emotion. In R. Davidson, K. Scherer, and H. Goldsmith (Eds.), *Handbook of affective sciences* (pp. 212–224). New York: Oxford University Press.

Levine, P., and Frederick, A. (1997). *Waking the tiger: Healing trauma*. Berkeley, CA: North Atlantic Books.

Lilienfeld, S. (2007). Psychological treatments that cause harm. *Perspectives on Psychological Science, 2*(1), 53–70.

Lupien, S., de Leon, M., de Santie, S., Convit, A., Tarshish, C., Nair, N., Thakur, M., McEwen, B., Hauger, R., and Meaney, M. (1998). Cortisol levels during human aging predict hippocampal atrophy and memory deficits. *Nature Neuroscience, 1*, 69–73.

Main, M. (1995). The organized categories of infant, child, and adult attachment: Flexible vs. inflexible attention under attachment-related stress. *Journal of the American Psychoanalytic Association, 48*, 1055–1096.

Malan, D. (1979). *Individual psychotherapy and the science of psychodynamics*. London: Butterworths.

McCullough, J. (2000). *Treatment for chronic depression: Cognitive behavioral analysis system of psychotherapy*. New York: Guilford Press.

McEwen, B., Bulloch, K., and Stewart, J. (1999). Parasympathetic function. Retrieved from http://www.macses.ucsf.edu/research /allostatic/notebook/parasym.php.

McEwen, B., and Lasley, E. (2002). *The end of stress as we know it.* Washington, DC: John Henry Press.

McEwen, B., and Sapolsky, R. (2000). Stress and cognitive function. In R. Squire and S. Kosslyn (Eds.), *Findings and current opinions in cognitive neuroscience* (pp. 173–184). Cambridge, MA: MIT Press.

Meissner, W. (1984). *Treatment of patients in the borderline spectrum.* New York: Jason Aronson.

Merzenich, M., and deCharms, R. (1996). Neural representations, experience, and change. In R. Llinas and P. Churchland (Eds.), *The mind-brain continuum: Sensory processes* (pp. 62–81). Cambridge, MA: MIT Press.

Miller, W., and Rollnick, S. (2002). *Motivational interviewing* (2nd ed.). New York: Guilford Press.

Mills, C., and Wooster, A. (1987). Crying in the counseling situation. *British Journal of Guidance and Counseling, 15*(2), 25–30.

Mitchell, C. (2007). *Effective techniques for dealing with highly resistant clients* (2nd ed.). Clifton, TN: Clifton Mitchell.

Monsen, J. Eilertsen, D., Melgard, T., and Odegard, P. (1996). Affects and affect consciousness: Initial experiences with the assessment of affect integration. *The Journal of Psychotherapy Practice and Research, 5,* 238–249.

Monsen, J., Odland, R., Faugli, A., Daae, E., and Eilertsen, D. (1995). Personality disorders: Changes and stability after intensive psychotherapy focusing on affect consciousness. *Psychotherapy Research, 5*(1), 33–48.

Nathanson, D. (1992). *Shame and pride: Affect, sex, and the birth of the self.* New York: Norton.

Nathanson, D. (1996). About emotion. In D. Nathanson (Ed.), *Knowing feeling: Affect, script, and psychotherapy* (pp. 1–21). New York: W. W. Norton.

Neborsky, R. (2001). Davanloo's method of intensive short-term dynamic psychotherapy. In M. Solomon, R. Neborsky, L.

McCullough, M. Alpert, F. Shapiro, and D. Malan (Eds.), *Short-term therapy for long-term change* (pp. 16–53). New York: W. W. Norton.

Neborsky, R. (2005). Understanding and overcoming instant repression—part III. The wailing prisoner: Self-punishment to self-pardon. Depression, somatization, and substance abuse: Overcoming blocks at stimulus and response. *Ad Hoc Bulletin of Short-Term Dynamic Psychotherapy, 9*(2), 34–53.

Nelson, J. (2000). Crying assessment based upon crying and crying inhibition based on attachment theory. *Bulletin of the Menninger Clinic, 64*(4), 509–529.

Nelson, M. C. (1962). Effect of paradigmatic tactics on the psychic economy of borderline patients. *Psychiatry, 25*(2), 119–134.

Nelson, M. C. (1968). Prescriptions for paradigms. In M. C. Nelson et al. *Roles and paradigms in psychotherapy*. New York: Grune and Stratton, Inc.

Newcomer, J., Selke, G., Melson, A., Hershey, T., Craft, S., Richards, K., and Alderson, A. (1999). Decreased memory performance in healthy humans induced by stress-level cortisol treatment. *Archives of General Psychiatry, 56*, 527–533.

Nunberg, H. (1955). *Principles of psychoanalysis*. New York: International Universities Press.

Ogden, P., Minton, K., and Pain, C. (2006). *Trauma and the body: A sensorimotor approach to psychotherapy*. New York: W. W. Norton.

Ogden, T. (1982). *Projective identification*. New York: Jason Aronson.

Ohman, A., and Wiens, S. (2003). On the automaticity of autonomic responses in emotion: An evolutionary perspective. In R. Davidson, K. Scherer, and H. Goldsmith (Eds.), *Handbook of affective sciences* (pp. 256–275). New York: Oxford University Press.

O'Keefe, J., and Nadel, L. (1978). *The hippocampus as a cognitive map*. Oxford: Clarendon Press.

Osho (1977). *The search*. Pune, India: Rajneesh Foundation.

Palombo, S. (1999). *The emergent ego: Complexity and co-evolution in the psychoanalytic process*. Madison, CT: International Universities Press.

Panksepp, J. (1998). *Affective neuroscience: The foundations of human and animal emotions*. Oxford: Oxford University Press.

Panksepp, J. (2009). Brain emotional systems and qualities of emotional life: From animal modes of affect to implications for psychotherapeutics. In D. Fosha, D. Siegel, and M. Solomon (Eds.), *The healing power of emotion: Affective neuroscience, development, and clinical practice* (pp. 1–26). New York: W. W. Norton.

Panksepp, J., and Biven, L. (2012). *The archaeology of mind: Neuroevolutionary origins of human emotions*. New York: W. W. Norton.

Piaget, J. (1970). *Genetic epistemology*. New York: W. W. Norton.

Porges, S. (1995). Emotion: An evolutionary by-product of the neural regulation of the autonomic nervous system. Retrieved from http://www.wam.umd.edu/~sporges/nyas/nyas.txt.

Porges, S. (2001a). The poly-vagal theory. In Porges, S. (2011). *The Polyvagal theory: Neurophysiological foundations of emotions, attachment, communication, self-regulation*. New York: W. W. Norton.

Porges, S. (2001b). The polyvagal theory: Phylogenetic substrates of a social nervous system. *International Journal of Psychophysiology, 42*, 123–146.

Porges, S. (2011). *The polyvagal theory: Neurophysiological foundations of emotions, attachment, communication, self-regulation*. New York: W. W. Norton.

Porges, S., and Bazhenova, O. (2006). Neurophysiological aspects of communications and learning disorders: Evolution and the autonomic nervous system: a neurobiological model of socioemotional and communication disorders. In Porges, S. (2011). *The Polyvagal theory: Neurophysiological foundations of emotions, attachment, communication, self-regulation*. New York: W. W. Norton.

Prins, A., Kaloupek, D., and Keane, T. (1995). Psychophysiological evidence of autonomic arousal and startle in traumatized adult populations. In M. Friedman and D. Charney (Eds.), *Neurobiological and clinical consequences of stress: From normal adaptation to post-traumatic stress disorder* (pp. 291–314). Philadelphia: Lippincott-Raven.

Prochaska, J., and Norcross, J. (2007). *Systems of psychotherapy: A trans-theoretical analysis.* (6th ed.). Pacific Grove, CA: Thomson/Brooks/Cole.

Racker, H. (1968). *Transference and countertransference.* Madison, CT: International Universities Press.

Rangell, L. (1985). Defense and resistance in psychoanalysis and life. In H. Blum (Ed.), *Defense and resistance: Historical perspectives and current concepts* (pp. 147–174). New York: International Universities Press.

Rank, O. (1936). *Will therapy: The therapeutic applications of will psychology.* New York: Alfred A. Knopf.

Rauch, S., Alpert, N., Fischman, A., Fisler, R., Jenike, M., Orr, S., et al. (1996). A symptom provocation study of posttraumatic stress disorder using positron emission tomography and script-driven imagery. *Archives of General Psychiatry, 53,* 380–387.

Reber, A. (1993). *Implicit learning and tacit knowledge: An essay on the cognitive unconscious.* Oxford: Oxford University Press.

Reich, W. (1933). *Character analysis.* (3rd ed.). New York: Farrar, Strauss, and Giroux.

Reiner, A. (2010). *The quest for conscience and the birth of the mind.* London: Karnac.

Reller, M. (2005). Fragile Ich-Struktur. I. Fragilitat bei Patientem mit regressive Abwehrstruktur. II. Fragiltat bei Patientem mit Obsessive Abwehrstruktur. Weiterbildungsseminare der Schweizerischen Gesellschaft fur Intensive Dynamik Kurzpsychotherapie. Zurich. Quoted in Troendle, P. (2005). *Psychotherapie: Dynamisch-intensiv-direkt: Lehrbuch zur Intensiven Dynamischen Kurzpsychother*apie. Giessen, Germany: Psychosozial-Verlag.

Robertson, D., et al. (Eds.). (2004). *Primer on the Autonomic Nervous System*. Amsterdam: Elsevier Academic Press.

Rosen, J., and Schulkin, J. (2004). Adaptive fear, allostasis, and the pathology of anxiety. In J. Schulkin (Ed.), *Allostasis, homeostasis, and the costs of physiological adaptation* (pp. 164–227). Cambridge: Cambridge University Press.

Roth, P. (2001). *The superego*. Cambridge: Totem Books.

Rothschild, B. (2003). *The body remembers casebook*. New York: W. W. Norton.

Rottenberg, J., Wilhelm, F., Gross, J., and Gotlib, I. (2003). Vagal rebound during resolution of tearful crying among depressed and non-depressed individuals. *Psychophysiology, 40*(1), 1–6.

Ryle, G. (1984). *The concept of mind*. Chicago: University of Chicago Press.

Safa-Gerard, D. (1998). Bearable and unbearable guilt: A Kleinian perspective. *Psychoanalytic Quarterly, 67*, 351–378.

Safran, J. (Ed.). (2003). *Psychoanalysis and Buddhism: An unfolding dialogue*. New York: Wisdom Publications.

Sandler, J., and Freud, A. (1985). *The analysis of defense: The ego and the mechanisms of defense revisited*. New York: International Universities Press.

Sapolsky, R. (2004). *Why zebras don't get ulcers*. New York: Henry Holt.

Sapolsky, R., Uno, H., Rebert, C., and Finch, C. (1990). Hippocampal damage with prolonged glucocorticoid exposure in primates. *The Journal of Neuroscience, 10*(9): 2897–2902. Quoted in Scaer, R., (2001). *The body bears the burden: Trauma, dissociation, and disease*. New York: Haworth Medical Press.

Scaer, R. (2001). *The body bears the burden: Trauma, dissociation, and disease*. New York: Haworth Medical Press.

Scaer, R. (2005). *The trauma spectrum: Hidden wounds and human resiliency*. New York: W. W. Norton.

Schore, A. (1991). Early superego development: The emergence of shame and narcissistic affect regulation in the practicing period. *Psychoanalysis and Contemporary Thought, 14*, 187–250.

Schore, A. (1994). *Affect regulation and the origin of the self.* Mahwah, NJ: Lawrence Erlbaum.

Schore, A. (2002). Dysregulation of the right brain: A fundamental mechanism of traumatic attachment and the psychopathogenesis of posttraumatic stress disorder. *Australian and New Zealand Journal of Psychiatry, 36,* 9–30.

Schore, A. (2003a). *Affect dysregulation and disorders of the self.* New York: W. W. Norton.

Schore, A. (2003b). *Affect regulation and the repair of the self.* New York: W. W. Norton.

Schore, A. (2009). Right brain affect regulation: An essential mechanism of development, trauma, dissociation, and psychotherapy. In D. Fosha, D. Siegel, and M. Solomon (Eds.), *The healing power of emotion: Affective neuroscience, development, and clinical practice* (pp. 112–144). New York: W. W. Norton.

Schulkin, J. (Ed.). (2004). *Allostasis, homeostasis, and the costs of physiological adaptation.* Cambridge: Cambridge University Press.

Schulkin, J. (2007). *A behavioral neuroscience perspective on the will.* Mahwah, NJ: Lawrence Erlbaum.

Schwartz, J., and Begley, S. (2002). *The mind and the brain: Neuroplasticity and the power of mental force.* New York: Harper Collins Publishers.

Segal, H. (1981). Notes on symbol formation. In *The work of Hannah Segal* (pp. 49–68). New York: Jason Aronson.

Sheline, Y., Gado, M., and Kraemer, H. (2003). Untreated depression and hippocampal volume loss. *American Journal of Psychiatry, 160,* 1516.

Sheline, Y., Wang, P., Gado, M., Csernansky, J., and Vannier, M. (1996). Hippocampal atrophy in recurrent major depression. *Proceedings of the National Academy of Sciences of the United States of America, 93*(9), 3908–4003.

Sherman, M. (1968). Siding with resistance rather than interpretation: Role implications. In M. Nelson et al. (Eds.), *Roles and paradigms in psychotherapy* (pp. 74–107). New York: Grune and Stratton.

Smith, G., Monson, R., and Ray, D. (1986). Patients with multiple un-explained symptoms: Their characteristics, functional health, and health care utilization. *Archives of Internal Medicine, 146,* 69–72.

Southwick, S., Rasmussen, A., Barron, J., and Arnsten, A. (2005). Neurobiological and neurocognitive alterations in PTSD: A focus on norepinephrine, serotonin, and the hypothalamic-pituitary-adrenal axis. In J. Vasterling and C. Brewin (Eds.), *The neuropsychology of PTSD* (pp. 27–58). New York: Guilford.

Spotnitz, H. (1985). *Modern psychoanalysis of the schizophrenic patient.* New York: Human Sciences Press.

Sroufe, L. (1989). Pathways to adaptation and maladaptation: Psychopathology as developmental deviation. In D. Cicchetti (Ed.), *Rochester symposium on developmental psychopathology. Vol.1: The emergence of a discipline* (pp. 13–40). Hillsdale, NJ: Lawrence Erlbaum.

Sroufe, L. (1996). *Emotional development: The organization of emotional life in the early years.* New York: Cambridge University Press.

Stekel, W. (1924). *Peculiarities of behavior* (Vols. 1–2). London: Williams and Norgate.

Sternberg, E. (2010). *My brain made me do it: The rise of neuroscience and the threat to moral responsibility.* Amherst, NY: Prometheus Books.

Strachey, J. (1934). The nature of the therapeutic action in psycho-analysis. *International Journal of Psychoanalysis, 15,* 127–159.

Sullivan, D., Block, L., and Pena, J. (1996). Influence of androgens and pituitary hormones on the structural profile and secretory activity of the lachrymal gland. *Acta Opthamalogica Scandinavica, 74*(5), 421–435.

Sullivan, H. S. (1953a). *Conceptions of modern psychiatry,* (2nd ed.). New York: W. W. Norton.

Sullivan, H. S. (1953b). *The interpersonal theory of psychiatry.* New York: W. W. Norton.

Ten Have de Labije, J. (1999). Maintaining Davanloo's discovery for uncovering the unconscious: An attempt at formulating the operational definitions of the dependent variables. *Ad Hoc Bulletin for Short-Term Therapy, 3*(1), 4–30.

Ten Have de Labije, J. (Ed.). (2001). *The working alliance: Whose intrapsychic crisis?* Amsterdam: VKDP.

Ten Have de Labije, J. (2005). Understanding and overcoming instant repression—part II. The hyena who drove a car: Overcoming blocks at stimulus and response. *Ad Hoc Bulletin of Short-Term Dynamic Psychotherapy, 9*(2), 10–33.

Ten Have de Labije, J. (2006). When patients enter with anxiety in the forefront. In *The collected writings of Josette ten Have de Labije* (pp. 37–80). Del Mar, CA: Unlocking Press.

Ten Have de Labije, J. (2009). Helping our patients to experience feelings: Understanding the role of defenses in emotion regulation and the implication for ISTDP practitioners—part I. *Ad Hoc Bulletin of Short-Term Dynamic Psychotherapy, 13*(1), 15–23.

Ten Have de Labije, J., and Neborsky, R. (2005). Understanding and overcoming instant repression—part I. *Ad Hoc Bulletin of Short-Term Dynamic Psychotherapy, 9*(2), 5–9.

Tomkins, S. (1962). *Affect, imagery, consciousness. Vol. 1: The positive affects.* New York: Springer.

Toner, B., Koyama, E., Garfinkel, P., and Jeejeebhoy, K. (1992). Social desirability and irritable bowel syndrome. *International Journal of Psychiatry in Medicine, 22,* 99–103.

Trevarthen, C. (2009). The functions of emotion in infancy: the regulation and communication of rhythm, sympathy, and meaning in human development. In Siegel, Dl, Fosha, D., and M. Solomon (Eds.), *The healing power of emotion: Affective neuroscience, development, and clinical practice* (pp. 55–85). New York: W. W. Norton.

Troendle, P. (2005). *Psychotherapie: Dynamisch-intensiv-direkt: Lehrbuch zur Intensiven Dynamischen Kurzpsychotherapie.* Giessen, Germany: Psychosozial-Verlag.

Trunnell, T. (1987). The management of the mechanisms of depression in intensive short-term dynamic psychotherapy. *International Journal of Short-Term Psychotherapy, 2,* 1–15.

Vaillant, G. (1993). *Wisdom of the ego.* Cambridge: Harvard University Press.

Waelder, R. (1960). *Basic theory of psychoanalysis.* New York: International Universities Press.

Wallerstein, R. (1985). Defenses, defense mechanisms, and the structure of the mind. In H. Blum (Ed.), *Defense and resistance: historical perspectives and current concepts* (pp. 201–226). New York: International Universities Press.

Walter, C. (2006). Why do we cry? *Scientific American Mind, 17*(6), 44–51.

Warshow, S. (2008). Compassionate interruption of defenses. Presentation at the Washington School of Psychiatry, Washington, DC.

Weeks, G. (Ed.). (1985). *Promoting change through paradoxical therapy.* New York: Brunner/Mazel.

Weeks, G., and L'Abate, L. (1982). *Paradoxical psychotherapy: Theory and practice with individuals, couples, and families.* New York: Brunner/Mazel.

Wegner, D. (2002). *The illusion of conscious will.* Cambridge, MA: MIT Press.

Wehrenberg, M., and Prinz, S. (2007). *The anxious brain: The neurobiological basis of anxiety disorders and how to effectively treat them.* New York: W. W. Norton.

Wexler, M. (1975). The evolution of a deficiency perspective on schizophrenia. In J. Gunderson and L. Mosher (Eds.), *Psychotherapy of schizophrenia* (pp. 161–174). New York: Jason Aronson.

Whittemore, J. (1996). Paving the royal road: An overview of conceptual and technical features in the graded format of Davanloo's ISTDP. *International Journal of Short-Term Dynamic Psychotherapy, 11*, 21–39.

Willick, M. (1985). On the concept of primitive defenses. In H. Blum (Ed.), *Defense and resistance: Historical perspectives and current concepts* (pp. 175–200). New York: International Universities Press.

Winnicott, D. W. (1965). *The maturational processes and the facilitating environment*. London: Hogarth Press.

Winnicott, D. W. (1971). *Playing and reality*. New York: Penguin Books.

Woolfolk, R., and Allen, L. (2007). *Treating somatization: A cognitive-behavioral approach*. New York: Guilford Press.

Worchel, J. (1986a).Transference in intensive short-term dynamic psychotherapy, part I: Technique of handling initial transference resistance. *International Journal of Short-Term Psychotherapy, 1*, 135–146.

Worchel, J. (1986b). Transference in intensive short-term dynamic psychotherapy, part II: Technique of handling initial transference resistance. *International Journal of Short-Term Psychotherapy, 1*, 205–215.

Wurmser, L. (1978). *The hidden dimension: Psychodynamics in compulsive drug use*. New York: Jason Aronson.

Wurmser, L. (2000). *The power of the inner judge: Psychodynamic treatment of the severe neuroses*. Northvale, NJ: Jason Aronson.

Wurmser, L. (2003). The annihilating power of absoluteness: Superego analysis in the severe neuroses, especially in character perversion. *Psychoanalytic Psychology, 20*(2), 214–235.

Wurmser, L. (2004). Superego revisited—relevant or irrelevant? *Psychoanalytic Inquiry, 24*, 183–205.

Ziegler, M. (2004). Psychological stress and the autonomic nervous system. In D. Robertson et al. (Eds.), *Primer on the autonomic nervous system* (pp. 189–190). Amsterdam: Elsevier Academic Press.

Index

About the Author

Jon Frederickson, MSW, is in private practice in Washington, DC. He is cochair of the Intensive Short-Term Dynamic Psychotherapy (ISTDP) Training Program at the Washington School of Psychiatry, where he has been on the faculty since 1988. He was previously chair of the Supervision Training and Advanced Psychotherapy Training Programs at the school as well as chair of the Faculty Clinical Council.

He is the chair of the ISTDP Core Training Program at the Norwegian ISTDP Society and on the faculty of the Laboratorium Psychoedukacji in Warsaw and the Italian Experiential Psychotherapy Association in Treviso. He is also the author of *Psychodynamic Psychotherapy: Learning to Listen from Multiple Perspectives*.

Jon gives clinical presentations ranging from half-day events to three-day sessions on many topics. In his presentations, he shows videos of his psychotherapy sessions so therapists can see and learn how to intervene effectively with a wide range of patients.

His topics include

- Treating depression and somatization
- Working with a dissociative patient
- Resolving resistance in the highly resistant patient
- Treatment of a recovering drug addict
- Restructuring projection in a borderline patient
- The man who had fourteen previous therapies

Jon also runs training groups in the United States, Sweden, Denmark, Norway, Poland, and Italy. Each group meets four times a year for three years. Jon and his teachers offer intensive skill-based training for therapists.

See the following for more information:

- *Speaking and training*: E-mail Jon at admin@istdpinstitute.com.
- *Webinars:* Visit www.istdpinstitute.com/webinars/ for a list of webinars offered by the ISTDP Institute.

- *DVDs:* Visit www.istdpinstitute.com/DVDs/ to purchase DVDs showing Jon working with patients.
- *Skill-building exercises:* Visit www.istdpinstitute.com /resources/20-skills-to-overcome-defenses/ for information on the "20 Skills to Overcome Defenses" audio course.
- *Clinical questions:* Visit www.facebook.com/Dynamic Psychotherapy/, where Jon answers clinical and theoretical questions in the ISTDP Institute learning community.